I0125308

THINK LIKE A ONE PERCENTER

THE UNCOMMON PATH TO WEALTH, WISDOM, AND KINGDOM PURPOSE

Joel Maxwell

Think Like A One Percenter: The Uncommon Path to Wealth, Wisdom, and Kingdom Purpose

Copyright © 2026 by Joel Maxwell

All rights reserved. No part of this book may be reproduced, stored in a retrieval system, or transmitted in any form or by any means—electronic, mechanical, photocopy, recording, or otherwise—without prior written permission of the publisher, except for brief quotations in critical reviews or articles.

The information contained in this book is for educational and informational purposes only. The author and publisher are not engaged in rendering legal, accounting, tax, investment, or other professional advice. Readers should consult with appropriate professionals regarding their individual circumstances. While the author has made every effort to provide accurate information at the time of publication, neither the publisher nor the author assumes any responsibility for errors or for changes that occur after publication. The stories and examples in this book are based on real events and real people, though some identifying details have been modified to protect privacy.

Scripture quotations are from the Tree of Life Version (TLV) and are used by permission.

Published by Amazon KDP
Physical Address: 410 Terry Ave N, Seattle, WA 98109
ISBN: 979-8-218-90071-7
Cover design by Rimsha Anwar
Printed in the United States of America
First Edition
10 9 8 7 6 5 4 3 2 1

DEDICATION

To Sara—

My partner in life, my fellow servant in God's Kingdom, and the one who believed in these principles before they bore fruit. Your wisdom, patience, and unwavering faith made this work possible.

To the Messianic community—

May we recover the biblical understanding of stewardship that our ancestors knew, building resources that advance Yeshua's Kingdom on earth.

And to those currently incarcerated who refuse to let circumstances define their futures—

This book proves that transformation begins in the mind, not in the circumstances. Your best years are still ahead.

TABLE OF CONTENTS

AUTHOR'S NOTE

I wrote this book in a place where most people would never expect a book about wealth building to be written—from inside a correctional facility in Florida. This is not the credential that opens doors or establishes credibility in personal finance circles. It is the credential that causes most people to dismiss everything that follows before reading a single word.

But I would argue that my perspective is valuable precisely because of where I am writing from, not in spite of it. I have made catastrophic mistakes that cost me years of my life and separated me from the people I love. I have experienced consequences that most people who write about success and wealth will never face. I have been stripped of everything except my mind, my faith, and my determination to ensure that my future differs radically from my past. This has given me clarity about what matters and what does not that is difficult to achieve when surrounded by comfort and conventional success.

I spent years studying the patterns that separate those who build substantial wealth from those who remain trapped in financial mediocrity despite comparable incomes and opportunities. I read hundreds of books on finance, investing, business, psychology, and persuasion. I've personally interrogated successful people about their decision-making processes. I analyzed the mistakes that destroy wealth and the disciplines that create it. I discovered that the difference between financial success and failure is not intelligence, education, family background, or luck—it is behavioral patterns sustained across decades.

The one percent implement optimal behaviors consistently. The ninety-nine percent know what optimal behaviors are but fail to implement them. This book explains those behaviors in meticulous detail across thirty-eight chapters covering every domain affecting wealth accumulation. The frameworks are not original to me—they are distilled from the work of researchers, investors, and practitioners who have studied these questions for generations. What I contribute is systematic organization, clear explanation, and integration of disparate insights into a coherent strategy that anyone can implement regardless of starting point.

I write from a Messianic Jewish perspective, which means I follow Yeshua (Jesus) while maintaining deep respect for the Torah and the Hebrew roots of our faith. This perspective shapes how I think about money, stewardship, and purpose. Wealth is not the ultimate goal—it is a tool that enables you to serve God's purposes more effectively. The person who builds wealth while remaining spiritually empty has failed regardless of their net worth. The person who builds wealth while advancing God's Kingdom has succeeded regardless of whether their wealth reaches levels that impress others.

This book is uncompromising in its directness. I do not soften hard truths to avoid offending readers. I do not pretend that building wealth is easy or that success comes without sacrifice. I do not offer shortcuts or secrets or hidden strategies that unlock wealth without effort. I offer frameworks that work when implemented with discipline across decades, and I explain precisely why most people fail to implement them despite understanding intellectually that they should.

Some readers will find my tone too harsh or my examples too extreme. They will object to my characterization of the ninety-nine percent as failing through behavioral patterns rather than through circumstances beyond their control. They will argue that my analysis ignores systemic barriers, discrimination, and economic structures that advantage some while disadvantaging others. These objections are understandable but they miss the point.

This book is not about whether the system is fair. It is about how to succeed within the system that actually exists. The person who spends their energy complaining about unfairness rather than implementing strategies that work within current reality guarantees their own failure. The person who acknowledges that the system is imperfect while still playing to win gives themselves the best chance of building wealth that can eventually be used to change the very systems they object to.

I acknowledge that I write from a position of advantage in some ways despite my current incarceration. I am educated. I speak English natively. I understand how systems work. I can write clearly and think strategically. These advantages are real and they matter. But they are not sufficient for success without behavioral discipline, and they are not necessary for success if you develop that discipline. I have encountered people with far fewer advantages than I possess who built substantial wealth through relentless implementation of basic principles. I have encountered people with far greater advantages than I possess who destroyed themselves through behavioral dysfunction.

The choice between implementation and intention is available to everyone regardless of advantages or disadvantages. The person who implements optimal financial behaviors starting from poverty will build more wealth than the person who knows those behaviors but never implements them despite starting from privilege. This book gives you the complete map. Whether you use it determines everything about your financial future.

A note on the stories and examples throughout this book: every story is based on real events involving real people. Some identifying details have been modified to protect privacy. The financial figures and timeframes are accurate. The outcomes described actually occurred. I selected examples that demonstrate principles clearly rather than examples that are statistically typical. The couple who built seven properties over thirty years is not typical—most people never purchase a single rental property. But their example demonstrates what becomes possible through sustained implementation better than a typical example of mediocre results would demonstrate.

I wrote this book for multiple audiences. I wrote it for young people early in their careers who can implement these principles for forty years and build wealth that transforms their families for generations. I wrote it for mid-career professionals who realize they are not on track for the retirement they want and who need frameworks for accelerating wealth building in their remaining working years. I wrote it for my fellow inmates who will eventually return to society and who need practical strategies for building legitimate wealth rather than returning to the paths that brought them here. I wrote it for my students and for educators who want to teach financial literacy but lack comprehensive resources explaining how money actually works.

Most importantly, I wrote it for my future self—for the man I will be when I leave this place and begin rebuilding my life with my wife Sara. This book is the foundation of the wealth-building strategy we will implement together. The principles I explain here are the principles I will live by. The mistakes I warn against are mistakes I will avoid. The disciplines I advocate are disciplines I will maintain. If I fail to implement what I have written, then the book is worthless regardless of whether others find it valuable.

I am aware that some readers will dismiss this book purely because of my current circumstances. They will argue that someone incarcerated cannot possibly teach others about success. I understand this objection and I will not attempt to refute it. The work speaks for itself. If the frameworks are sound and the explanations are clear and the evidence supports the conclusions, then the book has value regardless of my circumstances. If the frameworks are flawed or the explanations are confused or the evidence is weak, then the book deserves dismissal regardless of my credentials.

Judge the work on its merits. Implement what makes sense. Discard what does not. Test the frameworks in your own life. Measure the results. Adjust based on what you discover. That is all I ask.

May HaShem bless you with wisdom to distinguish between knowledge and implementation, between intention and action, between appearing successful and actually building wealth that serves His purposes.

—Maxwell

December 2025

PREFACE

Why I Wrote This Book

On a Tuesday morning in September 2019, I sat in a county jail cell watching my entire life collapse. The legal consequences that I had convinced myself would never actually materialize were materializing. The shortcuts that I had believed would lead to success had led to catastrophe. The behavioral patterns that I had maintained for years despite knowing better had finally extracted their full price.

I was twenty-one years old. I had no college degree. I had read dozens of books about investing and entrepreneurship and been around several people who were models of the same. I knew intellectually how to build wealth legitimately through discipline sustained across decades. And I had ignored everything I knew in favor of pursuing shortcuts that seemed faster and easier and that ultimately cost me everything.

The specific mistakes I made are less important than the pattern underlying them. I consistently chose short-term gratification over long-term benefit. I consistently prioritized appearing successful over actually building success. I consistently assumed I was smarter than the system and that I could beat odds that had destroyed countless people before me. These behavioral patterns produced exactly the outcomes that behavioral patterns always produce when sustained long enough: complete catastrophe.

Sitting in that cell, I had a choice. I could spend the next several years feeling sorry for myself, blaming circumstances, and emerging from prison with the same mindset that brought me there. Or I could use the time to systematically study the principles that actually create

wealth and to develop frameworks for implementing those principles regardless of starting circumstances. I chose the latter.

I spent the next several years reading everything I could access about investing, real estate, business, psychology, marketing, negotiation, and behavioral economics. I read the classics: The Intelligent Investor, A Random Walk Down Wall Street, The Millionaire Next Door, Influence, Scientific Advertising. I read modern works: Thinking Fast and Slow, Atomic Habits, The Psychology of Money. I read tax code. I read real estate analysis frameworks. I read everything written by people who had systematically studied how wealth is built.

I also studied people. I interviewed successful inmates who had built legitimate businesses before incarceration. I studied case histories of people who built substantial wealth from modest starting points. I analyzed what separated those who succeeded from those who failed despite similar opportunities. The patterns became clear through repeated observation: the successful implemented optimal behaviors consistently while the unsuccessful knew optimal behaviors but failed to implement them, or simply just did not know.

This book synthesizes everything I learned across thousands of hours of study. It is not original research—it is careful compilation and organization of insights from dozens of sources into a comprehensive system. Every framework, every principle, every mathematical calculation comes from authoritative sources that I have cited in the Notes and Sources section. My contribution is organization and synthesis, not discovery of new principles.

What makes this book different from other personal finance books is not that it contains secret information unavailable elsewhere. Everything in this book can be found in other sources if you read widely enough. What makes it different is comprehensiveness combined with unflinching directness about why people fail to implement what they know.

Most finance books assume that providing information creates behavior change. They explain compound interest, recommend index fund investing, suggest living below your means, and assume readers will implement these recommendations. Then they are puzzled when research shows that most readers implement nothing and that financial literacy education has minimal effect on financial behaviors.

This book starts from a different assumption: knowledge without implementation produces identical outcomes to ignorance. The person who knows they should save forty percent of their income but who saves nothing achieves identical wealth to the person who has never heard of savings rates. The person who knows they should invest in index funds but who keeps money in savings accounts earning one percent achieves identical returns to the person who has never heard of index funds. Knowledge without implementation is worthless.

The critical question is not "What should I do?" but "Why don't I do what I know I should do?" This book systematically addresses that question. Every chapter explains not only what to do but why people fail to do it and how to overcome the barriers preventing implementation. The barriers are psychological, emotional, social, and practical. Addressing them requires more than providing information—it requires understanding human nature deeply enough to work with it rather than against it.

I write from a Messianic Jewish perspective, which shapes how I think about money, wealth, and stewardship. I follow Yeshua (Jesus) as Messiah while maintaining deep respect for Torah and the Hebrew roots of our faith. This perspective prevents the common Christian error of treating poverty as spiritually superior to wealth or treating wealth building as worldly and unspiritual.

Scripture is clear that wealth is a blessing when stewarded properly and a curse when pursued selfishly or when acquired through oppression. The proverbs praise diligent planning and wealth accumulation. The Torah provides detailed instructions for managing property, for lending, for tithing, for ensuring the poor are cared for while also ensuring that irresponsibility is not rewarded. Yeshua's parables about stewardship commend those who invest resources wisely and produce returns, not those who bury resources out of fear.

Biblical stewardship means building wealth systematically through legitimate means and then deploying that wealth for Kingdom purposes: supporting ministries, helping the genuinely poor, leaving inheritance to descendants, funding education, and generally advancing God's purposes on earth. The person who remains financially illiterate and who fails to build wealth despite having the ability to do so is not being spiritual—they are being disobedient to clear biblical commands about stewardship.

This book provides the complete framework for biblical stewardship translated into modern financial terms. The thirty-eight chapters cover every domain affecting wealth accumulation. The progression is logical: mindset, then core strategies (living below means, index investing, tax optimization, real estate), then supporting strategies (career optimization, side income, expense management, health), then advanced topics (business building, negotiation, marketing, public speaking), and finally wisdom about silence and about raising the next generation.

Each chapter can stand alone. You can read the chapter on real estate without reading the chapter on index funds. You can read the chapter on negotiation without reading the chapter on tax planning. But the chapters are designed to work together as a system. The person who implements all thirty-eight chapters over a working lifetime will build substantially more wealth than the person who implements only a few chapters, and they will build it with less risk because diversification across strategies provides protection that concentration in any single strategy cannot match.

I am writing this book for several audiences simultaneously. I am writing it for young people early in their careers who can implement these principles for forty years and build generational wealth. I am writing it for mid-career professionals who realize they are behind where they should be and who need frameworks for accelerating wealth building. I am writing it for my fellow inmates who will eventually return to society and who need practical guidance for building legitimate wealth rather than returning to the paths that brought them to prison. I am writing it for educators who want to teach financial literacy but who lack comprehensive resources.

Most importantly, I am writing it for my future self. This book is the foundation of the wealth-building strategy I will continue implement with my wife when I leave this place. The principles I explain are the principles I live by. The mistakes I warn against are mistakes I avoid. The disciplines I advocate are disciplines I will maintain. If I fail to implement what I have written, the book is worthless to me regardless of whether others find it valuable.

I anticipate several objections to this book: "How can someone currently incarcerated teach others about success?" Judge the work on its merits. If the frameworks are sound and the evidence supports the conclusions, then the work has value regardless of my circumstances. Expertise comes from systematic study and pattern recognition, not from living a perfect life.

"This is too harsh and judgmental toward people who struggle financially." I am not judging people for struggling—I am explaining the behavioral patterns that create struggle versus the patterns that create wealth. The truth is often harsh, but softening it helps no one.

"The 1% have advantages that ordinary people cannot replicate." Some people do have advantages. But the behavioral differences I document—living below means, investing systematically, building multiple income streams, maintaining discipline across decades—are available to anyone regardless of starting advantages. The person who implements these behaviors from a disadvantaged starting point will build more wealth than the person who has advantages but who fails to implement the behaviors.

"Not everyone can become wealthy, so this advice only works for some people." Nearly everyone in developed countries can build substantially more wealth than they currently have by implementing the principles in this book. Most will not, because implementation requires sustained discipline that most people refuse to maintain. But the capacity exists even if the will does not.

"Building wealth is selfish and unbiblical." Building wealth for selfish accumulation is unbiblical. Building wealth to serve Kingdom purposes, to leave inheritance to descendants, to support ministries, and to help the genuinely poor is commanded by Scripture. The issue is motive and deployment, not accumulation itself.

I expect this book to offend some readers. If you read it and feel comfortable, you are missing the point. The gap between what you know and what you implement should create discomfort that motivates change. If it does not, you will remain in the 99% regardless of how many finance books you read.

I also expect this book to change some lives. The reader who implements even half of what is contained here will build substantially more wealth than their peers who ignore it. The reader who implements all of it systematically over decades will likely achieve financial independence and will leave substantial inheritance to their children. The frameworks work when implemented with discipline.

The question is whether you will implement them.

One final note: I have tried to make this book as practical and actionable as possible. Every chapter contains specific frameworks, calculations, and examples rather than vague platitudes about "being disciplined" or "thinking long-term." I explain exactly what to do, exactly how to calculate whether you are doing it correctly, and exactly what outcomes to expect if you sustain the behaviors across decades.

The worksheets in Appendix B allow you to track your progress. The resource guide in Appendix A points you to additional sources for deeper learning. The Notes and Sources section documents where every insight comes from so you can verify accuracy and explore topics further. I have attempted to create a complete resource rather than an introduction that requires you to purchase additional materials.

If you implement what this book teaches, you will build wealth. How much wealth depends on your starting income, how aggressively you implement the strategies, how long you sustain the discipline, and how market conditions develop over your wealth-building years. But the direction is certain even if the magnitude is uncertain. Implementation produces wealth. Failure to implement produces continued financial struggle regardless of how much you know.

The choice is yours. The knowledge has been provided and the frameworks are proven. What remains is the decision to implement or to remain on the sidelines watching others build wealth while you convince yourself that you will start tomorrow.

Tomorrow never comes. Today is all you have. Use it wisely.

—Joel
Florida
December 2025

INTRODUCTION:
THE GREAT DIVERGENCE

Picture, if you will, a boy of eleven years old sitting at a worn wooden desk, his fingers tracing columns of numbers in the financial pages of a newspaper. The year is 1941. While other children trade baseball cards and dream of comic book heroes, this boy studies stock prices with the intensity of a general surveying battlefield terrain. His name is Warren Buffett, and on this particular day, he makes his first stock purchase—three shares of Cities Service Preferred at thirty-eight dollars per share. He has saved every penny from delivering newspapers, selling golf balls he found in ponds, and operating pinball machines in barbershops. At eleven years old, he understands something that eludes most people until they reach their graves: money is not meant to be spent. It is meant to multiply.

Now contrast this with the average American, who makes their first stock market investment at age thirty-three. By that time, Warren Buffett has already accumulated millions. The divergence between these two paths is not one of luck, inheritance, or even intelligence. It is a divergence of thinking. One understands the game. The other does not know a game is being played.

I have spent more than two decades observing wealth—how it is built, how it is lost, and most importantly, how it transforms those who possess it. I have sat across tables from millionaires who drive fifteen-year-old trucks and from bankrupt executives who once owned expensive homes. I have watched fortunes rise from nothing and evaporate into nothing. And through all of this, I have come to understand a fundamental truth that no business school teaches and no financial advisor will tell you plainly: there are two distinct species

13

of human beings when it comes to money, and the chasm between them grows wider every year.

They are the ninety-nine percent and the one percent. But before you close this book thinking it is about income brackets or class warfare, understand this clearly—these categories have nothing to do with how much money you currently possess. They have everything to do with how you think about money, time, and value itself. I have known penniless immigrants who think like the one percent and will inevitably become wealthy. I have known doctors earning four hundred thousand dollars annually who think like the ninety-nine percent and will work until they die. Your current bank balance is merely a lagging indicator of your thinking. Change the thinking, and the balance will follow as surely as autumn follows summer.

The ninety-nine percent see money as something to be earned through labor and then spent on consumption. They trade their time for dollars in what they believe is a fair exchange, then trade those dollars for cars, homes, vacations, and a thousand other items that provide temporary satisfaction before requiring replacement. They view their paycheck as the finish line, the reward for their effort. They calculate their worth by their salary. They believe that security comes from steady employment, that wealth is for other people who got lucky or were born into privilege, and that the financial game is rigged against them. They are not entirely wrong about the rigging, but they are fatally wrong about what to do about it.

The ninety-nine percent wait. They wait for the right time to invest, wait for certainty before taking risks, wait for permission before pursuing opportunities. They wait for their employer to recognize their value and grant raises. They wait for the market to settle down before buying stocks. They wait for interest rates to drop before purchasing property. They wait for their children to finish college before thinking about retirement. And while they wait, time—their only irreplaceable asset—bleeds away like water through cupped hands.

The one percent understand that money is not a reward for labor but a tool that, properly deployed, multiplies itself while you sleep. They know that wealth is not built through the exchange of time for currency—there are only so many hours in a day and only so many years in a life. Wealth is built through the strategic deployment of capital into assets that generate returns exceeding inflation and taxes. The one percent study the rules of the financial game with the intensity of professional athletes studying playbooks. They recognize that the game has always had rules, that those rules are written by people who understand them, and that complaining about unfairness is merely the sound of spectators who refuse to learn the game.

Where the ninety-nine percent see obstacles, the one percent see rules to be learned and leveraged. Where the ninety-nine percent see risk, the one percent see calculated probabilities. Where the ninety-nine percent see stability in a paycheck, the one percent see the risk of concentrated dependence on a single income source. The perspectives are not merely different. They are inverted, like looking at the same landscape through opposite ends of a telescope.

Consider how each group approaches a windfall of ten thousand dollars. The ninety-nine percent see an opportunity— perhaps a vacation they have delayed, a car upgrade they have wanted, or a wedding they feel obligated to fund. The money arrives and disappears, converted into experiences or possessions that provide temporary elevation followed by return to baseline. Two years later, the ten thousand dollars is gone, transmuted into photographs and memories and depreciating goods.

The one percent see the same ten thousand dollars as soldiers to be deployed in their wealth-building campaign. They calculate that ten thousand dollars invested in index funds returning ten percent annually becomes sixteen thousand in five years, twenty-six thousand in ten years, sixty-seven thousand in twenty years, and one hundred seventy-five thousand in thirty years. They understand that this single decision—to deploy rather than spend—creates a quarter century's worth of additional labor-free capital. They make this calculation instinctively, the way a chess master sees three moves ahead without conscious effort. And so they invest the money, ignore it, and watch it multiply through the miracle of compound returns.

This is not about deprivation. The one percent often live well, but they live on a fraction of their income while their capital works in the background. The ninety-nine percent live on everything they earn and often more, borrowing from tomorrow to consume today, creating a treadmill from which they can never step down. They confuse income with wealth, failing to understand that wealth is not what you earn but what you keep and multiply.

Let me be direct about something that makes many people uncomfortable: becoming a one percenter is not fundamentally about money. It is about stewardship, purpose, and legacy. Those who seek wealth for its own sake—for the status symbols, for the power over others, for the ego gratification—inevitably lose it or discover it brings no satisfaction. The truly wealthy understand that capital is a tool for building something larger than themselves, for advancing purposes that outlive their own brief years, for creating margin in their lives to serve the Kingdom of God in ways that poverty makes impossible.

I have come to understand through both Scripture and experience that God cares deeply about how we handle resources. The parable of the talents was not a gentle suggestion but a stark warning: those who bury their resources in the ground out of fear, who fail to multiply what they have been given, face judgment. Stewardship requires multiplication, not merely preservation. This is not the prosperity gospel that promises God as a cosmic vending machine dispensing wealth to those who pray correctly. This is the ancient wisdom that recognizes wealth as responsibility, as test, as opportunity to advance purposes beyond our own comfort.

The one percent who maintain proper priorities understand that generosity and wealth-building are not opposed but complementary. They give strategically and often sacrificially, not from compulsion or legalistic ten-percent calculations, but from hearts aligned with Kingdom advancement. They support Israel, fund gospel work, strengthen their local congregations, and seize unexpected opportunities to demonstrate God's love through practical provision. And they do this before wealth arrives, proving through action during poverty that their hearts will remain aligned during prosperity. The heart revealed in scarcity is the heart that will govern in abundance.

This book exists because I have watched too many good people—people with noble intentions, strong work ethics, and generous hearts—remain trapped in financial mediocrity through nothing more than lack of knowledge. They were never taught to think about money correctly. Their parents did not know. Their schools did not teach it. Their churches avoided it as somehow unspiritual or crass. And so they stumbled through life making catastrophic financial decisions without realizing these decisions were catastrophic until decades had passed and options had evaporated.

I do not claim any special intelligence or virtue. What I possess is time—enough years to watch the consequences of different approaches play out across complete lifetimes. I have seen the results of patient compound investing versus stock picking. I have watched house hackers build rental empires while their neighbors accumulated mortgages. I have observed strategic career climbers multiply their incomes tenfold while their more talented peers stagnated through failure to negotiate or switch companies. Time reveals what youthful theories obscure.

What follows in these pages is not theory. It is tested wisdom, drawn from both personal experience and systematic study of those who have built wealth across generations. You will find no get-rich-quick schemes, no cryptocurrency speculation, no multilevel marketing fantasies. You will find the boring, proven, systematic approaches that actually build wealth: tax-advantaged investing, strategic real estate acquisition, careful career management, disciplined spending, and intelligent use of debt and leverage.

Some of what you read will challenge deeply held beliefs. You may discover that homeownership is not always wise, that paying off your mortgage early is often foolish, that life insurance is usually a scam, and that the very institutions you trusted to guide you financially have been selling you products that enrich them while impoverishing you. This will be uncomfortable. Comfort is the enemy of growth.

You will also discover that thinking like a one percenter does not require becoming someone you are not. It requires becoming more of who you are meant to be—a faithful steward who understands that resources entrusted to you carry responsibility, that talents buried in the ground face judgment, and that Kingdom advancement requires margin that poverty cannot provide.

The choice before you is simple but not easy. You can continue thinking like the ninety-nine percent, following the well-worn path of trading time for money and money for consumption, arriving at retirement age dependent on government programs and the generosity of children. Or you can adopt the thinking patterns of the one percent, building assets systematically, creating streams of income independent of your labor, and constructing a foundation of wealth that serves purposes beyond yourself.

The tools are available to everyone. The information is not secret. What remains rare is the willingness to act on that information, to delay gratification, to think in decades rather than days, and to make decisions others will question while you are on the path and celebrate once you have arrived.

This book will show you the way. Whether you walk it is your decision alone.

Let us begin.

CHAPTER 1:
FIRST THINGS FIRST—THE FOUNDATION OF ALL WEALTH

In 1895, a boy was born in a small Vermont town to a family of French immigrants who valued hard work above all else. By the age of fourteen, he had dropped out of school to work in his father's iron foundry. By thirty, he had founded his own company manufacturing earthmoving equipment. By fifty, he had revolutionized the construction industry and accumulated a fortune that would be worth hundreds of millions in today's currency. His name was Robert Gilmour LeTourneau, and he made a decision that financial advisors would have called insane: he gave away ninety percent of his income and lived on the remaining ten percent.

This was not the reckless generosity of a man with more money than sense. LeTourneau operated one of the most successful manufacturing enterprises in America, holding nearly three hundred patents for heavy machinery that built roads, airports, and infrastructure across the globe during and after World War II. He understood profit margins, capital allocation, and compound returns as well as any businessman of his era. Yet he structured his entire financial life in a way that inverted conventional wisdom. He did not give from his surplus after building wealth. He gave as he built wealth, proving through decades of consistent action that generosity and wealth accumulation were not opposing forces but complementary disciplines flowing from the same source.

When asked about his unusual arrangement, LeTourneau said something that captures the essence of what I want to establish before we discuss a single investment strategy or tax advantage: "The question is not how much of my money I give to God, but rather how much of God's money I keep for myself." This single statement reveals a foundation that must be laid before any other wealth-building principle can function properly. It is the foundation upon which everything else either stands or crumbles.

Before we discuss index funds, real estate strategies, or business ventures, we must establish first principles. And the first principle is this: you own nothing. Every dollar that passes through your hands, every asset you control, every opportunity you encounter exists as stewardship, not ownership. This is not religious sentiment designed to make you feel guilty about wanting financial security. This is the fundamental reality that shapes how the truly wealthy think about capital and its purposes.

The distinction between ownership and stewardship creates entirely different decision-making frameworks. Owners hoard, protect, and consume. Stewards multiply, deploy, and advance purposes larger than themselves. Owners build kingdoms centered on their own comfort and legacy. Stewards build outposts of an eternal Kingdom that will outlast every earthly empire. The former produces anxiety, greed, and eventual emptiness regardless of the account balances achieved. The latter produces peace, generosity, and purpose that transcends material outcomes.

I have observed both paths across decades of watching people build and lose fortunes. Those who approach wealth as owners inevitably discover that the wealth owns them. They become slaves to their portfolios, anxious about every market fluctuation, fearful of losing what they have accumulated, and unable to enjoy what they possess because they are too busy protecting it. Their relationships suffer because people become either threats to their wealth or instruments for increasing it. Their health deteriorates because the stress of protecting assets consumes the vitality those assets were supposed to provide. They arrive at the end of life with full bank accounts and empty souls, having won a game that provided no satisfaction in the winning.

Those who approach wealth as stewards experience something entirely different. They hold resources loosely, understanding that capital is meant to flow through them to accomplish purposes, not pool up in stagnant reservoirs. They make investment decisions based on long-term multiplication rather than short-term security. They give generously because they understand the resources do not originate with them and will not end with them. Most importantly, they sleep well regardless of market conditions because their identity is not tied to their net worth. The wealth serves them. They do not serve it.

This is not theoretical philosophy. It produces measurably different practical outcomes. Let me explain how this foundation affects every financial decision that follows.

When you understand that wealth is stewardship rather than ownership, your relationship with money fundamentally changes. You stop asking "What can I afford?" and start asking "What is the best use of these resources?" The first question leads to consumption at the edge of your means.

The second leads to multiplication and strategic deployment. You stop viewing your income as earned solely through your own effort and start recognizing it as provision entrusted to you for purposes beyond your own consumption. This recognition does not diminish your drive to increase income. It intensifies that drive while directing it toward different ends.

The proper heart toward God's plan must be demonstrated before wealth arrives, not merely professed after it accumulates. This is the test that reveals whether you will handle abundance faithfully. The servant who proves trustworthy with little will be entrusted with much. The servant who hoards or wastes the little will not be given more, and what he has will be taken away. This principle operates with mechanical consistency across every area of life, but nowhere more visibly than in finances.

I have watched people make promises about what they will do when they become wealthy. They will give generously, support gospel work, advance the Kingdom, help the poor. But in their current state of modest means, they give nothing. They explain that they need to achieve financial security first, build their foundation, ensure their own futures are settled before they can help others. This is the reasoning of the ninety-nine percent, and it leads to predictable outcomes. When such people acquire wealth, they discover that the foundation is never quite secure enough, the future never quite certain enough, the margin never quite sufficient to begin giving. The habit of hoarding, once established, does not reverse simply because the numbers in the account grow larger.

Contrast this with those who demonstrate kingdom alignment during poverty. They give when it makes no financial sense to give. They support their local congregation when they can barely pay their own bills. They fund mission work when they are eating beans and rice. They help Israel when their own circumstances are precarious. They pay a stranger's toll, buy groceries for a struggling family, or send money to a missionary despite having no surplus. These actions make no sense from a financial planning perspective. They make perfect sense from a stewardship perspective.

What such people are doing, whether they consciously recognize it or not, is proving that their hearts are aligned with Kingdom purposes regardless of their circumstances. They are establishing neural pathways of generosity that will remain open when wealth increases. They are demonstrating that giving flows from character rather than surplus, from values rather than convenience. And they are positioning themselves to be entrusted with more because they have proven faithful with less.

There is a mystery here that I do not fully understand even after decades of observation, but I have seen it operate too consistently to dismiss. Those who give sacrificially during poverty tend to experience what can only be described as supernatural provision. Opportunities appear that should not appear. Doors open that should remain closed. Resources materialize from unexpected sources. I am not speaking of prosperity gospel nonsense that treats God as a cosmic vending machine. I am speaking of a pattern so consistent that it demands acknowledgment even from skeptics.

LeTourneau understood this mystery and operated within it deliberately. His biographers document that even during the early years of his business when cash flow was tight and bankruptcy seemed likely, he maintained his commitment to giving ninety percent of his income. This was not reckless. It was the opposite of reckless. He recognized that his business success did not depend primarily on his own engineering genius or business acumen, though he possessed both in abundance. It depended on aligning himself with purposes larger than profit maximization.

The practical question becomes: how does one demonstrate proper heart alignment before wealth arrives? The answer is simpler than most people want to hear. You give according to your heart, not according to a percentage formula. The Pharisees loved their ten-percent calculations because legalism provides certainty and requires no examination of motives. They could tithe their mint and dill and cumin while their hearts remained far from God. Jesus condemned this approach precisely because it missed the entire point. Giving is not about satisfying an obligation. It is about revealing and shaping the heart.

If your heart is aligned with advancing God's kingdom, you will give even when it hurts. You will look for opportunities to demonstrate that alignment through practical action. You will support Israel because you understand the spiritual significance of the Jewish people and the importance of standing with them when the world does not. You will fund gospel work because you recognize that the eternal matters more than the temporal. You will help your local congregation because you understand that the body of Messiah requires practical support, not just theoretical affirmation. You will perform random acts of kingdom advancement—paying for someone's groceries, covering a toll, sending money to a missionary— because these actions train your heart to hold wealth loosely and see opportunities to advance purposes beyond yourself.

None of this should be done for show or to earn God's favor. You cannot purchase divine blessing through giving. What you can do is align your heart with divine purposes and position yourself to be trusted with resources that will be used for those purposes. This is not manipulation. It is the recognition of how stewardship operates.

The amount matters far less than the heart behind it. A widow giving two small coins gave more than wealthy donors contributing large sums, not because the amount was larger but because the sacrifice was greater and the heart was purer. You may be able to give only ten dollars monthly to kingdom work while you are building your foundation. Give that ten dollars faithfully, sacrificially, and with joy. The amount is almost irrelevant. The pattern is everything.

I want to address something that causes confusion for many people trying to navigate faith and finances. There exists a strain of teaching that treats poverty as virtue and wealth as inherently corrupting. This is not biblical wisdom but Greek philosophy that infiltrated early Christian thought and has never been fully expelled. The Scriptures are filled with wealthy people whom God used mightily: Abraham, Job, David, Solomon, Joseph of Arimathea, Lydia. Wealth itself is morally neutral. What matters is how it is acquired, how it is held, and how it is deployed.

God is not opposed to you building wealth. He is opposed to you being owned by wealth. He is not offended by your desire for financial security. He is offended when that desire becomes idolatry that displaces proper priorities. The distinction is crucial. You can pursue wealth building with intensity and discipline while maintaining proper heart alignment. What you cannot do is pursue wealth as ultimate security, as identity, or as an end in itself. The moment wealth becomes the point rather than the tool, you have lost proper orientation regardless of how much you accumulate.

This is why establishing first things first matters so profoundly. If you attempt to build wealth without proper foundation, you may succeed in accumulating assets, but you will fail at the deeper purpose those assets were meant to serve. You will arrive at financial independence only to discover you have built a prison rather than liberation. The wealthy who lack proper foundation become slaves to their wealth, consumed by fear of losing it, isolated by suspicion about others' motives, and empty despite abundance.

Those who build on proper foundation experience something entirely different. They pursue wealth with clarity about its purpose.

They accumulate assets knowing these assets are tools for kingdom advancement, not monuments to personal achievement. They give generously throughout the journey, proving continuously that their hearts remain aligned. They arrive at financial independence with margin to serve in ways poverty prevented. They deploy capital toward eternal purposes while enjoying the temporal blessings that stewardship produces. They sleep well, relate freely, and live purposefully because they understand who owns everything and what they have been called to do with what they steward.

Let me be practical about what this looks like during the building phase when resources are limited. You are making thirty thousand dollars annually and can barely cover basic expenses. The ninety-nine percent in this situation give nothing, explaining that they have nothing to give. The one percent in this situation examine their spending, find even small margin, and deploy that margin strategically toward kingdom purposes. Perhaps you commit ten dollars monthly to support Israel through organizations like Bridges for Peace or the Messianic Jewish Alliance of America. Perhaps you contribute twenty-five dollars monthly to your local congregation. Perhaps you keep fifty dollars available for random opportunities to demonstrate kingdom love through practical provision.

These amounts seem insignificant measured against your financial goals or against the needs they address. They are not insignificant measured against what they accomplish in your own heart. You are establishing patterns. You are proving trustworthiness with little. You are training yourself to see resources as tools for purposes rather than commodities for consumption. You are aligning your heart with eternal priorities while building temporal assets. This foundation, once laid properly, will support everything you build upon it.

As your income increases, your giving should increase. Not necessarily proportionally, but strategically. You may give ten percent at thirty thousand, fifteen percent at sixty thousand, twenty-five percent at one hundred thousand, and fifty percent at three hundred thousand. The percentages matter less than the direction and the heart. What you are demonstrating across years of increasing income is that wealth does not change your priorities or corrupt your purposes. You are proving that you can be trusted with more because you have remained faithful throughout the journey.

I have known people who gave away millions annually while living comfortable but modest lifestyles. I have known others who earned millions but gave nothing while justifying their hoarding through sophisticated rationalizations. The difference was not income level or investment returns. The difference was foundation. One group built on stewardship principles from the beginning. The other built on ownership assumptions and could not escape that framework even when their accumulation exceeded any rational need.

Here is what I want you to understand as we prepare to explore practical wealth-building strategies in the chapters that follow: every financial decision you make flows from your fundamental understanding of ownership versus stewardship. How you approach saving, investing, spending, giving, risk-taking, and wealth deployment will all be shaped by whether you see yourself as owner or steward. Get this foundation wrong and everything built upon it will be compromised. Get this foundation right and everything else becomes clearer.

The one percent who maintain proper priorities understand something the ninety-nine percent miss: generosity and wealth-building reinforce each other rather than compete. When you give sacrificially, you train yourself to live on less than you earn. This creates the savings rate necessary for wealth accumulation. When you view wealth as stewardship rather than ownership, you think in terms of multiplication and long-term deployment rather than short-term consumption. This produces the patient capital that generates compound returns. When you align your purposes with kingdom advancement, you gain clarity about what matters and what does not, which eliminates wasteful spending on status signaling and keeps lifestyle inflation in check.

The practical result is that those with proper foundation often accumulate wealth faster than those pursuing wealth for its own sake.

This seems paradoxical until you understand the mechanisms. Proper foundation creates discipline, patience, clarity of purpose, and freedom from the anxiety that causes poor decisions. These qualities produce better financial outcomes than raw ambition unconstrained by higher purposes.

LeTourneau built a manufacturing empire worth hundreds of millions while giving away ninety percent of his income. This was not despite his generosity but in significant part because of it. His generosity flowed from proper foundation, and that foundation shaped every business decision he made. He thought long-term because he was building for kingdom purposes, not personal consumption. He took calculated risks because he understood that the resources were not ultimately his to protect. He innovated relentlessly because he saw his business as service to purposes larger than profit maximization. The business succeeded wildly precisely because it operated on principles that transcended mere business.

I am not suggesting that everyone should give away ninety percent of their income. LeTourneau had unique circumstances, convictions, and capacity. What I am suggesting is that you establish proper foundation before pursuing wealth-building strategies. Determine in your heart that you will demonstrate kingdom alignment regardless of your circumstances. Commit to giving sacrificially even during poverty. Look for opportunities to advance gospel work, support Israel, strengthen your local congregation, and practice random acts of kingdom generosity. Establish these patterns now, not later when you imagine you will have surplus.

As we move forward into discussions of tax-advantaged accounts, real estate strategies, stock market investing, and business building, everything will rest on this foundation. If you build without it, you may accumulate assets but lose your soul in the process. If you build upon it, you will create not just wealth but legacy, not just financial independence but kingdom impact, not just security for yourself but provision for purposes that outlast your brief time on earth.

The choice is yours. You can pursue wealth like the ninety-nine percent who see money as the point. Or you can pursue wealth like the one percent who understand that money is the tool for accomplishing purposes far greater than personal comfort and security. The first path leads to accumulation without satisfaction. The second path leads to stewardship with purpose.

We have established first things first. God comes before investment strategies. Kingdom purposes come before retirement accounts. Stewardship comes before accumulation. Demonstrating proper heart during poverty comes before expecting to handle prosperity faithfully. This is the foundation. Everything else we discuss will build upon it.

Now let us turn to the practical mechanics of wealth building, secure in the knowledge that we have laid proper groundwork. The strategies that follow are powerful, but they are only as good as the foundation beneath them. With this foundation established, we can proceed with confidence that wealth built will be wealth stewarded faithfully for purposes that matter eternally.

CHAPTER 2:
ASSETS AND LIABILITIES—THE LANGUAGE OF WEALTH

In the winter of 1855, a boy was born in a modest wooden house in Richford, New York. His father was a con man and bigamist who spent more time avoiding creditors than providing for his family. His mother was a devout Baptist who taught her children that idleness was sin and that every penny mattered. By age sixteen, the boy had secured his first job as an assistant bookkeeper, earning fifty cents a day. He approached this position with religious intensity, arriving early, staying late, and recording every transaction with meticulous precision. His name was John Davison Rockefeller, and he was learning a language that most people never master: the language of assets and liabilities.

Rockefeller understood something at sixteen that most people never grasp at sixty. He recognized that dollars flowing through his hands could take two fundamentally different forms. They could be deployed into things that generated more dollars, or they could be spent on things that consumed dollars. The first category he pursued with methodical aggression. The second category he avoided with almost religious fervor. By age twenty-three, he had saved enough from his bookkeeping salary to invest four thousand dollars—a substantial fortune at the time—into a produce commission business. That business generated profits which he deployed into oil refining. The oil refining generated greater profits which he deployed into pipelines, distribution networks, and eventually vertical integration of the entire petroleum industry.

By the time Rockefeller reached his fifties, he controlled ninety percent of America's oil refining capacity and had become the wealthiest person in modern history. Yet he lived in the same house for decades, wore suits until they needed patching, and famously said that he would rather earn interest than pay it. His fortune was not built through high income alone—many of his contemporaries earned comparable salaries. His fortune was built through understanding the fundamental distinction between assets and liabilities and structuring his entire life to maximize the former while minimizing the latter.

This distinction sounds simple. It is simple. Yet the vast majority of people spend their entire lives getting it backwards, accumulating things they believe are building their wealth when those things are actually destroying it. They work for forty years, earn millions of dollars in aggregate, and arrive at retirement with nothing because they never learned the language that Rockefeller mastered as a teenager. They speak English, they conduct transactions, they manage budgets, but they are functionally illiterate in the only language that actually matters for wealth building.

Let me define the terms clearly because confusion about these definitions has impoverished more people than any economic recession. An asset is something that puts money into your pocket. A liability is something that takes money out of your pocket. This is not my definition. This is the operational definition that separates those who build wealth from those who merely circulate money. An asset generates positive cash flow. A liability generates negative cash flow.

Everything you own or might purchase falls into one of these two categories. Your financial future depends entirely on which category dominates your balance sheet.

The confusion begins with the largest purchase most people ever make: their home. The ninety-nine percent believe their primary residence is an asset. They have been told this by parents, real estate agents, mortgage brokers, and financial advisors. They repeat it confidently when discussing their finances. They are completely wrong. Your primary residence is a liability. It does not matter if it appreciates in value over time. It does not matter if you could sell it for more than you paid. What matters for this definition is the direction of cash flow, and cash flows relentlessly out of your pocket to maintain a primary residence.

Consider the complete picture. You purchase a home for three hundred thousand dollars, putting down sixty thousand and financing two hundred forty thousand at four percent interest over thirty years. Your monthly mortgage payment is approximately twelve hundred dollars, of which roughly eight hundred initially goes to interest. You pay three thousand annually in property taxes. You pay twelve hundred annually in homeowner's insurance. You spend two percent of the home's value annually on maintenance and repairs— another six thousand dollars. Your utilities, landscaping, and incidental costs add another three thousand annually. The total annual cost of owning this home is approximately twenty-seven thousand dollars, or twenty-two hundred fifty dollars monthly.

Now ask yourself honestly: does this home put money into your pocket or take money out? The answer is obvious. It consumes twenty-seven thousand dollars annually. The fact that it might appreciate to three hundred fifty thousand over ten years does not change the cash flow direction. You are still writing checks every month. Money flows from you to others. This is the definition of a liability, not an asset.

The one percent understands this distinction and think about housing accordingly. They ask whether the money consumed by a primary residence could generate better returns deployed elsewhere. They calculate the opportunity cost of that sixty-thousand-dollar down payment sitting in a house instead of an index fund returning ten percent annually. They recognize that over thirty years, that sixty thousand invested instead of used as a down payment would grow to over one million dollars. They understand that the twenty-seven thousand spent annually on housing costs represents two hundred seventy thousand in foregone investment capital over just ten years, capital that would have grown to over seven hundred thousand by retirement.

This does not mean you should never buy a home. It means you should understand what you are buying. You are purchasing consumption, not an investment. You are buying shelter, comfort, stability, and the freedom to paint walls whatever color you choose. These things have value. They are not assets. The one percent make this purchase with eyes open, understanding the true cost and choosing it deliberately rather than stumbling into it while believing they are building wealth.

The same principle applies to automobiles, but here the delusion is even more destructive because cars depreciate rapidly while homes at least maintain some value. The average new car costs forty-five thousand dollars today. Financed at six percent over five years, the total cost is fifty-two thousand dollars. The car loses twenty percent of its value—nine thousand dollars—the moment you drive it off the lot. It continues depreciating by fifteen percent annually for the next several years. Within five years, your fifty-two-thousand dollar total expenditure has purchased a car worth perhaps twenty thousand dollars. You have spent thirty-two thousand dollars, or six thousand four hundred annually, for the privilege of driving a depreciating asset.

The truly devastating part is the opportunity cost. That fifty-two thousand spent on a car represents capital that will never compound. Had it been invested at ten percent returns, it would grow to $135,000 in twenty years, $350,000 in forty years. Every expensive car purchase is a choice to destroy hundreds of thousands in eventual wealth. The ninety-nine percent make this trade unconsciously, believing that a nice car is somehow connected to their financial success. The one percent understand that the connection runs in precisely the opposite direction: expensive cars are obstacles to financial success, not markers of it.

Rockefeller understood this instinctively. Even after becoming the world's wealthiest person, he drove modest cars and often had them driven by employees while he sat in back reading financial reports. He was not being cheap. He was being rational. The transportation function could be served by any reliable vehicle. Spending more on transportation generated no return and therefore made no sense. Every dollar unnecessarily spent on a car was a dollar not deployed into assets that generated returns. The math was simple. Most people cannot do this math, or more accurately, they do the math and then ignore its implications because they want the car more than they want the wealth.

Let me be clear about what constitutes an actual asset. A rental property that generates $500 monthly in positive cash flow after all expenses is an asset. It puts money in your pocket. The property might appreciate or depreciate, but regardless of what happens to its value, it generates monthly income that increases your wealth. A portfolio of dividend-paying stocks that yields 3% annually is an asset. It sends you checks that you did not work for. A business that operates profitably without requiring your constant presence is an asset. It generates income whether you show up or not. Intellectual property that earns royalties is an asset. Someone else performs the work while you collect the checks.

These are assets. They share a common characteristic: money flows from them to you, not from you to them. This is the only definition that matters. The one percent structure their entire financial lives to maximize true assets and minimize everything else. They view every potential purchase through this lens. Before buying anything, they ask a simple question: will this generate income or consume it? If the answer is consumption, they evaluate whether the consumption is worth the opportunity cost of the capital that could be deployed into income generation instead.

This framework explains behaviors that seem bizarre to the ninety-nine percent. Why does the millionaire drive a fifteen-year-old Toyota while his neighbor with fifty thousand in credit card debt drives a brand new BMW? Because the millionaire understands the cost is not the monthly payment but the foregone investment returns +on the capital. Why does the wealthy executive rent a modest apartment in an expensive city rather than buying a luxury condo? Because he has calculated that the premium for ownership exceeds any reasonable return and that capital deployed into income generating assets will produce superior outcomes. Why does the successful entrepreneur live in a small home while building a rental portfolio? Because she understands her residence is consumption while her rentals are assets, and she deliberately minimizes consumption to maximize assets. These decisions are not about frugality for its own sake or some ascetic lifestyle philosophy. They are about understanding mathematics and structuring life accordingly.

The one percent are not necessarily cheap. They spend freely on things that generate returns and sparingly on things that do not. They fly first class when time saved generates income exceeding the cost difference. They pay for education and skills that increase earning capacity. They invest in tools and equipment that improve business productivity. These expenditures generate returns and therefore make economic sense. Buying expensive cars, oversized houses, and status symbols that impress others generates no return and therefore makes no sense regardless of whether they can afford it.

The ninety-nine percent operate from a completely inverted framework. They minimize investment in assets because investing feels like sacrifice, like money disappearing into abstract accounts that provide no immediate gratification. They maximize spending on liabilities because spending feels like success, like reward for their labor, like tangible proof they are moving forward financially. They finance furniture, lease cars, mortgage houses, and accumulate consumer goods that provide temporary satisfaction followed by the need for upgrade or replacement. They believe they are building wealth because they own things. They are actually destroying wealth because they own the wrong things.

I want to address something that causes resistance when people first encounter this framework. Some argue that quality of life matters, that you cannot put a price on living in a nice home or driving a reliable car, that denying yourself basic comforts while building wealth is no way to live. This objection misses the point entirely. No one is advocating poverty or deprivation. What the one percent understand is that true wealth—the kind that provides lasting security, freedom, and options—comes from owning assets that generate income. Once you have built sufficient asset base, you can afford any lifestyle you choose because the assets pay for it.

The sequence matters profoundly. The ninety-nine percent try to live like they are wealthy before building the asset base that generates wealth. They buy the house, the cars, the lifestyle first, then attempt to save and invest from whatever remains. There is never anything remaining. They spend forty years on this treadmill, always feeling behind, always stressed about money despite solid incomes, never understanding why wealth eludes them.

The one percent inverts the sequence. They minimize consumption during the building phase, deploying maximum capital into assets. They live modestly not because they are poor but because they are strategically prioritizing asset accumulation over lifestyle inflation. They drive old cars and live in small apartments while their net worth grows exponentially. Then, after building sufficient asset base, they allow lifestyle to expand—but only to the level their passive income supports. They earn the lifestyle through assets rather than financing it through labor.

This approach requires delayed gratification, which is perhaps the single characteristic that most clearly distinguishes the one percent from the ninety-nine percent. The ability to forego immediate pleasure for greater future reward is not personality quirk or genetic gift. It is learned discipline that anyone can develop. Rockefeller was not born with this ability. He developed it through his mother's teaching and his own observation of how wealth was built or destroyed. He watched his father squander money on schemes and vices while his mother stretched every penny to keep the family fed. He learned which approach produced which outcomes.

You can develop the same discipline by understanding what you are actually trading when you make financial decisions. That new car is not just $45,000. It is the $350,000 that $45,000 would become if invested over forty years. That house upgrade is not just the additional thirty thousand in down payment. It is the $600,000 that thirty thousand would grow into over the same period. Every spending decision is a choice between present consumption and future abundance. The ninety-nine percent consistently choose present consumption while wondering why future abundance never arrives. The one percent consistently choose future abundance and discover that after years of patient accumulation, present consumption becomes effortlessly affordable.

Let me provide a practical framework for evaluating every potential purchase. Before acquiring anything, ask yourself three questions. First, does this generate income? If yes, it is potentially an asset worth acquiring. Evaluate it based on return relative to risk and alternative uses of capital. If no, proceed to the second question. Second, is this consumption necessary or valuable enough to justify the opportunity cost? Sometimes consumption is necessary—you need shelter, transportation, food. Sometimes consumption is valuable even if not strictly necessary—experiences with family, health maintenance, education. Calculate the true cost including opportunity cost, then decide consciously. Third, if acquiring this consumption, how can I minimize the cost? Buy used instead of new. Rent instead of own. Choose function over status. Negotiate aggressively.

Apply this framework consistently and you will find yourself accumulating assets while others accumulate liabilities. Your net worth will grow while theirs stagnates or declines. Within a decade, the gap will be substantial. Within two decades, it will be enormous. Within three decades, you will have financial independence while they are still working and worried about retirement.

The mathematics are inexorable once you understand the compounding effect of consistently choosing assets over liabilities. Consider two individuals, both earning seventy thousand annually. The first follows conventional wisdom: buys a home with a large mortgage, finances a new car every few years, accumulates furniture and possessions, takes vacations on credit cards, and saves whatever remains after spending. This person might save 5% of income—thirty-five hundred annually—and accumulates modest retirement accounts over forty years.

The second person thinks in assets and liabilities. He rents modestly, drives a used car purchased with cash, owns minimal possessions, takes inexpensive vacations paid in cash, and saves thirty-five percent of income—twenty-four thousand five hundred annually. After twenty years, the first person has perhaps two hundred thousand in retirement accounts and a home with some equity offset by remaining mortgage debt. The second person has over one million four hundred thousand in invested assets generating passive income. After forty years, the first person has perhaps eight hundred thousand and hopes Social Security fills the gap. The second person has over 10 million and has lived on passive income for the last decade.

These are not hypothetical numbers. They are mathematical results of different frameworks applied consistently. The difference is not income. The difference is understanding assets versus liabilities and structuring life accordingly. One person spent forty years accumulating things that consumed money. The other spent forty years accumulating things that generated money. The outcomes diverge precisely as the framework predicts.

Rockefeller built his empire through relentless application of this principle. Every decision was evaluated based on whether it would increase or decrease his asset base. He purchased oil refineries not because he liked oil but because they generated profits that could be deployed into more refineries. He built pipelines not for the prestige of infrastructure ownership but because they increased margins on his refining operations. He integrated vertically not for empire building but because controlling supply chains increased returns on capital. Everything was assets. Nothing was wasted on liabilities.

This created a compounding effect that his contemporaries could not match. While competitors spent profits on mansions and yachts and conspicuous consumption, Rockefeller deployed profits into more assets that generated more profits. His wealth compounded exponentially while theirs grew linearly or not at all. By the time his competitors recognized what was happening, the gap was unbridgeable. They had spent their building years on consumption. He had spent his building years on accumulation. The outcomes were predetermined by the frameworks.

You have the same choice available today. You can follow the conventional path that leads to forty years of work and insufficient retirement savings. Or you can adopt the framework that Rockefeller understood at sixteen and that every genuinely wealthy person practices whether they articulate it this way or not. The framework is simple: maximize assets, minimize liabilities. Measure every decision by this standard. Deploy capital into things that generate returns. Avoid deploying capital into things that generate expenses.

This does not mean living like a pauper. It means living strategically. You can have nice things once your asset base generates sufficient passive income to pay for nice things. What you cannot do is finance nice things through labor income during your building years and then expect to build wealth from the scraps that remain. The math does not work. It has never worked. It will never work. Pretending otherwise is financial delusion.

The language of assets and liabilities is not difficult to learn. What is difficult is acting on what the language teaches, especially when everyone around you speaks a different language and makes different choices. Your friends buy houses, so you feel pressure to buy a house. Your colleagues lease luxury cars, so you feel inadequate driving your paid-off sedan. Your neighbors upgrade their lifestyles with every raise, so you question whether you are missing out by banking yours. This is the social pressure that keeps the ninety-nine percent trapped in their framework. Breaking free requires not just understanding the language but having the discipline to speak it when everyone else is speaking something different.

Rockefeller faced similar pressure. His contemporaries mocked his frugality, laughed at his old clothes, and questioned why the wealthiest man in America lived so modestly. He ignored them completely. He understood what they did not: wealth is not displayed through consumption but built through accumulation. Those who understand this language join him in the one percent. Those who never learn it remain in the ninety-nine percent regardless of their incomes.

We have established the fundamental distinction. Assets generate income. Liabilities consume income. Your financial future depends on which dominates your balance sheet. In the chapters ahead, we will explore specific types of assets and how to acquire them systematically. We will examine the vehicles for investing, the strategies for real estate, the approaches to business building. Everything will rest on this foundation: assets versus liabilities, income generation versus income consumption, strategic accumulation versus reactive spending.

Learn this language. Speak it fluently. Structure your financial life around its principles. Do this and wealth becomes inevitable. Ignore it and wealth becomes impossible, regardless of how much you earn or how hard you work. The choice, as always, is yours.

CHAPTER 3:
THE COMPANY YOU KEEP—ENGINEERING YOUR ENVIRONMENT

In the summer of 1998, a group of young men gathered in a cramped office on University Avenue in Palo Alto, California. They were building a company that would allow people to send money through email—a concept most observers dismissed as impractical or unnecessary. The company was called Confinity, and it would eventually merge with a competitor to become PayPal. What made this gathering significant was not the technology they were developing but the constellation of talent assembled in that small space. Peter Thiel, Elon Musk, Reid Hoffman, Max Levchin, and several others who would go on to create or fund companies worth hundreds of billions of dollars were working side by side, arguing about product features, debating business strategy, and absorbing lessons about how to build companies that changed the world.

When eBay acquired PayPal in 2002 for one and a half billion dollars, this group dispersed into the broader business world. What happened next became one of the most remarkable demonstrations of environmental influence in modern business history. Thiel founded Palantir and became the first outside investor in Facebook, turning a five-hundred-thousand-dollar investment into billions. Musk founded SpaceX and Tesla, revolutionizing both space exploration and automotive industries. Hoffman founded LinkedIn, creating a professional network worth tens of billions. Levchin founded multiple successful companies including Affirm. Others from that original group started YouTube, Yelp, and dozens of other ventures that collectively created trillions in market value.

This phenomenon became known as the PayPal Mafia, and business analysts have spent years trying to understand what made this particular group so successful. Was it superior intelligence? Many smart people work at companies that fail to generate even one billionaire founder. Was it luck? The odds of one company producing so many successful entrepreneurs by chance are astronomically small. Was it the internet boom? Plenty of people had access to the same opportunities during the same period and achieved nothing comparable. The answer lies not in any single factor but in the environment these individuals created together and the way that environment shaped their thinking, raised their standards, and expanded their sense of what was possible.

You become the average of the five people you spend the most time with. This statement has been repeated so often it borders on cliché, yet most people treat it as motivational rhetoric rather than statistical reality. It is not metaphor. It is measurable fact. Your income will approximate the average income of your five closest associates. Your health habits will mirror those of your social circle. Your ambitions will be constrained or expanded by what the people around you consider normal and achievable. Your risk tolerance, your work ethic, your standards of excellence, and your capacity for delayed gratification will all trend toward the mean of your environment. Fighting against this gravitational pull requires constant effort. Moving with it requires none.

The one percent understand this principle and engineer their environments accordingly. They do not wait for productive peer groups to form organically around them. They do not hope that their current social circle will elevate to match their ambitions. They deliberately place themselves in proximity to people who think bigger, work harder, know more, and expect more than they currently do. They understand that environment is not background scenery but active force that shapes outcomes as surely as compound interest shapes investment returns.

The ninety-nine percent, by contrast, allow their environments to form through accident and convenience. They maintain relationships from high school or college not because these relationships serve their growth but because these relationships are familiar and comfortable. They spend time with family members whose values and ambitions may be radically misaligned with their own goals. They work in organizations where mediocrity is tolerated and excellence is viewed with suspicion. They wonder why their finances never improve while spending their leisure time with people who think saving ten percent of income is extreme and who mock the discipline required for wealth building.

I want to be clear about something that makes people uncomfortable. This is not about abandoning people you care about or treating relationships as purely transactional. Family remains family. Old friends can be valued for history and affection even if they do not share your financial ambitions. What changes is the understanding that proximity determines influence. You can love people from a distance. You can maintain relationships without allowing those relationships to shape your daily thinking and behavior. The one percent make these distinctions consciously. They decide who belongs in their inner circle based on where they want to go, not where they have been.

Consider what happened in that PayPal office. These young men were not just working together on a product. They were engaged in constant intellectual combat, challenging each other's assumptions, debating strategy and philosophy, and pushing each other toward higher standards. Thiel brought libertarian political philosophy and contrarian thinking. Musk brought engineering ambition and refusal to accept conventional constraints. Hoffman brought network thinking and understanding of social dynamics. Levchin brought mathematical rigor and security expertise. Each raised the others' level of thinking simply through proximity and interaction.

More importantly, they normalized ambition. When everyone around you thinks building a company worth tens of millions is a massive achievement, building a company worth billions seems impossible or delusional. When everyone around you is planning to build companies worth billions, that becomes the standard against which you measure yourself. The PayPal Mafia created an environment where massive ambition was not extraordinary but expected. This environmental standard explains more about their subsequent success than any individual genius or unique insight.

The practical question becomes: how does someone without access to Silicon Valley or elite networks engineer a productive environment? The answer is that environment is more accessible today than at any point in human history, but it requires investment and intentionality that most people will not make. The one percent pay for proximity to people who think differently. They attend conferences, join masterminds, purchase coaching, and strategically relocate themselves to cities or neighborhoods where wealth-building conversations occur naturally.

Masterminds deserve particular attention because they represent the most efficient mechanism for environmental engineering. A mastermind is a deliberately formed group of people at similar or slightly higher levels of business or financial success who meet regularly to share knowledge, provide accountability, and solve problems collectively. The structure varies, but the principle remains constant: you bring your challenges to a group of peers who have relevant experience, they provide perspectives you cannot see from inside your situation, and the collective intelligence exceeds what any individual could generate alone.

The most powerful masterminds charge substantial fees for participation. This is not exploitation but filtering mechanism. Those willing to invest five figures or more annually in mastermind membership signal both seriousness and financial capacity that makes peer relationships productive. The group becomes self-selecting for people who are either already successful or so committed to becoming successful that they will prioritize mastermind investment over consumption. These groups provide not just tactical advice but environmental immersion in different thinking patterns.

I have observed people transform their financial trajectories within eighteen months of joining the right mastermind. Not because they learned some secret strategy unavailable elsewhere, but because they were suddenly surrounded by people for whom earning two hundred thousand annually was considered modest, for whom buying rental properties was standard practice, for whom starting businesses was normal rather than remarkable. The mastermind reset their baseline expectations. What seemed impossible from inside their previous environment became merely difficult but achievable from inside the new one. The strategies and tactics could be learned from books. The environmental shift could only come from proximity to people already operating at higher levels.

Beyond paid masterminds, you can create informal peer groups with similar effect. Identify three to five people in your city or industry who are one to two steps ahead of where you want to be. Not twenty steps ahead—that gap is too large for productive peer relationships. One to two steps ahead means they recently solved the problems you are currently facing and can provide actionable guidance. Propose meeting monthly for breakfast or lunch, with each person bringing their current challenges and the group providing perspective and accountability. This costs nothing except time and ego. Most people will not do it because asking for help feels like weakness and organizing requires effort. The one percent do it because they understand the return on that effort exceeds almost any other time investment they could make.

You must also become ruthless about limiting exposure to people who drain your energy, normalize mediocrity, or undermine your ambitions. This is where the distinction between family and proximity becomes crucial. You cannot choose your family, and maintaining those relationships serves important purposes even when they do not align with your financial goals. What you can choose is how much influence those relationships have on your daily thinking and decision-making. You can love your brother who thinks investing is gambling and business ownership is too risky while ensuring that you do not spend three hours every Sunday absorbing his worldview and defending your choices.

I have watched people sabotage their own wealth-building efforts by remaining embedded in environments that punished rather than rewarded their ambitions. The family that mocks them for living frugally while building their investment portfolio. The friends who call them greedy for wanting to earn more than a comfortable middle-class income. The colleagues who view their side business efforts as betrayal of the company or proof they are unhappy with their jobs. These environmental forces exert constant pressure to conform to group norms. Resisting that pressure requires either exceptional strength of will or physical distance from the pressure sources. Most people overestimate their own strength and underestimate the power of environmental influence.

The PayPal Mafia succeeded in part because they insulated themselves from conventional thinking about what was possible. They were not surrounded by people telling them that starting a company was too risky, that their ambitions were unrealistic, or that they should be satisfied with stable jobs and comfortable lives. They were surrounded by people who shared their ambitions and raised rather than lowered their standards. This created a reinforcing cycle where each person's success raised the bar for the others and validated the approach that generated that success.

You can create similar dynamics on a smaller scale. The key is understanding that you are looking for people who share your values around wealth building, delayed gratification, and long-term thinking. Shared interests or history or likability matter far less than shared values around the specific domain where you seek growth. You can enjoy recreational friendships with people who do not think about money the way you do. You should not seek wealth-building advice or accountability from them. That advice and accountability must come from people whose financial results demonstrate they understand what you are trying to accomplish.

Location matters more than most people want to acknowledge. Some cities attract people who think about wealth building constantly. Others attract people who prioritize lifestyle, culture, or comfort over financial ambition. This is not about superiority of one value system over another but about alignment between environment and goals. If you want to build significant wealth, living in a city where that ambition is normal rather than remarkable provides measurable advantage. The conversations you overhear in coffee shops, the opportunities that arise through casual networking, and the baseline expectations of your peer group all shift based on geography.

The one percent often make strategic relocation decisions that seem extreme to the ninety-nine percent. They move to cities where their industries cluster, even when that means leaving family and familiar surroundings. They choose neighborhoods based on the professional networks they provide access to rather than school districts or proximity to relatives. They understand that environment is not just about comfort or convenience but about positioning themselves where wealth-building conversations and opportunities occur with high frequency. The short-term discomfort of relocation creates long-term advantage through environmental optimization.

Within whatever location you choose, you must position yourself in rooms where higher-level conversations occur. This is partially about money—paying to attend the conferences, join the clubs, or access the networks where successful people gather. But it is more fundamentally about mindset. You must be willing to be the least successful person in the room, at least initially. Most people avoid this positioning because it feels uncomfortable or embarrassing. They prefer being big fish in small ponds, where their accomplishments stand out and their egos remain protected. The one percent deliberately place themselves in rooms where they are small fish in big ponds, understanding that the discomfort of that position drives growth.

When you are the most successful person in your peer group, you stop growing. There is no one to learn from, no one to be challenged by, no standard higher than your own current achievement to pursue. You become complacent without realizing it because everyone around you thinks you are doing remarkably well. The praise feels good. The status feels comfortable. Growth stops. The one percent recognize this trap and escape it by constantly upgrading their environments as their own capacities increase.

This creates a progression. Early in your wealth-building journey, you might join a local real estate investment club where people discuss their first rental properties. As you acquire several properties, you move to regional conferences where people discuss portfolio management and scaling strategies. As your portfolio grows larger, you join national mastermind groups where people discuss syndications and institutional relationships. At each level, you are again among the least experienced in the room. At each level, that inexperience relative to your peers drives you to grow faster than you would if you had remained comfortable in your previous environment.

The mechanism is simple but powerful. Humans are social creatures who unconsciously calibrate their behavior to match group norms. When the group norm is saving ten percent and considering that excellent discipline, you will save approximately ten percent even if you are capable of saving forty percent. When the group norm is building seven-figure businesses, you will not be satisfied with building a six-figure side income. The group sets the standard, and individuals conform to that standard without conscious decision-making. Fighting this conformity requires exhausting amounts of willpower. Aligning with it makes achievement effortless.

I recognize that what I am describing sounds mercenary or calculating. There is discomfort in thinking about relationships in terms of what they provide rather than purely emotional connection. But I am not advocating that you abandon authentic relationship or reduce all human interaction to utility maximization. I am stating a reality about how influence operates and suggesting you become conscious and deliberate about forces that most people allow to operate unconsciously and accidentally. You will have close relationships with people regardless. The question is whether those relationships support or undermine the goals you have set for yourself.

The wealthy understand this distinction and make it consciously. They maintain warm relationships with family and old friends while ensuring that their closest advisors, accountability partners, and daily associates are people aligned with their wealth-building trajectory. They love their parents without adopting their parents' financial habits. They enjoy recreational friendships with people who have different values while seeking strategic counsel from people who share their values. They do not confuse emotional connection with ideological alignment.

There is also the matter of what you contribute to others as your own capacity grows. The PayPal Mafia succeeded not just because each individual absorbed from the group but because each contributed unique perspectives that made the collective stronger. As you develop expertise and experience, you become valuable to peer groups not just as learner but as contributor. This creates reciprocal relationships where value flows in both directions. You provide tactical guidance in your areas of strength. Others provide tactical guidance in theirs. Everyone grows faster than they would working in isolation.

This reciprocal dynamic is what separates genuine peer relationships from transactional networking. You are not collecting contacts or using people for advancement. You are engaging in mutual elevation where everyone benefits from everyone else's growth. The one percent build networks based on this principle of mutual value creation. They connect people who can help each other, share insights that advance others' goals, and provide accountability that makes their peers better. This generosity of contribution is what makes them valuable members of elite networks rather than outsiders trying to extract value from those networks.

Environment is not static background against which your life unfolds. It is dynamic force that shapes who you become and what you achieve. The PayPal Mafia demonstrated this truth dramatically, but the same principle operates at every level of wealth and success. You cannot control all aspects of your environment, but you can control far more than most people realize. You can choose which relationships receive your time and attention. You can choose which groups you join and which you leave. You can choose where you live and how you position yourself within that location. You can choose whether to invest in conferences, masterminds, and networks that provide access to people thinking at higher levels than you currently operate.

These choices accumulate into environmental engineering that either accelerates or impedes your wealth-building trajectory. The one percent engineer deliberately. The ninety-nine percent accept whatever environments form around them through accident and convenience. The results diverge accordingly. You have established proper foundation regarding stewardship in Chapter One. You have learned the language of assets and liabilities in Chapter Two. Now you must engineer an environment where those principles are reinforced rather than undermined by the people you interact with daily.

This requires action. Identify three people in your current network who are building wealth according to principles similar to those we have discussed. Propose monthly meetings for mutual accountability and problem-solving. Identify one conference or event in the next six months where people at the level you aspire to reach will gather. Register and attend. Identify one person in your city or industry who is two steps ahead of where you want to be. Ask to buy them lunch and learn from their experience. These actions seem small. Their cumulative effect over years is extraordinary.

The one percent understand that time spent with the right people is the highest-leverage activity they can engage in. An hour with someone who has solved the problem you are facing is worth more than a hundred hours of independent research. A mastermind meeting that provides perspective on a strategic decision can be worth tens or hundreds of thousands in improved outcomes. A conference conversation that leads to a key relationship can be worth millions over time. This is not hyperbole. These are documented returns that occur regularly for people who invest in environmental engineering.

Conversely, time spent with people who normalize mediocrity, reinforce limiting beliefs, or drain your energy carries massive negative returns. The family dinner where everyone complains about money while doing nothing to improve their situations plants seeds of similar thinking in your mind. The friends who mock your frugality while financing lifestyles they cannot afford make your own discipline more difficult to maintain. The colleagues who view ambition as character flaw create environments where hiding your drive becomes necessary for social acceptance.

These negative returns compound just like positive returns, creating widening gaps between those who engineer productively and those who accept what surrounds them.

You are now three chapters into this education. You understand that God and kingdom purposes come first, that stewardship rather than ownership is the proper frame for wealth. You understand that assets generate income while liabilities consume it, and that your balance sheet must favor the former. You now understand that environment determines trajectory more than individual willpower, and that engineering environment deliberately is essential for achieving goals that differ from cultural norms. These three foundations work together. Proper spiritual foundation provides the why. Asset versus liability thinking provides the what. Environmental engineering provides the how.

In the chapters ahead, we will explore specific vehicles and strategies for wealth building. Everything will be easier, more natural, and more likely to succeed if you have engineered an environment where these strategies are normal practice among your peers rather than strange behaviors you must sustain through isolated effort. Make that investment now. The return will exceed almost anything else you do.

CHAPTER 4:
THE TAX-ADVANTAGED ARSENAL—WEAPONS OF
WEALTH BUILDING

In 1999, a young lawyer and entrepreneur named Peter Thiel opened a Roth IRA account and contributed two thousand dollars—the maximum allowed that year. This was unremarkable. Millions of Americans do the same annually, following conventional financial advice to save for retirement through tax-advantaged accounts. What made Thiel's account different was not the contribution but what he did with it. As one of the founders of PayPal, he had access to founder's shares before the company went public. He used his Roth IRA to purchase 1.7 million shares of PayPal at a fraction of a penny per share, a valuation available only to company insiders during early funding rounds.

When eBay acquired PayPal in 2002, those shares inside Thiel's Roth IRA were suddenly worth twenty-eight million dollars. But the story does not end there. Thiel continued using the account to invest in early-stage companies, including a small social network started by a Harvard undergraduate named Mark Zuckerberg. His five-hundred-thousand-dollar investment in Facebook from his Roth IRA eventually became worth over a billion dollars. By 2027, financial disclosures revealed that Thiel's Roth IRA contained approximately five billion dollars—all of which will eventually be withdrawn completely tax-free.

Most Americans will contribute diligently to their Roth IRAs for forty years and accumulate perhaps five hundred thousand dollars by retirement, which represents excellent discipline and will serve them well. Thiel turned his into five billion in less than two decades. The difference was not luck or even exceptional investment returns, though he certainly achieved those. The difference was understanding what these vehicles actually are and how they can be used by those who study the rules carefully. The tax code is not neutral. It is a detailed instruction manual written by the wealthy to benefit the wealthy, and it provides specific mechanisms for those who learn to read it.

I have spent decades watching people handle tax-advantaged accounts, and the pattern is consistent. The ninety-nine percent treat them as savings vehicles where money disappears until retirement. They make their contributions, select conservative investment options, ignore the accounts for years, and hope everything works out. The one percent treat them as weapons in a systematic wealth-building campaign. They understand the specific advantages of each account type, they maximize every benefit available, and they structure their entire financial lives to extract maximum value from the opportunities the tax code provides.

What I want to establish at the outset is that we are not discussing tax evasion or even aggressive tax avoidance. We are discussing the use of vehicles that Congress specifically created to encourage certain behaviors. The government wants you to save for retirement, so it provides tax benefits for doing so. It wants you to save for healthcare expenses, so it provides triple tax advantages for HSAs. It wants you to give to charity, so it provides immediate deductions for contributions to donor-advised funds. These are not loopholes to be exploited guiltily. They are explicit invitations to participate in systems designed to reward specific actions.

The wealthy accept these invitations. Everyone else either remains unaware they exist or considers them too complicated to bother with. This single difference—using the vehicles available versus ignoring them—creates gaps of hundreds of thousands or even millions of dollars over working lifetimes. The math is not subtle. The vehicles are not hidden. What is missing is education about what exists and discipline to use it systematically.

Let me walk through the arsenal in order of power and utility, starting with the most overlooked vehicle that provides advantages exceeding even the Roth IRA when used properly. The Health Savings Account was created in 2003 as part of Medicare legislation, and it remains the least understood and most underutilized tool available to ordinary wealth builders.

An HSA provides three distinct tax advantages that no other vehicle can match. Contributions reduce your current taxable income, exactly like a traditional IRA. The money grows tax-free inside the account, exactly like a Roth IRA. Withdrawals for qualified medical expenses are tax-free, which no other vehicle provides. This triple advantage makes HSAs the single most powerful wealth-building tool available to those who qualify and use them correctly.

The requirements for accessing an HSA are straightforward but specific. You must be enrolled in a high-deductible health plan, which the IRS defines each year with specific minimum deductible amounts. For 2024, that means a deductible of at least sixteen hundred dollars for individual coverage or thirty-two hundred dollars for family coverage. Most people avoid high-deductible plans because they fear the out-of-pocket costs. The one percent choose high-deductible plans specifically to gain access to HSAs, understanding that the tax advantages far exceed the risk of higher medical expenses, especially for healthy individuals who rarely need significant medical care.

Once you have access to an HSA, you can contribute up to the annual limits—currently forty-one hundred dollars for individuals and eighty-three hundred for families, with an additional thousand-dollar catch-up contribution allowed after age fifty-five. These contributions come directly off your taxable income. If you earn seventy thousand and contribute the family maximum of eighty-three hundred, your taxable income drops to sixty-one thousand two hundred. At a twenty-two percent marginal tax rate, that is an immediate eighteen hundred twenty-six dollars in tax savings. This is identical to the benefit provided by a traditional 401k contribution.

Where HSAs diverge from other retirement accounts is in how they treat both growth and withdrawals. The money inside an HSA can be invested exactly like an IRA, growing through stocks, bonds, or mutual funds. Most people miss this entirely. They leave their HSA funds in cash accounts earning minimal interest, treating the HSA as a spending account for immediate medical expenses. This is catastrophically wrong. The optimal strategy is to maximize HSA contributions annually, invest the funds aggressively in index funds, pay all current medical expenses out of pocket from your regular checking account, and allow the HSA to grow untouched for decades.

Here is where the strategy becomes remarkable. You can reimburse yourself for medical expenses at any point in the future with no time limit, provided you kept the receipts. That dental work you paid for in 2025? You can reimburse yourself from your HSA in 2055 if you choose, withdrawing the money completely tax-free. Meanwhile, that money has been growing tax-free for thirty years. If you contributed eighty-three hundred annually to an HSA starting at age thirty and invested it in index funds returning ten percent, by age sixty-five you would have over two million dollars in the account. All withdrawals for medical expenses—and medical expenses in retirement are substantial—come out tax-free. Any withdrawals after age sixty-five for non-medical expenses are simply taxed as ordinary income, exactly like a traditional IRA, so the worst-case scenario is that your HSA functions identically to a traditional retirement account while providing the upside of tax-free withdrawals for medical costs.

This makes the HSA superior to both traditional and Roth IRAs for those who have access to one, yet I have watched countless people pass up this opportunity because they do not want to deal with high-deductible insurance. They are trading thousands of dollars in annual tax benefits for the psychological comfort of a low deductible they will likely never use. This is precisely the kind of decision that separates those who build wealth from those who merely hope to build wealth.

Moving to the more familiar territory of retirement accounts, the Roth IRA deserves its reputation as one of the most powerful wealth-building vehicles ever created. The concept is simple: you contribute after-tax dollars now and receive tax-free growth and withdrawals forever. For 2024, you can contribute up to seven thousand dollars annually if under age fifty, eight thousand if over fifty. The account grows without taxation, and when you withdraw funds after age fifty-nine and a half, you pay zero taxes on either the contributions or the growth.

The mathematics of tax-free compounding are extraordinary. Seven thousand dollars contributed annually from age twenty-five to age sixty-five, growing at ten percent, becomes over three million four hundred thousand dollars. Every penny of that three million four hundred thousand can be withdrawn tax-free. Compare this to a taxable brokerage account where the same contributions and returns would face annual taxes on dividends and capital gains, plus taxes on final withdrawal. The tax burden would easily exceed five hundred thousand dollars over that forty-year period. This is found money, captured simply by using the correct vehicle for long-term investing.

The question I am asked most frequently about Roth IRAs is whether to choose them over traditional tax-deferred accounts. The conventional wisdom says to use traditional accounts when your tax rate is high and Roth accounts when your tax rate is low, with the theory being that you want the deduction when it is worth more and the tax-free withdrawal when you would otherwise pay at lower rates. This conventional wisdom is wrong for most people building significant wealth, and Peter Thiel's five-billion-dollar Roth IRA demonstrates why.

The traditional versus Roth decision should be based on expected future tax rates and account sizes, not current tax rates alone. If you believe tax rates will rise—and given federal debt levels and demographic trends, this seems highly probable—paying taxes now at today's rates and receiving tax-free withdrawals at tomorrow's higher rates makes obvious sense. More importantly, if you expect to build substantial wealth, Roth accounts eliminate the risk that your retirement account success creates a massive tax liability. Traditional accounts require minimum distributions starting at age seventy-three, forcing you to withdraw money and pay taxes whether you need the money or not. Roth accounts have no such requirements. The money can grow tax-free for your entire life and pass tax-free to your heirs.

This makes Roth IRAs particularly valuable for those who follow the principles we have discussed in previous chapters. If you are systematically building wealth through multiple vehicles and expect to have substantial assets by retirement, having a large pool of money that can be accessed tax-free provides flexibility that traditional accounts cannot match. You might need capital for a business opportunity, a real estate investment, or simply to manage your tax liability by blending tax-free Roth withdrawals with taxable traditional account withdrawals. The Roth IRA is a Swiss Army knife that becomes more valuable the wealthier you become.

The traditional 401k or 403b remains relevant primarily for the employer match, which is the only genuinely free money in personal finance. If your employer offers to match your contributions dollar-for-dollar up to six percent of your salary, you must contribute at least enough to capture that full match. This is a one-hundred-percent immediate return on your investment before any market growth. There is no other opportunity in finance that provides this return with this certainty. I do not care if you are in debt, building an emergency fund, or saving for a house down payment. Capture the full employer match first. Everything else is secondary.

Beyond the match, whether to continue contributing to a traditional 401k depends on your income level and access to other vehicles. If you earn enough that you cannot contribute directly to a Roth IRA due to income limits—and those limits are surprisingly low for high earners—you may need to use the backdoor Roth conversion strategy where you contribute to a traditional IRA and immediately convert to Roth. This maintains your ability to build Roth assets despite exceeding income thresholds. If your 401k offers Roth contributions, that may be preferable to traditional contributions for the reasons already discussed, though you lose the immediate tax deduction.

The sequencing of contributions matters enormously and yet receives little attention in conventional financial advice. The optimal order for most people building wealth is: first, contribute enough to your 401k to capture the full employer match. Second, maximize your HSA contribution if you have access to one. Third, maximize your Roth IRA contribution either directly or through backdoor conversion. Fourth, return to your 401k and contribute additional funds up to the annual maximum if you have remaining capital to invest. Fifth, move to taxable brokerage accounts for any additional investment capital. This sequence captures free money first, then triple tax advantage, then tax-free growth, then tax-deferred growth, and finally taxable growth.

The taxable brokerage account is often overlooked in retirement planning advice, which focuses almost exclusively on tax-advantaged retirement accounts. This is a mistake that limits wealth-building potential. Taxable brokerage accounts provide something that retirement accounts cannot: liquidity and flexibility without penalties. You can access the money before age fifty-nine and a half without penalty. You can use it for opportunities that arise—business investments, real estate acquisitions, or simply bridging income needs if you pursue early retirement. The tax treatment is actually superior to traditional retirement accounts for long-term holdings, since qualified dividends and long-term capital gains face maximum rates of fifteen or twenty percent, lower than ordinary income tax rates that apply to traditional retirement account withdrawals.

The one percent always maintain substantial assets in taxable brokerage accounts alongside their retirement accounts. They understand that flexibility has value and that not all wealth building should be locked behind retirement account restrictions. If you want to retire at fifty instead of sixty-five, you need assets you can access without penalty. If you want to start a business at forty-five, you need capital that is not trapped in retirement accounts. The taxable brokerage account provides this optionality while still offering tax-efficient growth through index funds that generate minimal taxable events.

The 529 education savings plan represents one of the most misunderstood and underutilized vehicles for those raising children, yet it provides advantages that compound over decades when used properly. Created in 1996 and named after the section of tax code authorizing them, 529 plans allow you to invest after-tax dollars for education expenses with all growth occurring tax-free and all withdrawals for qualified education expenses coming out tax-free at the federal level. Many states provide additional state income tax deductions for contributions, creating immediate tax benefits that enhance the already substantial advantages of tax-free growth.

The mechanics are straightforward. You open a 529 account designating a beneficiary—typically your child, though it can be yourself, a grandchild, or anyone else. You contribute after-tax money up to very high annual limits that vary by state but that typically allow total contributions exceeding three hundred thousand dollars per beneficiary across all accounts. The money is invested in mutual funds or age-based portfolios that automatically shift from aggressive to conservative allocations as the beneficiary approaches college age. When you withdraw funds to pay for qualified education expenses— tuition, fees, books, room and board at accredited institutions—the growth comes out completely tax-free.

The power of tax-free compounding over eighteen years is substantial. Someone who contributes three thousand dollars annually to a 529 plan from their child's birth until age eighteen, earning eight percent returns, accumulates approximately ninety thousand dollars despite contributing only fifty-four thousand. That thirty-six thousand in growth comes out tax-free when used for college, saving perhaps five thousand four hundred dollars in federal taxes at a fifteen percent capital gains rate, plus additional savings from avoiding state taxes on the growth. This is found money captured through using the appropriate vehicle rather than saving in a taxable account.

The state tax deduction available in many states enhances these benefits significantly. Over thirty states provide full or partial tax deductions for 529 contributions, with some states allowing deductions for the full amount contributed regardless of size. New York, for instance, allows married couples filing jointly to deduct up to ten thousand dollars in annual 529 contributions. At New York's top marginal rate of ten point nine percent, this provides an immediate tax savings of one thousand ninety dollars annually. Over eighteen years, this creates nearly twenty thousand dollars in tax savings before accounting for any growth benefits. The combination of immediate state tax deduction plus decades of tax-free federal growth makes 529 plans extraordinarily powerful for those who utilize them fully.

The one percent understand a strategy called superfunding that most people never learn about. IRS rules allow you to contribute five years' worth of annual gift tax exclusions in a single year without triggering gift taxes, provided you elect to treat the contribution as spread over five years. For 2024, with annual gift tax exclusions at eighteen thousand dollars per person, this allows contributing ninety thousand dollars per beneficiary in a single year—or one hundred eighty thousand per beneficiary if married couples combine their exclusions. A wealthy grandparent can superfund 529 accounts for multiple grandchildren, moving hundreds of thousands of dollars out of their taxable estate while providing education funding that grows tax-free.

This superfunding strategy provides estate planning benefits beyond the education funding itself. The money is removed from the contributor's estate immediately while they retain control over the account. If the grandparent dies, the account remains intact for the beneficiary. If the beneficiary does not use all the funds, the grandparent or other account owner can change beneficiaries to other family members. This combination of estate tax reduction plus education funding plus retained control makes superfunding one of the most effective wealth transfer strategies available to high-net-worth families.

The objection I encounter most frequently regarding 529 plans is the fear that the child will not attend college or will receive scholarships making the 529 unnecessary. This concern causes many parents to avoid 529 plans entirely, leaving substantial tax benefits uncaptured. The concern is misplaced for several reasons. First, you can change the beneficiary to another family member—a sibling, a cousin, even yourself if you decide to pursue additional education.

The money is not trapped for one specific person's education. Second, if the beneficiary receives scholarships, you can withdraw an amount equal to the scholarship from the 529 and pay only income taxes on the growth portion without the additional ten percent penalty that normally applies to non-qualified withdrawals. Third, recent changes allow up to ten thousand dollars from 529 plans to be used for K-12 tuition at private schools, expanding the qualified uses beyond just college.

Fourth, and most importantly, starting in 2024, unused 529 funds can be rolled over to a Roth IRA for the beneficiary subject to certain conditions. Up to thirty-five thousand dollars of unused 529 funds accumulated over at least fifteen years can be transferred to the beneficiary's Roth IRA without taxes or penalties, subject to annual Roth IRA contribution limits. This provision transforms 529 plans from education-only vehicles into tools that can serve either education funding or retirement funding depending on the beneficiary's path. The fear that money will be trapped if your child does not attend college has been largely eliminated through these various provisions.

The one percent establish 529 plans for their children at birth and contribute systematically throughout childhood, understanding that eighteen years of tax-free compounding creates assets that would be impossible to accumulate in the final few years before college. They often fund 529s before funding their own retirement accounts beyond the employer match because the time horizon for education savings is shorter—money needed in eighteen years benefits from immediate investment more than money needed in forty years benefits from slightly higher contributions. They utilize state tax deductions fully by contributing at least up to the deduction limit annually. They invest aggressively in stock-heavy allocations during the child's early years, understanding that eighteen years provides sufficient time to recover from market volatility.

The common mistakes with 529 plans mirror the mistakes people make with retirement accounts: contributing too conservatively because they fear market declines, selecting actively managed funds with high fees rather than low-cost index funds, timing contributions sporadically rather than systematically, and checking account balances too frequently during market volatility and making emotional decisions to shift to conservative allocations at exactly the wrong times. Someone who contributes three thousand dollars annually but invests it in money market funds earning two percent accumulates only sixty-seven thousand over eighteen years instead of the ninety thousand they would have accumulated at eight percent. The difference of twenty-three thousand dollars—enough to pay for a full year at many state universities—is surrendered through excessive conservatism driven by fear of short-term volatility.

The one percent who use 529 plans invest aggressively during the child's early years, maintain those allocations through market downturns, and only shift toward conservative allocations when college attendance is imminent and the money will be needed within two to three years. They understand that a 529 account for a newborn has an eighteen-year time horizon that fully justifies stock-heavy allocations, and that shifting to bonds when the child is five years old because of fear of market crashes costs them thirteen additional years of equity returns for no good reason.

The coordination of 529 plans with other education funding sources requires thought that most families skip. Many families save in both 529 plans and in taxable accounts or custodial accounts for education expenses. The optimal strategy is to maintain 529 accounts for tax-free growth while keeping minimal funds in custodial accounts that count against the student's financial aid eligibility at far higher rates than parent-owned 529 accounts. A student with ten thousand dollars in a custodial account under their name will see their financial aid reduced by two thousand dollars annually because student assets are assessed at twenty percent. The same ten thousand in a parent-owned 529 account reduces aid by only five hundred sixty dollars because parent assets are assessed at five point six percent.

This difference means that families should fund 529 plans fully before contributing anything to custodial accounts or to taxable accounts designated for the child's education. The 529 provides superior tax treatment plus superior financial aid treatment, making it strictly better than alternatives for education savings. The only exception is if you expect your child will not attend college at all and you do not want to deal with the complications of changing beneficiaries or taking non-qualified withdrawals. Even in that case, the new Roth IRA rollover provision largely eliminates the concern.

The Donor-Advised Fund represents the final vehicle in this arsenal, deserving attention from anyone serious about charitable giving. A DAF functions as a charitable investment account. You contribute cash or appreciated securities to the fund and receive an immediate tax deduction for the full fair market value of the contribution. The assets then remain in the fund, where they can be invested and grow tax-free. You can recommend grants from the fund to qualified charities at any time, and the fund distributes those grants on your behalf.

The advantages are multiple and substantial. First, you receive the tax deduction immediately, even though you may not distribute the funds to charities for years. This allows you to time deductions for years when they provide maximum tax benefit—perhaps a year with unusually high income or when you have capital gains from selling a business or property. Second, if you contribute appreciated securities rather than cash, you avoid paying capital gains tax entirely while still receiving a deduction for the full value. Third, the money grows tax-free inside the fund while you decide which organizations to support. Fourth, you can make grants anonymously if you prefer privacy. Fifth, your heirs can inherit the ability to recommend grants from the fund, creating a vehicle for teaching children about stewardship and philanthropy.

I recognize that donor-advised funds may seem relevant only to the wealthy, but they become valuable at more modest wealth levels than most people realize. If you are contributing three thousand dollars annually to various ministries and Christian organizations, consolidating that giving into a DAF provides administrative simplicity and allows you to invest the funds for growth between distributions. If you have appreciated stock in your brokerage account—perhaps shares you purchased years ago that have substantial gains—donating those shares to a DAF instead of selling them and donating cash saves you the capital gains tax on the appreciation.

The combination of these vehicles creates an ecosystem for tax-efficient wealth building. You minimize current taxes through HSA and traditional 401k contributions. You eliminate future taxes through Roth IRA contributions. You fund education tax-efficiently through 529 plans. You maintain flexibility through taxable brokerage accounts. You optimize charitable giving through donor-advised funds. Each vehicle serves specific purposes, and using all of them in proper sequence and proportion maximizes the after-tax wealth you can accumulate over a working lifetime.

The dollar amounts involved are not trivial. Consider someone who earns eighty thousand annually and follows the optimization sequence. They contribute enough to capture a six percent employer match—four thousand eight hundred dollars that costs them only four thousand eight hundred from their salary but creates nine thousand six hundred in their 401k. They maximize their family HSA contribution—eighty-three hundred dollars that reduces their taxable income and compounds tax-free for decades. They maximize a Roth IRA—seven thousand dollars in after-tax contributions that grow tax-free forever. They contribute three thousand annually to their child's 529 plan, capturing state tax deductions and building education funding through tax-free growth. This totals twenty-seven thousand six hundred dollars invested annually with maximum tax efficiency. If they maintain this pattern from age thirty to age sixty-five and earn ten percent returns, they will have approximately seven point eight million dollars across their various accounts. The tax advantages captured through proper vehicle selection easily exceed one point two million dollars compared to investing the same amounts in purely taxable accounts.

Most people will never approach these amounts because they do not maximize their contributions, do not use all available vehicles, and do not maintain discipline over decades. That is precisely what creates the divergence between the one percent and the ninety-nine percent. The vehicles are available to everyone. The knowledge of how to use them is readily accessible. What remains rare is the combination of knowledge and discipline to implement the strategy year after year regardless of competing demands for current consumption.

Peter Thiel's five-billion-dollar Roth IRA is an extreme example that demonstrates what becomes possible when you understand the rules and use them creatively within legal boundaries. Most people will not have access to founder's shares in companies that become worth billions. But the principle applies at every level: these vehicles exist, they provide enormous advantages, and using them systematically creates wealth that would be impossible to accumulate through any other means. The tax code is not your enemy. It is a detailed map showing exactly where the treasure is buried.

The one percent read that map carefully and dig in the marked locations. The ninety-nine percent complain the map is too complicated and never bother learning to read it.

I want to address one final point that causes paralysis for many people. They read advice about Roth versus traditional accounts, HSA strategies versus traditional health insurance, 529 plans versus taxable savings, and donor-advised funds versus direct giving, and they become overwhelmed by the complexity. They conclude that getting the strategy exactly right is essential and that making a mistake will be catastrophic. This is false. Perfect optimization matters far less than simply using any of these vehicles consistently. A Roth IRA is better than a traditional IRA for most people, but a traditional IRA is infinitely better than no retirement account at all. A 529 plan provides advantages over taxable education savings, but taxable education savings is infinitely better than no education savings at all. A donor-advised fund provides advantages over direct giving, but direct giving is infinitely better than no giving at all.

The goal is not perfection but consistent action using the best vehicles available to you. Open the accounts. Make the contributions. Invest the funds properly. Maintain the discipline for decades. The tax advantages will accumulate. The compound returns will multiply.

The wealth will build. Do this and you will arrive at retirement with more assets than most of your peers despite similar incomes, simply because you used vehicles that captured tax benefits they ignored.

The tax code is filled with thousands of pages specifically because it contains thousands of provisions designed to reward specific behaviors. The one percent study those provisions the way generals study terrain before battle. They know where the advantages lie, how to access them, and how to combine them for maximum effect. You now know the essential vehicles and how they function. What remains is the choice to use them or to continue operating as though they do not exist. The former leads to wealth captured through legal tax optimization. The latter leads to wealth unnecessarily surrendered to taxes that could have been avoided.

CHAPTER 5:
REAL ESTATE—THE WEALTH-BUILDING MACHINE THE MIDDLE CLASS IGNORES

In 1992, a young couple named John and Jane purchased a modest duplex in Portland, Oregon for eighty-five thousand dollars. They put down seventeen thousand—twenty percent to avoid private mortgage insurance—and financed the remaining sixty-eight thousand at seven point five percent interest. They moved into one unit and rented the other unit to tenants who paid six hundred fifty dollars monthly. Their total mortgage payment including property taxes and insurance was seven hundred eighty dollars monthly. The rental income covered eighty-three percent of their housing costs, meaning their actual out-of-pocket expense to live in half of a duplex was one hundred thirty dollars monthly while their tenants paid down their mortgage and covered most of their ownership costs.

This was house hacking before the term existed, and it represented the beginning of a wealth-building journey that would transform John and Jane's financial lives. They lived in that duplex for four years while saving aggressively. The rental income plus their minimal living expenses allowed them to save over forty percent of their combined income of fifty-five thousand dollars annually. By 1996, they had accumulated enough for another down payment. They purchased a second duplex for one hundred fifteen thousand dollars, moved into one unit, and rented both units of their first duplex plus one unit of their second duplex. They now had three rental units producing income while living essentially for free in the fourth unit.

They repeated this pattern every three to four years throughout the late 1990s and early 2000s, eventually accumulating seven properties containing fourteen total units by 2008. When the financial crisis hit and property values collapsed, they faced the same crisis that destroyed thousands of real estate investors—some of their properties were underwater, meaning they owed more than the properties were worth. But they had structured their purchases conservatively enough that the rental income covered their mortgages even during the recession when some units sat vacant for months. They never missed a mortgage payment. They never sold during the panic. They maintained their properties and their tenants through the crisis.

By 2024, thirty-two years after their first duplex purchase, John and Jane owned all seven properties free and clear. The mortgages were paid off through a combination of rental income, extra principal payments, and refinancing during low interest rate periods. The properties that they had purchased for a combined total of approximately eight hundred fifty thousand dollars were now worth over four million dollars. More importantly, those properties generated approximately fifteen thousand dollars monthly in rental income—one hundred eighty thousand annually—with no mortgage payments consuming that income. They had built a passive income stream exceeding what most people earn from full-time employment, and they had done it systematically through repeated application of simple principles sustained across three decades.

John and Jane were not brilliant real estate investors. They were not developers or flippers or syndicators doing complex deals. They were schoolteachers who understood that real estate builds wealth through multiple simultaneous mechanisms that no other investment provides in combination: leverage allowing you to control assets worth five times your investment, mortgage paydown where tenants pay your debt, cash flow generating monthly income, appreciation building equity over decades, and tax advantages that shelter income from taxation. They implemented these principles consistently despite market volatility, despite inevitable tenant problems, despite repairs and vacancies and all the complications that real estate ownership creates. Their discipline produced financial independence while their colleagues who earned similar salaries remained dependent on employment income into their sixties.

This chapter examines why real estate represents one of the most reliable paths to substantial wealth for ordinary people, how to analyze properties to distinguish investments from money pits, what strategies allow you to acquire properties even with limited capital, what mistakes destroy real estate investors, and why most people never build wealth through real estate despite understanding intellectually that it works. The frameworks are straightforward and the mathematics are clear, yet the implementation rate remains extraordinarily low because real estate requires active management and tolerance for complications that stock investing does not require. The one percent accept these complications as the price of accessing returns and leverage that passive investments cannot provide. The ninety-nine percent avoid real estate entirely or buy single properties that they manage poorly and eventually sell out of frustration, never accessing the compounding that creates transformative wealth.

The five simultaneous wealth-building mechanisms that real estate provides explain why it has created more millionaires than perhaps any other investment class. Understanding each mechanism and how they interact is essential to appreciating why real estate is powerful and to avoiding the mistakes that prevent people from capturing these benefits.

The first mechanism is leverage—the ability to control assets worth five to ten times your invested capital through mortgage financing. When you purchase a two hundred thousand dollar property with twenty percent down, you invest forty thousand dollars but control an asset worth two hundred thousand. If that property appreciates five percent annually, it increases in value by ten thousand dollars. That ten thousand dollar gain on your forty thousand dollar investment represents a twenty-five percent return on your invested capital, even though the property itself only appreciated five percent. This is the mathematical power of leverage—your returns are calculated on the full property value but your investment is only the down payment.

Compare this to stock investing where you must purchase stocks entirely with your own capital. If you invest forty thousand in stocks and they appreciate five percent, you gain two thousand dollars—a five percent return on your investment. The real estate investor with identical capital invested and identical asset appreciation rate achieved a twenty-five percent return while the stock investor achieved a five percent return. This five-to-one difference in returns from identical asset appreciation is leverage at work, and it is the primary reason that real estate builds wealth faster than most other investments for those who use it correctly.

The second mechanism is mortgage paydown—the fact that tenants pay your debt through their rent payments. Every month that tenants pay rent, a portion of that rent goes toward your mortgage principal, reducing your debt and increasing your equity in the property. In the early years of a mortgage, most of each payment goes toward interest and only small amounts reduce principal. But over time, the principal portion increases while the interest portion decreases. Across thirty years, tenants pay off hundreds of thousands in debt that you borrowed but never personally paid back. This forced savings mechanism operates independently of whether the property appreciates—you build equity through debt reduction even if property values remain flat.

The third mechanism is cash flow—the monthly income remaining after all expenses are paid. A property generating two thousand dollars in monthly rent with one thousand dollars in mortgage payment, two hundred dollars in property taxes, one hundred fifty dollars in insurance, one hundred dollars in maintenance reserves, and fifty dollars in property management fees produces five hundred dollars monthly in positive cash flow. This five hundred dollars monthly—six thousand annually—is real income that you can spend, reinvest, or use to accelerate mortgage paydown. Cash flow provides current benefit while leverage and mortgage paydown build future equity.

The fourth mechanism is appreciation—the increase in property values over time. Historically, real estate in desirable locations has appreciated at approximately three to five percent annually, though this varies enormously by location and time period.

Some markets appreciate ten percent or more during boom periods. Some markets decline during busts. Over multi-decade holds, most properties in decent locations appreciate substantially, building equity that eventually can be accessed through sale or refinancing. The combination of leverage multiplying appreciation returns plus mortgage paydown plus cash flow creates wealth accumulation rates that are difficult to match through other investments.

The fifth mechanism is tax advantages that allow real estate investors to generate income while paying minimal taxes. Depreciation allows you to deduct the theoretical wearing out of the property over twenty-seven and a half years, creating paper losses that offset rental income even when you are generating positive cash flow. Mortgage interest is deductible, reducing taxable income further. Operating expenses including repairs, maintenance, property management, insurance, and property taxes are all deductible. The result is that you can generate substantial cash flow while showing little to no taxable income, sometimes even showing losses that offset other income. When you eventually sell, you can defer capital gains taxes indefinitely through 1031 exchanges where you sell one property and purchase another of equal or greater value, pushing taxes into the future.

These five mechanisms operate simultaneously, compounding each other to create wealth accumulation that exceeds what any single mechanism could provide. The property that you purchased with twenty percent down appreciates while tenants pay down your mortgage while generating monthly cash flow while creating tax deductions that shelter income from taxation. After ten years, you have built substantial equity through appreciation and mortgage paydown, you have collected tens of thousands in cash flow, and you have reduced your tax liability through depreciation and expense deductions. This combination is extraordinarily powerful when sustained across decades.

In 1973, a recent college graduate named Sam Zell purchased his first apartment building in Ann Arbor, Michigan using money he had saved managing student housing during college. The property was distressed—the owner was motivated to sell and the building needed work. Zell purchased it below market value, improved it, increased rents to market rates, and refinanced to extract his capital. He used the extracted capital to purchase another property and repeated the pattern. Over the following five decades, Zell built Equity Residential and Equity LifeStyle Properties into real estate empires worth billions. He became known as the "grave dancer" for his willingness to buy properties during market crashes when others were panicking.

Zell's success came from understanding that real estate cycles through boom and bust periods, and that the greatest wealth is built by those who buy during busts and hold through the subsequent recoveries. During the 1970s recession, the early 1990s savings and loan crisis, the 2008 financial crisis, and the 2020 COVID panic, Zell purchased properties that frightened sellers were desperate to unload. He improved them, held them through the recovery periods, and either sold at peaks or refinanced to extract equity while maintaining ownership. His returns came not from brilliant property selection but from contrarian timing—buying when others sold and selling when others bought.

The average person cannot replicate Zell's scale, but the principles apply at any level. The investor who purchased rental properties in 2010 and 2011 when the market was still depressed from the 2008 crisis achieved extraordinary returns as the market recovered through the 2010s. Properties purchased for one hundred fifty thousand in 2010 were worth three hundred thousand by 2020, doubling in value while generating cash flow the entire time and having substantial mortgage principal paid down by tenants. The investor who waited until 2021 when the market had fully recovered paid three hundred thousand for properties that had been available for one hundred fifty thousand eleven years earlier, cutting their potential returns in half.

This timing advantage requires courage to buy when markets are depressed and when the conventional wisdom is that prices will fall further. It also requires capital available when opportunities appear, which means maintaining reserves and not being fully invested during boom periods when everyone else is aggressively buying. The one percent maintain dry powder—cash reserves and available credit—specifically so they can act when opportunities emerge during panics. The ninety-nine percent are fully invested during booms and have no capital available during busts, missing the opportunities that create generational wealth.

The analysis framework for evaluating rental properties determines whether you purchase wealth-building assets or money-losing disasters. The framework is mathematical rather than emotional, and it requires collecting specific data and running calculations before making offers. The one percent analyze dozens of properties before purchasing one, walking away from deals that do not meet their criteria regardless of how much time they invested in analysis. The ninety-nine percent fall in love with properties based on aesthetics or location and then rationalize the numbers to justify emotional decisions, purchasing properties that will never generate adequate returns.

The rental income analysis begins with determining market rent—what tenants will actually pay, not what you hope they will pay. This requires researching comparable properties in the same area with similar bedrooms, bathrooms, and amenities. Zillow, Rentometer, and similar sites provide rental estimates, but the most reliable data comes from calling property management companies and asking what they could rent a property like yours for, or from studying current rental listings for comparable properties. If comparable properties are listing for one thousand eight hundred monthly, your property will likely rent for approximately that amount. Hoping you can charge two thousand two hundred because you plan to upgrade the property is speculation, not analysis.

The expense estimation must include all costs, not just mortgage and property taxes. Property taxes and insurance are easily determined from listing information and insurance quotes. Maintenance and repairs typically run one percent of property value annually—on a two hundred thousand dollar property, budget two thousand annually or one hundred sixty-seven monthly. Property management fees are typically eight to ten percent of collected rent if you use professional management, which you should unless you want property management to become your job. Vacancy allowance should be five to eight percent of rent to account for periods between tenants. HOA fees, if applicable, must be included. Capital expenditures for major replacements like roofs, HVAC systems, and appliances should be budgeted at one to two percent of property value annually.

The total monthly expense calculation for a two hundred thousand dollar property renting for two thousand monthly might look like:

- Mortgage (eighty percent loan-to-value at seven percent for thirty years): one thousand sixty-four dollars
- Property taxes (one point two percent annually): two hundred dollars
- Insurance: one hundred dollars
- Maintenance (one percent of value annually): one hundred sixty-seven dollars
- Property management (eight percent of rent): one hundred sixty dollars
- Vacancy allowance (five percent of rent): one hundred dollars
- Capital expenditures (one percent of value annually): one hundred sixty-seven dollars
- Total monthly expenses: one thousand nine hundred fifty-eight dollars
- Monthly rent collected: two thousand dollars
- Monthly cash flow: forty-two dollars

This property generates minimal cash flow—only forty-two dollars monthly or five hundred four dollars annually on a forty thousand dollar down payment. That represents a one point two six percent cash-on-cash return, which is terrible compared to what you could earn in index funds or money market accounts. This is not a property you should purchase unless you are confident that rents will increase substantially or that appreciation will compensate for weak cash flow. The one percent would walk away from this property and continue searching for better opportunities. The ninety-nine percent would purchase it because it is "only" slightly negative or barely positive, then discover that unexpected repairs or longer vacancy periods turn those minimal returns negative and that they are subsidizing tenants to live in their property.

The one percent rule provides a quick filter for identifying properties worth analyzing in detail. The rule states that monthly rent should equal at least one percent of the purchase price. A two hundred thousand dollar property should generate at least two thousand dollars monthly in rent. A three hundred thousand dollar property should generate three thousand monthly. Properties meeting the one percent rule typically generate adequate cash flow to justify the investment and the management effort required. Properties below the one percent rule often generate inadequate returns and should be avoided unless appreciation prospects are exceptional.

The one percent rule is violated in most expensive coastal markets where property prices have appreciated faster than rents. In San Francisco or Los Angeles or New York, properties routinely sell for prices requiring only point four to point six percent monthly rents—a million dollar property might rent for only four to six thousand monthly. These properties can still build wealth through appreciation and mortgage paydown, but they typically generate negative cash flow requiring owners to subsidize them monthly. The one percent avoid negative cash flow properties unless they have high confidence in continued appreciation and unless they have reserves allowing them to sustain negative cash flow through market cycles without forced sales.

The mortgage structure you select affects your returns and your risk substantially. The standard thirty-year fixed-rate mortgage provides stability—your payment never changes regardless of market conditions, making budgeting predictable and protecting you from interest rate increases. The fifteen-year fixed-rate mortgage requires higher monthly payments but builds equity far faster and costs dramatically less in total interest paid. The adjustable-rate mortgage offers lower initial rates that can increase substantially after the fixed period expires. The interest-only mortgage minimizes monthly payments but builds no equity through principal paydown.

The one percent typically use thirty-year fixed-rate mortgages for rental properties because the payment stability allows them to weather market downturns without facing payment increases that would turn positive cash flow into negative cash flow. They accept that thirty-year mortgages cost more in total interest than fifteen-year mortgages because the lower monthly payment provides safety margin and because they can always make extra principal payments to accelerate payoff if they choose. They avoid adjustable-rate mortgages on rental properties because the risk of payment increases during market downturns creates foreclosure risk that fixed-rate mortgages eliminate.

The house hacking strategy that John and Jane used represents the most accessible entry point into real estate investing for those with limited capital. House hacking means purchasing a property with multiple units, living in one unit while renting the others, and using rental income to cover most or all of your housing costs. This strategy allows you to live for free or nearly free while building equity in a property and learning landlording with minimal risk because you live on-site and can address issues immediately.

The most common house hacking approach uses FHA financing to purchase a two-to-four unit property with only three point five percent down payment. FHA loans require owner occupancy, meaning you must live in the property for at least one year, but they allow you to rent the other units immediately. Someone purchasing a two hundred fifty thousand dollar fourplex with three point five percent down invests only eighty-seven hundred fifty dollars plus closing costs. If three units rent for one thousand dollars each and the total mortgage payment plus expenses is twenty-five hundred dollars monthly, the rental income covers most of the housing costs while the owner lives in the fourth unit. After one year of owner occupancy, the owner can purchase another property with another FHA loan, move into the new property, and rent the fourth unit of the original property, converting it to a fully-rented investment property.

This strategy allows someone to acquire multiple properties over several years using low down payment financing that would not be available for pure investment properties. After five years of purchasing one property annually and living in each for one year before moving to the next, the investor owns five properties with minimal capital invested and has tenants paying mortgages on all of them. The equity built through appreciation and mortgage paydown over this period often provides enough capital to begin purchasing additional properties with conventional financing without needing to live in them.

The one percent who start with limited capital use house hacking as their entry point into real estate investing. They accept the inconvenience of living in rental properties and dealing with tenants in close proximity as the temporary price of accessing financing and building initial equity. They view the one-year owner occupancy requirement not as a burden but as a mechanism allowing them to acquire multiple properties over several years that they could never have afforded to purchase as pure investments. They recognize that living modestly while building equity positions them to eventually own enough properties that they can move wherever they want while their properties generate passive income.

The location selection for rental properties matters more than almost any other factor because location determines appreciation, rental demand, tenant quality, and management difficulty. The one percent follow a simple rule: buy in areas where they would be willing to live themselves, not in areas they consider beneath them but suitable for tenants. The properties in desirable areas with good schools, low crime, and strong employment attract responsible tenants who maintain properties and pay rent consistently. The properties in deteriorating areas with poor schools, high crime, and weak employment attract problem tenants who damage properties and default on rent regularly.

The false economy that destroys many beginning real estate investors is purchasing cheap properties in cheap areas and believing they are getting good deals because purchase prices are low and initial cash flow looks good. A fifty thousand dollar house renting for eight hundred monthly appears to meet the one percent rule easily. But properties that cheap are cheap for reasons—they are in areas where employment is declining, where crime is high, where schools are failing, and where tenants have limited options and limited income. The maintenance costs on these properties are astronomical because tenants damage them and because the properties are often old and poorly maintained. The vacancy rates are high because good tenants move to better areas as soon as they can afford to. The appreciation is minimal or negative because these areas are declining.

The one percent avoid these value traps by purchasing in areas with strong fundamentals—growing employment, good schools, declining crime, increasing property values. They pay more per property but they accept higher purchase prices as the cost of accessing appreciation, stable tenants, and reasonable maintenance costs. They understand that a three hundred thousand dollar property in a good area will build more wealth over twenty years than a fifty thousand dollar property in a bad area, even though the initial cash flow from the cheap property looks better on paper.

The property management decision determines whether real estate investing enhances your life or consumes it. Self-management saves the eight to ten percent property management fee but requires you to handle tenant calls, coordinate repairs, show properties to prospective tenants, collect rent, and manage all the complications that rental properties create. Professional management costs money but eliminates these responsibilities, making rental property ownership genuinely passive. The decision is not primarily financial but rather about whether you want to operate a property management business or whether you want to own real estate as an investment that others manage for you.

The one percent typically use professional property management because their time is worth more than the management fees they pay. Someone earning one hundred thousand annually in their primary career earns approximately forty-eight dollars per hour. Spending ten hours monthly managing rental properties costs them four hundred eighty dollars in opportunity cost—time they could have spent earning money in their primary career or investing in activities that generate more value than saving property management fees. They gladly pay two hundred dollars in management fees to avoid four hundred eighty dollars in opportunity cost plus the stress and inconvenience of managing tenants themselves.

The ninety-nine percent often try to self-manage to save money, not realizing that their time has value and that dealing with tenant issues at midnight or on weekends destroys the quality of life that building wealth is supposed to improve. They burn out on real estate investing after a few years of dealing with problem tenants and constant maintenance issues, selling their properties and never building the portfolio that creates financial independence. The eight percent they saved in management fees cost them the entire opportunity because they quit before the compounding really accelerated.

The property acquisition during market downturns creates the opportunity for life-changing returns that buying during stable markets cannot provide. During the 2008 financial crisis, foreclosures flooded markets in cities across the country. Properties that sold for three hundred thousand dollars in 2006 were available for one hundred fifty thousand dollars in 2009. Investors who had cash or access to financing could purchase properties at fifty percent discounts to peak prices. Those properties recovered to exceed their previous peaks by 2015, doubling the investors' money in six years while generating cash flow the entire time.

The challenge is maintaining capital and courage during market peaks so that you have resources available when crashes occur. Most investors are fully invested during boom periods, buying at peak prices and then facing losses when markets decline. They have no capital available when opportunities emerge during crashes because they spent everything during the boom. The one percent maintain reserves and credit capacity specifically to exploit crashes. They sell marginal properties during peaks, building cash reserves. They maintain credit lines that they can tap during crashes. They avoid becoming overleveraged during booms so that downturns do not force them to sell at losses.

In 2020, when COVID-19 lockdowns crashed the economy and created panic in real estate markets, many predicted that property values would collapse. Investors who panicked and sold in March and April 2020 realized losses. Investors who maintained their properties through the panic and who purchased additional properties during the brief period when sellers were desperate generated extraordinary returns as the market recovered rapidly and then exploded upward through 2021 and 2022. Properties purchased in mid-2020 during the panic appreciated thirty to fifty percent within two years in many markets. This eighteen-month period created more wealth for those who had capital and courage than the previous decade had created for those who bought during stable conditions.

The tax advantages that real estate provides separate it from almost every other investment and create the possibility of generating substantial income while paying minimal taxes. The depreciation deduction allows you to treat the property as though it is wearing out over twenty-seven point five years, deducting approximately three point six four percent of the property value annually. On a two hundred thousand dollar property (excluding land value, which is not depreciable), you can deduct approximately seven thousand dollars annually in depreciation. This is a paper loss—you did not actually spend seven thousand dollars—but it offsets rental income for tax purposes.

If that property generates ten thousand dollars in annual cash flow, the seven thousand dollar depreciation deduction means your taxable income from the property is only three thousand dollars instead of ten thousand. At a twenty-two percent tax bracket, this saves you fifteen hundred forty dollars in taxes annually. Over ten years of ownership, this is over fifteen thousand dollars in tax savings from a deduction for an expense you never actually incurred. This is legal, encouraged by tax policy designed to incentivize real estate investment, and available to anyone who owns rental property.

The 1031 exchange allows you to sell a property, purchase another property of equal or greater value, and defer all capital gains taxes indefinitely. Someone who purchased a property for two hundred thousand dollars that is now worth five hundred thousand dollars has a three hundred thousand dollar capital gain. Selling would trigger approximately forty-five thousand dollars in federal capital gains taxes plus state taxes. Through a 1031 exchange, they can sell the property, use all proceeds to purchase a six hundred thousand dollar property, and pay zero taxes. The gain is not forgiven—it carries forward into the new property's cost basis—but the taxes are deferred, potentially for decades.

The one percent use 1031 exchanges to continuously upgrade their portfolios without paying taxes. They sell smaller properties and exchange into larger properties, building equity across decades while deferring all taxation. They understand that deferring taxes is nearly as valuable as eliminating them because the tax money that would have been paid to the government instead remains invested and continues compounding. Someone who defers forty-five thousand dollars in taxes and invests that forty-five thousand at eight percent for twenty years turns it into two hundred nine thousand dollars. The tax deferral created one hundred sixty-four thousand dollars in additional wealth.

The mistake patterns that destroy real estate investors are predictable and avoidable, yet they are repeated constantly by people who enter real estate without understanding what they are doing. The first mistake is purchasing properties that do not generate adequate cash flow, hoping that appreciation will compensate. Appreciation is uncertain and cyclical. Cash flow is knowable at purchase based on current rents and expenses. The property that barely breaks even or that requires monthly subsidies might appreciate substantially, or it might not. If it does not appreciate and you are subsidizing it monthly for years, you have destroyed wealth rather than building it.

The second mistake is underestimating expenses, particularly maintenance and capital expenditures. First-time investors routinely budget only for mortgage, taxes, and insurance, forgetting that roofs need replacing, HVAC systems fail, appliances break, and tenants damage properties. When these expenses hit, the investors have no reserves and must either fund repairs from personal income or allow properties to deteriorate. The one percent budget conservatively for all expenses and maintain reserves covering six months of expenses per property. When inevitable repairs occur, reserves cover them without creating financial stress.

The third mistake is poor tenant selection, allowing anyone willing to pay first month's rent and deposit to move in without thorough screening. Problem tenants damage properties, default on rent, disturb neighbors, and create legal complications through evictions. Screening tenants through criminal background checks, credit checks, employment verification, and previous landlord references eliminates most problems before they occur. The one percent use professional property management companies that have systematic screening processes. The ninety-nine percent try to save money by skipping screening and end up losing far more through property damage and lost rent than they would have spent on proper screening.

The fourth mistake is emotional attachment to properties, treating real estate as though it is a home when it is actually an investment that should be evaluated purely on financial performance. The investor who refuses to sell a poorly performing property because they "love the house" or because they have "put so much work into it" allows emotion to override mathematics. The property that generates three percent cash-on-cash returns should be sold and the capital redeployed into properties generating eight percent returns. The one percent evaluate properties purely on returns and sell underperformers without hesitation. The ninety-nine percent hold onto poor investments for years because of emotional attachment that has no place in investment decisions.

The fifth mistake is excessive leverage, purchasing properties with minimal down payments and maximum loan amounts, creating situations where any decline in rents or increase in vacancy rates produces negative cash flow that the investor cannot sustain. The investor who purchased ten properties with five percent down payments across two million dollars in property value has only one hundred thousand invested but one million nine hundred thousand in debt. If the market declines ten percent, they are underwater on all ten properties. If several units go vacant simultaneously, the negative cash flow exceeds their ability to cover it and they face foreclosure. The one percent use conservative leverage, typically twenty to twenty-five percent down payments, maintaining equity cushions that protect them during downturns.

The question of whether to invest in real estate versus investing only in stocks cannot be answered universally because it depends on individual circumstances, risk tolerance, and willingness to actively manage investments. Real estate provides leverage, cash flow, and tax advantages that stocks cannot match. Stocks provide liquidity, simplicity, and truly passive returns that real estate cannot match. The optimal strategy for most people building substantial wealth is to use both, allocating capital across stocks through index funds and across real estate through rental properties, gaining the benefits of both asset classes.

The one percent typically build wealth through multiple asset classes rather than concentrating entirely in one. They maintain stock portfolios providing liquidity and passive growth. They maintain real estate portfolios providing cash flow and tax advantages. They maintain business equity providing the highest potential returns. This diversification across asset classes protects them from having everything at risk in one investment type and allows them to exploit opportunities in whichever market is offering the best risk-adjusted returns at any given time.

John and Jane's journey from purchasing their first duplex to owning seven properties generating one hundred eighty thousand dollars annually demonstrates that real estate wealth building is not about brilliant individual deals but about systematic acquisition and long-term holding sustained through market cycles. They purchased decent properties in decent areas at reasonable prices. They maintained them adequately. They kept good tenants. They refinanced when rates dropped. They made extra principal payments when possible. They held through the 2008 crisis when they were tempted to sell. They did this for three decades and built financial independence.

The frameworks have been provided. You understand the five mechanisms that make real estate powerful. You understand how to analyze properties to distinguish investments from disasters. You understand house hacking as an entry strategy requiring minimal capital. You understand why location matters more than purchase price. You understand the tax advantages that shelter income. You understand the mistakes that destroy investors and how to avoid them. You understand why market timing matters and why maintaining capital for opportunities during crashes creates disproportionate returns.

What remains is the decision to implement or to remain on the sidelines watching others build wealth through real estate while you convince yourself it is too complicated or too risky or not worth the effort. Real estate is not passive like stock index funds. It requires active management even when you hire property managers. It creates headaches that stocks never create. It ties up capital in illiquid assets that cannot be sold instantly if you need money. These are real drawbacks that anyone considering real estate must accept.

But the returns available through real estate exceed what you can achieve through stocks alone for most people willing to accept the complications. The combination of leverage multiplying returns, tenants paying your debt, monthly cash flow providing current income, appreciation building long-term equity, and tax advantages sheltering income creates wealth accumulation that is difficult to match through any other investment available to ordinary people. The one percent accept the complications as the price of accessing these returns. The ninety-nine percent avoid real estate because they prioritize convenience over returns and then wonder why their wealth accumulation through stocks alone never provides the cash flow needed for financial independence.

CHAPTER 6:
THE MARKET—LONG-TERM WEALTH CREATION THROUGH OWNERSHIP

In 1944, a woman named Anne Scheiber retired from the Internal Revenue Service after twenty-three years as a low-level auditor. She had never married, lived frugally in a small rent-controlled apartment in Manhattan, and had saved five thousand dollars from her modest government salary. She was fifty-one years old and faced a future with a small pension and no significant assets. Most women in her circumstances would have spent their remaining years in genteel poverty, clipping coupons and worrying about expenses. Anne Scheiber had different plans. She opened a brokerage account and began buying shares of American companies.

She had no formal investment training beyond what she observed during her years auditing tax returns at the IRS. She had seen which strategies generated wealth and which generated audit flags. She noticed that those who traded frequently paid substantial taxes and often showed losses. She noticed that those who held quality stocks for decades paid minimal taxes and showed steady wealth accumulation. She understood that the tax code itself was revealing investment wisdom to anyone who bothered to pay attention. So she bought stocks in companies she understood—pharmaceutical firms, entertainment companies, consumer brands—and she never sold them. She reinvested every dividend. She added to positions when she had spare capital. She ignored market fluctuations, economic recessions, and the countless reasons brokers gave for why she should change her strategy.

When Anne Scheiber died in 1995 at age 101, her five thousand-dollar initial investment had grown to twenty-two million dollars. She left the entire sum to Yeshiva University to fund scholarships for women, an institution she had no connection to during her life but chose because she believed in education and opportunity. Her attorney was shocked. Her neighbors had no idea. She had lived in the same small apartment, worn the same modest clothes, and maintained the same frugal habits until the end. The wealth existed entirely on paper, growing silently for fifty-one years through the simple mechanism of owning pieces of productive American enterprises and refusing to sell them.

The stock market is the greatest wealth-creation tool ever devised for ordinary people. This is not hyperbole or sales pitch. It is mathematical and historical fact. The market allows anyone with spare capital to own fractional pieces of the world's most profitable enterprises. You can own portions of companies that employ thousands, generate billions in revenue, and dominate their industries. You can participate in their profits without working there, without understanding their operations in detail, and without any special connections or credentials. The market democratizes ownership in ways that would have been inconceivable for most of human history.

Yet the ninety-nine percent approach the market as though it were a casino, a place where speculation and luck determine outcomes, where mysterious forces move prices unpredictably, and where ordinary people are destined to lose money to sophisticated insiders. This perspective is precisely backwards. The market is not a casino. It is the mechanism by which ownership of productive assets is exchanged. Those who understand this and act accordingly build wealth with statistical certainty over sufficient time periods. Those who view it as speculation or gambling create precisely the outcomes they expect—random results, emotional decisions, and eventual losses.

I have spent time studying individuals who lived over half a century interact with the stock market, and the pattern is depressingly consistent. When prices are rising and everyone is making money, the ninety-nine percent become convinced that they understand investing and should take control of their portfolios. They chase performance, buying whatever has recently performed best. They trade frequently, convinced that they can time entries and exits. They consume financial media constantly, believing that staying informed provides advantage. When prices inevitably fall, they panic and sell, locking in losses and missing the subsequent recovery. They repeat this cycle for decades, consistently buying high and selling low, then concluding that the stock market is rigged against ordinary investors.

The one percent operate from an entirely different framework. They understand that the stock market has returned approximately ten percent annually for the past century. This is not a guarantee, not a promise, and not even a prediction about the next year or five years. It is an observation about what ownership of American enterprise has returned over long periods despite world wars, depressions, recessions, technological disruptions, political upheavals, and every other crisis that has occurred. The ten-percent figure represents the growth rate of American capitalism itself, the rate at which productive enterprise has expanded value over time. Those who own pieces of that enterprise participate in that expansion. Those who trade in and out capture nothing but transaction costs and tax liabilities.

The mathematics of compound growth at ten percent annually are extraordinary, yet most people have never actually calculated what they mean. I want you to understand these numbers viscerally, not abstractly. If you invest ten thousand dollars at age twenty-five and earn ten percent annually without adding another dollar, that ten thousand becomes twenty-six thousand by age thirty-five, sixty-seven thousand by age forty-five, one hundred seventy-five thousand by age fifty-five, and four hundred fifty-three thousand by age sixty-five. You did nothing. The money simply participated in the growth of American enterprise for forty years. One dollar became forty-five dollars.

Now consider consistent monthly contributions. If you invest five hundred dollars monthly—six thousand annually—starting at age twenty-five and maintain that exact contribution until age sixty-five while earning ten percent returns, you will accumulate three million nine hundred seventy-five thousand dollars. You will have contributed two hundred forty thousand of your own money over those forty years. The other three million seven hundred thirty-five thousand is growth, the expansion of value that occurs when you own productive assets for long periods. This is not theoretical. This is not best-case scenario. This is the actual return that patient investors in diversified American stocks have achieved for a century.

The reason most people never experience these returns despite their mathematical reliability is that they cannot tolerate the path required to achieve them. The journey from point A to point B is not a smooth upward line. It is a chaotic series of advances and retreats, periods of euphoria followed by periods of terror, years when your portfolio doubles and years when it drops by forty percent. The one percent understand that volatility is the cost of admission for superior returns. They accept that cost because they understand the destination is statistically certain if they refuse to abandon the path. The ninety-nine percent demand certainty at every step and therefore never reach any destination worth arriving at.

Let me be specific about what volatility means in practice. If you invested one hundred thousand dollars in a diversified portfolio of American stocks in 2008, by March 2009 that portfolio was worth approximately fifty-five thousand dollars. You had lost forty-five percent of your capital. Your friends and family were telling you to sell before you lost everything. Financial media was predicting depression and the end of capitalism as we knew it. Every instinct in your body was screaming to stop the pain by selling. If you sold, you locked in a forty-five-thousand-dollar loss and permanently impaired your ability to participate in the recovery.

If you did nothing—if you simply held your positions and continued making your regular monthly contributions—by 2013 your original hundred thousand was worth approximately one hundred sixty thousand. By 2018 it was worth approximately three hundred thousand. By 2024 it was worth approximately six hundred thousand. The same capital that appeared to have been cut in half during the crisis had multiplied six-fold over fifteen years. Those who sold in panic because they could not tolerate temporary losses never participated in the recovery. Those who held through the discomfort captured the full return that patient ownership provides.

This psychological tolerance for volatility cannot be taught through theory alone. It must be developed through experience and reinforced through understanding of what you actually own. When you buy an index fund tracking the S&P 500, you are buying ownership stakes in five hundred of the largest, most profitable companies in America. You own Apple, Microsoft, Google, Amazon, and hundreds of other enterprises that generate billions in annual profits. When the stock price of that index fund drops by twenty percent, the underlying companies have not disappeared. They continue manufacturing products, providing services, generating revenue, and earning profits. What has changed is the price other investors are willing to pay for ownership stakes at that particular moment.

Anne Scheiber understood this distinction instinctively. She held shares in pharmaceutical companies that developed medications treating diseases. She held shares in entertainment companies that produced films audiences wanted to see. She held shares in consumer brands that sold products people purchased repeatedly. When stock prices fell, the companies did not stop producing medications, films, or consumer goods. They did not stop generating revenue and profits. The business value remained intact even when the stock price

fluctuated. So she held her positions, collected her dividends, reinvested those dividends, and allowed the compounding to operate uninterrupted for five decades.

The question arises repeatedly about whether to select individual stocks or buy index funds. This debate has consumed more words than almost any other topic in personal finance, yet the answer for most people is straightforward. Index funds provide superior outcomes for all but the most sophisticated and dedicated investors. The reasons are both mathematical and behavioral.

Mathematically, most professional money managers who spend every working hour analyzing companies and markets fail to beat index fund returns after accounting for their fees. If professionals cannot consistently select winning stocks, the odds that you will do so while working a full-time job in an unrelated field are negligible.

Behaviorally, individual stock selection encourages exactly the emotional decision-making that destroys returns—chasing performance, panic selling, overconfidence following wins, and despair following losses.

That said, there exists a narrow category of people for whom individual stock selection makes sense. If you work in an industry and develop genuine expertise about which companies within that industry are positioned for success, you may have an informational advantage worth exploiting. If you have both the intellectual capacity and the emotional discipline to analyze companies fundamentally, ignore price movements, and hold positions for decades regardless of volatility, you may achieve superior returns. If you genuinely enjoy the research process and view it as productive use of leisure time rather than burden, the effort may be worthwhile even if the returns only match index performance. But understand that you are selecting a harder path that is statistically unlikely to produce better outcomes, and most who choose it eventually conclude that the effort exceeds the return.

For everyone else, the strategy is simple to the point of seeming unsophisticated. Purchase low-cost index funds that track broad market indices. The S&P 500 represents large American companies. A total stock market index represents the entire American market across all sizes. An international index provides exposure to developed markets outside America. An emerging markets index provides exposure to developing economies. You can construct a complete portfolio from three to five index funds that provides global diversification, requires minimal maintenance, and will deliver market returns with statistical reliability.

The allocation between these categories depends primarily on age and risk tolerance. The conventional wisdom suggests holding your age in bonds and the remainder in stocks—a thirty-year-old holds thirty percent bonds and seventy percent stocks, while a sixty-year-old holds sixty percent bonds and forty percent stocks. This rule of thumb is not terrible but is probably too conservative for most people building wealth. Bonds provide stability but deliver returns barely exceeding inflation. Stocks provide volatility but deliver the returns that build actual wealth. If you have decades until retirement, you can tolerate substantial stock allocation—perhaps eighty or ninety percent—because you have time to recover from market declines. As you approach retirement, you gradually shift toward more bonds to reduce volatility when you will soon need to draw on the portfolio.

International exposure deserves consideration even though American stocks have dominated global returns for decades. The one percent understand that past performance is not predictor of future results, and that maintaining some international diversification provides insurance against the possibility that American dominance does not continue indefinitely. A reasonable approach is holding seventy to eighty percent in American stocks and twenty to thirty percent in international developed and emerging markets. This provides global diversification without abandoning the market that has historically delivered superior returns.

The specific funds you select matter less than the costs you pay. Expense ratios—the annual fees charged by fund companies—directly reduce your returns. A fund charging one percent annually costs you hundreds of thousands over a career compared to a fund charging point-oh-three percent annually. This seems trivial but compounds exactly like returns compound. Vanguard pioneered low-cost index funds and remains the gold standard, though competitors like Schwab and Fidelity now offer comparable products at similar costs. Choose funds with expense ratios below point-one percent. Avoid any fund charging more than point-five percent unless you have specific reasons to accept those costs. Most investors do not.

The maintenance required for this approach is minimal. You establish automatic monthly contributions from your paycheck to your investment accounts. You allocate those contributions according to your target percentages across your selected index funds. Once or twice annually, you rebalance by selling a small portion of whatever has grown above your target allocation and buying whatever has fallen below it. This forces you to sell high and buy low mechanically, without emotional decision-making. The total time required is perhaps two hours annually. The rest of the time you ignore the accounts entirely, focusing on earning income, building your career, and living your life.

This sounds too simple to work. The ninety-nine percent are convinced that building wealth must require constant attention, specialized knowledge, and sophisticated strategies. They cannot accept that simply owning diversified American enterprise through low-cost index funds and never selling delivers superior results to nearly every alternative approach. So they add complexity, seek out active managers who promise to beat the market, chase hot sectors and trending stocks, and consume financial media that profits from convincing them they need constant advice. They turn a simple process into a complicated one and achieve worse results while expending more effort.

I recognize that what I am describing requires faith in capitalism itself—faith that human beings will continue creating value through enterprise, that innovation and productivity will continue expanding, and that ownership of that expanding enterprise will continue generating returns. If you believe capitalism is dying or that developed economies have reached permanent stagnation, then you should not invest in stocks at all. But if you believe that humans will continue solving problems, creating products, serving needs, and building companies that generate profits, then you should own pieces of those companies and hold them for as long as that fundamental reality continues.

Anne Scheiber placed her faith in American capitalism in 1944 and maintained that faith until 1995. Fifty-one years of uninterrupted ownership converted five thousand dollars into twenty-two million. She did not time the market. She did not trade around positions. She did not panic during the bear markets of 1973, 1987, or 1990. She simply owned quality companies and refused to sell them. This is not genius. It is patience. But patience consistently applied over decades produces results that appear genius in retrospect.

I want to address the most common objection I encounter when presenting this strategy. People argue that the market is too high, that valuations are stretched, that a crash is imminent, and that waiting for better entry points makes sense. This reasoning has cost more people more money than any other investment mistake. The market always appears too high to those looking for reasons not to invest. In 1995, when the S&P 500 was at six hundred, investors said it was too high and waited for a crash. In 2000 it reached fifteen hundred. Those who stayed out missed a one hundred fifty percent gain while waiting for better prices. Yes, it then crashed to eight hundred in 2002, but those who had been invested since 1995 were still ahead. And those who waited and then bought at eight hundred rode it to fifteen hundred again by 2007, then watched it crash to six hundred seventy-seven in 2009, then participated as it rose to fortynine hundred by 2024.

The pattern is clear to anyone who studies market history. Prices rise, fall, rise again to higher levels, fall again but not as low as before, and gradually trend upward over decades. Trying to time these movements is a fool's errand. The optimal entry point is always whatever point you have capital available to invest. The optimal exit point is when you need the money for living expenses in retirement. Everything in between is noise that you should ignore completely.

The strategy I have described works regardless of market conditions at your entry point, provided you maintain it long enough for the compounding to operate. If you begin investing right before a major bear market, you will buy the entire decline, accumulating shares at decreasing prices, then capturing the full recovery when it comes. If you begin investing right before a major bull market, you will immediately see gains, then continue buying during the inevitable corrections that follow. Either path leads to wealth accumulation if you refuse to deviate from the strategy.

What destroys people is not the strategy but their inability to maintain it. They begin investing, encounter a decline, lose faith, and stop contributing or sell positions. They miss the recovery. Or they begin investing, see strong gains, become convinced they understand investing, and start making individual stock picks that lose money. Or they begin investing, become bored because nothing seems to be happening, and seek excitement through day trading or cryptocurrency speculation. The account exists. The strategy exists.

The discipline to maintain both simultaneously for decades is what separates outcomes.

You have now been provided the foundation in previous chapters—proper stewardship, understanding assets and liabilities, engineering your environment, and utilizing tax-advantaged vehicles. This chapter provides the investment strategy that operates within those vehicles. You now know what to buy, where to buy it, and how to maintain it. What remains is the psychological capacity to hold this strategy through every market condition for decades until the compounding transforms your regular contributions into financial independence. No one can give you that capacity. You must develop it through understanding what you own, why you own it, and the statistical certainty that patient ownership of productive enterprise generates wealth over sufficient time periods.

Anne Scheiber was not brilliant. She was patient. She was not sophisticated. She was consistent. She was not lucky. She was disciplined. She understood that owning quality companies for long periods was the only investment strategy proven across centuries and cultures. She implemented that understanding without deviation for five decades. The result was twenty-two million dollars built from five thousand, proving that the market rewards patience more generously than it rewards any other quality. You have the same opportunity.

CHAPTER 7:
REAL ESTATE MASTERY—HOUSE HACKING AND BEYOND

In 2008, a twenty-four-year-old restaurant manager in Colorado found himself staring at a financial crossroads. Brandon Turner was earning thirty-two thousand dollars annually and living in a small apartment that consumed a substantial portion of his modest income. He had recently discovered the concept of real estate investing through books and podcasts, but with minimal savings and no investment experience, the path forward seemed unclear. Traditional advice would have told him to continue renting, save diligently, and perhaps purchase a small single-family home in five or ten years when he had accumulated a proper down payment. Turner rejected this conventional timeline entirely.

Instead, he found a small duplex listed for ninety-seven thousand dollars in a working-class neighborhood. He secured an FHA loan requiring only three and a half percent down— approximately thirty-four hundred dollars he had managed to scrape together. He moved into one unit and rented the other. The rental income from his tenant covered his entire mortgage payment, property taxes, and insurance. Turner was living completely free while building equity in an appreciating asset. Within a year, he repeated the process with a fourplex, then another small multifamily property. By 2012, he owned multiple properties, had left his restaurant job, and was generating more passive income from real estate than he had earned in active employment. By his mid-thirties, his rental portfolio provided complete financial independence.

Turner's journey demonstrates a fundamental truth that challenges conventional housing wisdom: your primary residence does not need to be a liability. Through strategic structuring, it can become your first income-generating asset. This approach, known as house hacking, represents perhaps the most accessible entry point into real estate investing for people with limited capital. It requires neither substantial savings nor extensive experience. It requires only willingness to make housing decisions based on investment logic rather than lifestyle preference, and discipline to live somewhat unconventionally during the wealth-building phase.

We have established in previous chapters that your home typically functions as a liability, consuming cash flow rather than generating it. We have discussed how the wealthy think in terms of assets and how environment shapes outcomes. Real estate investing brings these principles together in concrete form. Unlike stocks that exist as electronic entries in brokerage accounts, real estate is tangible, controllable, and susceptible to deliberate value creation through informed decision-making. Unlike business ownership that requires building something from nothing, real estate investing begins with purchasing existing assets that already generate income. This combination of tangibility, control, and existing cash flow makes real estate uniquely suited for wealth building by those willing to educate themselves about how property markets operate.

The house hacking concept is simple but requires mental recalibration for most people. Instead of purchasing a single-family home where you alone occupy the property and bear the entire cost, you purchase a multifamily property—a duplex, triplex, or fourplex—where you occupy one unit and rent the remaining units to tenants. The rental income from those tenants pays most or all of your housing costs. In the best scenarios, the rental income exceeds your total housing expense and you live for free while actually generating positive cash flow. In more typical scenarios, the rental income substantially reduces your housing costs compared to renting or owning a traditional home.

The financing mechanism that makes house hacking accessible to people with limited capital is the FHA loan program. The Federal Housing Administration insures loans for owner-occupied properties, allowing lenders to offer terms requiring as little as three and a half percent down payment. This applies not just to single-family homes but to properties with up to four units, provided the buyer occupies one unit as their primary residence. This is critical: you can purchase a fourplex with three and a half percent down and immediately have three tenants paying rent that covers most or all of your mortgage payment. This same financing would not be available for a pure investment property, which typically requires twenty to twenty-five percent down. The FHA loan is explicitly designed to help people become homeowners, and the government does not distinguish between a single-family home and a small multifamily property for this purpose.

The mathematics are straightforward. A duplex priced at two hundred thousand dollars requires seven thousand in down payment with an FHA loan, plus perhaps three thousand in closing costs. With ten thousand dollars in capital—an amount most people earning moderate incomes can save within a year or two through disciplined saving—you can purchase a property where one unit houses you and the other generates rental income. If each unit could rent for one thousand monthly on the open market, and your total housing expense including mortgage, taxes, insurance, and maintenance is eighteen hundred monthly, you are living for eleven hundred monthly rent-free and paying only eight hundred in net housing costs. Compared to renting an apartment for one thousand monthly, you are saving two hundred monthly in immediate cash flow while building equity in an appreciating asset.

The objections arise immediately. People worry about being a landlord, about tenant problems, about maintenance emergencies, about losing privacy by living in such proximity to renters. These concerns are legitimate but manageable, and they represent the price paid for living free while building wealth. The alternative is paying full freight for housing while building nothing. Turner dealt with difficult tenants, handled maintenance calls at inconvenient hours, and sacrificed some privacy during his house hacking years. He viewed these as temporary costs of admission to wealth building, not permanent lifestyle impositions. After several years of house hacking and using the savings to acquire additional properties, he moved into a single-family home while his rental portfolio generated sufficient income to cover his housing costs there as well.

The progression from initial house hack to substantial rental portfolio follows a logical sequence, though the timeline varies based on market conditions and individual circumstances. You begin with house hacking, using the combination of minimal down payment requirements and rental income to acquire your first property while living there. You build equity through mortgage paydown and property appreciation while saving additional capital from the reduced housing costs. After twelve months—the minimum occupancy period required by FHA—you can purchase another property using another FHA loan, move into that property, and convert your first property to a full rental. Now you have two properties, both generating rental income, and you live in the second property with reduced or eliminated housing costs.

This can continue for several cycles, though the FHA requirement that you occupy the property limits how quickly you can scale using that specific financing method. After several house hacks, you transition to conventional financing for additional purchases, using equity built in your existing properties to fund down payments on new acquisitions. Some investors refinance existing properties to extract equity through cash-out refinancing. Others use home equity lines of credit secured by appreciated properties to fund additional purchases. The specific mechanisms matter less than the pattern: you start with house hacking, build a foundation of several properties, then leverage that foundation to acquire additional properties more rapidly.

The analysis required to evaluate potential house hack properties differs from the analysis you would conduct when purchasing a primary residence for lifestyle reasons. Location matters, but not primarily for school districts or neighborhood aesthetics. You care about rental demand, employment stability in the area, crime rates that affect tenant quality and insurance costs, and proximity to amenities that make units attractive to renters. Property condition matters, but not primarily for your personal preferences. You care about maintenance costs, remaining useful life of major systems, and potential for value-added improvements that increase rental income relative to cost. Purchase price matters enormously, but not relative to what you can afford in mortgage payments. You care about whether the rent you can collect exceeds your total monthly costs, creating positive cash flow that builds wealth rather than merely providing shelter.

The one percent who build wealth through real estate develop systematic approaches to property analysis. They calculate the one-percent rule as a rough filter: monthly rent should equal at least one percent of purchase price. A two-hundred-thousand-dollar property should generate two thousand monthly in total rent to pass this initial test. This is not a guarantee of good returns but a threshold below which deals rarely work. They calculate cash-on-cash return: annual cash flow divided by total cash invested. A ten-thousand-dollar investment generating one thousand two hundred annually in positive cash flow produces a twelve-percent cash-on-cash return, which is excellent. They project total returns including cash flow, mortgage paydown, and appreciation, understanding that real estate wealth comes from multiple simultaneous sources rather than any single factor.

Most importantly, they underwrite conservatively, assuming higher expenses and lower rents than optimistic projections suggest. Real estate investing punishes optimism. The property will require more maintenance than you expect. Tenants will occasionally not pay rent. Vacancies will last longer than anticipated. Insurance and property taxes will increase. Underwriting conservatively by adding ten to twenty percent to your expense estimates and reducing your rent projections by five to ten percent protects you from deals that appear profitable on paper but destroy cash flow in reality. The one percent would rather pass on marginal deals than close on deals that become cash flow drains.

The tenant management aspect of house hacking creates anxiety for most people contemplating this strategy. You are living in the same building as people paying you rent. What if they are difficult? What if they complain constantly? What if they fail to pay? These scenarios occur, and they are more uncomfortable when the tenant lives thirty feet away from you rather than across town. The mitigation comes through rigorous tenant screening before accepting anyone, establishing clear expectations through comprehensive leases, and maintaining professional boundaries even though you share a building.

Tenant screening should verify income of at least three times the monthly rent, check credit history for patterns of financial responsibility, contact previous landlords to assess whether they paid on time and maintained properties well, and conduct criminal background checks to identify serious concerns. This process eliminates the majority of potential problem tenants before they move in. The remaining problems typically stem from life circumstances that change after move-in rather than from inadequate screening. The one percent who succeed in rental property understand that their most important decision is who they allow to live in their properties. They set high standards and reject applicants who do not meet them, even when vacancies extend longer than comfortable.

The value creation opportunity in real estate distinguishes it from stock market investing, where you own pieces of companies but cannot control their operations. With real estate, you can directly improve the asset through renovations that increase rental income or reduce expenses. You can add washer-dryer hookups that allow higher rents. You can upgrade kitchens and bathrooms to attract better tenants willing to pay premiums. You can improve landscaping and curb appeal to reduce vacancy periods. You can separately meter utilities to eliminate the expense of paying for tenant consumption. Each improvement that increases rental income or decreases operating expense increases the property value directly, since real estate is valued based on the income it produces.

This creates opportunities for forced appreciation that do not exist in stock investing. If you buy a duplex where each unit rents for eight hundred monthly, invest twenty thousand in renovations that allow you to charge one thousand per unit, you have increased annual rental income by forty-eight hundred dollars. Investment properties are typically valued using capitalization rates—the ratio of net operating income to property value. At a seven-percent cap rate, increasing net income by forty-eight hundred dollars increases property value by approximately sixty-nine thousand dollars. You invested twenty thousand and created sixty-nine thousand in value. This is wealth creation through informed action rather than passive market appreciation.

Turner built much of his wealth through exactly this approach. He identified underperforming properties where rents were below market, purchased them at prices reflecting the current low rents, made strategic improvements, raised rents to market rates, and either refinanced to extract equity or sold at profits reflecting the improved income. This required work that stock investing does not require. It also generated returns that stock investing rarely produces over short time periods. The combination of cash flow, mortgage paydown through tenant rent payments, tax benefits from depreciation, and forced appreciation through improvements produces total returns that often exceed twenty percent annually for skilled investors in favorable markets.

The progression beyond house hacking leads to different property types and strategies. Some investors prefer single-family homes for their liquidity and ease of management. When you need to sell, individual homeowners represent a much larger pool of potential buyers than investors alone. When you need to manage, a single tenant household is simpler than multiple units. Other investors prefer small multifamily properties because the income diversification reduces risk—one vacancy in a fourplex costs you twenty-five percent of income, while one vacancy in a single-family home costs you one hundred percent. Larger apartment buildings provide economies of scale but require more capital and expertise.

The financing structures available change as you move beyond owner-occupied properties into pure investment properties. Conventional investment property loans require twenty to twenty-five percent down payments and charge higher interest rates than owner occupied financing. This dramatically affects the cash-on-cash returns you can achieve. A two-hundred-thousand-dollar fourplex purchased with an FHA loan and seven thousand down might produce excellent cash flow. The same property purchased with a conventional investment loan requiring fifty thousand down might produce negative cash flow or barely break even. This is why the house hacking entry point is so valuable—it allows you to acquire properties with financing terms that make cash flow possible on your first several purchases, building equity and experience before transitioning to higher down payment requirements.

Creative financing strategies deserve mention for those willing to invest time in learning mechanisms beyond conventional mortgages. Seller financing, where the property owner acts as the bank and you make payments directly to them, can provide terms unavailable through traditional lenders. Lease options, where you lease a property with an option to purchase at a predetermined price, allow you to control properties with minimal upfront capital. Partnerships, where you provide sweat equity finding and managing deals while partners provide capital, allow you to acquire properties despite limited personal funds. Each strategy carries specific risks and requires more sophisticated understanding than simply obtaining a conventional mortgage. The one percent who scale rapidly often employ these strategies, but beginners should master conventional approaches first.

The mistakes that destroy novice real estate investors are predictable and avoidable. The first is inadequate reserves. A property that cash flows one hundred dollars monthly seems profitable until a roof needs replacement costing ten thousand dollars. Without reserves to handle that expense, you face either going into debt or losing the property to foreclosure. The one percent maintains reserves of at least six months of operating expenses per property, understanding that major expenses are inevitable and planning breaks the amateur investor. The second mistake is overestimating rents and underestimating expenses. Wishful thinking about what tenants will pay and how little maintenance will cost turns projected profits into actual losses. Conservative underwriting protects against this. The third mistake is poor tenant screening driven by desire to fill vacancies quickly. A bad tenant costs more in missed rent, property damage, and legal expenses than months of vacancy. The screening process exists to prevent catastrophic tenants, not merely to fill units.

The fourth mistake deserves extended treatment because it represents a fundamental misunderstanding of what makes real estate attractive. Many novice investors chase appreciation—buying properties in hot markets where prices are rising rapidly, expecting to profit from price increases alone. This is speculation, not investment. When your returns depend entirely on appreciation, you have no margin of safety and no income while you wait for prices to rise.

Markets that have appreciated rapidly often correct violently, wiping out years of paper gains. The one percent focus on cash flow—buying properties where rental income exceeds all expenses from day one. The property pays for itself while you own it, and any appreciation is bonus rather than the basis for the investment. This approach survived the 2008 financial crisis while appreciation-focused investors lost everything.

Real estate investing is not passive income. This phrase is used frequently and is technically false. Real estate is less-active income than employment but more active than stock market investing. You must find properties, analyze deals, secure financing, manage tenants, handle maintenance, and eventually sell or refinance properties. This requires time, attention, and often direct involvement in activities that are genuinely unpleasant—dealing with tenant complaints, coordinating repairs, pursuing late rent payments. The one percent who succeed in real estate either accept these realities as costs of building wealth or systematize and delegate them once their portfolios reach sufficient scale to justify professional property management.

The role of property managers deserves consideration. Professional management typically costs eight to twelve percent of collected rent plus markup on maintenance work. This expense dramatically affects cash flow, often turning profitable deals into break-even or negative situations. For this reason, most investors self-manage their first several properties, learning the business while keeping all the income. As portfolios grow, the time demands become unsustainable and the opportunity cost of self-managing exceeds the expense of professional management. The transition point varies, but it typically arrives somewhere between five and fifteen properties depending on property types and personal circumstances.

The tax advantages of real estate deserve brief mention here, though they receive fuller treatment in the following chapter on advanced strategies. You can depreciate buildings over twenty-seven and a half years for residential property, creating paper losses that shelter actual income from taxation. You can deduct all operating expenses, mortgage interest, and travel related to property management. You can defer taxes on appreciation through 1031 exchanges that allow you to sell properties and reinvest proceeds without triggering capital gains taxes. These advantages make real estate uniquely tax-efficient compared to most other investment categories, increasing actual after-tax returns substantially above the pre-tax returns that casual analysis suggests.

Brandon Turner's progression from restaurant manager to financially independent real estate investor required approximately four years of dedicated house hacking and strategic property acquisition. He lived modestly, managed properties himself, educated himself constantly through books and networking with experienced investors, and reinvested profits into additional properties rather than upgrading his lifestyle. This is the pattern among those who succeed. The timeline varies based on market conditions, starting capital, and individual circumstances, but the pattern remains constant: acquire the first property through house hacking, build experience and equity, acquire additional properties systematically, maintain discipline through the building phase, and eventually reach the point where passive income from the portfolio exceeds living expenses.

The objection that real estate requires too much capital deserves final consideration. Turner started with approximately ten thousand dollars. In higher-cost markets, that amount proves insufficient, but the principle remains available through adjustment. You might need twenty-five thousand or even fifty thousand in expensive markets, but these are amounts that someone earning moderate income can accumulate through one to three years of disciplined saving using the principles discussed in earlier chapters. The bigger obstacle is not capital but conviction—the belief that this approach will work and the discipline to execute it despite social pressure, family skepticism, and personal doubt.

Real estate has created more millionaires than any asset class in history. This is not accident or luck but the natural result of combining leverage, cash flow, appreciation, tax advantages, and forced appreciation through improvements. Those who master house hacking as an entry point, then systematically build rental portfolios, create wealth faster than stock market investing alone typically allows. Those who attempt real estate without proper education, adequate reserves, and conservative underwriting destroy capital and conclude the asset class is too risky. The difference lies not in the asset class but in the approach, which you now understand.

CHAPTER 8:

ADVANCED REAL ESTATE TAX STRATEGY—1030IS, AUGUSTA RULE, AND LEGAL LOOPHOLES

In 1978, a young real estate developer in Manhattan faced a problem that would have devastated most people in his position. Donald Trump had acquired the Commodore Hotel near Grand Central Terminal for a nominal sum, converted it into the Grand Hyatt, and watched the property appreciate substantially. The success created a dilemma: selling the property would generate millions in profit but also trigger massive capital gains taxes that would consume roughly a third of those gains. Holding the property meant maintaining exposure to a single asset rather than diversifying into new opportunities. Most developers would have chosen one path or the other, either accepting the tax burden or foregoing the new opportunities.

Trump chose neither. He discovered a provision in the Internal Revenue Code—Section 1031—that allowed him to sell appreciated property and defer all capital gains taxes indefinitely by reinvesting the proceeds into similar property within specific timeframes. He sold the Grand Hyatt partnership interest, used the proceeds to acquire other properties, sold those when they appreciated, and rolled the gains into still more properties. He repeated this cycle for decades, continuously upgrading his portfolio while never paying capital gains taxes on the appreciation. By the time financial disclosures revealed the extent of his holdings in the 1990s, he had built an empire worth billions while deferring hundreds of millions in taxes through systematic use of 1031 exchanges. The taxes were not evaded illegally. They were deferred legally using mechanisms Congress specifically created for this purpose.

This chapter examines the tax provisions that make real estate the most tax-advantaged asset class available to ordinary wealth builders. These are not loopholes in the sense of unintended gaps that clever lawyers exploit. They are explicit incentives Congress wrote into the tax code to encourage specific behaviors—property investment, property improvement, and long-term holding of real estate assets. The one percent study these provisions with the intensity that professionals study their crafts. They structure their real estate activities to maximize every available benefit. The ninety-nine percent either remain unaware these provisions exist or consider them too complicated to bother understanding. This knowledge gap creates wealth disparities that compound over decades into differences of millions of dollars.

The 1031 exchange stands as the single most powerful wealthbuilding tool in the real estate tax code. Named for Section 1031 of the Internal Revenue Code, this provision allows real estate investors to sell properties and defer all capital gains taxes by reinvesting proceeds into similar properties within specific timeframes. The deferral is not temporary. If structured properly and repeated systematically, you can defer taxes for your entire life, continuously upgrading your portfolio without ever paying capital gains on the appreciation. When you die, your heirs receive a stepped-up basis, meaning they inherit the properties at current market value and the deferred gains disappear entirely. You have used other people's capital—the money you would have paid in taxes— to build wealth across your lifetime, then passed that wealth tax-free to the next generation.

The mechanics require attention to detail but are not complex. You must identify replacement property within forty-five days of selling your relinquished property. You must close on the replacement property within one hundred eighty days of the sale. The properties must be held for investment or business purposes, not personal use. The replacement property must be of equal or greater value than the property sold. You cannot receive the proceeds directly—they must flow through a qualified intermediary who holds them during the exchange period. These rules are rigid and unforgiving. Miss the forty-five-day identification deadline by even one day and the entire transaction becomes taxable. Fail to reinvest all proceeds and you pay taxes on the portion not reinvested, called boot in exchange terminology.

The strategic implications are profound. Consider an investor who purchases a rental property for two hundred thousand dollars, holds it for ten years while it appreciates to four hundred thousand dollars, then sells. Without a 1031 exchange, federal capital gains taxes at fifteen or twenty percent plus state taxes consume roughly sixty to eighty thousand dollars, leaving three hundred twenty to three hundred forty thousand to reinvest. With a 1031 exchange, the full four hundred thousand rolls into the replacement property. That extra sixty to eighty thousand of retained capital continues compounding. Over multiple cycles across decades, this creates exponential differences in wealth accumulation.

The true power emerges through serial exchanges that continuously upgrade portfolio quality. You begin with a modest duplex purchased for two hundred thousand. It appreciates to three hundred thousand over seven years. You exchange into a small apartment building worth six hundred thousand, using the three hundred thousand as down payment and financing the remainder. That building appreciates to nine hundred thousand over another seven years. You exchange into a larger commercial property worth one million eight hundred thousand. Each cycle, you move into higher-quality assets generating greater income while deferring all taxes on the appreciation. After three decades of this pattern, you control millions in real estate while having paid zero capital gains taxes. The deferred tax money has instead been deployed into additional property purchases, multiplying your wealth through leverage and compound appreciation.

Congress permits this because they want investment capital flowing into real estate rather than sitting idle or being consumed by taxation. Real estate investment creates construction jobs, provides housing, generates property tax revenue for local governments, and contributes to economic activity. The 1031 exchange encourages continuous investment and portfolio improvement rather than encouraging investors to hold properties indefinitely to avoid triggering taxes. This aligns private incentives with public policy goals. The wealthy understand this alignment and exploit it systematically. Those who fail to use 1031 exchanges pay hundreds of thousands or millions in unnecessary taxes across their investing careers, permanently impairing their wealth-building capacity.

The limitations deserve mention because misunderstanding them creates problems. You cannot exchange into property you intend to immediately flip or use personally. The IRS expects you to hold investment property for investment purposes, though no specific holding period is mandated. Most tax advisors recommend holding at least two years to demonstrate investment intent clearly. You cannot exchange vacation homes where you spend significant personal time unless you carefully document rental activity and limit personal use. You cannot exchange from real estate into other asset classes—stocks, bonds, or business interests do not qualify as like-kind property. The exchange is specifically for real estate to real estate, though the definition of like-kind is remarkably broad. You can exchange raw land for apartment buildings, residential rentals for commercial properties, or properties in different states. What matters is that both properties are held for investment or business use within the United States.

The Augusta Rule represents an entirely different tax advantage that remains obscure to most real estate investors despite its remarkable benefits. Named for the city of Augusta, Georgia, which persuaded Congress to exempt homeowners from taxation on short-term rentals during the Masters golf tournament, Section 280A allows any homeowner to rent their primary residence for up to fourteen days annually without reporting the rental income. This seems minor until you understand the implications for business owners.

If you own a business and need meeting space, you can rent your personal home to your own business for up to fourteen days annually. The business pays market-rate rent to you personally. The business deducts the rent as a legitimate business expense, reducing business taxable income. You receive the rent personally but do not report it as income under the Augusta Rule. The money has moved from a taxable business entity to you personally without taxation, while simultaneously reducing the business tax burden. Executed properly with appropriate documentation, this is entirely legal and explicitly permitted by the tax code.

The amounts can be substantial. Market-rate rental for a suitable home for business meetings might be five hundred to one thousand dollars per day in many markets. Fourteen days at seven hundred fifty dollars per day generates ten thousand five hundred dollars in tax-free income while creating a ten thousand five hundred dollar business deduction. At a thirty-five percent combined federal and state tax rate for the business, this saves roughly three thousand six hundred dollars in business taxes. You receive the ten thousand five hundred dollars personally tax-free. The total benefit exceeds fourteen thousand dollars created through understanding and using a provision most people have never heard of.

The requirements are straightforward but must be followed meticulously. The rental must be at fair market value—you cannot charge your business five thousand dollars per day for a home that would rent for five hundred. You must actually use the property for legitimate business purposes—board meetings, strategic planning sessions, client entertainment. You must document everything

through rental agreements, payment records, and business purpose documentation. You cannot exceed fourteen days. The IRS audits these arrangements when they appear abusive, but legitimate use following the rules survives scrutiny because Congress explicitly permits this exact structure.

Business owners who understand the Augusta Rule build it into their annual tax planning. They schedule their most important meetings at their homes, document the business purpose carefully, pay themselves fair market rent from their business accounts, and capture thousands in tax benefits that remain invisible to competitors who do not know this provision exists. Over a career, this single strategy can save or generate hundreds of thousands in after-tax wealth. The knowledge is freely available. The discipline to implement it properly is rare.

Depreciation represents perhaps the most significant ongoing tax benefit in real estate investing. When you purchase investment property, the IRS allows you to deduct the building value—not the land—over twenty-seven and a half years for residential property or thirty-nine years for commercial property. This creates paper losses that shelter actual cash flow from taxation. You receive positive cash flow from rental income exceeding expenses, but you report a loss on your tax return due to depreciation deductions. This loss can offset other income depending on your circumstances, reducing your total tax burden while you simultaneously build wealth through rental income and appreciation.

The mechanics are straightforward. You purchase a rental property for three hundred thousand dollars. The land represents twenty percent of the value—sixty thousand dollars—and cannot be depreciated. The building represents eighty percent—two hundred forty thousand dollars—and depreciates over twenty-seven and a half years. Your annual depreciation deduction is approximately eighty-seven hundred dollars. If your rental income after all operating expenses but before depreciation is six thousand dollars, you report a loss of twenty-eight hundred dollars on your tax return. You keep the six thousand dollars in actual cash flow while showing a loss that potentially reduces taxes on your other income.

The benefit multiplies across multiple properties. If you own ten rental properties each generating similar cash flow and depreciation, you have sixty thousand dollars in actual cash flow while reporting twenty-eight thousand dollars in total losses. This is not fraud or aggressive tax avoidance. This is using depreciation exactly as Congress intended—to account for the theoretical wear and deterioration of buildings over time and to encourage investment in rental housing by making it tax-efficient.

The catch arrives when you eventually sell. Depreciation must be recaptured, meaning you pay taxes on the depreciation you claimed during ownership. The recapture rate is currently twenty-five percent, lower than ordinary income tax rates but higher than long-term capital gains rates. This creates a tax liability that many investors fail to anticipate. The solution is to never sell, instead using 1031 exchanges to continuously defer both capital gains and depreciation recapture. If you hold property until death, your heirs receive stepped-up basis and the depreciation recapture obligation disappears entirely along with the capital gains.

Cost segregation studies take depreciation benefits to another level. Normal depreciation treats the entire building as a single asset depreciating over twenty-seven and a half or thirty-nine years. Cost segregation involves hiring specialized engineers to analyze the property and separate components that can be depreciated over shorter periods. Carpeting, appliances, landscaping, parking lots, and certain building systems can be classified as five-year, seven-year, or fifteen-year property rather than twenty-seven-and-a-half-year property. This accelerates depreciation into early years, creating larger deductions when they provide maximum benefit.

The costs for cost segregation studies range from five thousand to fifteen thousand dollars for typical properties, though larger commercial buildings might require more expensive analysis. The studies only make economic sense when you have sufficient income to benefit from the accelerated deductions and when the property is large enough that the increased deductions exceed the study cost. For most investors, this becomes relevant once they have acquired properties worth at least five hundred thousand dollars and have other income that the depreciation losses can offset.

Opportunity Zones represent the newest addition to the real estate tax advantage arsenal. Created by the Tax Cuts and Jobs Act of 2017, Opportunity Zones allow investors to defer and potentially eliminate capital gains taxes by investing gains into designated economically distressed areas. You sell any asset producing capital gains—stocks, business interests, or real estate. You invest those gains into a Qualified Opportunity Fund that deploys capital into Opportunity Zone properties or businesses. You defer paying taxes on the original gains until 2026 or until you sell the Opportunity Zone investment, whichever comes first. If you hold the Opportunity Zone investment for ten years, all appreciation on that investment becomes permanently tax-free.

The mathematics are compelling for those with substantial capital gains. You sell stock generating a one million dollar gain. Rather than paying two hundred thousand in capital gains taxes, you invest the full one million into an Opportunity Zone fund. The two hundred thousand tax obligation is deferred until 2026. If your Opportunity Zone investment appreciates to two million over ten years, that entire one million dollars of appreciation is tax-free. You have converted a taxable gain into deferred taxation on the original gain plus permanent tax-free treatment of the new gains. The wealthbuilding potential is extraordinary for those who can identify quality Opportunity Zone investments and maintain the discipline to hold for the required decade.

The risks deserve acknowledgment. Opportunity Zones are economically distressed by definition. Not all distressed areas will experience revitalization. Some Opportunity Zone investments will fail, wiping out capital rather than growing it. The legislation created incentives but cannot guarantee outcomes. The one percent approach Opportunity Zones as they approach any investment—with careful due diligence, conservative underwriting, and clear exit strategies. The tax benefits provide margin for error but do not justify investing in fundamentally flawed opportunities.

These strategies—1031 exchanges, Augusta Rule, depreciation optimization through cost segregation, and Opportunity Zone investing—exist independently but create powerful effects when combined systematically. You begin acquiring rental properties, capturing depreciation benefits that shelter cash flow from taxation. You use the Augusta Rule to extract additional tax-free income if you own businesses. When properties appreciate substantially, you use 1031 exchanges to upgrade into larger properties while deferring all taxes. You conduct cost segregation studies on larger properties to accelerate depreciation and create larger losses offsetting other income. When you have major capital gains events from non-real-estate investments, you deploy gains into Opportunity Zones to defer and potentially eliminate those taxes while diversifying your real estate holdings.

This systematic approach creates compounding tax efficiency across decades. You build wealth through real estate cash flow, appreciation, and mortgage paydown. You simultaneously minimize taxation through depreciation, defer taxation through 1031 exchanges, eliminate taxation through Augusta Rule and Opportunity Zone strategies, and eventually pass wealth to heirs with stepped-up basis that erases all deferred tax obligations. The result is wealth accumulation at rates that would be impossible in fully taxable scenarios.

Donald Trump built much of his fortune through exactly this approach. He acquired properties using aggressive leverage, improved them to force appreciation, captured depreciation benefits to shelter income, used 1031 exchanges to continuously upgrade his holdings without paying capital gains, and structured his businesses to maximize deductible expenses while minimizing taxable income. Critics called this tax avoidance. He correctly called it tax planning using provisions Congress explicitly created for these exact purposes. The difference in perspective reflects the difference between those who study the tax code as a roadmap to wealth building and those who view it as an incomprehensible burden to be endured.

I want to emphasize something that creates confusion and sometimes ethical concerns for people encountering these strategies. Everything described in this chapter is legal, tested through decades of IRS scrutiny, and explicitly intended by Congress. You are not cheating or exploiting loopholes when you use 1031 exchanges, claim depreciation, apply the Augusta Rule, or invest in Opportunity Zones. You are accepting invitations that Congress extended to encourage behaviors they view as economically beneficial. The tax code is not neutral. It is deliberate policy expressing through financial incentives what activities Congress wants to encourage. Real estate investment receives favorable treatment because Congress believes real estate investment generates broader economic benefits.

The one percent understand this and feel no guilt about using every available provision. They recognize that paying more tax than legally required is not virtue but waste. They hire competent tax advisors who stay current on changing regulations, structure transactions to maximize benefits while maintaining clear legal boundaries, and document everything meticulously to withstand potential audits. They view tax optimization as professional discipline equivalent to any other business skill requiring mastery.

The ninety-nine percent either remain ignorant that these strategies exist or feel vaguely uncomfortable using them even after learning about them. This discomfort costs them hundreds of thousands or millions across investing careers. The money they unnecessarily pay in taxes does not fund better government services or create public benefit. It simply reduces their wealth-building capacity while transferring resources to the government. The one percent keep those resources, deploy them into additional investments, and build exponentially greater wealth as a result.

The complexity of these strategies requires professional guidance. You should not attempt 1031 exchanges without qualified intermediaries and experienced tax advisors. You should not implement Augusta Rule strategies without proper documentation and legal review. You should not conduct cost segregation studies without engineering firms specializing in this analysis. You should not invest in Opportunity Zones without understanding the specific regulations governing these investments. The cost of professional guidance is modest relative to the benefits captured and the risks avoided. The one percent pay for expertise because they understand that amateur implementation of sophisticated strategies creates audit risk and potential liability that far exceeds any savings from avoiding professional fees.

The progression for most real estate investors begins with simple depreciation on their first rental properties. As portfolios grow and properties appreciate, 1031 exchanges become relevant for upgrading holdings without triggering taxes. If you own businesses, the Augusta Rule becomes available for additional tax-free income. Once properties reach sufficient scale, cost segregation studies make economic sense for accelerating depreciation benefits. If you experience major liquidity events creating large capital gains, Opportunity Zones provide mechanisms for deferring and eliminating taxes on those gains. Each strategy becomes relevant at different stages of wealth building, but all rest on the foundation of understanding that tax optimization is not optional for those serious about building significant wealth.

The information is available. The strategies are legal. The benefits are substantial. What separates those who capture these benefits from those who do not is willingness to invest time understanding the rules, discipline to structure transactions properly, and comfort accepting that using legal tax provisions is prudent financial management rather than unethical manipulation. Trump demonstrated over decades that real estate tax provisions can convert good investments into extraordinary wealth-building machines. His specific business practices and personal conduct are separate matters, but his use of real estate tax strategies exemplifies what becomes possible when you master the code and use it systematically.

You have now been provided the foundation for real estate wealth building through house hacking and rental property acquisition in the previous chapter. This chapter provides the tax optimization framework that makes real estate the most tax-efficient wealth-building vehicle available to ordinary investors. Stock market returns face taxation on dividends and capital gains. Business income faces self-employment taxes and ordinary income rates. Real estate provides mechanisms for deferring, reducing, and sometimes eliminating taxation while building wealth through multiple simultaneous channels. The combination of cash flow, appreciation, leverage, depreciation benefits, and strategic tax deferral through 1031 exchanges creates wealth-building potential that no other asset class can match.

The choice before you is whether to build real estate wealth with or without tax optimization. Both approaches work. One builds wealth perhaps fifty percent faster than the other by retaining capital that would otherwise disappear into tax payments. That fifty percent differential compounds over decades into millions of dollars of difference in terminal wealth. The effort required to capture that difference is learning rules, hiring competent advisors, and structuring transactions properly. This is not difficult work. It is detail-oriented work that most people will not bother with because it seems complicated or because they lack conviction that the benefits justify the effort. The one percent make that effort and capture those benefits. The ninety-nine percent do not and wonder why their real estate investments produce inferior results despite similar starting points. The rules are written. The benefits are available. Whether you claim them remains your decision.

CHAPTER 9:
THE RENT VERSUS BUY DECISION—STRATEGIC HOUSING CHOICES

In 1901, Andrew Carnegie sold his steel company to J.P. Morgan for four hundred eighty million dollars, making him the wealthiest man in the world. His fortune would equal approximately three hundred billion in today's currency, dwarfing the net worth of most contemporary billionaires. With this incomprehensible wealth, Carnegie could have purchased any residence in America. He could have built palatial estates in every major city, accumulated properties as trophies, or constructed monuments to his success. Instead, he rented an apartment in New York City for the remainder of his life. When asked why the wealthiest man in America chose to rent rather than own his primary residence, Carnegie responded that the mathematics of renting versus buying in Manhattan made ownership economically irrational, and he saw no reason to make irrational financial decisions regardless of his capacity to absorb the losses.

This statement contradicts everything most Americans believe about housing and wealth. We are told from childhood that renting is throwing money away, that homeownership builds equity and represents the foundation of middle-class wealth, that landlords get rich while tenants stay poor. These beliefs are so deeply embedded in American culture that challenging them produces visceral reactions. People become defensive, even angry, when you suggest that renting might be financially superior to buying. They interpret the suggestion as an attack on their life choices or their intelligence. What they are actually experiencing is cognitive dissonance—the discomfort that arises when new information conflicts with existing beliefs.

The one percent make housing decisions based on mathematics rather than cultural programming. They calculate the true cost of ownership including opportunity costs, compare those costs to rental expenses, and choose whichever option provides superior financial outcomes. Sometimes that choice is ownership. Sometimes it is renting. The decision depends on specific market conditions, personal circumstances, and intended duration of residence. What the one percent never do is assume that ownership is automatically superior simply because everyone says it is. They run the numbers, and they believe the numbers over the cultural narrative.

I want to establish at the outset that I am not arguing against homeownership categorically. I am arguing against the reflexive assumption that ownership is always superior to renting. In many markets and circumstances, ownership makes excellent financial sense. In many other markets and circumstances, ownership destroys wealth compared to renting while investing the difference. The distinguishing characteristic of one-percent thinking is the willingness to analyze each situation independently rather than applying universal rules that may not fit particular circumstances.

The framework for making this decision rationally begins with understanding the complete cost of ownership. The ninety-nine percent compare mortgage payments to rent payments and conclude that buying makes sense when the mortgage is similar to rent. This analysis is incomplete to the point of being worthless. The true cost of ownership includes mortgage principal and interest, property taxes, homeowners insurance, maintenance and repairs, homeowners association fees where applicable, opportunity cost of the down payment, and transaction costs for both purchase and eventual sale. When you account for all these factors, the actual cost of ownership typically exceeds the mortgage payment by fifty to one hundred percent.

Let me provide specific numbers to illustrate this reality. You consider purchasing a home for four hundred thousand dollars with a twenty-percent down payment of $80,000. You finance $320,000 at

4 percent interest over 30 years, creating a monthly mortgage payment of approximately $1,500. At first glance, this compares favorably to renting a similar property for $2,000 monthly. The analysis seems to favor buying. Now include the complete picture.

Property taxes in many jurisdictions run one to two percent of property value annually—four thousand to eight thousand dollars for a four-hundred-thousand-dollar home, or three hundred thirty to six hundred seventy dollars monthly. Homeowners insurance costs approximately one thousand to fifteen hundred annually, or eighty-five to one hundred twenty-five monthly. Maintenance and repairs average one to two percent of property value annually—another four thousand to eight thousand annually, or three hundred thirty to six hundred seventy monthly. If the property is in a community with homeowners association fees, add another two hundred to five hundred monthly. The sum of these additional costs is approximately one thousand to two thousand dollars monthly beyond the mortgage payment. Your total monthly cost of ownership is twenty-five hundred to thirty-five hundred dollars, substantially exceeding the two-thousand-dollar rental cost for an equivalent property.

The comparison worsens when you account for opportunity cost. That eighty-thousand-dollar down payment could have been invested in index funds. At ten percent annual returns, that eighty thousand would grow to approximately two hundred eight thousand over ten years, five hundred forty thousand over twenty years, and one million four hundred thousand over thirty years. By using it as a down payment instead, you forego all that growth. The opportunity cost compounds annually and represents real wealth you sacrifice by choosing ownership over investing.

Transaction costs amplify the disadvantage. Purchasing a home typically costs two to five percent of the purchase price in closing costs—eight thousand to twenty thousand dollars for a four-hundred-thousand-dollar home. Selling the home costs another six to eight percent including real estate agent commissions and closing costs—twenty-four thousand to thirty-two thousand dollars. If you buy a four-hundred-thousand-dollar home and sell it five years later, you have paid forty-two thousand to sixty-two thousand in total transaction costs before accounting for any other expenses. You could have rented for two thousand monthly for five years—one hundred twenty thousand total—and still come out ahead when you factor in all the hidden costs of ownership.

The mathematical tool that professionals use to evaluate rent versus buy decisions is the price-to-rent ratio. This metric divides the purchase price by the annual rent for equivalent properties. A four-hundred-thousand-dollar home that would rent for two thousand monthly costs four hundred thousand to purchase versus twenty-four thousand annually to rent, producing a price-to-rent ratio of 16.7. This is the multiplier—how many years of rent equal the purchase price.

Historically, price-to-rent ratios between twelve and fifteen indicate rough equilibrium where buying and renting produce similar financial outcomes over time. Ratios below twelve favor buying because you are purchasing future housing consumption at a discount to rental costs. Ratios above twenty favor renting because you are paying substantial premiums for ownership that rental markets do not justify. The four-hundred-thousand-dollar home with a 16.7 ratio falls in the gray zone where the decision depends on additional factors including expected appreciation, duration of residence, and alternative uses for the down payment capital.

These ratios vary dramatically across markets and over time within the same markets. In 2012, following the housing market collapse, many markets saw price-to-rent ratios drop below ten. Buying was obviously superior to renting in those circumstances. By 2021, following rapid appreciation during the pandemic, many markets showed price-to-rent ratios exceeding twenty-five. Renting was obviously superior in those circumstances. Most people bought houses in 2021 anyway because they were following cultural programming rather than mathematical analysis. They purchased at precisely the moment when ownership made least financial sense, locking themselves into expensive mortgages that will take decades to pay off while their wealth-building capacity remains permanently impaired.

Carnegie understood this principle in his era just as clearly as it operates today. Manhattan real estate in the early twentieth century commanded premiums that made ownership economically irrational compared to renting. The capital required to purchase equivalent housing could generate returns elsewhere that far exceeded any appreciation or equity building through ownership. Carnegie deployed his capital into investments generating superior returns while renting his living space. This was not about affordability—he could have purchased buildings easily. This was about optimizing capital allocation, which is how the wealthy think about every financial decision including housing.

The emotional and psychological dimensions of homeownership deserve acknowledgment because they influence decisions regardless of mathematical analysis. Owning a home provides stability, control over your living environment, the ability to modify property to suit preferences, protection from rental increases, and psychological satisfaction that many people value highly. These benefits are real and legitimate. The question is whether they justify the financial cost, and that question has different answers depending on circumstances and personal values.

For families with children seeking stability and planning to remain in an area for a decade or more, homeownership often makes sense even when the pure financial analysis is neutral or slightly negative. The non-financial benefits justify the financial costs. For young professionals uncertain about career trajectories and geographic location, for individuals who value flexibility and freedom from maintenance responsibilities, or for anyone in markets with price-to-rent ratios exceeding twenty, renting provides superior outcomes both financially and practically. The one percent make this assessment consciously. The ninety-nine percent follow cultural scripts without asking whether those scripts serve their interests.

The opportunity cost analysis deserves deeper examination because it represents the clearest distinction between one-percent thinking and conventional assumptions. When you invest eighty thousand in a down payment, you are choosing to deploy that capital into residential real estate rather than into index funds, rental properties, business opportunities, or any other investment. The return on that investment is whatever combination of appreciation, mortgage paydown, and imputed rent you receive from owning rather than renting. The alternative return is whatever you could have earned by investing that same eighty thousand elsewhere while paying rent for housing.

Run this comparison over realistic time periods with realistic assumptions. The eighty-thousand-dollar down payment invested in index funds at ten percent annual returns becomes two hundred eight thousand after ten years. During those same ten years, if the house appreciates at three percent annually—the historical average for residential real estate—your four-hundred-thousand-dollar home becomes approximately five hundred thirty-seven thousand. Your equity in the home is your original eighty thousand down payment, plus the one hundred thirty-seven thousand in appreciation, plus approximately fifty thousand in mortgage principal paydown, minus transaction costs of approximately forty thousand for purchase and another forty thousand you will eventually pay when you sell. Your net equity is approximately one hundred eighty-seven thousand compared to two hundred eight thousand you would have by investing the down payment and renting.

This comparison actually understates the advantage of renting because it ignores the higher monthly costs of ownership versus renting. If ownership costs you five hundred dollars more monthly than renting would cost, and you invest that five hundred dollars monthly difference at ten percent returns, you accumulate an additional seventy-six thousand after ten years. Your total wealth from renting and investing is two hundred eighty-four thousand compared to one hundred eighty-seven thousand from owning. Renting produces fifty-two percent more wealth over the decade despite conventional wisdom insisting that ownership builds wealth while renting wastes money.

The scenarios where buying produces superior outcomes require either home prices appreciating substantially faster than historical averages or rental costs increasing much faster than ownership costs. Neither assumption is reliable. In markets where homes appreciate rapidly, rents typically also increase rapidly, maintaining the price-to-rent ratio relationship. In markets where ownership costs remain stable, home prices typically appreciate slowly because the economic fundamentals supporting rapid appreciation are absent. The mathematical edge consistently favors renting in high price-to-rent markets and favoring buying in low price-to-rent markets, with neutral zones where personal preferences legitimately determine outcomes.

The flexibility advantage of renting becomes particularly valuable during periods of economic or career uncertainty. When you own a home and need to relocate for employment, you face the choice of selling at whatever price the market offers or attempting to rent the property and become a remote landlord. Selling quickly often means accepting discounts and paying full transaction costs. Renting the property while you live elsewhere means managing tenants from a distance, carrying two housing costs simultaneously if rental income falls short of ownership expenses, and maintaining exposure to a single property market you no longer live in. Both options are suboptimal.

When you rent your housing, relocation becomes simple. You notify your landlord, fulfill your lease obligations, and move. Your capital remains liquid and portable. You are not anchored to a specific geography by an illiquid asset that may take months to sell. This flexibility has measurable economic value, particularly early in careers when mobility often drives income growth. The one percent understand that the ability to pursue opportunities without property constraints can be worth more than any equity you might build through ownership.

I have observed a pattern across decades of watching people make housing decisions. Those who buy homes in their twenties and early thirties often realize by their late thirties or early forties that they purchased in the wrong location, at the wrong time, or based on circumstances that have since changed. They feel trapped by properties that no longer serve their needs but that they cannot easily exit without substantial financial losses. They either stay in suboptimal situations or take significant financial hits to escape. Those who rented during those same years maintained flexibility to move as careers evolved, relationships changed, and preferences clarified. They deployed their capital into investments generating returns rather than illiquid housing. By their forties, they have accumulated significantly more investable wealth than their homeowning peers despite paying rent continuously.

The objection arises immediately that landlords extract profit from tenants, and that profit must mean tenants are getting poor deals. This reasoning is flawed. Landlords extract profit by purchasing properties at the right times in the right markets, holding them long enough for appreciation and mortgage paydown to generate equity, maintaining properties efficiently, and managing tenants professionally. Their profit comes primarily from leverage, appreciation, and tax advantages discussed in previous chapters, not from overcharging tenants relative to market rates. In markets with high price-to-rent ratios, landlords who recently purchased properties often lose money monthly even while collecting rent from tenants. Their bet is that future appreciation will eventually generate returns that justify current negative cash flow. Tenants in those markets benefit by paying below ownership costs while landlords absorb losses hoping for future appreciation.

The house-hacking strategy discussed in Chapter Seven represents the exception where ownership can produce superior outcomes even in high price-to-rent markets. When you live in one unit of a multifamily property and collect rent from other units that offset most or all of your housing costs, you have converted your primary residence from a liability into an asset or at least a minimal expense. This approach requires willingness to manage tenants and sacrifice some privacy, but it provides the best of both worlds—building equity through ownership while eliminating or minimizing housing costs through rental income. For those willing to live this way during their building years, house hacking deserves serious consideration even in markets where traditional single-family home purchases make poor financial sense.

The geographic dimension of this analysis cannot be ignored. Markets like San Francisco, New York, Los Angeles, and Seattle have sustained price-to-rent ratios exceeding twenty-five for extended periods. In these markets, renting is mathematically superior to buying for most people most of the time. Markets like Cleveland, Detroit, Memphis, and many smaller cities maintain price-to-rent ratios below fifteen consistently. In these markets, buying generally makes more sense than renting, provided you plan to stay long enough to justify transaction costs. The challenge is that high-ratio markets tend to be where career opportunities concentrate, while low-ratio markets often have fewer employment options and lower income growth potential.

This creates a strategic consideration beyond pure housing costs. You might rent in an expensive city during your high-income years, accumulating wealth through saving and investing while paying steep rent. Once you reach financial independence or transition to remote work, you relocate to a low-cost market where you purchase housing with cash or minimal leverage. This pattern allows you to earn in expensive markets while building wealth rather than consuming it through overpriced housing, then retire in affordable markets where your accumulated wealth supports comfortable lifestyles. The one percent execute this strategy regularly. The ninety-nine percent either never consider it or reject it because they are anchored to specific locations by family, relationships, or unwillingness to disrupt established routines.

The taxation differences between renting and owning deserve brief mention. Homeowners can deduct mortgage interest and property taxes when they itemize deductions, though the 2017 tax reform limited these benefits substantially. The standard deduction now exceeds itemized deductions for most taxpayers, meaning many homeowners receive no tax benefit from ownership. Additionally, the mortgage interest deduction primarily benefits high-income households with expensive mortgages, while providing minimal or no benefit to moderate-income households. Homeowners also receive capital gains exclusions allowing them to exclude two hundred fifty thousand dollars individually or five hundred thousand dollars for married couples when they sell their primary residence, provided they meet residency requirements. These tax benefits are real but generally insufficient to overcome the wealth-building advantages of renting in high price-to-rent markets while investing the difference.

The timing of the buy decision matters enormously and yet receives insufficient attention. Buying at the peak of a market cycle locks you into elevated prices and maximum debt right before values decline. Buying during or after market corrections allows you to purchase at lower prices while avoiding peak-market debt levels. The problem is that most people make housing decisions based on life events—marriage, children, job changes—rather than market timing. They buy when they need housing, which may be the worst possible time from a market perspective. The one percent delay gratification when markets are overheated, continuing to rent and invest until prices correct, then purchasing when valuations become reasonable. This requires discipline to resist social pressure and willingness to maintain unconventional living arrangements longer than peers.

Carnegie's decision to rent in Manhattan reflected this exact thinking. He understood that purchasing overpriced real estate to satisfy social expectations would reduce his ability to deploy capital into more productive investments. He chose wealth over status. The amusing irony is that his wealth eventually provided more status than property ownership ever could. Those who bought homes to signal success owned depreciating structures while owing money to banks. Carnegie owned industrial enterprises generating millions annually while paying rent that represented a trivial percentage of his income. The cultural programming insisted ownership meant wealth while renting meant poverty. The mathematics demonstrated precisely the opposite in his specific circumstances.

The duration of intended residence provides perhaps the clearest guidance for making rational buy versus rent decisions. If you know you will remain in a location for less than five years, renting almost always produces superior financial outcomes because transaction costs consume any equity you might build through appreciation and mortgage paydown. If you expect to remain ten years or longer, buying in markets with reasonable price-to-rent ratios generally makes sense because you have sufficient time for equity building to overcome transaction costs. The five-to-ten-year middle range depends on specific market conditions and personal circumstances. The one percent make these assessments honestly rather than rationalizing buying decisions based on optimistic assumptions about how long they will stay.

I want to address the psychological difficulty many people experience when considering renting long-term or choosing to rent when they could afford to buy. There is genuine social pressure that treats homeownership as a marker of adult success. Family members ask when you are going to stop throwing money away on rent. Friends discuss home purchases and renovations, and you have nothing to contribute to these conversations. Colleagues assume you are struggling financially if you rent while they own. This social pressure drives people to make economically irrational decisions because the psychological cost of going against cultural norms exceeds the financial cost of overpaying for housing.

The one percent develop immunity to this pressure through conviction that their financial analysis is correct and through confidence that wealth building matters more than status signaling. They recognize that explaining their housing choices to skeptical family members or defending their decisions to colleagues is temporary discomfort, while the financial consequences of poor housing decisions compound for decades. They become comfortable being misunderstood by people who do not think about money the way they do. This immunity is not natural. It is developed through education, experience, and commitment to goals that transcend social approval.

The goal is not to rent forever or to own forever. The goal is wealth. Sometimes renting advances that goal more effectively than owning. Sometimes owning advances it more effectively than renting.

The distinguishing feature of one-percent thinking is making this assessment based on mathematics and circumstances rather than cultural programming and social pressure. You calculate price-to-rent ratios, you account for opportunity costs, you assess intended duration of residence, you evaluate career flexibility needs, and you make the choice that optimizes wealth building even if that choice contradicts conventional wisdom.

Andrew Carnegie died in 1919 after giving away ninety percent of his fortune to libraries, universities, and cultural institutions. He lived his final years in the same rented New York apartment he had occupied for decades, having never seen reason to change a housing arrangement that served him perfectly well. He left a legacy of wealth creation and strategic philanthropy that would have been impossible had he followed conventional wisdom about property ownership. His approach to housing was not about cheapness or eccentricity. It was about maintaining intellectual honesty in the face of cultural pressure to conform to suboptimal financial practices.

You face the same choice in your circumstances. You can follow the cultural script that insists homeownership is essential for building wealth, purchasing property whenever you are financially able regardless of market conditions or price-to-rent ratios. Or you can think independently, analyze your specific situation, and make housing decisions that optimize wealth building even when those decisions conflict with what everyone around you is doing. The first path is comfortable socially but often destructive financially. The second path is uncomfortable socially but frequently superior financially. The one percent choose the second path because they care more about actual wealth than about appearing to build wealth through homeownership.

We have now progressed through the foundations of wealth building—proper stewardship, asset versus liability thinking, environmental engineering, tax-advantaged investing, stock market wealth creation, real estate investing, and advanced tax strategies. This chapter challenges perhaps the most sacred assumption in American financial culture: that homeownership is always superior to renting. The reality is more nuanced. In some markets and circumstances, buying builds wealth. In others, renting and investing the difference builds significantly more wealth. The one percent assess which situation they face and act accordingly. The ninety-nine percent buy regardless of circumstances because everyone says they should. The wealth divergence that results from these different approaches compounds over decades into differences of hundreds of thousands or millions of dollars. You now have the framework to make this decision rationally. Whether you use it or default to cultural programming remains your choice.

CHAPTER 10:
INSURANCE WISDOM—PROTECTION WITHOUT WASTE

In 2007, a Lebanese-American mathematician and former derivatives trader named Nassim Nicholas Taleb published a book titled "The Black Swan" that warned of catastrophic risks lurking in complex financial systems. Most readers focused on his philosophical arguments about randomness and prediction. Those who understood his deeper message recognized that Taleb was describing an approach to risk management fundamentally different from conventional wisdom. He structured his entire financial life around a simple principle: protect aggressively against catastrophic losses that would destroy your wealth permanently, while accepting completely the minor losses that occur frequently but never threaten your survival. In insurance terms, this meant carrying massive liability coverage and high deductibles on everything else.

When the 2008 financial crisis arrived exactly as Taleb's framework predicted it eventually would, his investment fund gained eighty-five percent while most investors lost thirty to fifty percent of their wealth. The protection against catastrophe that everyone else had dismissed as paranoid or unnecessary proved to be the only rational approach when the improbable-but-inevitable disaster finally materialized. Taleb had spent years paying premiums for protection that appeared wasteful right up until the moment it became priceless. He understood something that most people never grasp about insurance: it exists to transfer risks you cannot afford to absorb, not to make small problems slightly more convenient.

The ninety-nine percent approach insurance backwards. They buy policies for minor losses because those policies feel productive—you pay premiums, you file claims, you receive checks that make the expense feel worthwhile. They skip or minimize coverage for catastrophic losses because those policies feel wasteful—

you pay premiums year after year and nothing happens, creating the impression that you are being robbed. This is exactly wrong. Insurance for minor losses is almost always a losing proposition where the insurance company prices policies to guarantee profit over large populations. Insurance for catastrophic losses is the one form of insurance that consistently provides value by protecting against events that would destroy you financially even though they occur rarely.

The framework begins with distinguishing between frequency and severity of potential losses. High-frequency, low-severity risks should be self-insured. You will experience these losses regularly, and insurance companies know this. They price policies to collect more in premiums than they pay in claims, plus administrative costs and profit margins. When you buy insurance for high-frequency events, you are systematically paying more than the expected cost of the events themselves. This is guaranteed wealth destruction over time. Low-frequency, high-severity risks should be insured aggressively. You may never experience these losses, but if you do, they will destroy your financial life. Insurance companies must price these policies competitively because few policyholders ever file claims, meaning they can offer meaningful protection at reasonable costs relative to the potential loss.

This principle applies across every insurance category, yet most people violate it consistently. They buy extended warranties on appliances and electronics—high-frequency, low-severity coverage priced to guarantee manufacturer profits. They choose low deductibles on auto and home insurance—coverage for minor accidents and repairs that they could easily pay out of pocket. They skip or minimize umbrella liability insurance—coverage for lawsuits and liability claims that could wipe out their entire net worth. They have optimized for feeling protected against minor inconveniences while leaving themselves exposed to financial catastrophe.

Life insurance provides the clearest example of this inverted thinking. The purpose of life insurance is replacing income that dependents rely on. If you die prematurely, your family loses your future earning capacity. Life insurance transfers that risk to an insurance company, which pays a death benefit that replaces some portion of those lost earnings. This is valuable and necessary protection for anyone with dependents who rely on their income. The question is not whether to buy life insurance but what type to buy and how much.

The insurance industry makes extraordinary profits selling whole life insurance, which combines a death benefit with an investment component that builds cash value. Agents present whole life as superior to term insurance because it provides both protection and savings. They show projections of cash value growth and explain how you can borrow against the policy or eventually surrender it for cash. They describe term insurance as renting protection while whole life means owning it. This sales pitch succeeds because it sounds sophisticated and appeals to people's desire to feel they are building something rather than merely renting protection.

The mathematics tell a different story. Whole life insurance costs approximately ten times as much as term insurance for equivalent death benefit coverage. A healthy thirty-five-year-old male might pay fifty dollars monthly for a one-million-dollar twenty-year term policy or five hundred dollars monthly for a one-million-dollar whole life policy. Over twenty years, the term policy costs twelve thousand dollars. The whole life policy costs one hundred twenty thousand dollars. The difference of one hundred eight thousand dollars is the amount you paid for the investment component of the whole life policy.

Now examine what that investment component provides. The cash value growth inside whole life policies typically yields three to four percent annually after expenses. If you had instead purchased term insurance for fifty dollars monthly and invested the four-hundred-fifty-dollar monthly difference in a low-cost index fund returning ten percent annually, after twenty years you would have accumulated approximately three hundred forty thousand dollars. The whole life policy might have one hundred thousand dollars in cash value after twenty years. You paid one hundred eight thousand dollars more in premiums to accumulate one hundred thousand in cash value when you could have accumulated three hundred forty thousand dollars by buying term insurance and investing the difference yourself.

The whole life policy makes sense for the insurance company, which collects massive premiums and invests your money at market rates while paying you a fraction of those returns. It makes sense for the agent, who earns a commission of fifty to one hundred percent of the first year's premium—twenty-five hundred to six thousand dollars on that five-hundred-dollar monthly policy. It makes no sense for you except in narrow circumstances involving estate planning for the very wealthy who need permanent insurance to pay estate taxes. For everyone else, term life insurance provides the protection you need at a fraction of the cost, allowing you to invest the difference and build actual wealth rather than enriching insurance companies.

The amount of term life insurance you need depends entirely on your dependents' financial situation if you die. The standard recommendation of six to ten times annual income provides a rough guideline but lacks precision. A better approach calculates the actual income replacement your family would need. If you earn eighty thousand annually and your family needs seventy thousand to maintain their lifestyle after accounting for your personal expenses that would disappear, they need to replace seventy thousand annually. At a four-percent withdrawal rate from invested assets, they need one million seven hundred fifty thousand dollars in capital. This is the insurance amount required to fully replace your income through invested returns without depleting principal.

As your net worth grows, your life insurance need declines. When you have accumulated five hundred thousand in investments, you need only one million two hundred fifty thousand in coverage. When you reach one million in net worth, you need only seven hundred fifty thousand. Once your net worth exceeds the amount your dependents would need to maintain their lifestyle indefinitely, you need no life insurance at all. You have become self-insured through wealth accumulation. This progression is why term insurance makes more sense than permanent insurance. You need large death benefits during your working years when dependents rely on your income. You need no coverage once you have accumulated sufficient wealth. Term insurance provides large coverage when you need it and expires when you no longer do. Whole life provides modest coverage forever, including decades when you need no insurance at all.

Disability insurance receives insufficient attention despite representing greater risk than premature death for most working-age people. You are far more likely to become disabled and unable to work than to die before retirement. Disability eliminates your income while leaving all your expenses intact and often adding substantial medical costs. For anyone whose income depends on their capacity to work—which is nearly everyone not yet financially independent—disability insurance is more important than life insurance. Yet most people either skip it entirely or carry inadequate coverage because they do not understand the risk or because employer-provided coverage seems sufficient.

Employer disability policies typically replace fifty to sixty percent of salary and define disability narrowly as inability to perform any occupation rather than your specific occupation. If you are a surgeon who loses fine motor control in your hands, you are disabled from surgery but not from any occupation according to these policies. They would deny benefits if you could perform any work, even if that work pays a fraction of your surgical income. Individual disability policies purchased outside employment define disability as inability to perform your specific occupation and replace up to sixty to seventy percent of income with benefits paid tax-free if you paid premiums with after-tax dollars.

The cost varies based on occupation, age, and health, but professionals should expect to pay approximately two to three percent of income for quality coverage. Someone earning one hundred thousand might pay two thousand to three thousand annually for disability coverage replacing sixty thousand annually until age sixty-five. This seems expensive until you calculate the value of protection. If you become disabled at age forty, you are protecting twenty-five years of income—one million five hundred thousand dollars in

THINK LIKE A ONE PERCENTER

benefits for someone replacing sixty thousand annually. The premiums you paid over previous years are trivial compared to the benefit received. Yet most people skip this coverage because nothing seems to be happening and the premiums feel like waste.

Liability insurance represents perhaps the most underutilized protection available. Umbrella policies provide additional liability coverage beyond the limits of your auto and homeowners insurance. These policies typically provide one to five million dollars in coverage for remarkably low premiums—often one hundred fifty to three hundred dollars annually for one million in coverage, with additional millions costing less incrementally. If you are sued and found liable for damages exceeding your underlying insurance limits, the umbrella policy pays the excess up to its limits. Without this coverage, plaintiffs can pursue your personal assets to satisfy judgments.

The risk increases as your net worth grows. When you have minimal assets, there is limited reason for plaintiffs to pursue you aggressively—you cannot pay more than you have. As you accumulate wealth, you become an attractive target for litigation. An auto accident where you are at fault and someone is seriously injured can easily generate claims exceeding one million dollars. Without umbrella coverage, a judgment that large could wipe out years of accumulated wealth. With umbrella coverage costing perhaps three hundred dollars annually, you have transferred that entire risk to an insurance company for less than the cost of a dinner for two at a nice restaurant.

The one percent carry umbrella coverage as reflexively as they carry any insurance. The cost is negligible relative to their assets, and the protection is comprehensive. The ninety-nine percent skip it because they do not understand the risk or because three hundred dollars seems like an expense they can avoid. This is precisely the kind of thinking that keeps people trapped in the ninety-nine percent. They nickel-and-dime themselves on catastrophic protection that costs almost nothing while freely spending on consumption that provides no lasting value.

Health insurance deserves extended treatment because it represents the most complex and expensive insurance most people purchase. We have discussed Health Savings Accounts in Chapter Four as powerful wealth-building vehicles. The vehicle depends on pairing an HSA with a high-deductible health plan. For healthy individuals and families, high-deductible plans almost always provide superior outcomes compared to traditional low-deductible plans when you account for the combination of premium savings and HSA contribution benefits.

The conventional approach to health insurance prioritizes low deductibles and low out-of-pocket maximums because people fear medical expenses. They pay substantially higher premiums to minimize the possibility of paying for care directly. This is expensive protection against small losses—exactly the category of insurance that consistently destroys wealth. A low-deductible plan might charge six hundred dollars monthly in premiums with a five-hundred-dollar deductible. A comparable high-deductible plan might charge three hundred dollars monthly with a three-thousand-dollar deductible. Over a year, the low-deductible plan costs seven thousand two hundred dollars in premiums. The high-deductible plan costs thirty-six hundred dollars in premiums.

If you have a year with minimal medical expenses, the low-deductible plan cost you seven thousand two hundred dollars while the high-deductible plan cost you perhaps four thousand dollars including out-of-pocket expenses. You saved thirty-two hundred dollars, which you contributed to your HSA where it grows tax-free forever. If you have a year with substantial medical expenses hitting your deductible, the low-deductible plan cost you seven thousand seven hundred dollars in total expenses. The high-deductible plan cost you sixty-six hundred dollars in total expenses. You saved one thousand one hundred dollars while contributing that amount and more to your HSA. The high-deductible plan wins in both scenarios, yet people choose low-deductible plans because they make emotional rather than mathematical decisions about insurance.

The selection process for health insurance requires comparing total potential costs across realistic scenarios. Start with the premium—what you pay regardless of whether you use healthcare.

Add the deductible—what you must pay before insurance covers anything. Add the out-of-pocket maximum—the most you can pay in a year including deductible and coinsurance. Calculate the best-case scenario where you use minimal healthcare and the worst-case scenario where you hit your out-of-pocket maximum. Compare these total costs across available plans while accounting for any employer contributions to HSAs that pair with high-deductible plans. The plan with the lowest total cost in both best-case and worst-case scenarios is almost always the optimal choice.

Auto insurance follows similar principles but with some variation. You need substantial liability coverage because auto accidents can cause serious injuries with enormous costs. You should carry liability limits of at least one hundred thousand per person and three hundred thousand per occurrence, preferably higher if you have substantial assets to protect. This coverage is relatively inexpensive because the insurance company is betting you will not cause serious accidents, which is statistically a good bet for most drivers. You should minimize or eliminate collision and comprehensive coverage on older vehicles worth less than a few thousand dollars. If your vehicle is worth three thousand dollars and collision coverage costs eight hundred annually, you are paying substantial premiums to protect minimal value. After four years, you have paid more in premiums than the vehicle is worth. You should self-insure by dropping collision coverage and accepting the risk of having to replace the vehicle out of pocket if you total it.

The deductible selection matters enormously. Raising your deductible from five hundred dollars to one thousand dollars might reduce your premium by one hundred fifty dollars annually. You are paying one hundred fifty dollars annually to avoid five hundred dollars of potential out-of-pocket expense. Over four years, you pay six hundred dollars in higher premiums to protect against five hundred dollars in deductible exposure. This is paying one hundred twenty percent of the protected amount for coverage you may never use. The rational choice is taking the higher deductible and investing the premium savings. Over twenty years of driving, you will almost certainly come out ahead even if you experience one or two accidents requiring you to pay the higher deductible.

Homeowners insurance follows identical logic. You need substantial dwelling coverage to rebuild your home if it is destroyed completely. This is catastrophic protection that justifies whatever premium is required. You need liability coverage for accidents that occur on your property, which is why you should pair homeowners insurance with umbrella liability coverage. You should take the highest deductible you can afford comfortably. Moving from a one-thousand-dollar deductible to a five-thousand-dollar deductible might save three hundred to five hundred dollars annually in premiums. That savings accumulates to six thousand to ten thousand dollars over twenty years. You are self-insuring the first five thousand dollars of any claim and pocketing the premium difference. Unless you file multiple claims over those twenty years, you come out ahead financially while still maintaining protection against the catastrophic loss of your home.

The insurance industry profits from people's inability to distinguish between frequency and severity, between affordable losses and catastrophic losses. They price policies assuming most people will choose low deductibles for the psychological comfort of minimizing out-of-pocket expenses. This allows them to collect premium dollars far exceeding the claims they pay. The one percent understand this dynamic and refuse to participate. They self-insure everything they can afford to lose and transfer only the risks that would impair their wealth permanently. This requires maintaining reserves to cover the higher deductibles they carry, but we have established in previous chapters that maintaining reserves is fundamental to sound financial management regardless of insurance decisions.

The process for buying insurance at the lowest cost begins with understanding that insurance companies use different underwriting models and price identical coverage differently. Shopping multiple carriers for the same coverage specifications can produce quotes varying by thirty to fifty percent. Most people either accept their current carrier's renewal without shopping or obtain one or two quotes and choose based on limited comparison. The one percent obtain at least four to five quotes for any major insurance purchase, ensuring they have captured the low end of the pricing distribution for their risk profile.

Independent insurance agents who represent multiple carriers provide more efficient shopping than contacting each carrier directly. These agents submit your information to their carrier network and return multiple quotes simultaneously. The concern is that independent agents may be incentivized to sell policies providing them higher commissions rather than lowest cost to you. Combat this by being explicit that you are choosing based solely on price for specified coverage and that you are obtaining quotes from multiple sources. This forces the agent to show you the genuinely lowest-cost options rather than steering you toward more profitable policies.

The timing of insurance purchases affects cost substantially. Auto insurance rates consider your prior insurance history, making continuous coverage essential even when you are not driving regularly. Homeowners insurance is cheapest when bundled with auto insurance through the same carrier, though you should still compare bundled pricing across carriers rather than assuming bundling always provides the best value. Life and disability insurance cost less when purchased while young and healthy, though you should avoid purchasing more coverage than you need simply because it is cheap while young. Term life insurance should match your actual protection needs, which change as your net worth and family situation evolve.

The claims process requires understanding when to file claims and when to pay out of pocket despite having coverage. Every claim you file is recorded and affects your future insurability and pricing. Multiple claims over a few years can result in cancellation or substantial premium increases that exceed the value of the claims paid. For this reason, you should file claims only for losses exceeding your deductible by substantial margins. If you have a one-thousand-dollar deductible and suffer a fifteen-hundred-dollar loss, filing a claim nets you five hundred dollars but creates a claim record that might cost you substantially more in future premium increases. The rational decision is often paying the fifteen hundred out of pocket and preserving your claims-free status. This is another reason higher deductibles make sense—they force you to self-insure minor losses that should not be claimed anyway.

The insurance needs evolve as wealth accumulates. Early in your career with minimal assets, you need substantial life and disability insurance but minimal liability coverage beyond basic policy limits. Your earning capacity is your most valuable asset, and insurance protects that capacity. You have few assets for plaintiffs to pursue, so umbrella liability coverage is less critical. As you accumulate wealth, life insurance needs decline while liability coverage needs increase. Your assets can replace your income for dependents, reducing the death benefit required. Those same assets become targets for litigation, making umbrella coverage essential. By the time you reach financial independence, you likely need no life or disability insurance but should carry substantial umbrella liability coverage. You have become self-insured for mortality and disability risk but remain exposed to liability risk that no amount of wealth can fully self-insure against.

Nassim Taleb's approach to insurance extends beyond formal insurance policies to a broader philosophy about risk management. He structures his investment portfolio to survive any market crisis, accepting lower returns during normal times in exchange for protection during catastrophic times. He maintains redundancy in critical systems, ensuring that no single failure can destroy him. He avoids concentration in any risk category, spreading exposure across multiple independent factors. This is insurance thinking applied to all aspects of life. Protect aggressively against catastrophe. Accept fully the minor setbacks that occur frequently but never threaten survival. This philosophy builds antifragility—the capacity to benefit from disorder and stress rather than merely surviving it.

The psychological barrier most people face with proper insurance strategy is that it feels wasteful when nothing goes wrong. You pay premiums for umbrella coverage year after year and never file a claim. You carry high deductibles and pay out of pocket for minor losses. You buy term insurance that expires worthless. All of this feels like money disappearing with nothing to show for it. The one percent reframe this entirely. Insurance premiums are not consumption. They are the cost of transferring catastrophic risk. The value is not receiving claims payments but rather eliminating the possibility of financial catastrophe. You are paying to know with certainty that no insurable event can destroy your wealth permanently. That certainty is worth whatever the premium costs.

This reframing requires accepting that insurance should feel wasteful most of the time. If you are filing claims regularly, you either have catastrophically bad luck or you are insuring high-frequency events that should be self-insured. Properly structured insurance produces peace of mind through decades of premium payments that generate no claims. Then, if catastrophe strikes, the insurance performs exactly as intended, transferring a loss you could not absorb to a company that can. The one percent pay for this transfer without complaint because they understand that wealth preservation requires it.

The integration of insurance strategy with wealth-building strategy should now be clear. You maintain high-deductible health insurance to access HSAs that build tax-free wealth. You carry sufficient life and disability insurance to protect your earning capacity during wealth accumulation. You purchase umbrella liability coverage to protect accumulated assets from litigation. You self-insure minor losses through higher deductibles, capturing premium savings that can be invested for compound growth. You avoid wealth-destroying products like whole life insurance and extended warranties that enrich sellers while impoverishing buyers. Each decision follows from the fundamental principle of insuring catastrophes while accepting minor losses.

The total cost of properly structured insurance is substantially less than most people currently pay while providing superior protection. The savings from eliminating whole life insurance, choosing high deductibles, and skipping unnecessary coverage products typically exceeds one thousand dollars monthly for a family.

That thousand dollars monthly invested at ten percent returns for thirty years becomes two million two hundred seventy thousand dollars. This is wealth you build by thinking rationally about insurance rather than emotionally. The protection you need costs far less than the protection you are sold when you understand the distinction between frequency and severity, between affordable losses and catastrophic risks.

You have now been provided the framework every financial decision in previous chapters assumes is in place. Proper stewardship in Chapter One, asset versus liability thinking in Chapter Two, environmental engineering in Chapter Three, tax-advantaged vehicles in Chapter Four, market investing in Chapter Six, real estate in Chapter Seven, advanced tax strategies in Chapter Eight, and housing decisions in Chapter Nine all assume you are protecting the wealth you build through appropriate risk transfer. Insurance is not the exciting part of wealth building. It is the foundation that ensures what you build cannot be destroyed by events beyond your control. The one percent establish this foundation early and maintain it permanently. The ninety-nine percent either skip it entirely or implement it backwards, insuring minor losses while remaining exposed to catastrophic risks. The result is that unexpected events regularly destroy wealth that took years to accumulate. Proper insurance strategy prevents this. The cost is modest. The value is preservation of everything else you accomplish. You now understand how to structure protection without waste. Implementation remains your responsibility.

CHAPTER 11:
CARS—TRANSPORTATION WITHOUT FINANCIAL SUICIDE

In 1998, two Stanford graduate students named Sergey Brin and Larry Page were developing a search algorithm they believed could revolutionize how people found information on the internet. They needed funding to transform their academic project into a commercial venture. They approached David Cheriton, a Stanford professor who had made a fortune from previous technology investments, and presented their vision for what would become Google. Cheriton was immediately impressed by their technical sophistication and business potential. He wrote them a check for one hundred thousand dollars and introduced them to other investors who provided the capital necessary to launch the company.

That hundred-thousand-dollar investment eventually became worth billions when Google went public in 2004. Cheriton's stake in the company, combined with his other successful technology investments, placed his net worth comfortably in the billions. Yet when journalists tracked him down to write profiles about his remarkable investment success, they invariably noted a detail that seemed to contradict everything about the wealth he had accumulated. David Cheriton drove a 1986 Honda Civic, a vehicle he had owned for more than a decade and showed no intention of replacing despite its age and his capacity to purchase any automobile in the world.

When pressed to explain why a billionaire would drive a twenty-year-old economy car, Cheriton responded with an observation that captures everything you need to understand about automobile ownership and wealth building. He noted that the car served its transportation function perfectly well, that purchasing an expensive vehicle would not improve his quality of life in any measurable way, and that the capital he did not waste on automotive consumption remained available for investments generating actual returns. The difference between his net worth and that of his peers who drove luxury vehicles could be measured in millions of dollars attributable directly to this single category of spending discipline maintained across decades.

This example contradicts the deep cultural programming most Americans receive about automobiles and their relationship to success. We are taught that cars signal status, that successful people drive expensive vehicles, and that upgrading your car as your income rises represents normal and expected behavior. The automotive industry spends billions annually reinforcing these messages through advertising that associates vehicle ownership with identity, achievement, and social position. The financing industry enables this consumption by making monthly payments seem affordable even when the total cost is catastrophic. The result is that the average American destroys more wealth through automobile purchases than through almost any other category of spending except housing.

The mathematics are brutal and yet somehow remain invisible to most people making these decisions. A new car loses approximately twenty percent of its value the moment you drive it from the dealership. This is not metaphor or exaggeration. If you purchase a vehicle for forty thousand dollars and attempt to sell it the following day, you will receive offers around thirty-two thousand dollars. Eight thousand dollars has vanished permanently, converted into the transaction costs of new car sales and the premium buyers pay for factory-fresh vehicles. This loss occurs before you have driven a single mile beyond the delivery trip home.

The depreciation continues relentlessly. The typical new car loses roughly fifteen percent of its remaining value annually for the first five years. Your forty-thousand-dollar vehicle becomes thirty-two thousand after year one, twenty-seven thousand two hundred after year two, twenty-three thousand one hundred after year three, nineteen thousand six hundred after year four, and sixteen thousand seven hundred after year five. You have paid forty thousand dollars for a vehicle now worth sixteen thousand seven hundred dollars. The difference of twenty-three thousand three hundred dollars is wealth you destroyed through new car ownership over five years. This is consumption, not investment. This is value permanently eliminated from your balance sheet with nothing to show for it except transportation you could have obtained far more cheaply.

Now layer financing costs onto this depreciation. Most people finance new car purchases because they cannot afford to pay cash for forty-thousand-dollar vehicles. At six percent interest over five years, the total payments on a forty-thousand-dollar car loan exceed fortysix thousand dollars. You are paying forty-six thousand dollars for a vehicle that becomes worth sixteen thousand seven hundred dollars. The difference of twenty-nine thousand three hundred dollars represents wealth destruction through the combination of depreciation and financing costs. This is before accounting for insurance, maintenance, registration fees, and fuel costs that add thousands annually to the true cost of ownership.

The opportunity cost dwarfs even these direct costs. That forty-six thousand dollars paid over five years for a depreciating vehicle could have been invested in index funds. At ten percent returns, forty-six thousand dollars becomes approximately seventy-five thousand dollars over five years through compound growth. Instead of building seventy-five thousand in wealth, you destroyed twenty-nine thousand three hundred in direct costs, for a net difference of over one hundred four thousand dollars. That single vehicle purchase cost you more than one hundred thousand dollars in total wealth impact when you account for what you paid, what you lost to depreciation, and what you foregone by not investing the capital instead.

Extend this pattern across a working lifetime and the numbers become staggering. Someone who purchases a new forty-thousand dollar vehicle every five years from age twenty-five to age sixty-five has made eight vehicle purchases totaling three hundred twenty thousand dollars in purchase costs. The depreciation losses exceed one hundred eighty thousand dollars. The opportunity cost of not investing that capital approaches two million dollars. The total wealth impact of this automotive consumption pattern is approximately two million three hundred thousand dollars. This is wealth destroyed through a single category of spending that could have been reduced by seventy percent or more through rational vehicle acquisition strategies.

The alternative approach begins with understanding that vehicles are transportation tools, not investments or status symbols. Their purpose is moving you reliably from origin to destination at the lowest possible total cost. Everything beyond this basic function is consumption that you can choose to indulge if it provides value you consider worth the cost, but you must acknowledge honestly that you are choosing expensive consumption over wealth building. Most people cannot make this acknowledgment honestly because they have convinced themselves that expensive vehicles are somehow connected to their financial success or professional credibility.

The optimal vehicle acquisition strategy purchases quality used vehicles three to five years old where someone else absorbed the steepest portion of the depreciation curve. A three-year-old vehicle that sold for forty thousand dollars new typically costs twenty-five thousand dollars on the used market. The first buyer paid forty thousand and absorbed fifteen thousand in depreciation. You are purchasing the same vehicle with the same useful life remaining for twenty-five thousand. Over the next five years, this vehicle depreciates from twenty-five thousand to approximately fourteen thousand, a loss of eleven thousand compared to the twenty-three thousand three hundred you would have lost buying new. You saved twelve thousand three hundred dollars in depreciation alone by purchasing used rather than new.

The financing costs also decrease because you are borrowing twenty-five thousand rather than forty thousand. At six percent over five years, the total payments are approximately twenty-nine thousand dollars rather than forty-six thousand. The interest paid is four thousand rather than six thousand. The cash outflow is seventeen thousand dollars less over the five-year ownership period. Combined with the twelve thousand three hundred in depreciation savings, you have reduced your total cost by twenty-nine thousand three hundred dollars through the single decision to purchase used rather than new. This is found money captured through patience and willingness to drive a vehicle that is three years old rather than brand new.

The vehicle selection process should prioritize reliability over appearance or features. Certain manufacturers and models have demonstrated superior longevity and lower maintenance costs across decades of production. Honda, Toyota, and to a lesser extent Mazda and Subaru produce vehicles that regularly exceed two hundred thousand miles with proper maintenance. Their used vehicles command premium prices precisely because informed buyers recognize their superior value retention and reliability. These premium prices are justified by the reduced likelihood of major repairs and the extended useful life compared to vehicles from manufacturers with inferior reliability records.

The one percent study reliability data from sources like Consumer Reports and J.D. Power before making vehicle purchases. They identify specific models with documented histories of minimal problems and they purchase those models regardless of whether they are exciting or prestigious. A ten-year-old Toyota Camry with one hundred fifty thousand miles but comprehensive maintenance records is a superior financial decision to a five-year-old luxury sedan with half the mileage but a history of expensive repairs and poor reliability ratings. The former will likely provide another hundred thousand miles of service at minimal cost beyond routine maintenance. The latter will consume thousands in repairs while depreciating faster and eventually requiring replacement sooner.

The total cost of ownership includes categories beyond purchase price and depreciation that most people fail to calculate before buying vehicles. Insurance costs vary dramatically based on vehicle type and value. Sports cars and luxury vehicles carry premium insurance rates because repairs are expensive and theft is common. Economy vehicles from reliable manufacturers cost substantially less to insure because parts are cheap and theft is rare. The difference can exceed one thousand dollars annually, adding ten thousand dollars to the total cost of ownership over a decade.

Fuel costs compound daily and receive insufficient attention during purchase decisions. A vehicle averaging twenty-five miles per gallon versus one averaging thirty-five miles per gallon creates annual fuel cost differences of five hundred to eight hundred dollars at current fuel prices for typical driving distances. Over ten years of ownership, this seemingly minor efficiency difference costs an additional five thousand to eight thousand dollars. Maintenance costs follow similar patterns, with luxury vehicles requiring expensive synthetic oils, premium replacement parts, and dealer service that economy vehicles do not require. The annual maintenance differential can easily reach one thousand to two thousand dollars, adding another ten thousand to twenty thousand dollars to lifetime ownership costs.

The financing decision between buying and leasing receives substantial attention in automotive advertising, with manufacturers offering lease deals that appear attractive compared to purchase financing. The lease mathematics almost always favor the manufacturer rather than the consumer. When you lease a vehicle, you are financing the depreciation that occurs during your lease term plus interest on that depreciation. The manufacturer calculates the expected depreciation, adds their profit margin and interest charges, and divides the total by the lease term to determine your monthly payment. You pay for the full depreciation during your possession of the vehicle but never own the asset. At lease end, you return the vehicle with nothing to show for your payments except the transportation you consumed during the lease period.

The scenarios where leasing makes financial sense are narrow and specific. If you need a vehicle for business purposes and can deduct lease payments as business expenses, the tax benefits may justify the premium cost compared to purchasing. If you have unusual need for consistently new vehicles with the latest safety or technology features and you are willing to pay the premium for this preference, leasing provides that option while avoiding the transaction costs of frequent purchase and resale. For everyone else, leasing is expensive consumption that transfers wealth from you to automotive manufacturers and finance companies.

The negotiation process for vehicle purchases determines whether you pay fair market price or overpay by thousands of dollars. Dealerships structure their pricing to maximize profit through multiple mechanisms that most buyers fail to understand or recognize. They separate the negotiation into four components: vehicle price, trade-in value, financing terms, and add-on products. By negotiating each component independently and obscuring the relationships between them, they create opportunities to extract profit even when they appear to offer favorable terms on one component by offsetting it through less favorable terms on others.

The defense against this manipulation is conducting extensive research before entering any negotiation. Online resources provide invoice costs showing what the dealer paid for the vehicle, allowing you to establish a reasonable target price that provides the dealer modest profit while preventing price gouging. These same resources provide fair market values for your trade-in vehicle, preventing dealers from offering below-market trade values to offset apparent discounts on purchase price. You should secure financing from banks or credit unions before visiting dealers, ensuring you have a baseline interest rate that dealer financing must beat to be competitive. You should decline all add-on products including extended warranties, fabric protection, and dealer-installed accessories that carry enormous markups and provide minimal value.

The optimal negotiation approach contacts multiple dealers via email with specific vehicle requirements and requests their best out-the-door price including all fees. This creates competition between dealers without requiring you to visit showrooms or engage in face-to-face negotiations where psychological pressure and time investment bias you toward accepting suboptimal terms. The dealers know they are competing directly and typically offer aggressive pricing to win your business. You select the lowest offer, verify that it matches the terms stated, and complete the purchase. This process requires perhaps three to five hours of research and email communication compared to the eight to twelve hours many people spend visiting multiple dealers and negotiating in person for worse outcomes.

The timing of vehicle purchases affects prices materially. Dealers face monthly and quarterly sales targets that influence their willingness to discount. The final days of months and quarters typically offer the most aggressive discounting as dealers attempt to meet targets. The final days of model years offer substantial discounts as dealers clear inventory to make room for new model year vehicles. December offers advantages as dealers simultaneously face calendar year-end targets and model year clearance pressures. Someone flexible about timing their purchase can capture discounts of two thousand to five thousand dollars through strategic timing compared to purchasing during slow periods when dealers feel no pressure to negotiate.

The psychology of vehicle ownership creates the most significant barrier to rational decision-making in this category. People derive identity and status from the vehicles they drive in ways that make objective financial analysis nearly impossible. A physician believes he should drive a luxury sedan because his colleagues do and his patients expect it. An executive believes her vehicle reflects her corporate standing and that driving a modest car would undermine her professional credibility. A young man believes an expensive sports car will attract romantic partners and signal his success to friends. These beliefs are false, but they are deeply held and they drive decisions that destroy hundreds of thousands of dollars in wealth over lifetimes.

David Cheriton's continued driving of a 1986 Honda Civic demonstrated immunity to these status concerns. He apparently did not care whether colleagues were impressed by his vehicle or whether strangers judged his success based on what he drove. He had achieved actual wealth measured in billions and felt no need to signal that wealth through automotive consumption. This psychological freedom is characteristic of genuine one-percent thinking. Those who are secure in their actual financial position feel no compulsion to prove anything through consumption. Those who are insecure about their financial position attempt to compensate through consumption that creates the appearance of success while preventing actual accumulation of wealth.

The progression most people follow is predictable and destructive. They graduate college and secure employment offering modest income. They purchase a new economy car because their old college vehicle is unreliable and they need dependable transportation. They finance the purchase over five years. Three years into the loan, they receive a promotion and salary increase. They decide this success warrants a better vehicle. They trade the partially paid loan for a larger loan on an expensive vehicle. This new loan requires six or seven years to repay. Four years later, another promotion arrives with another salary increase. The cycle repeats with an even more expensive vehicle and even larger loan. After twenty years of this pattern, they have perpetually carried automotive debt consuming ten to fifteen percent of gross income, they have destroyed hundreds of thousands in wealth through depreciation and interest costs, and they have never owned a vehicle free and clear except briefly between loan payoff and trading for the next vehicle.

The alternative progression purchases a quality used vehicle with cash or minimal financing, pays off any loan aggressively within two to three years, drives that vehicle until major repairs become necessary or until the vehicle no longer meets needs reliably, then replaces it with another quality used vehicle purchased with cash saved during the years of debt-free ownership. This pattern eliminates interest costs entirely after the first vehicle, minimizes depreciation losses through used purchases, and creates periods of years where vehicle costs consist only of insurance, fuel, and routine maintenance. The wealth preserved through this approach accumulates through investments that compound over decades.

The calculation determining when to replace a vehicle requires honest assessment of repair costs versus replacement costs. A vehicle worth five thousand dollars that needs three thousand dollars in repairs to remain reliable for another three years is a rational repair decision. You are paying three thousand dollars for three years of transportation, approximately one thousand annually. A replacement vehicle costs at minimum ten thousand dollars for equivalent reliability, requiring depreciation and carrying costs substantially exceeding the one thousand annual cost of maintaining your existing vehicle. The repair is the obvious financial choice even though writing a three-thousand-dollar check for repairs feels painful while signing financing documents for a replacement vehicle feels less immediate.

Most people make replacement decisions based on frustration with aging vehicles and desire for something newer rather than rational cost comparisons. They trade vehicles with relatively minor issues for much more expensive replacements, destroying wealth through unnecessary depreciation. The one percent maintain vehicles longer precisely because they understand that the marginal cost of continued ownership decreases substantially once depreciation slows and major systems have been replaced or maintained. A fifteen-year-old vehicle that has received a new transmission and timing belt has eliminated the major mechanical risks and likely offers several more years of economical service despite its age.

The exception to the used vehicle purchasing strategy applies to individuals who maintain vehicles for extreme durations. If you intend to drive a vehicle for fifteen to twenty years and two hundred thousand miles or more, purchasing new provides certain advantages over purchasing used. You control the complete maintenance history, you receive manufacturer warranty coverage during early years when defects typically emerge, and you avoid inheriting deferred maintenance or abuse from previous owners. The depreciation losses from new purchases are offset by extended ownership periods that spread those losses across many more years. Someone who purchases a thirty-thousand-dollar vehicle and drives it for twenty years pays fifteen hundred annually in depreciation. This is lower than someone who purchases three-year-old vehicles every eight years and pays higher average annual depreciation despite avoiding the steepest initial decline.

This extended ownership approach requires selecting vehicles known for exceptional longevity and committing to meticulous maintenance regardless of cost. You are essentially operating a single vehicle for your entire working career rather than cycling through multiple vehicles. The economic benefits are substantial, the environmental benefits are considerable, and the simplicity of never shopping for vehicles or negotiating purchases has value beyond pure economics. This is not the path most people choose because vehicles become boring after years of ownership and the desire for something new overwhelms rational long-term thinking.

The one percent recognize this psychological pattern and defend against it through conscious commitment to extended ownership regardless of temporary desire for novelty.

The electric vehicle transition introduces new variables to vehicle ownership economics that deserve consideration. Electric vehicles carry purchase price premiums over comparable gasoline vehicles but offer substantially lower operating costs through reduced fuel and maintenance expenses. The total cost of ownership analysis depends heavily on driving distances, electricity costs in your region, and expected ownership duration. Current federal tax credits of up to seven thousand five hundred dollars for new electric vehicle purchases substantially improve their economics, though these credits phase out after manufacturers sell specific quantities and may not exist indefinitely.

The strategic approach to electric vehicles purchases them used rather than new, allowing someone else to absorb the depreciation premium while you capture the operating cost benefits. A three-year-old electric vehicle costs thirty to forty percent less than new while retaining most battery capacity and benefit. The combination of used purchase pricing and low operating costs creates favorable total cost of ownership compared to either new electric vehicles or used gasoline vehicles in many scenarios. The one percent analyze these numbers for their specific circumstances rather than making ideological decisions about vehicle propulsion technology.

The relationship between income and vehicle expenses provides useful guidance for those uncertain whether their automotive spending is reasonable. The general recommendation suggests total vehicle expenses including loan payments, insurance, fuel, maintenance, and depreciation should not exceed fifteen to twenty percent of gross income. Someone earning sixty thousand annually should spend no more than nine thousand to twelve thousand annually on total vehicle costs. This includes depreciation, meaning if you are driving a vehicle losing four thousand annually in value, your remaining budget for all other expenses is five thousand to eight thousand. Most people violate this guideline substantially, spending twenty-five to thirty-five percent of gross income on vehicles through expensive purchases, long-term financing, and premature replacement cycles.

David Cheriton's automotive spending likely consumed less than one percent of his income during his years of driving the 1986 Honda Civic. The vehicle was fully paid for, insurance on an old economy car cost minimal amounts, and fuel and maintenance represented his only significant expenses. This freed ninety-nine percent of what he could have spent on automotive consumption for investment instead. The compound returns on that capital over decades explain more about his current net worth than most people realize. He built billions not primarily through genius investment selection but through systematic avoidance of wealth-destroying consumption that his peers indulged freely.

You face the same choice in your circumstances with your income level. You can follow cultural programming that treats expensive vehicles as rewards for professional achievement, financing new cars every few years and destroying wealth through depreciation and interest costs. Or you can recognize vehicles as transportation tools, purchase quality used vehicles for cash, maintain them properly, and drive them until replacement becomes economically rational. The first path leads to decades of automotive debt and hundreds of thousands in destroyed wealth. The second path leads to minimal automotive expenses and hundreds of thousands in accumulated investment assets. The vehicles provide identical transportation function in both scenarios. The wealth outcomes diverge by amounts that determine whether you reach financial independence or work until forced retirement.

The one percent make this choice consciously. They understand that every dollar unnecessarily spent on automotive consumption is a dollar not available for investment and compound growth. They feel no need to prove their success through expensive vehicles because they have actual wealth rather than merely the appearance of wealth. They experience genuine freedom from both automotive debt and status anxiety that drives peers to make financially destructive decisions. This is not deprivation. This is liberation from consumption that provides minimal satisfaction while preventing wealth accumulation.

We have now established the principles governing every major spending category in wealth building. Housing received examination in Chapter Nine. Insurance received analysis in Chapter Ten. Vehicles complete the triad of major expenses that determine whether your spending supports or undermines wealth accumulation. The pattern is consistent across all three: the one percent minimize costs in these categories through strategic decision-making and patient capital deployment while the ninety-nine percent maximize costs through emotional decisions and cultural conformity. The wealth gap that results from these different approaches compounds over decades into differences measured in millions of dollars. You now understand the rational approach to vehicle acquisition and ownership. Use this information to your advantage.

CHAPTER 12:
POLITICAL THINKING—UNDERSTANDING POWER AND POLICY

In 1873, a railroad magnate named Cornelius Vanderbilt faced a problem that threatened to destroy the empire he had spent decades building. The New York State Legislature, responding to public anger about railroad monopolies and rising freight rates, was preparing to pass legislation that would regulate railroad operations and limit the rates Vanderbilt's companies could charge. The proposed laws would devastate his profit margins and potentially trigger the collapse of the complex financial structures he had created through consolidation of competing rail lines. Most businessmen in his position would have hired lawyers to argue against the regulations, written editorials defending free markets, or perhaps accepted the inevitable reduction in profits as the cost of operating in a democracy.

Vanderbilt chose a different approach. He recognized that legislators respond to incentives just as businessmen do, and that understanding those incentives provides leverage that moral arguments cannot match. He identified the key legislators whose votes would determine whether the regulatory bills passed or failed. He arranged for certain of these legislators to purchase shares in railroad companies at artificially low prices shortly before announcing mergers or expansions that drove share prices upward. He ensured that other legislators received appointments to lucrative positions within railroad companies or their subsidiary enterprises. He made generous contributions to political organizations aligned with legislators whose votes he needed. The regulatory legislation died in committee. Vanderbilt's empire continued generating extraordinary profits for another two decades.

This example makes modern readers uncomfortable because it describes what we now recognize as corruption. The specific mechanisms Vanderbilt employed are illegal today and properly so. But the underlying principle he understood remains completely valid and essential for anyone serious about building and preserving wealth: policy determines the environment in which economic activity occurs, those who influence policy shape that environment to their advantage, and ignoring politics while focusing solely on business or investing is a choice to accept whatever environment others create rather than participating in its formation.

I am not advocating bribery, corruption, or illegal influence of public officials. I am stating that the one percent understand politics as a system of incentives and power relationships that shape economic outcomes, and they engage with that system strategically to protect and advance their interests. The ninety-nine percent either ignore politics entirely while complaining about its results, or they engage with politics emotionally through outrage and partisan loyalty that generates no practical benefit to their wealth-building efforts. Neither approach serves their economic interests.

The foundation of political thinking begins with understanding that government is not neutral. Every law, regulation, tax provision, and policy decision creates winners and losers. Zoning regulations determine which properties increase in value and which become restricted in use. Tax codes determine which activities receive favorable treatment and which face punitive rates. Licensing requirements determine who can enter certain professions and who is excluded. Permitting processes determine which construction projects proceed quickly and which face delays that destroy their economics. Environmental regulations determine which properties can be developed and which must remain undeveloped. Educational policies determine property values in specific neighborhoods based on school quality. Infrastructure investments determine which areas experience growth and which stagnate.

These are not abstract policy questions. They are concrete economic decisions that transfer wealth from some parties to others.

When a city rezones an area to allow higher density development, property owners in that area receive windfalls as their land becomes more valuable. Property owners in adjacent areas may lose value if the new development brings traffic or changes neighborhood character. When the federal government provides tax credits for solar panel installation, companies in that industry benefit while taxpayers subsidize their profits. When a state legislature raises minimum wages, some workers receive higher incomes while other workers lose jobs as employers reduce headcount. Every policy choice involves trade-offs and wealth transfers.

The one percent recognize these dynamics and position themselves accordingly. They do not wait for policy changes to affect them randomly. They anticipate policy directions, they influence policy formation where possible, and they structure their affairs to benefit from favorable policies while minimizing exposure to unfavorable ones. This is not manipulation of democracy. This is participation in democracy by those who understand how the system operates and choose to engage rather than remaining passive.

The most accessible level of political engagement involves local government, where small numbers of active participants exert disproportionate influence over decisions affecting property values, business regulations, and tax rates. Most people never attend city council meetings, planning commission hearings, or school board sessions. This absence creates a vacuum that organized interests fill easily. A handful of residents who attend meetings consistently and speak during public comment periods can materially influence outcomes on issues affecting entire communities.

Consider zoning decisions that determine how property can be used. If you own real estate or plan to acquire it, you have direct financial interest in zoning policies that either restrict or enable development. A duplex zoned for single-family residential use cannot be converted to a triplex or fourplex without zoning variance or change. If you understand that multi-family zoning would increase your property value substantially, you can attend planning commission meetings, speak in favor of upzoning your neighborhood, build relationships with commissioners who decide these matters, and potentially influence the outcome. If you remain uninvolved, the outcome will be determined by others whose interests may conflict with yours.

The same pattern applies to business licensing, permit approvals, infrastructure investments, and countless other decisions made by local officials. Someone who wants to start a home-based business may discover that local ordinances prohibit commercial activity in residential zones. Rather than accepting this restriction, you can petition for variance, propose ordinance changes that would allow specified home businesses, and build support among neighbors who might also benefit from such changes. The process requires time and persistence, but the alternative is accepting constraints that others imposed without your input.

The strategic value of local political engagement extends beyond immediate economic interests. Relationships built through participation in local government create networks that provide advantage in multiple domains. When you are known to planning commissioners because you regularly attend their meetings and engage thoughtfully on issues, you have access they do not provide to strangers who appear only when seeking personal favors. When you have established credibility with city council members through sustained involvement, your phone calls receive responses that others' calls do not. When you have demonstrated understanding of local issues and willingness to participate in civic processes, officials consult you on matters where they seek informed input.

These relationships are not purchased through contributions or created through influence peddling. They are earned through consistent engagement, substantive knowledge, and demonstration that you care about community outcomes beyond your narrow self-interest. The one percent build these relationships as a matter of course in jurisdictions where they live and invest. They understand that local officials are accessible, that competition for their attention is minimal, and that small investments of time generate outsized returns through both direct influence on specific decisions and general access to decision-makers.

The question arises whether to seek elected office yourself. The answer depends entirely on your specific circumstances, career flexibility, tolerance for public scrutiny, and the particular offices available in your jurisdiction. Local offices rarely require full-time commitment and often involve minimal competition. A city council seat in a town of twenty thousand might receive three candidates for two open positions. A school board seat might go unopposed. These positions provide direct influence over budgets, policies, and appointments while requiring perhaps ten to twenty hours monthly of attendance at meetings and constituent interactions.

The benefits extend beyond policy influence. Elected officials build networks with other officials, business leaders, and community stakeholders that would require years to develop through other means. They gain understanding of government operations that provides advantage in dealing with bureaucracy for personal or business purposes. They establish public profiles that benefit business ventures, particularly those involving local customers or requiring community support. These advantages accumulate over years of service and persist long after leaving office.

The costs are equally real. You sacrifice privacy as your finances, statements, and actions become subject to public scrutiny. You allocate time to meetings, constituent communications, and campaign activities that could be spent on business or investing. You expose yourself to criticism from opponents and constituents who disagree with your positions. You may face conflicts between your financial interests and your official duties that require careful navigation or recusal from decisions. These costs are manageable for some people and prohibitive for others.

The strategic approach evaluates specific opportunities based on competitive environment, time requirements, and alignment with wealth-building objectives. A planning commission appointment requiring one evening monthly and providing direct influence over development decisions that affect your real estate investments might be worth pursuing aggressively. A mayoral race requiring year-long campaigning and full-time service if elected might not be worth pursuing unless you have independent income sources and genuine interest in public service beyond economic benefit.

For most people focused primarily on wealth building, the optimal level of political engagement stops short of seeking office but exceeds passive voting. This middle ground involves regular attendance at relevant government meetings, relationship building with elected officials and staff, participation in public comment periods on issues affecting your interests, and strategic contributions to candidates who support policies favorable to your economic activities. This level of engagement requires perhaps five to ten hours monthly but generates meaningful influence on decisions affecting property values, business regulations, and tax policies.

The national political level operates differently because individual influence is negligible for all but the extremely wealthy who can fund campaigns at scales that create access to federal officials. Presidential campaigns cost billions. Senate races cost tens of millions. House races in competitive districts cost millions. Your contribution of one thousand dollars or even ten thousand dollars registers as statistical noise in these races. The return on investment from national political contributions is negative for ordinary wealth builders because you receive no meaningful access or influence in exchange for your money.

The exception involves single-issue advocacy where organized groups can influence policy through collective action even when individual members lack significant wealth. Organizations focused on specific tax provisions, regulatory frameworks, or policy areas can achieve results through coordinated lobbying that individual action cannot. If your business operates in an industry with effective trade associations, membership and participation in those associations' political efforts may provide positive returns. If you have strong convictions on specific policy issues that affect your economic interests, supporting organizations that lobby effectively on those issues may be worthwhile. But general political contributions to candidates based on party affiliation or vague policy agreement rarely generate economic benefit to the contributor.

The understanding of political thinking requires recognizing the distinction between policy preferences and personal economics. You may have strong views on foreign policy, social issues, or cultural matters that influence your voting decisions. These preferences are legitimate and important. What I am addressing is the separate question of how political engagement affects wealth building. The one percent distinguish clearly between their political preferences as citizens and their political engagement as economic actors. They support candidates and policies that advance their economic interests regardless of whether those candidates or policies align with their personal political philosophy.

This sounds cynical to those who believe politics should be about principles rather than interests. But every participant in politics pursues interests—labor unions support policies that benefit workers, environmental groups support policies that protect natural resources, business associations support policies that benefit industries. The one percent simply recognize that their economic interests constitute legitimate concerns worthy of advocacy, and they engage politically to advance those interests while maintaining whatever other political activities their citizenship or values inspire.

The practical implementation begins with identifying which policies affect your wealth-building activities most directly. If you own rental properties, housing regulations, property tax rates, landlord-tenant laws, and zoning policies are your primary concerns. If you operate a business, licensing requirements, employment regulations, tax rates, and permit processes are paramount. If you invest primarily through financial markets, tax treatment of capital gains, retirement account regulations, and securities laws matter most. You focus your political attention on the governmental levels and specific officials who control these policy areas.

Once you have identified relevant policy domains and officials, you establish relationships through the mechanisms available at that level of government. For local officials, this means attending meetings, speaking during public comment periods, volunteering for advisory committees, and requesting individual meetings to discuss issues of concern. For state officials, this means joining industry associations that lobby at the state level, attending town halls and constituent meetings, and communicating through email and phone on specific legislation. For federal officials, this means supporting advocacy organizations that lobby on issues affecting your interests and, if you have the resources, contributing to campaigns at levels that provide at least minimal access.

The communication with officials requires understanding how they process information and make decisions. Elected officials respond to constituents who vote, to organizations that mobilize voters, to contributors who fund campaigns, and to businesses that provide employment in their jurisdictions. Your leverage with officials depends on demonstrating that you represent one or more of these constituencies. A meeting with a city council member is more productive when you mention that you employ twenty people in the district than when you present yourself as an isolated individual with opinions. A conversation with a state legislator is more effective when you represent an industry association with thousands of members than when you speak only for yourself.

The testimony and advocacy you provide should be factual, specific, and focused on how proposed policies would affect real people and businesses rather than on abstract principles. Officials hear plenty of ideological arguments from both sides of every issue. What they often lack is concrete understanding of how policies would actually operate in practice. If you can explain clearly how a proposed regulation would affect your business operations, including specific cost increases or operational changes required, you provide information that influences decisions. If you can only argue that the regulation violates free market principles or represents government overreach, you add nothing to what officials have already heard repeatedly.

The timing of political engagement matters enormously. Attempting to influence policy after legislation has been drafted and is moving toward votes is far less effective than engaging early in the process when issues are being framed and options are being considered. Officials develop positions based on their early research and consultations. Once they have taken public positions, changing their minds requires admitting error or inconsistency that most avoid. Early engagement, before positions have hardened, allows you to shape the framework within which decisions will be made.

This requires monitoring of governmental agendas, which is easier at local levels where meeting agendas are published online and proceedings are accessible. Reading planning commission agendas weekly takes fifteen minutes and alerts you to upcoming decisions affecting property development. Monitoring city council agendas similarly requires minimal time while ensuring you know when issues affecting your interests are being considered. At state and federal levels, this monitoring is more complex but industry associations and advocacy organizations provide alerts on relevant legislation to their members.

The ethics of political engagement deserve direct address. I have described mechanisms through which individuals and businesses influence policy to serve their economic interests. This is legal and democratic participation that is available to everyone and should not require apology. But the line between legitimate advocacy and corruption is clear, and crossing it destroys both reputation and wealth. Bribes are illegal and properly so. Quid pro quo arrangements where contributions are explicitly tied to specific official actions are illegal. Conflicts of interest where officials benefit personally from decisions they make in their official capacity are illegal. You must remain scrupulously on the legal side of these lines regardless of the economic benefits that might flow from crossing them.

The legitimate tools of political influence are sufficient for protecting and advancing your interests without resorting to illegal methods. Campaign contributions within legal limits demonstrate support and create opportunities for access. Informed participation in public processes demonstrates seriousness and builds credibility. Clear communication of how policies affect real businesses and people provides information officials need. Organizing with others who share your interests multiplies your voice beyond what you can achieve individually. These legal methods generate meaningful influence when applied consistently and strategically.

The broader principle underlying political thinking is understanding that power operates according to consistent rules across different domains. Those who control resources have power. Those who can grant or deny permissions have power. Those who can mobilize groups have power. Those who understand what others want and can help them obtain it have power. Politics is simply one arena where these power dynamics operate, and the one percent study those dynamics the way they study any other system affecting their wealth.

Vanderbilt's methods were corrupt and illegal by modern standards, but his understanding of political incentives was accurate. Legislators respond to pressures and inducements that affect their own interests, whether those interests involve reelection, reputation, ideology, or personal gain. Your task is not to bribe or corrupt officials but to understand what legitimately motivates them and to position your interests in alignment with those motivations. A local official who cares about economic development responds to evidence that your proposed business will create jobs. A state legislator who represents agricultural districts responds to concerns about how regulations affect farmers. A federal official who prioritizes deficit reduction responds to arguments about fiscal impacts of proposed programs.

The distinction between the one percent and the ninety-nine percent in political engagement is that the one percent recognize politics as a system affecting their wealth that deserves strategic attention, while the ninety-nine percent treat politics as entertainment or moral crusade unconnected to their economic interests. The former study the system, identify leverage points, and engage strategically to protect and advance their interests. The latter watch political news for entertainment, argue with relatives about partisan issues, and wonder why policy outcomes consistently favor others while harming their financial position.

We have now examined the foundations of wealth building through proper stewardship, asset accumulation, environmental engineering, and strategic use of tax-advantaged vehicles. We have explored specific wealth-building strategies through stock market investing and real estate acquisition. We have analyzed how to minimize wealth destruction through rational decisions about housing, insurance, and vehicles. This chapter addresses how policy shapes the environment in which all other wealth-building activities occur and how strategic political engagement protects the wealth you build from adverse policy changes while positioning you to benefit from favorable ones.

The one percent understand that wealth building does not occur in a vacuum but within legal and regulatory frameworks that government creates and modifies continuously. They engage with the political system that creates those frameworks rather than passively accepting whatever frameworks others establish. This engagement requires time, attention, and occasional discomfort from public exposure or conflict with those holding opposing views. The alternative is allowing others to shape policy environments that may damage your interests while you focus exclusively on business and investing activities that operate within whatever constraints those others impose.

CHAPTER 13:
CHOOSING A LIFE PARTNER—THE MOST IMPORTANT FINANCIAL DECISION

In 1864, a twenty-five-year-old oil refinery owner in Cleveland, Ohio, began courting a young schoolteacher named Laura Spelman. John D. Rockefeller had already demonstrated the discipline and business acumen that would eventually make him the wealthiest man in America, but he was not yet rich. He lived frugally, reinvested every dollar of profit into his expanding business, and maintained account books tracking every penny he spent with meticulous precision. Most young women of that era would have considered him an unappealing prospect—intense, abstemious, and more interested in compound interest than romance.

Laura Spelman was not most young women. She came from a family of abolitionists who valued education, purposeful living, and moral clarity above social position or material comfort. She had been raised to view money as a tool for accomplishing good rather than as an end in itself. When she observed Rockefeller's disciplined approach to business and his habit of tithing ten percent of even his modest early earnings to his Baptist church, she recognized a man whose values aligned with her own. She saw not a miser but a man who understood stewardship. She accepted his proposal not despite his austere habits but in part because of them.

The marriage that followed lasted fifty-one years until Laura's death in 1915. During those decades, she managed the household finances with the same rigor Rockefeller applied to his business empire, ensuring that even as his wealth grew into the hundreds of millions, their personal spending remained modest and purposeful.

173

She guided his philanthropic efforts, helping him develop the systematic approach to giving that eventually distributed ninety percent of his fortune to universities, medical research, and cultural institutions. She raised their children to understand wealth as responsibility rather than privilege, preventing the dissolution of family fortune that consumed the inheritances of Rockefeller's wealthy contemporaries within a single generation.

More than any business decision, more than any investment strategy, more than any operational innovation in his oil empire, Rockefeller's choice of Laura Spelman as his wife determined his capacity to build and preserve the wealth that made him a historical figure. A different choice would have produced different outcomes. A wife who valued social position over purpose would have pressured him to display wealth rather than compound it. A wife who did not share his view of money as stewardship would have undermined his disciplined reinvestment of profits. A wife who raised their children to believe wealth entitled them to lives of leisure would have destroyed in one generation what Rockefeller spent a lifetime building.

This chapter addresses what may be the most uncomfortable truth in this entire book: your choice of spouse will affect your financial outcome more than your investment returns, more than your career decisions, more than your savings rate, and more than any other single factor you control. Divorce destroys more accumulated wealth than market crashes, business failures, or medical catastrophes. Marriage to the right partner accelerates wealth building beyond what either partner could achieve independently. Marriage to the wrong partner creates decades of friction, misaligned priorities, and eventual financial catastrophe that leaves both parties substantially worse off than they would have been remaining single.

I recognize that discussing marriage in financial terms strikes many people as unromantic or even mercenary. We are taught that love conquers all, that marriage should be about emotional connection rather than practical compatibility, and that considering financial implications when choosing a spouse is somehow impure or calculating. These romantic notions have destroyed more wealth and caused more human misery than perhaps any other cultural mythology. The one percent understand that marriage is simultaneously a romantic partnership and an economic union that will either build or destroy wealth based on the alignment of values between partners. Acknowledging the economic dimension does not diminish the romantic dimension. It prevents the romantic dimension from blinding you to practical realities that will determine whether the marriage succeeds or fails.

The statistics on divorce and wealth destruction are sobering. Approximately forty percent of first marriages end in divorce, with higher rates for subsequent marriages. The financial impact of divorce includes legal costs averaging fifteen thousand to thirty thousand dollars for contested divorces, division of marital assets that typically results in each party retaining forty to fifty percent of what they would have accumulated together, establishment of separate households that doubles housing and living costs, and potential alimony or child support obligations that transfer wealth from higher-earning to lower-earning spouses for years or decades. The total wealth impact of divorce frequently exceeds fifty percent of what the couple would have accumulated had they remained married, with some studies suggesting the wealth destruction reaches seventy to eighty percent when accounting for all direct and indirect costs.

Beyond these measurable financial costs, divorce destroys wealth through the emotional distraction and life disruption that impairs earning capacity, investment discipline, and business performance during and after the divorce process. I have watched successful business owners lose their companies during divorces that consumed their attention for months or years. I have seen investors make catastrophically poor decisions while going through divorces because their judgment was impaired by emotional turmoil. I have observed high-earning professionals experience career setbacks during divorces that cost them hundreds of thousands in lost income and advancement opportunities. These indirect costs often exceed the direct financial costs of the divorce itself.

The obvious conclusion is that avoiding divorce preserves wealth. The less obvious but more important conclusion is that avoiding divorce requires choosing the right partner initially rather than attempting to make incompatible partnerships work through effort and compromise. Most divorces are not caused by unexpected events or changes in circumstances. They are caused by fundamental incompatibilities that existed before marriage but were ignored, minimized, or believed to be surmountable through love and commitment. The time to address compatibility is before marriage, not after.

The framework for evaluating compatibility begins with values rather than interests or personalities. Interests change over time. Personalities can adapt to circumstances. Values are the deep assumptions about what matters and how life should be lived, and they rarely change substantially in adulthood. Two people with aligned values but different interests can build successful marriages because they agree on fundamental priorities even when they pursue different activities. Two people with aligned personalities but conflicting values will experience constant friction over decisions large and small because their basic assumptions about life are incompatible.

The specific values that matter most for wealth-building partnerships are attitudes toward money, faith, politics, children, and life philosophy. I will address each category because misalignment in any of them predicts marital failure with depressing reliability.

Attitudes toward money encompass beliefs about earning, spending, saving, investing, risk, and the purpose of wealth. Someone who views money as a tool for building security and funding future objectives thinks fundamentally differently than someone who views money as a resource for experiencing life and enjoying the present. Someone who believes in living below one's means and investing the difference cannot build a successful partnership with someone who believes in consuming all available resources and financing additional consumption through debt. Someone who sees wealth building as important life work that justifies present sacrifice for future abundance will experience constant conflict with someone who sees wealth building as greed that sacrifices meaningful living for abstract future benefits.

These are not small differences that can be bridged through compromise. They represent opposed worldviews that will generate conflict over every financial decision the marriage encounters. The person focused on building wealth will resent the partner's spending. The person focused on present enjoyment will resent the partner's frugality. Neither is objectively wrong, but they are incompatible in partnership. The one percent identify these incompatibilities before marriage through extended conversations about money values, observation of spending patterns, and honest assessment of whether alignment exists.

The evaluation includes attitude toward capitalism itself. Someone who believes that free markets, private property, and wealth creation through enterprise are moral goods that benefit society thinks differently than someone who believes capitalism is exploitation that concentrates wealth unjustly. These philosophical differences will manifest in countless practical decisions about careers, investments, business ownership, philanthropy, politics, and child-rearing. A marriage between someone who wants to build businesses and someone who believes business ownership is morally problematic will experience perpetual tension that cannot be resolved because the tension stems from irreconcilable first principles.

Faith represents perhaps the deepest category of values because it encompasses assumptions about reality itself, about purpose and meaning, about moral frameworks and ultimate accountability. Someone whose faith shapes their entire worldview including their approach to wealth and stewardship cannot build a successful long-term partnership with someone who views faith as private preference separate from practical life decisions or with someone whose faith tradition contains fundamentally different assumptions about money and material goods.

For those of particular faith convictions, the specificity matters enormously. Someone who follows Yeshua as Messiah and maintains connection to Israel and Jewish roots thinks differently about

Scripture, about the role of faith in daily life, about the significance of Israel, and about the relationship between Old and New Covenant than someone who identifies as culturally Christian but maintains no particular conviction or practice. These are not differences that can be managed through respectful disagreement. They will shape every major life decision from how to raise children to where to give charitably to how to observe holy days to what community you participate in. Misalignment creates either constant conflict or one partner subordinating their deepest convictions to maintain peace, neither of which produces thriving marriages.

A couple whose political perspectives are deeply misaligned may find themselves in conflict over the very purpose of wealth. One partner might view capital primarily as a means to ensure security, legacy, and personal independence, advocating for strategies that preserve and gradually grow assets. The other might see wealth as a tool for social impact, immediate lifestyle enhancement, or systemic change, preferring allocations that support these goals, even at the expense of traditional metrics of growth. They will support ideologies which aligns with "taxing the rich" while scrutinizing them. This divergence can lead to persistent tension in everyday financial decisions—from budgeting and charitable giving to investment choices and long-term planning.

For instance, differing views on the role of government and economic systems directly influence financial behavior. A spouse with a more progressive outlook may prioritize policies and personal spending that support social safety nets, collective responsibility, and addressing inequality, which can manifest in a higher comfort with taxation for public programs or investing with strong ESG (Environmental, Social, and Governance) criteria. Conversely, a spouse with a more conservative leaning may emphasize personal responsibility, free-market principles, and wealth preservation, directing resources toward private investment, tax-advantaged accounts, and intergenerational wealth transfer.

When these underlying philosophies clash, it can create a destabilizing friction. Financial unity requires agreement not just on numbers, but on the values those numbers serve. Constant disagreement on these foundational issues can lead to inefficient financial strategies, conflicting priorities that dilute resource accumulation, and, in severe cases, legal fees and asset division that actively destroy wealth.

Therefore, political compatibility serves as a crucial proxy for deeper financial harmony. It indicates a shared framework for evaluating opportunity, risk, and responsibility. A couple aligned in their worldview can present a unified front, making consistent, disciplined decisions that compound over time. They avoid the costly internal debates that can stall progress or lead to contradictory actions. In essence, choosing a spouse with compatible political values is less about ideological purity and more about ensuring a partnership built on a cohesive economic strategy, turning the marital unit into a far more powerful and efficient vehicle for building and sustaining wealth.

The approach to children encompasses beliefs about whether to have children, how many to have, how to raise them, what values to instill, what level of parental involvement is appropriate, and what obligations parents have to fund children's education and adult establishment. These decisions involve hundreds of thousands of dollars in direct costs and influence wealth building capacity for decades. Someone who wants multiple children and plans to fund their complete education through graduate school is making radically different financial commitments than someone who wants no children or who believes children should be financially independent after high school. Someone who believes children should be raised with clear discipline, high expectations, and graduated responsibility thinks differently than someone who believes in minimal structure and maximum freedom. These differences cannot be compromised because every day of child-rearing requires countless decisions that reflect one philosophy or the other.

Life philosophy includes questions about ambition, risk tolerance, geographic flexibility, work-life balance, social obligations, and purpose. Someone whose life purpose involves building substantial wealth and using that wealth to advance specific causes needs a partner who shares that purpose or at least supports it fully. Someone who derives identity from career achievement and professional advancement needs a partner who accepts the time commitments and relocations that career advancement may require. Someone who values geographic stability and proximity to extended family cannot thrive in partnership with someone who views frequent relocation as opportunity rather than disruption. These philosophical differences will create friction over every major life decision from career changes to geographic moves to time allocation to social commitments.

The evaluation of these values requires more than surface-level conversation. Most people can state values they believe they hold or values they think they should hold. What matters is revealed values demonstrated through actual decisions and behavior patterns. Someone who claims to value saving and investing but consistently spends everything earned reveals that their stated values differ from their actual values. Someone who claims faith is central to their life but never participates in religious community or allows faith to influence practical decisions reveals that faith is aspiration rather than reality for them. Someone who claims to want children but shows no interest in spending time with nieces, nephews, or friends' children reveals possible misalignment between stated desires and genuine preference.

The observation period required to evaluate revealed values is measured in years, not months. People can maintain false impressions for short periods through conscious effort. Over extended time, true patterns emerge. The person who initially appears financially disciplined but gradually reveals patterns of impulsive spending and debt accumulation. The person who initially presents as sharing your faith convictions but gradually reveals that attendance and participation are performed for your benefit rather than from genuine conviction. The person who initially agrees that children are important but gradually reveals ambivalence or reluctance to accept the sacrifices parenthood requires. These revelations typically emerge between eighteen months and three years into relationships if both parties are paying attention rather than seeing what they want to see.

The red flags that predict marital failure and financial disaster are often visible before marriage but ignored because of emotional attachment or investment in the relationship. Different political philosophies indicate different underlying values about individual responsibility versus collective obligation, about the role of government, about property rights, and about how society should be organized. These are not trivial differences. They reflect fundamentally different assumptions about human nature and social organization that will manifest in disagreement about career choices, philanthropic priorities, and child-rearing approaches. The couple that dismisses political differences as unimportant during courtship will discover those differences create irreconcilable conflicts over major life decisions.

Hostility toward wealth building or capitalism indicates incompatibility with anyone serious about accumulating substantial assets. Someone who views your business ambitions as greed rather than legitimate life work will undermine those ambitions through criticism and lack of support. Someone who believes wealthy people are inherently exploitative will resent your success even while enjoying the benefits it provides. Someone who thinks entrepreneurs take advantage of workers rather than creating value and employment will never support your business ventures enthusiastically. These attitudes can sometimes be expressed subtly through comments about other people's success or through patterns of negative reaction to stories about business achievement, but they predict spousal resistance to your wealth-building efforts if you marry despite these warning signs.

Lukewarm or performative faith in a potential partner who knows your own faith is important to you represents a form of deception that will eventually produce conflict. Someone who attends religious services and discusses faith topics because they know these matter to you but who shows no independent commitment or personal practice is performing for your benefit. After marriage, when the performance is no longer necessary to maintain your commitment, the genuine lack of faith conviction will emerge. You will then face the choice between compromising your own practice to reduce household friction or maintaining your practice while your spouse's lack of participation creates distance and difference. Neither outcome produces thriving marriage.

Different visions for child-rearing create inevitable conflict that cannot be resolved through compromise because every interaction with children embodies one philosophy or the other. You cannot simultaneously raise children with firm boundaries and minimal boundaries. You cannot simultaneously instill the belief that achievement requires work and the belief that children deserve provision regardless of effort. You cannot simultaneously teach children that faith should shape all of life and teach them that faith is private preference separate from practical decisions. Every decision about discipline, activities, education, and expectations will become a negotiation or conflict if parents hold fundamentally different philosophies.

The difficult conversations about these topics should occur well before engagement and certainly before marriage. The framework for these conversations begins with establishing that you are evaluating compatibility rather than trying to convince the other person to change. If major values differences exist, the goal is identifying them honestly so both parties can make informed decisions about whether to continue the relationship, not convincing the other person to adopt your values so you can proceed toward marriage. Most people avoid these conversations because they fear the relationship will end if differences emerge. This is precisely backwards. Better to end a relationship before marriage than to discover incompatibility after legal and financial union makes separation catastrophically expensive.

The specific questions that reveal values include asking about financial histories and current approaches to money. What debts do you carry and how did you acquire them? What percentage of your income do you save? What are your long-term financial goals? What was the last major purchase you made and what was your decision process? These questions reveal actual relationship with money rather than aspirational statements about values. Someone who carries substantial consumer debt, saves nothing, has no concrete financial goals, and makes major purchases impulsively has demonstrated their true values regardless of what they claim to believe about financial responsibility.

Questions about faith should probe depth of conviction rather than mere affiliation. How does your faith affect your daily decisions? What does it mean to you that Yeshua is Messiah? How do you observe Sabbath or holy days? What role does Scripture play in your life? What is your relationship with the broader body of Messiah? What is your understanding of Israel's role in God's plan? These questions distinguish between genuine conviction that shapes life and cultural identification that carries no practical implications. The person who cannot articulate how faith influences practical decisions or who views questions about theological understanding as overly serious is revealing that faith is not actually central to their life regardless of claims otherwise.

Questions about children should address not just whether to have them but complete philosophy of child-rearing. How many children do you envision? What values do you want to instill? What does good parenting look like? How should children be disciplined? What role should extended family play in children's lives? What financial obligations do parents have to adult children? These questions reveal assumptions that will govern thousands of decisions over decades of child-rearing. Misalignment on these questions predicts constant conflict that many couples do not anticipate because they focus only on whether both want children without exploring the far more important question of how children should be raised.

Questions about life philosophy should explore purpose, ambition, geography, and priorities. What do you want to accomplish in life? How important is career advancement versus other life domains? How do you feel about relocating for opportunities? What role should extended family play in our life decisions? How do you think about work-life balance? These questions reveal whether fundamental assumptions about how to structure life are compatible. The person who wants to build businesses and accumulate substantial wealth needs a partner who supports that ambition or at least accepts it fully. The person who views career as means to fund non-work priorities needs a partner who shares that view rather than one who sees career as primary source of identity and meaning.

The prenuptial agreement deserves consideration not as sign of distrust but as business contract between partners building something larger than themselves. The agreement specifies how assets will be divided if the marriage ends, establishing clear expectations that reduce conflict and legal costs if divorce occurs. This seems unromantic to those who believe marriage should involve complete merging of lives and finances without contemplation of potential failure. The one percent recognize that marriage involves both romantic partnership and economic union, and that the economic union deserves the same careful documentation that any business partnership would receive.

The prenuptial agreement is particularly important when one partner brings substantially more assets or earning capacity into the marriage, when one or both partners own businesses that should not be subject to division in divorce, or when either partner has children from previous relationships whose inheritance rights should be protected. The agreement does not indicate lack of commitment or expectation of failure. It indicates recognition that circumstances sometimes change in ways that end marriages, and that establishing clear expectations about financial consequences reduces the damage when endings occur.

The resistance to prenuptial agreements typically comes from the partner who would benefit financially from divorce without such agreement, which itself reveals something about motivations and values. Someone who refuses to marry unless they will receive substantial portion of their partner's assets in divorce is revealing that they view marriage at least partially as financial transaction rather than purely as commitment to shared life. This revelation should inform your decision about whether to proceed. The partner who readily agrees to prenuptial agreement protecting assets each party brought to marriage while sharing equitably in assets accumulated during marriage is demonstrating confidence in the relationship itself rather than in financial security divorce would provide.

The process of working through prenuptial agreements, difficult as it may be, serves as useful test of whether the couple can navigate difficult conversations about money and expectations. If you cannot discuss prenuptial agreements without the conversation devolving into accusations or emotional manipulation, you certainly cannot navigate the far more numerous difficult conversations that marriage will require about spending, career decisions, child-rearing, and countless other topics. The ability to discuss prenuptial agreements calmly and reach mutually acceptable terms while both parties have independent legal counsel predicts capacity to navigate marital challenges. The inability to have these conversations predicts relationship dysfunction that will eventually destroy the marriage regardless of whether prenuptial agreement exists.

The decision about whether to proceed toward marriage after evaluating compatibility should be made rationally rather than emotionally. If substantial values misalignment exists in any of the core categories—money, faith, children, politics, or life philosophy— the rational decision is ending the relationship regardless of emotional attachment or time invested. The emotional pain of ending a relationship is temporary and finite. The financial and emotional pain of divorce is severe and often permanent in its effects. Better to experience the former than guarantee the latter.

The one percent make this assessment consciously and honestly. They evaluate potential partners using the same rigorous analysis they would apply to business partnerships or major investments. They recognize that romantic feelings, while important and valuable, are insufficient basis for legal and financial union that will determine their wealth outcomes for decades. They end relationships when misalignment becomes clear rather than hoping love will somehow overcome fundamental incompatibilities. This appears cold or calculating to the ninety-nine percent who make marriage decisions based primarily on emotion and then wonder why forty percent of marriages end in divorce and many of the remaining ones involve unhappy people staying together for financial reasons or fear of starting over.

The parallel to business partnerships is precise. You would not enter business partnership with someone whose values about money, risk, purpose, and management differ fundamentally from yours regardless of how much you like them personally or how well you work together on limited projects. You would insist on evaluating compatibility thoroughly, documenting expectations clearly, and ensuring alignment on fundamental questions before entering legal partnership that binds you financially. Marriage deserves identical rigor because the stakes are higher and the consequences of failure are more severe.

Bill and Melinda Gates built a partnership that created the largest private foundation in history despite their marriage eventually ending. What made their partnership successful for decades was not perfect compatibility or absence of differences but rather shared commitment to using their wealth to address global health and poverty. This shared sense of purpose allowed them to build something larger than either could have built alone and to maintain effective collaboration even after their romantic relationship ended. Their example demonstrates that what matters most is alignment on core values and purposes rather than agreement on every detail or perfect romantic chemistry.

The broader principle is that successful marriage requires shared mission that transcends both individuals and provides purpose beyond personal happiness or material success. For those who hold faith as central, that shared mission involves using whatever resources and opportunities God provides to advance His kingdom purposes. This could manifest through business building that provides employment and serves customers, through systematic wealth accumulation that funds gospel work and supports Israel, through raising children who will themselves advance kingdom purposes, or through any number of other expressions. What matters is that both partners share the understanding that marriage serves purposes beyond the partners themselves and that wealth exists as tool for accomplishing those purposes rather than as end in itself.

This shared mission prevents the inward focus that destroys many marriages. Couples who view marriage primarily as vehicle for personal happiness and fulfillment discover that no partner can satisfy all needs and desires continuously. They experience disappointment, they blame their partners for failing to meet their expectations, and they eventually divorce in search of partners who will somehow succeed where previous partners failed. Couples who view marriage as partnership in service of purposes beyond themselves have external focus that reduces pressure on the relationship itself while providing shared work that binds them together through accomplishment rather than merely through emotion.

The wealth building that occurs within properly aligned marriages exceeds what either partner could accomplish independently through several mechanisms. Two incomes allow for higher savings rates while maintaining reasonable lifestyle. Complementary skills and knowledge allow for better decisions across domains from investing to tax planning to business strategy. Emotional support during inevitable setbacks provides resilience that solo wealth builders often lack. Division of labor allows specialization where each partner focuses on areas of strength rather than both attempting to master all domains. Most importantly, shared values and purpose prevent the internal conflict that undermines focus and creates stress that impairs decision-making.

I have watched couples build eight-figure net-worths over twenty to thirty years through nothing more extraordinary than consistent income earning, high savings rates, disciplined investing, and complete alignment on priorities. Neither partner earned exceptional income. Neither possessed unusual investment insights. What they had was agreement on goals, mutual support through the long journey, and absence of the financial friction that destroys wealth building for couples with misaligned values. The compounding occurred not just in their investment accounts but in their relationship itself, as each year of working together toward shared objectives strengthened their capacity to continue.

You stand now at a point where you understand the foundations of wealth building through proper stewardship, asset accumulation, environmental engineering, and strategic decision-making about major spending categories. You understand specific strategies for building wealth through stock market investing, real estate acquisition, and business operations. You understand how policy shapes economic environment and how strategic political engagement protects your interests. None of these strategies will generate their full potential if you choose a life partner whose values undermine your wealth-building efforts or whose presence creates financial friction that consumes the wealth you build.

The decision about whom to marry is yours alone. No framework can remove the uncertainty or guarantee outcomes. What I can provide is clear statement that this decision matters more than any other financial decision you will make, and that you should approach it with at least the rigor you would apply to business partnerships or major investments. Evaluate values honestly. Have difficult conversations early. Identify misalignments before they become legal and financial obligations. Choose a partner who shares your views on money, faith, children, politics, and life philosophy. Establish clear expectations through prenuptial agreements when appropriate. Build your marriage around shared mission that transcends both partners.

Do this and marriage becomes force multiplier for wealth building and life satisfaction. Fail to do this and marriage becomes wealth destroyer and source of perpetual conflict. The one percent understand these stakes and choose accordingly. The ninety-nine percent follow romantic impulses and hope everything works out, then express surprise when forty percent of marriages end in divorce and many others persist unhappily because divorce would be too costly. You now understand what separates these outcomes.

CHAPTER 14:
DAY TRADING—SPECULATION VERSUS INVESTMENT

In October 1987, a thirty-three-year-old commodities trader named Paul Tudor Jones sat in his Manhattan office watching market indicators that suggested the stock market was catastrophically overvalued and due for violent correction. He had spent years studying market history, particularly the patterns preceding the 1929 crash, and he recognized similar technical formations developing in current price charts. Most traders ignored these signals or dismissed them as irrelevant to modern markets with circuit breakers and sophisticated risk management. Jones did something different. He built massive short positions betting that the market would collapse, risking his fund's capital and his reputation on analysis that contradicted prevailing sentiment.

On Monday, October 19, 1987, the stock market fell twenty-two percent in a single day—the largest one-day percentage decline in history. Fortunes evaporated. Brokerage firms failed. Investors lost billions. Paul Tudor Jones made approximately one hundred million dollars. His fund gained sixty percent during October while the broader market lost more than twenty percent. This single month of trading success established his reputation and launched a career that would generate billions in returns over subsequent decades.

This outcome appears to validate day trading as a path to wealth. Before you conclude that studying charts and timing market movements can generate similar results, understand what separated Jones from the thousands of traders who attempted similar strategies during the same period and lost everything. Jones had spent years developing expertise in market microstructure, technical analysis, and

189

mass psychology. He had studied every major market crash in history to identify patterns that preceded them. He employed rigorous risk management that limited his maximum loss on any position to one percent of capital. He had the emotional discipline to maintain positions that appeared wrong for months while the market continued rising, enduring criticism and doubt from investors who questioned his judgment. Most importantly, he understood that he was speculating rather than investing, and he structured his entire approach around surviving long enough to be positioned correctly when the rare catastrophic event eventually materialized.

Day trading is not investing. This distinction must be established clearly before discussing anything else about this activity. Investing involves purchasing assets that generate cash flows or appreciate based on fundamental value creation. You buy ownership stakes in productive enterprises through stocks. You acquire properties that produce rental income through real estate. You build or buy businesses that generate profits through operations. The value of these assets derives from their capacity to produce income, and that income provides margin of safety even when market prices fluctuate. You can hold these investments indefinitely because they generate returns independent of whether you sell them.

Day trading involves purchasing securities with the sole intention of selling them at higher prices within hours or days. You are not investing in productive enterprises. You are speculating on short-term price movements driven by supply and demand imbalances, momentum from other traders, or technical patterns that may or may not predict future price direction. The securities you trade generate no income during your holding period. Your only source of return is selling at a higher price than you paid. If you cannot sell at higher prices, you lose money. This is speculation, and it operates under completely different rules than investment.

The first rule of speculation is that it is a negative-sum game after accounting for transaction costs. For every trader who makes money, another trader loses money, and the brokerage firms and exchanges collect fees on every transaction regardless of who wins.

This means that the total returns to all traders must be negative after fees. Contrast this with investing in stocks, which is a positive-sum game because the underlying companies generate profits that create value for all shareholders over time. The market can rise consistently for decades because productive enterprise creates genuine wealth. Day trading cannot produce consistent positive returns across all participants because no wealth is being created—only redistributed from losers to winners, with friction costs extracted by intermediaries.

The implication is that day trading is a competition where your profits come from other traders' losses. You are not participating in economic growth. You are taking money from less skilled traders. This requires that you possess skills or information advantages that allow you to consistently identify opportunities before other traders do and execute faster than they can respond. Most people attempting day trading do not have these advantages. They are the less skilled traders from whom the professionals extract profits.

The statistics on day trading success rates support this reality. Studies examining thousands of day traders over multi-year periods consistently find that approximately ninety percent lose money after accounting for all costs. Of the ten percent who are profitable, most generate returns below what they would have earned through simple index fund investing without the stress and time commitment day trading requires. Perhaps one to two percent of day traders generate returns substantially exceeding index fund alternatives consistently enough to justify the activity on purely economic grounds.

These statistics do not improve over time as traders gain experience. Studies tracking individual traders across multiple years find that most who are profitable in early periods eventually blow up and lose their accumulated gains plus more. The traders who succeed initially often do so through luck rather than skill, and they mistake luck for skill, increase their position sizes, and eventually encounter market conditions where their approach fails catastrophically. The rare traders who sustain success over decades do so because they understand they are managing risk rather than predicting prices, and they structure their trading to survive the inevitable periods when their approaches stop working.

Paul Tudor Jones succeeded not because he could predict market movements consistently but because he understood risk management, position sizing, and the importance of asymmetric bets where potential gains far exceeded potential losses. His October 1987 success resulted from a trade where he risked small amounts of capital over months while building positions that would generate enormous gains if his thesis proved correct. He was wrong for much of 1987 as the market continued rising. He lost money monthly as his short positions declined in value. His risk management prevented these losses from becoming catastrophic. When the crash finally arrived, his correct positioning for that single event more than compensated for months of losses.

This is not a strategy that most aspiring day traders can implement because it requires capital sufficient to withstand extended periods of losses, emotional discipline to maintain positions that appear wrong, and analytical frameworks for identifying rare events worth betting on. Most day traders attempt instead to generate consistent returns through frequent trading based on technical patterns or momentum, strategies that are far more difficult to sustain profitably because they require being correct more often than you are wrong while transaction costs erode returns from every trade.

If you are considering day trading despite these warnings, you must understand what separates the small percentage who succeed from the large percentage who fail. The successful day traders treat trading as a business requiring constant study, rigorous record-keeping, and systematic improvement. They develop specific trading strategies based on identifiable edge—some informational, technical, or executional advantage they possess over other market participants. They test these strategies extensively through paper trading before risking real capital. They implement strict position sizing rules that prevent any single trade from destroying their accounts. They maintain detailed journals documenting every trade including the rationale, execution, and outcome. They review these journals regularly to identify patterns in their mistakes and successes.

The edge you need to succeed in day trading takes different forms depending on your approach. Some traders develop expertise in specific sectors or securities, understanding the fundamental drivers and typical trading patterns better than generalist traders. Some traders identify technical patterns that predict short-term price movements with statistical reliability slightly better than random chance, which is sufficient for profitability if coupled with proper position sizing and risk management. Some traders exploit execution advantages through superior technology or market access that allows them to enter and exit positions faster than competitors. Some traders understand market microstructure—how orders flow through markets and how large institutional trades affect short-term prices—in ways that allow them to position ahead of predictable price movements.

None of these edges are obvious or easy to develop. You cannot attend a weekend seminar and learn to trade profitably. You cannot purchase indicator software that will generate consistent returns. You cannot follow trading gurus on social media and replicate their supposed success. The edge required for day trading success takes months or years to develop through study, practice, and painful learning from losses. Most people attempting day trading never develop any edge at all. They trade based on feelings, tips from others, or pattern recognition that has no statistical validity. They lose money consistently and either quit or continue losing until their capital is exhausted.

The psychological requirements for successful day trading exceed the analytical requirements. You must maintain emotional equilibrium while watching positions move against you by thousands of dollars within minutes. You must execute trades according to your system even when your emotions scream to do something different. You must accept losses as routine cost of trading rather than as personal failures that generate shame or anger. You must resist the temptation to deviate from your strategy after losses in attempts to recover money quickly. You must avoid overconfidence after wins that leads to position sizes exceeding your risk parameters. Most people do not possess this psychological profile naturally, and most cannot develop it even with training and experience.

The practical implementation of day trading begins with education that does not involve risking capital. You must understand market structure, order types, technical analysis, and basic statistics before attempting to trade. Books, courses, and mentorship from successful traders can provide this foundation, though you must be skeptical of anyone selling education who claims day trading is easy or that their methods guarantee success. The legitimate educators acknowledge the difficulty and low success rates while providing frameworks that give you fighting chance of joining the small minority who succeed.

After education, you must practice through simulated trading using paper trading platforms that execute against real market data without risking capital. This practice should continue for months minimum, ideally six to twelve months, until you demonstrate consistent profitability in your paper trading account. Many aspiring traders skip this step or abbreviate it because they are impatient to begin making real money. This impatience virtually guarantees failure because you are attempting to compete against professional traders who have years of experience while you are still learning basic execution and emotional management.

The capital you eventually risk in day trading must be money you can afford to lose completely without affecting your lifestyle or long-term financial security. This cannot be stated strongly enough. Day trading should never involve money needed for living expenses, emergency funds, retirement savings, house down payments, or any other essential purpose. The capital should be purely speculative money that you have set aside knowing you may lose it entirely. For most people, this means day trading should not begin until you have established emergency funds, maximized retirement contributions, built substantial investment portfolios, and accumulated surplus capital beyond these essential categories.

The amount of capital required to day trade effectively is larger than most people realize. You need sufficient capital to withstand normal losing periods without your account falling below minimum balances required by brokers. You need enough capital to size positions large enough that winning trades generate meaningful profits after transaction costs. You need reserves to add to your trading account when inevitable drawdowns occur. The minimum realistic amount for serious day trading is probably twenty-five thousand dollars, with fifty thousand or more being preferable. Attempting to day trade with smaller amounts virtually guarantees failure because transaction costs consume too large a percentage of your capital and because you cannot size positions appropriately for your strategy.

The risk management rules that separate successful traders from failed traders center on position sizing and maximum loss parameters. Successful traders never risk more than one to two percent of their total capital on any single trade. If you have fifty thousand dollars, your maximum loss on any trade is five hundred to one thousand dollars. This means you must size positions and set stop losses such that if the trade moves against you to your stop loss level, you lose only this predetermined amount. This rule prevents any single trade or even a series of bad trades from destroying your account. You can be wrong ten consecutive times, losing one thousand dollars on each trade, and still have eighty percent of your capital remaining to continue trading.

Most aspiring day traders violate this rule constantly. They risk five or ten percent per trade because they believe they need larger positions to generate meaningful profits. They override their stop losses when trades move against them because they believe the positions will eventually recover. They add to losing positions to lower their average cost. These behaviors are precisely how traders lose entire accounts rapidly. Professional traders accept small losses repeatedly because they understand that survival is prerequisite to eventually being positioned correctly for the trades that generate large gains.

The transaction costs of day trading receive insufficient attention from most aspiring traders. Every trade you make incurs costs through commissions, bid-ask spreads, and potential market impact if you are trading large enough size to move prices. These costs seem small on individual trades but compound rapidly when you are making dozens or hundreds of trades monthly. A trader making fifty trades monthly with ten dollars in total transaction costs per trade pays six thousand dollars annually in costs. This trader must generate returns exceeding six thousand dollars just to break even. If the trader has a fifty-thousand-dollar account, this represents a twelve-percent return requirement just to cover costs before generating any profit.

High-frequency trading where you enter and exit positions multiple times daily multiplies these costs dramatically. Some day traders make hundreds or thousands of trades monthly, paying tens of thousands annually in transaction costs. Unless you possess genuine edge that allows you to overcome these costs, you are guaranteeing negative returns regardless of how well you select trades. This is why the vast majority of active traders underperform simple buy-and-hold strategies. The transaction costs and bid-ask spreads they pay overwhelm whatever skill they might have in timing trades.

The tax treatment of day trading creates additional burdens that most aspiring traders do not anticipate. Profits from securities held less than one year are taxed as ordinary income rather than at preferential long-term capital gains rates. If you are a successful day trader earning fifty thousand dollars annually from trading while in the twenty-four percent federal tax bracket, you pay approximately twelve thousand dollars in federal taxes plus state taxes on those profits. This is substantially more than the capital gains taxes you would pay on equivalent returns from long-term investing. Day trading profits are also potentially subject to self-employment taxes if you qualify as a trader in securities for tax purposes, adding another fifteen percent to your tax burden on profits.

The relationship between day trading and long-term wealth building is inverse rather than complementary. The time and attention day trading requires prevents you from focusing on activities that actually build wealth—increasing your income through career advancement, building businesses, acquiring rental properties, or systematically accumulating diversified investment portfolios. The psychological patterns day trading reinforces—focus on short-term price movements, emotional reactions to gains and losses, constant monitoring of positions—are precisely the opposite of the patterns required for long-term wealth building through patient capital deployment and compound returns.

I have watched people spend years attempting to become successful day traders, destroying tens or hundreds of thousands of dollars in capital while learning that they do not possess the skills or psychological profile required for success. These same people could have spent those years building businesses, advancing careers, or simply investing systematically in index funds. The opportunity cost of time spent on day trading often exceeds the capital lost through trading itself because time spent developing a trading edge that you may never acquire is time not spent on activities that would reliably increase your wealth.

The scenarios where day trading might be justified for someone interested in wealth building are narrow. If you have genuine passion for markets and trading independent of profit potential, day trading can be pursued as expensive hobby funded with capital you can afford to lose. If you possess unusual analytical gifts combined with the psychological profile required for successful speculation, and you have already established financial security through other means, day trading might provide intellectual challenge and potential additional income. If you work in financial markets professionally and can develop edge through your employment that translates to profitable personal trading, the activity might make economic sense within appropriate risk parameters.

For everyone else, day trading represents distraction from wealth building at best and path to rapid capital destruction at worst. The statistics are unambiguous. Ninety percent of day traders lose money. Most of the remaining ten percent would have been better off investing in index funds. The one to two percent who generate substantial profits possess combinations of skill, discipline, and psychological makeup that are extraordinarily rare. The odds are overwhelming that you do not fall into this rare category, and attempting to discover whether you do by risking capital is expensive test with predictable outcomes.

Paul Tudor Jones represents the extreme positive outcome of speculation done expertly with superior risk management, analytical frameworks, and emotional discipline developed over years. For every Paul Tudor Jones, there are thousands of traders who attempted similar approaches and failed completely. The survivorship bias in trading success stories is extreme. We hear about the rare successes and almost never hear about the legions of failures. This creates false impression that trading success is more achievable than it actually is.

If you proceed with day trading despite these warnings, you must do so with complete honesty about what you are doing. You are not investing. You are speculating. You are competing in a negative-sum game where your profits come from other traders' losses. You will most likely lose money. You are risking capital that could be deployed into activities that reliably build wealth. You are spending time that could be used to increase earning capacity or build businesses. These are costs you must accept if you choose this path, and you must do so with money and time you can afford to lose without affecting your long-term financial security.

The alternative to day trading is simple, boring, and statistically certain to produce superior outcomes over decades. You invest systematically in diversified index funds. You focus on earning high income through your career or business. You maintain high savings rate by controlling spending in major categories. You allow compound returns to multiply your wealth over time. You ignore daily price fluctuations and short-term market movements. You never sell except when you need capital for living expenses in retirement. This approach requires no special skills, no constant monitoring, minimal time investment, and produces wealth building for the vast majority who implement it consistently. It generates no excitement, provides no validation of your analytical abilities, and offers no opportunity to prove you are smarter than other market participants.

The one percent understand that day trading is entertainment masquerading as wealth building for most who attempt it. They recognize that the time and capital required to potentially succeed at day trading are better deployed into activities that reliably generate wealth. They understand that speculation requires edges that most people do not possess and psychological capacities that most cannot develop. They see day trading as distraction from systematic wealth accumulation through patient capital deployment, high savings rates, and focus on increasing earning capacity. They leave day trading to the tiny minority of professional traders who compete in that arena while they build wealth through proven methods that require no special gifts beyond discipline and time.

You have now been provided comprehensive education about wealth building through proper foundations in stewardship and values, strategic decisions about major spending categories, systematic accumulation through stock and real estate investing, tax optimization, and partner selection. Day trading does not fit within this framework except as warning about what to avoid. The activity consumes capital that should be invested for long-term growth. It demands time that should be spent on career advancement or business building. It reinforces psychological patterns opposite to those required for patient wealth accumulation. The rare individuals who succeed at day trading do so despite these obstacles through extraordinary combinations of skill and discipline that you almost certainly do not possess.

The choice is whether to accept this reality and focus your efforts on proven wealth-building approaches, or to spend years discovering through expensive experience that you are part of the ninety percent who lose money through day trading. The one percent make this choice rationally based on statistics and honest assessment of their capacities. The ninety-nine percent ignore the statistics, overestimate their abilities, and learn through losses what they could have learned through education.

CHAPTER 15:
THE LANGUAGE OF SUCCESS—CONVERSING WITH THE ELITE

In 1981, a homeless man named Chris Gardner stood in a brokerage firm office in San Francisco, having convinced the manager to grant him an interview for a competitive stockbroker training program despite arriving in paint-stained clothes and worn shoes. He had been evicted from his apartment the previous week and was sleeping in subway bathrooms with his young son. His formal education consisted of a high school diploma and some military training. He had no business background, no finance degree, and no network in the industry. What he did have was an understanding of how successful people communicated and the ability to mirror that communication convincingly enough to gain entry to their world.

During the interview, Gardner did not discuss his homelessness or desperate circumstances. He did not apologize for his appearance or make excuses. Instead, he spoke precisely about why he wanted to enter finance, referenced specific aspects of the firm's business he had researched, asked sophisticated questions about the training program structure and career progression, and demonstrated through his language patterns and conversational approach that he belonged in that environment despite his circumstances suggesting otherwise. The manager accepted him into the program. Within five years, Gardner had built a seven-figure business. Within fifteen years, he had sold that business for millions and established himself as successful entrepreneur and motivational speaker. His story became the basis for the film "The Pursuit of Happyness" starring Will Smith.

What Gardner understood instinctively is that the one percent speak a different language than the ninety-nine percent. This is not about vocabulary size or grammatical correctness, though both matter. This is about patterns of communication that signal membership in a particular class. The way you phrase questions, the assumptions embedded in your statements, the references you make, the stories you tell, and the conversational frameworks you employ all communicate volumes about your background, experience, and thinking patterns. Those who master the language of the elite gain access to rooms and opportunities that remain closed to those who sound like they do not belong, regardless of their actual capabilities or potential.

The foundation of elite communication is precision. The ninety-nine percent communicate in generalizations and approximations because they have not developed the habit of thinking precisely about what they want to express. They say a project will take "a while" rather than estimating three to six weeks based on specific work requirements. They describe something as "expensive" rather than stating the actual cost and whether it fits within budget parameters. They claim that "everyone" holds a particular opinion rather than specifying which relevant stakeholders have expressed that view. This imprecision signals unclear thinking, lack of preparation, or unwillingness to commit to specific positions.

The one percent communicate in specifics because their thinking is precise. They state timeframes with ranges that account for uncertainty while providing concrete targets. They discuss costs in actual figures and relate those costs to value delivered or budgets available. They identify specific individuals or groups when discussing opinions rather than hiding behind vague collective assertions. This precision signals that they have thought carefully about what they are saying, that they are prepared to defend their statements with evidence, and that they take responsibility for the positions they articulate. The effect is credibility that vague communication cannot establish.

The vocabulary differences between classes are real but not in the way most people assume. The one percent do not use unnecessarily complex words to demonstrate intelligence. They use technical terminology appropriate to specific domains because that terminology communicates concepts efficiently to others who understand the same language. When discussing investments, they reference alpha, beta, Sharpe ratios, and basis points not to impress but because these terms convey specific meanings that would require paragraphs to explain using general vocabulary. When discussing business operations, they reference EBITDA, runway, burn rate, and unit economics because these concepts are fundamental to business analysis and using precise terminology prevents confusion.

The error most people make when attempting to adopt elite language is using technical terms they do not fully understand. Nothing exposes an outsider more quickly than misusing specialized vocabulary or using such terminology in contexts where it is inappropriate. The person who references "synergies" without explaining what specific operational improvements would result from combining entities, or who discusses "disrupting an industry" without identifying what specific aspect of current business models their approach would replace, signals that they are mimicking language they have heard without understanding the substance beneath it. The one percent recognize this immediately and dismiss such speakers as pretenders rather than peers.

The path to developing authentic facility with specialized language is studying domains deeply rather than collecting impressive-sounding terms. When you genuinely understand financial concepts, the appropriate terminology emerges naturally from that understanding because you need efficient ways to express the concepts you are thinking about. When you have built or analyzed businesses, terms like contribution margin and customer acquisition cost become part of your working vocabulary because these metrics matter for the analysis you conduct regularly. The vocabulary is byproduct of substance rather than substitute for it.

The conversational frameworks the one percent employ differ fundamentally from those the ninety-nine percent use. The ninety-nine percent structure conversations around themselves, focusing on their own experiences, opinions, and needs. They talk about what they have done, what they think, and what they want. The one percent structure conversations around understanding others, focusing on asking questions that reveal information useful for building relationships or identifying opportunities. They talk about what interests their conversation partners, what challenges those partners face, and how they might add value to those partners' situations.

This distinction manifests in the types of questions asked during networking or business conversations. The ninety-nine percent ask questions focused on extracting value for themselves. They want to know how the other person can help them, whether opportunities exist that they can pursue, or what connections the other person can provide. These questions signal that the questioner views the conversation as transactional and that they are seeking to extract value without necessarily providing value in return. The one percent ask questions focused on understanding the other person's situation. They want to know what challenges the person faces, what they are working on currently, what outcomes they seek, and what constraints limit their progress. These questions signal genuine interest and often reveal opportunities to provide value that builds reciprocal relationships.

The framework for professional conversations that build relationships rather than merely exchange information begins with research before the conversation occurs. You learn what you can about the person's background, current role, company, and relevant recent developments. This allows you to ask informed questions rather than basic questions that anyone could ask without preparation. When you reference a recent company announcement, a career transition, or a professional accomplishment during your conversation, you signal that you considered this person important enough to research. This is flattering and it establishes that you enter the conversation with context rather than requiring the other person to provide complete background.

The questions you ask should be open-ended rather than yes-or-no questions because open-ended questions encourage elaboration that reveals useful information. Rather than asking whether someone enjoyed their previous role, you ask what aspects of that role they found most rewarding and what prompted their transition to their current position. Rather than asking whether their company faces challenges in a particular area, you ask how they are approaching specific aspects of their business that you know from research are likely pain points. These questions demonstrate that you have thought about their situation and that you are interested in understanding their perspective rather than simply filling conversational space.

The listening during these conversations matters as much as the questions asked. The ninety-nine percent listen selectively, waiting for openings to interject their own experiences or opinions. They view listening as temporary pause before speaking rather than as opportunity to gather information and understand the other person's thinking. The one percent listen actively, asking follow-up questions that demonstrate engagement with what was said, noting specific details that can be referenced later, and allowing silence when the other person is thinking rather than rushing to fill every pause with words. This active listening signals respect for the speaker and often reveals information that superficial listening would miss.

The art of storytelling separates effective communicators from those who merely convey information. The ninety-nine percent relate events chronologically, providing excessive detail about context and process while failing to emphasize the key point or lesson. They tell stories about what happened to them rather than stories that illustrate principles or demonstrate capabilities relevant to their audience. The one percent structure stories to support specific points, eliminating irrelevant details and emphasizing the elements that matter for their communication objective. They tell stories that demonstrate how they think, how they handle challenges, and what they have accomplished in ways that are specific and memorable.

The structure for effective professional storytelling follows the STAR framework, though the one percent internalize this structure rather than consciously applying it.

- **Situation** describes the context briefly without excessive detail.
- **Task** identifies what needed to be accomplished or what challenge was faced.
- **Action** explains what you did specifically, emphasizing your thinking process and decision-making rather than just describing activities.
- **Result** states the outcome clearly with specific metrics or impacts where possible.

This structure ensures that stories demonstrate your capabilities through concrete examples rather than through general claims about your qualities.

The preparation of these stories should occur before networking events, interviews, or important meetings rather than attempting to construct them spontaneously during conversations. You identify key themes you want to communicate about your capabilities, experience, or thinking approach. You develop two or three stories that illustrate each theme using specific examples from your work or life. You practice these stories until you can deliver them naturally without seeming rehearsed. When conversations provide openings where these stories are relevant, you deploy them smoothly rather than struggling to remember examples or organizing your thoughts in real time while speaking.

The references you make during conversations signal your education, experience, and the communities you participate in. The ninety-nine percent reference popular culture that everyone knows or niche interests that only small groups care about. The one percent reference books, ideas, and frameworks that are known within professional communities but not necessarily by general audiences. When you reference Clayton Christensen's work on disruptive innovation, Daniel Kahneman's research on cognitive biases, or Ray

Dalio's principles for management, you signal that you read serious business literature and think about frameworks rather than merely reacting to circumstances. When you reference specific podcasts, conferences, or publications that professionals in your field engage with regularly, you signal that you are part of that professional community.

These references should emerge naturally from your actual reading and intellectual engagement rather than being deployed as signaling devices. The person who name-drops books they have not read or references concepts they do not understand will be exposed quickly through follow-up questions or through misapplication of the concepts. The authentic approach is reading widely in your field and adjacent fields, engaging with ideas seriously enough to form opinions about them, and allowing those ideas to surface naturally when conversations touch on relevant topics. This requires actual intellectual work rather than merely collecting impressive-sounding references.

The discussion of compensation and money separates those comfortable in elite environments from those who are not. The ninety-nine percent either avoid discussing money entirely because they consider it impolite or they discuss it crudely in ways that signal discomfort with the topic. The one percent discuss compensation and financial matters matter-of-factly as topics that require attention but not emotional charge. They state salary expectations precisely, they discuss equity and benefits structures knowledgeably, and they negotiate compensation terms directly without apologizing or becoming defensive.

This comfort with money discussions develops through recognizing that compensation is an exchange of value rather than a judgment of your worth as a person. When you are negotiating salary, you are determining the market rate for your skills and experience in that particular role, not establishing your value as a human being. When you discuss investment opportunities or business valuations, you are analyzing financial structures, not making moral judgments. The one percent maintain this emotional separation between money and identity, allowing them to discuss financial matters with the same calm precision they apply to any other business topic.

The ability to disagree professionally without creating conflict is essential for operating in elite environments where strong opinions and healthy debate are expected. The ninety-nine percent either avoid disagreement entirely to prevent conflict or they express disagreement in ways that attack the person rather than the idea. The one percent disagree regularly but do so by focusing on reasoning and evidence rather than on personalities. They phrase disagreements as questions that probe assumptions rather than as assertions that someone is wrong. They acknowledge valid points in arguments they ultimately disagree with rather than dismissing positions entirely. They separate the quality of reasoning from the conclusion reached, crediting good analysis even when they believe it leads to incorrect conclusions.

The phrases that signal professional disagreement without personal attack include frameworks like "I see it differently because," "Have you considered," "My concern with that approach is," and "In my experience, that works best when." These phrases allow you to express disagreement while maintaining respect for the other person and focusing the conversation on substantive differences rather than on who is right or wrong. The goal is identifying the best answer through collaborative analysis rather than winning an argument.

The networking conversations that build valuable relationships over time differ from transactional exchanges that seek immediate benefit. The ninety-nine percent view networking as collecting contacts who might help them in the future. They attend events, exchange business cards, connect on LinkedIn, and then reach out when they need something. This creates relationships that exist only when the person needs something, which means the relationships provide minimal value because no foundation of mutual respect and reciprocal value exchange has been built. The one percent view networking as building a community of people they can help and who can help them over extended time periods. They look for ways to provide value before asking for anything. They stay in touch with people when they do not need anything because the relationship itself is valuable independent of immediate transactional benefit.

The practical implementation of relationship building requires systems for staying in touch rather than relying on memory or spontaneous contact. You maintain lists of people you want to stay connected with, organized by relationship strength and relevance. You schedule periodic outreach where you send brief messages checking in, sharing relevant articles or opportunities, or asking how their current projects are progressing. These communications require only minutes but they maintain relationships that would otherwise atrophy through neglect. When you eventually need something from these contacts, the foundation of mutual goodwill created through consistent small touches makes them far more likely to respond positively.

The follow-up after networking events or meaningful conversations separates those who build relationships from those who merely collect contacts. The ninety-nine percent might send a generic message saying they enjoyed meeting or suggesting they stay in touch. The one percent send personalized messages referencing specific topics discussed, providing promised information or introductions, or asking follow-up questions about projects or challenges the person mentioned. These substantive follow-ups demonstrate that you were paying attention during the conversation and that you view the relationship as potentially valuable enough to invest additional time nurturing it.

The etiquette surrounding introductions and requests demonstrates social sophistication that the one percent employ reflexively. When asking for introductions to someone in your network's contacts, you provide specific context about why you want the introduction and what value you believe the meeting would provide for the person you are asking to meet. You make the introduction easy by offering to draft the introduction email that your contact can edit and forward. You follow up after introductions to thank the person who made the connection and to report briefly on how the meeting went. These practices demonstrate respect for people's time and social capital while making it easy for them to help you.

When introducing two people to each other, you provide context about why you believe they should know each other and what value the connection might provide to each party. You highlight relevant background and shared interests that give them starting points for conversation. You make clear whether you are introducing them because they specifically should meet or because one requested the introduction, as this affects expectations about who should follow up and how quickly. These details prevent awkward situations where both parties wait for the other to reach out or where one party is unclear about why they were introduced.

The management of professional reputation through your communication patterns operates continuously whether you are conscious of it or not. Every email you send, every presentation you deliver, every meeting you participate in, and every casual conversation you have contributes to how others perceive your capabilities and professionalism. The ninety-nine percent treat some communications as important and others as casual, maintaining different standards based on perceived significance. The one percent maintain consistent standards across all communications because they recognize that you cannot control which interactions others will remember or discuss with their own networks.

The email communication that builds professional reputation is concise, well-organized, and action-oriented. You state your purpose in the opening sentence. You provide necessary context efficiently. You make clear requests with specific deadlines when you need something from the recipient. You use paragraph breaks and formatting to make the email easy to scan. You proofread before sending to eliminate errors that suggest carelessness. These practices seem basic but they are violated constantly by people who write rambling emails that bury key points in multiple paragraphs, who make vague requests without deadlines, who send messages containing obvious typos or grammatical errors. The person who consistently sends professional emails stands out simply by meeting standards that should be universal but are not.

The presentations that establish credibility are structured logically with clear narrative flow from problem to analysis to recommendation. You open with the conclusion rather than building to it because busy professionals want to know your recommendation immediately and can dig into supporting analysis if they choose. You use visuals that clarify rather than decorate, ensuring that every chart or graphic adds information rather than merely making slides visually interesting. You anticipate questions and address them preemptively in your supporting materials. You practice sufficiently that you can deliver smoothly without reading slides or notes. These practices distinguish professional presentations from the amateur presentations that most people deliver despite their importance for career advancement.

The development of elite communication skills requires years of conscious practice rather than merely accumulating experience. You must pay attention to how successful people in your field communicate, noting specific patterns and phrases they employ. You must solicit feedback about your own communication from mentors or colleagues whose judgment you trust. You must deliberately practice skills like storytelling, active listening, and professional disagreement rather than hoping they will develop naturally. You must read extensively to develop the vocabulary and frameworks that informed professionals reference. This is work that most people will not do because it requires acknowledging that their current communication patterns are inadequate and investing time in improvement that could be spent on immediately productive activities.

Chris Gardner developed these communication skills through observation and conscious practice despite his lack of formal education and desperate circumstances. He listened carefully to how stockbrokers spoke, noted the questions they asked and the frameworks they referenced, and practiced these patterns until he could deploy them authentically. His success had little to do with his intelligence or work ethic, which were not unusual. It had everything to do with his ability to communicate in ways that signaled he belonged in professional environments despite external circumstances suggesting otherwise. The language opened doors that credentials or circumstances would have kept closed.

You face similar opportunities to develop communication patterns that provide access to opportunities and relationships that your current patterns do not support. The elite language is not secret or inaccessible. It is documented in business books, demonstrated in professional podcasts, modeled by successful people you can observe. What separates those who develop fluency from those who do not is willingness In 1981, a homeless man named Chris Gardner stood in a brokerage firm office in San Francisco, having convinced the manager to grant him an interview for a competitive stockbroker training program despite arriving in paint-stained clothes and worn shoes. He had been evicted from his apartment the previous week and was sleeping in subway bathrooms with his young son. His formal education consisted of a high school diploma and some military training. He had no business background, no finance degree, and no network in the industry. What he did have was an understanding of how successful people communicated and the ability to mirror that communication convincingly enough to gain entry to their world.

During the interview, Gardner did not discuss his homelessness or desperate circumstances. He did not apologize for his appearance or make excuses. Instead, he spoke precisely about why he wanted to enter finance, referenced specific aspects of the firm's business he had researched, asked sophisticated questions about the training program structure and career progression, and demonstrated through his language patterns and conversational approach that he belonged in that environment despite his circumstances suggesting otherwise. The manager accepted him into the program. Within five years, Gardner had built a seven-figure business. Within fifteen years, he had sold that business for millions and established himself as successful entrepreneur and motivational speaker. His story became the basis for the film "The Pursuit of Happyness" starring Will Smith.

What Gardner understood instinctively is that the one percent speak a different language than the ninety-nine percent. This is not about vocabulary size or grammatical correctness, though both matter. This is about patterns of communication that signal membership in a particular class. The way you phrase questions, the assumptions embedded in your statements, the references you make, the stories you tell, and the conversational frameworks you employ all communicate volumes about your background, experience, and thinking patterns. Those who master the language of the elite gain access to rooms and opportunities that remain closed to those who sound like they do not belong, regardless of their actual capabilities or potential.

The foundation of elite communication is precision. The ninety-nine percent communicate in generalizations and approximations because they have not developed the habit of thinking precisely about what they want to express. They say a project will take "a while" rather than estimating three to six weeks based on specific work requirements. They describe something as "expensive" rather than stating the actual cost and whether it fits within budget parameters. They claim that "everyone" holds a particular opinion rather than specifying which relevant stakeholders have expressed that view. This imprecision signals unclear thinking, lack of preparation, or unwillingness to commit to specific positions.

The one percent communicate in specifics because their thinking is precise. They state timeframes with ranges that account for uncertainty while providing concrete targets. They discuss costs in actual figures and relate those costs to value delivered or budgets available. They identify specific individuals or groups when discussing opinions rather than hiding behind vague collective assertions. This precision signals that they have thought carefully about what they are saying, that they are prepared to defend their statements with evidence, and that they take responsibility for the positions they articulate. The effect is credibility that vague communication cannot establish.

The vocabulary differences between classes are real but not in the way most people assume. The one percent do not use unnecessarily complex words to demonstrate intelligence. They use technical terminology appropriate to specific domains because that terminology communicates concepts efficiently to others who understand the same language. When discussing investments, they reference alpha, beta, Sharpe ratios, and basis points not to impress but because these terms convey specific meanings that would require paragraphs to explain using general vocabulary. When discussing business operations, they reference EBITDA, runway, burn rate, and unit economics because these concepts are fundamental to business analysis and using precise terminology prevents confusion.

The error most people make when attempting to adopt elite language is using technical terms they do not fully understand. Nothing exposes an outsider more quickly than misusing specialized vocabulary or using such terminology in contexts where it is inappropriate. The person who references "synergies" without explaining what specific operational improvements would result from combining entities, or who discusses "disrupting an industry" without identifying what specific aspect of current business models their approach would replace, signals that they are mimicking language they have heard without understanding the substance beneath it. The one percent recognize this immediately and dismiss such speakers as pretenders rather than peers.

The path to developing authentic facility with specialized language is studying domains deeply rather than collecting impressive-sounding terms. When you genuinely understand financial concepts, the appropriate terminology emerges naturally from that understanding because you need efficient ways to express the concepts you are thinking about. When you have built or analyzed businesses, terms like contribution margin and customer acquisition cost become part of your working vocabulary because these metrics matter for the analysis you conduct regularly. The vocabulary is byproduct of substance rather than substitute for it.

The conversational frameworks the one percent employ differ fundamentally from those the ninety-nine percent use. The ninety-nine percent structure conversations around themselves, focusing on their own experiences, opinions, and needs. They talk about what they have done, what they think, and what they want. The one percent structure conversations around understanding others, focusing on asking questions that reveal information useful for building relationships or identifying opportunities. They talk about what interests their conversation partners, what challenges those partners face, and how they might add value to those partners' situations.

This distinction manifests in the types of questions asked during networking or business conversations. The ninety-nine percent ask questions focused on extracting value for themselves. They want to know how the other person can help them, whether opportunities exist that they can pursue, or what connections the other person can provide. These questions signal that the questioner views the conversation as transactional and that they are seeking to extract value without necessarily providing value in return. The one percent ask questions focused on understanding the other person's situation. They want to know what challenges the person faces, what they are working on currently, what outcomes they seek, and what constraints limit their progress. These questions signal genuine interest and often reveal opportunities to provide value that builds reciprocal relationships.

The framework for professional conversations that build relationships rather than merely exchange information begins with research before the conversation occurs. You learn what you can about the person's background, current role, company, and relevant recent developments. This allows you to ask informed questions rather than basic questions that anyone could ask without preparation. When you reference a recent company announcement, a career transition, or a professional accomplishment during your conversation, you signal that you considered this person important enough to research. This is flattering and it establishes that you enter the conversation with context rather than requiring the other person to provide complete background.

The questions you ask should be open-ended rather than yes-or-no questions because open-ended questions encourage elaboration that reveals useful information. Rather than asking whether someone enjoyed their previous role, you ask what aspects of that role they found most rewarding and what prompted their transition to their current position. Rather than asking whether their company faces challenges in a particular area, you ask how they are approaching specific aspects of their business that you know from research are likely pain points. These questions demonstrate that you have thought about their situation and that you are interested in understanding their perspective rather than simply filling conversational space.

The listening during these conversations matters as much as the questions asked. The ninety-nine percent listen selectively, waiting for openings to interject their own experiences or opinions. They view listening as temporary pause before speaking rather than as opportunity to gather information and understand the other person's thinking. The one percent listen actively, asking follow-up questions that demonstrate engagement with what was said, noting specific details that can be referenced later, and allowing silence when the other person is thinking rather than rushing to fill every pause with words. This active listening signals respect for the speaker and often reveals information that superficial listening would miss.

The art of storytelling separates effective communicators from those who merely convey information. The ninety-nine percent relate events chronologically, providing excessive detail about context and process while failing to emphasize the key point or lesson. They tell stories about what happened to them rather than stories that illustrate principles or demonstrate capabilities relevant to their audience. The one percent structure stories to support specific points, eliminating irrelevant details and emphasizing the elements that matter for their communication objective. They tell stories that demonstrate how they think, how they handle challenges, and what they have accomplished in ways that are specific and memorable.

The structure for effective professional storytelling follows the STAR framework, though the one percent internalize this structure rather than consciously applying it.

- **Situation** describes the context briefly without excessive detail.

- **Task** identifies what needed to be accomplished or what challenge was faced.

- **Action** explains what you did specifically, emphasizing your thinking process and decision-making rather than just describing activities.

- **Result** states the outcome clearly with specific metrics or impacts where possible.

This structure ensures that stories demonstrate your capabilities through concrete examples rather than through general claims about your qualities.

The preparation of these stories should occur before networking events, interviews, or important meetings rather than attempting to construct them spontaneously during conversations. You identify key themes you want to communicate about your capabilities, experience, or thinking approach. You develop two or three stories that illustrate each theme using specific examples from your work or life. You practice these stories until you can deliver them naturally without seeming rehearsed. When conversations provide openings where these stories are relevant, you deploy them smoothly rather than struggling to remember examples or organizing your thoughts in real time while speaking.

The references you make during conversations signal your education, experience, and the communities you participate in. The ninety-nine percent reference popular culture that everyone knows or niche interests that only small groups care about. The one percent reference books, ideas, and frameworks that are known within professional communities but not necessarily by general audiences.

When you reference Clayton Christensen's work on disruptive innovation, Daniel Kahneman's research on cognitive biases, or Ray Dalio's principles for management, you signal that you read serious business literature and think about frameworks rather than merely reacting to circumstances. When you reference specific podcasts, conferences, or publications that professionals in your field engage with regularly, you signal that you are part of that professional community.

These references should emerge naturally from your actual reading and intellectual engagement rather than being deployed as signaling devices. The person who name-drops books they have not read or references concepts they do not understand will be exposed quickly through follow-up questions or through misapplication of the concepts. The authentic approach is reading widely in your field and adjacent fields, engaging with ideas seriously enough to form opinions about them, and allowing those ideas to surface naturally when conversations touch on relevant topics. This requires actual intellectual work rather than merely collecting impressive-sounding references.

The discussion of compensation and money separates those comfortable in elite environments from those who are not. The ninety-nine percent either avoid discussing money entirely because they consider it impolite or they discuss it crudely in ways that signal discomfort with the topic. The one percent discuss compensation and financial matters matter-of-factly as topics that require attention but not emotional charge. They state salary expectations precisely, they discuss equity and benefits structures knowledgeably, and they negotiate compensation terms directly without apologizing or becoming defensive.

This comfort with money discussions develops through recognizing that compensation is an exchange of value rather than a judgment of your worth as a person. When you are negotiating salary, you are determining the market rate for your skills and experience in that particular role, not establishing your value as a human being. When you discuss investment opportunities or business valuations, you are analyzing financial structures, not making moral judgments. The one percent maintain this emotional separation between money and identity, allowing them to discuss financial matters with the same calm precision they apply to any other business topic.

The ability to disagree professionally without creating conflict is essential for operating in elite environments where strong opinions and healthy debate are expected. The ninety-nine percent either avoid disagreement entirely to prevent conflict or they express disagreement in ways that attack the person rather than the idea. The one percent disagree regularly but do so by focusing on reasoning and evidence rather than on personalities. They phrase disagreements as questions that probe assumptions rather than as assertions that someone is wrong. They acknowledge valid points in arguments they ultimately disagree with rather than dismissing positions entirely. They separate the quality of reasoning from the conclusion reached, crediting good analysis even when they believe it leads to incorrect conclusions.

The phrases that signal professional disagreement without personal attack include frameworks like "I see it differently because," "Have you considered," "My concern with that approach is," and "In my experience, that works best when." These phrases allow you to express disagreement while maintaining respect for the other person and focusing the conversation on substantive differences rather than on who is right or wrong. The goal is identifying the best answer through collaborative analysis rather than winning an argument.

The networking conversations that build valuable relationships over time differ from transactional exchanges that seek immediate benefit. The ninety-nine percent view networking as collecting contacts who might help them in the future. They attend events, exchange business cards, connect on LinkedIn, and then reach out when they need something. This creates relationships that exist only when the person needs something, which means the relationships provide minimal value because no foundation of mutual respect and reciprocal value exchange has been built. The one percent view networking as building a community of people they can help and who can help them over extended time periods. They look for ways to provide value before asking for anything. They stay in touch with people when they do not need anything because the relationship itself is valuable independent of immediate transactional benefit.

The practical implementation of relationship building requires systems for staying in touch rather than relying on memory or spontaneous contact. You maintain lists of people you want to stay connected with, organized by relationship strength and relevance. You schedule periodic outreach where you send brief messages checking in, sharing relevant articles or opportunities, or asking how their current projects are progressing. These communications require only minutes but they maintain relationships that would otherwise atrophy through neglect. When you eventually need something from these contacts, the foundation of mutual goodwill created through consistent small touches makes them far more likely to respond positively.

The follow-up after networking events or meaningful conversations separates those who build relationships from those who merely collect contacts. The ninety-nine percent might send a generic message saying they enjoyed meeting or suggesting they stay in touch. The one percent send personalized messages referencing specific topics discussed, providing promised information or introductions, or asking follow-up questions about projects or challenges the person mentioned. These substantive follow-ups demonstrate that you were paying attention during the conversation and that you view the relationship as potentially valuable enough to invest additional time nurturing it.

The etiquette surrounding introductions and requests demonstrates social sophistication that the one percent employ reflexively. When asking for introductions to someone in your network's contacts, you provide specific context about why you want the introduction and what value you believe the meeting would provide for the person you are asking to meet. You make the introduction easy by offering to draft the introduction email that your contact can edit and forward. You follow up after introductions to thank the person who made the connection and to report briefly on how the meeting went. These practices demonstrate respect for people's time and social capital while making it easy for them to help you.

When introducing two people to each other, you provide context about why you believe they should know each other and what value the connection might provide to each party. You highlight relevant background and shared interests that give them starting points for conversation. You make clear whether you are introducing them because they specifically should meet or because one requested the introduction, as this affects expectations about who should follow up and how quickly. These details prevent awkward situations where both parties wait for the other to reach out or where one party is unclear about why they were introduced.

The management of professional reputation through your communication patterns operates continuously whether you are conscious of it or not. Every email you send, every presentation you deliver, every meeting you participate in, and every casual conversation you have contributes to how others perceive your capabilities and professionalism. The ninety-nine percent treat some communications as important and others as casual, maintaining different standards based on perceived significance. The one percent maintain consistent standards across all communications because they recognize that you cannot control which interactions others will remember or discuss with their own networks.

The email communication that builds professional reputation is concise, well-organized, and action-oriented. You state your purpose in the opening sentence. You provide necessary context efficiently. You make clear requests with specific deadlines when you need something from the recipient. You use paragraph breaks and formatting to make the email easy to scan. You proofread before sending to eliminate errors that suggest carelessness. These practices seem basic but they are violated constantly by people who write rambling emails that bury key points in multiple paragraphs, who make vague requests without deadlines, who send messages containing obvious typos or grammatical errors. The person who consistently sends professional emails stands out simply by meeting standards that should be universal but are not.

The presentations that establish credibility are structured logically with clear narrative flow from problem to analysis to recommendation. You open with the conclusion rather than building to it because busy professionals want to know your recommendation immediately and can dig into supporting analysis if they choose. You use visuals that clarify rather than decorate, ensuring that every chart or graphic adds information rather than merely making slides visually interesting. You anticipate questions and address them preemptively in your supporting materials. You practice sufficiently that you can deliver smoothly without reading slides or notes. These practices distinguish professional presentations from the amateur presentations that most people deliver despite their importance for career advancement.

The development of elite communication skills requires years of conscious practice rather than merely accumulating experience.

You must pay attention to how successful people in your field communicate, noting specific patterns and phrases they employ. You must solicit feedback about your own communication from mentors or colleagues whose judgment you trust. You must deliberately practice skills like storytelling, active listening, and professional disagreement rather than hoping they will develop naturally. You must read extensively to develop the vocabulary and frameworks that informed professionals reference. This is work that most people will not do because it requires acknowledging that their current communication patterns are inadequate and investing time in improvement that could be spent on immediately productive activities.

Chris Gardner developed these communication skills through observation and conscious practice despite his lack of formal education and desperate circumstances. He listened carefully to how stockbrokers spoke, noted the questions they asked and the frameworks they referenced, and practiced these patterns until he could deploy them authentically. His success had little to do with his intelligence or work ethic, which were not unusual. It had everything to do with his ability to communicate in ways that signaled he belonged in professional environments despite external circumstances suggesting otherwise. The language opened doors that credentials or circumstances would have kept closed.

You face similar opportunities to develop communication patterns that provide access to opportunities and relationships that your current patterns do not support. The elite language is not secret or inaccessible. It is documented in business books, demonstrated in professional podcasts, modeled by successful people you can observe. What separates those who develop fluency from those who do not is willingness to acknowledge that communication matters, to invest time learning patterns that differ from what comes naturally, and to practice these patterns until they become automatic rather than forced. This is not about being inauthentic or pretending to be someone you are not. This is about developing the communication tools that allow you to express your actual capabilities and thinking in ways that others can recognize and value.

We have now examined how to build wealth through strategic decisions about money, investments, real estate, and major spending categories. We have discussed how to choose a life partner whose values support wealth building and how to avoid speculation disguised as investing. This chapter has addressed how to communicate in ways that provide access to the networks and opportunities where wealth is built. The pattern across all these domains is that the one percent operate according to principles that are knowable and learnable but that most people never discover or never implement despite their availability. Communication is no different. The frameworks exist. The patterns are observable. The improvement is achievable through deliberate practice. to acknowledge that communication matters, to invest time learning patterns that differ from what comes naturally, and to practice these patterns until they become automatic rather than forced. This is not about being inauthentic or pretending to be someone you are not. This is about developing the communication tools that allow you to express your actual capabilities and thinking in ways that others can recognize and value.

We have now examined how to build wealth through strategic decisions about money, investments, real estate, and major spending categories. We have discussed how to choose a life partner whose values support wealth building and how to avoid speculation disguised as investing. This chapter has addressed how to communicate in ways that provide access to the networks and opportunities where wealth is built. The pattern across all these domains is that the one percent operate according to principles that are knowable and learnable but that most people never discover or never implement despite their availability. Communication is no different. The frameworks exist. The patterns are observable. The improvement is achievable through deliberate practice.

CHAPTER 16:

INTERVIEW MASTERY—SELLING YOURSELF AT MAXIMUM VALUE

In 2001, a thirty-one-year-old woman named Sheryl Sandberg sat across from Eric Schmidt in a conference room at Google's Mountain View headquarters. Schmidt had recently become CEO and was building his executive team for what was still a relatively small technology company that most people had never heard of. Sandberg had an unusual background for a technology executive—she had worked at the World Bank, served as Chief of Staff to the Treasury Secretary under President Clinton, and most recently had been managing online sales operations at a business consulting firm. She had no computer science degree, no engineering background, and no experience at internet companies during the height of the dot-com boom.

What Sandberg did have was a clear understanding of what Schmidt needed even if he had not fully articulated it himself. During their conversation, she asked questions about Google's business model, its revenue challenges, and its plans for monetizing search traffic. She identified gaps in the company's commercial operations that her background made her uniquely qualified to address. She explained how her experience building teams at Treasury and managing operations at her previous company had prepared her to build Google's advertising business from essentially nothing into a systematic revenue engine. She did not focus on what she had done. She focused on what she could do for Google specifically, based on what she had learned about their situation through her research and through the questions she asked during the interview itself.

Schmidt offered her a position that day. Sandberg spent the next seven years building Google's advertising operation from generating approximately quarter of a billion dollars annually to generating over twenty billion dollars annually. That success established her reputation and led to her recruitment as Chief Operating Officer of Facebook, where she helped build another technology empire while accumulating personal wealth in the hundreds of millions of dollars. Her career trajectory began not with her impressive resume but with her ability to conduct an interview that demonstrated she understood what the employer needed and could deliver results in that specific context.

Interviews are not conversations. They are sales presentations where you are the product being sold. This fundamental reframing changes everything about how you approach these interactions. The ninety-nine percent view interviews as examinations where they must answer questions correctly to pass some threshold of acceptability. They prepare by reviewing their own backgrounds and practicing answers to common questions. They hope to avoid mistakes that might disqualify them. They wait passively for the interviewer to determine whether they are adequate for the role. This defensive, reactive approach produces adequate results at best and fails entirely when competing against candidates who understand what is actually happening in the room.

The one percent view interviews as opportunities to demonstrate value and to close a sale. They prepare by researching the company, the role, the interviewers, and the business context that makes this position necessary. They construct a narrative about how their background uniquely positions them to solve the specific problems this role exists to address. They ask questions that demonstrate understanding while gathering additional information to refine their pitch. They close the interview by making clear their interest and their confidence that they can deliver the results the company needs. This active, strategic approach produces multiple offers at maximum compensation because you are not waiting for someone to select you—you are persuading them that selecting you is the obvious correct decision.

The preparation for effective interviews begins days or weeks before you enter the room, not the night before or during the drive to the office. You research the company through annual reports if publicly traded, through news coverage of recent developments, through industry analysis that provides context about competitive pressures and market trends. You research the specific role by analyzing the job description for clues about what problems need solving, what the previous person in the role accomplished or failed to accomplish, and what success would look like in the first year. You research the interviewers through LinkedIn to understand their backgrounds, their career paths within the company, and what they likely care about based on their responsibilities.

This research provides three critical advantages. First, it allows you to ask informed questions that demonstrate you have invested time understanding their situation rather than walking in blind and expecting them to educate you. When you reference a recent strategic initiative the company announced, a challenge the industry faces that affects their business, or a metric that matters for measuring success in this role, you signal immediately that you are prepared and serious. Second, the research reveals how to position your background in ways that align with their specific needs rather than presenting your experience generically. Third, research uncovers concerns or objections they are likely to have about your candidacy, allowing you to address these preemptively rather than being caught unprepared when they arise.

The stories you prepare before the interview determine whether you can demonstrate your capabilities convincingly or whether you fumble through vague generalizations about your experience. The STAR framework—Situation, Task, Action, Result— provides structure for these stories, though you should internalize the framework rather than mechanically applying it in ways that sound rehearsed. You identify the key capabilities or qualities the role requires based on the job description and research. You develop two or three specific stories that demonstrate each capability through concrete examples from your experience. You practice these stories until you can deliver them smoothly while adapting them based on the specific questions asked.

The situation component should be brief, providing only context necessary to understand the challenge. The ninety-nine percent spend excessive time on situation, describing organizational structures, historical background, and peripheral details that dilute the impact of their story. The one percent provide one or two sentences establishing context, then move immediately to the problem that needed solving. The interviewer does not need to understand your entire organizational structure. They need to understand what challenge you faced.

The task component identifies what needed to be accomplished and why it mattered. This is where you establish the stakes and the difficulty level. A story about organizing a small team event carries different weight than a story about leading a cross-functional project affecting company revenue. You want the interviewer to understand that what you accomplished required real capability rather than merely showing up and executing obvious tasks. The common error is understating the difficulty or importance of what you did, which makes your accomplishment seem routine rather than impressive.

The action component is where most candidates lose the opportunity to demonstrate their thinking and decision-making process. The ninety-nine percent describe what they did using language like "we implemented" or "the team developed" without explaining their specific contribution or the reasoning behind their approach. The one percent describe their thinking process, the alternatives they considered, the factors they weighed, and the specific decisions they made. They use "I" language when discussing their contributions even when working on teams because the interviewer is evaluating them individually, not evaluating the team. They explain why they chose their approach rather than merely describing what they did.

The result component must be specific and quantified wherever possible. Saying you "improved performance" is meaningless. Saying you "increased sales by thirty-two percent over six months" or "reduced processing time from four hours to ninety minutes" provides concrete evidence of impact. The interviewer can evaluate whether this level of improvement matters for the challenges they face. When results cannot be quantified easily, you should still provide specific evidence of impact through stakeholder feedback, recognition received, or subsequent opportunities that resulted from your success.

The questions you ask during interviews distinguish candidates who are merely competent from candidates who think strategically. The ninety-nine percent ask generic questions about company culture, work-life balance, or advancement opportunities that could be asked at any company. These questions provide minimal information and they signal that you have not thought carefully about this specific opportunity. The one percent ask questions that demonstrate research and insight while gathering information useful for evaluating the opportunity and refining their pitch.

The strategic questions begin with understanding the context that makes this role necessary. You ask what prompted the company to create this role or what happened with the previous person who held it. This reveals whether you are filling a vacancy created by growth and expansion, replacing someone who failed, or stepping into a newly created position addressing emerging needs. Each scenario carries different implications for expectations, support, and likelihood of success. You ask what success looks like in the first ninety days and first year. This reveals the true priorities versus what appeared in the job description and it allows you to assess whether their expectations are realistic given the resources and authority the role provides.

You ask about the team you would lead or work with, about the resources available, about the decision-making authority you would have, and about how performance is measured. These questions reveal whether the role as described matches the role as it actually exists. Many positions sound impressive in job descriptions but turn out to have minimal authority, inadequate resources, or unrealistic expectations that make success unlikely. Asking these questions during interviews allows you to identify situations you should decline rather than discovering problems after you have accepted an offer.

The questions about your interviewers' experiences with the company provide both useful information and opportunities to build rapport. You ask what they find most rewarding about working there, what surprised them when they joined, and what advice they would give someone entering the role you are discussing. These questions make the interview conversational rather than interrogatory, they provide genuine insight into company culture and challenges, and they allow interviewers to reflect on their own experiences in ways that often make them more favorably disposed toward you because you have shown interest in their perspectives.

The reading of interview dynamics in real time separates sophisticated candidates from those who follow scripts regardless of how conversations develop. You pay attention to which topics generate energy and engagement from interviewers versus which topics they respond to perfunctorily. When you mention an aspect of your background or ask a question that clearly resonates, you explore that area more deeply rather than moving mechanically through your prepared material. When an interviewer seems distracted or disengaged, you adjust your approach by asking questions that require their participation rather than continuing to present information they are not absorbing.

The body language and verbal cues interviewers provide reveal their concerns and interests if you attend to them carefully. When they lean forward and ask follow-up questions, they are genuinely interested in what you are discussing. When they glance at the clock or give brief responses, they are ready to move to different topics or the interview is not going well. When they express concern about a particular aspect of your background, they are telling you what objection you need to address before they can advocate for hiring you. Most candidates miss these signals entirely because they are focused on delivering their prepared responses rather than engaging dynamically with what is actually happening in the conversation.

The addressing of objections or concerns requires direct acknowledgment rather than evasion. If you are transitioning from a different industry, the interviewer is wondering whether your skills transfer to their environment. Rather than hoping they do not raise this concern, you raise it yourself and explain specifically why your background applies to their context. If you lack a credential or experience they might expect, you acknowledge this directly and explain either why it does not matter for this role or how you have compensated through other experiences. This direct approach prevents objections from festering unspoken and it demonstrates confidence that you have thought through potential concerns rather than hoping they go unnoticed.

The close of the interview matters as much as any other component. The ninety-nine percent thank the interviewer for their time and ask about next steps in the process. This passive close leaves the interviewer with no particular impression beyond what your answers provided. The one percent close by summarizing why they believe they are strong candidates for this role specifically, by expressing genuine enthusiasm for the opportunity, and by asking directly whether the interviewer has any concerns about their candidacy that they should address. This active close accomplishes multiple objectives simultaneously.

First, the summary allows you to reinforce key messages about your fit for the role, connecting specific aspects of your background to specific needs you have identified through the conversation. Second, expressing enthusiasm signals genuine interest rather than treating this as one of many options you are evaluating. Third, asking directly about concerns gives you one final opportunity to address objections while demonstrating confidence and willingness to engage difficult topics directly. Even when interviewers demur and claim they have no concerns, the question itself makes a positive impression by showing that you care about addressing their evaluation criteria rather than merely hoping you performed adequately.

The salary negotiation determines whether you maximize your compensation or leave substantial money on the table through poor negotiation. The research you conducted before the interview

231

should include market rates for similar roles at comparable companies in your geography. Websites like Glassdoor, Levels.fyi, and Payscale provide data points, though you should supplement these with conversations with recruiters and people in your network who have visibility into compensation at various companies. This research establishes your baseline understanding of what the role should pay and what represents fair compensation versus what represents an attempt to underpay you.

The timing of salary discussions matters enormously. You want to delay specific compensation conversations until after you have demonstrated your value and ideally until the company has decided they want to hire you. The ninety-nine percent state their salary requirements early in the process, often during initial screening calls, which gives the employer information without having received corresponding information about budget and without having had opportunity to demonstrate full value. The one percent deflect early salary questions by stating they are focused on finding the right opportunity and that they are confident fair compensation can be negotiated once mutual fit is established. This preserves flexibility while preventing you from being screened out based on salary mismatches before you have had opportunity to interview.

When the company makes an offer, your first response should never be immediate acceptance regardless of how attractive the offer appears. You thank them for the offer, express enthusiasm about the opportunity, and ask for time to review the complete package including benefits, equity, and other components beyond base salary. This pause accomplishes several objectives. It prevents you from accepting an offer that could have been negotiated higher. It signals that you take the decision seriously and have other options to consider. It provides time to evaluate the complete compensation picture rather than reacting solely to the base salary figure.

The negotiation itself should focus on total compensation rather than base salary alone. Equity, bonuses, benefits, flexible work arrangements, professional development budgets, and other components all have value that can be negotiated. Some companies have rigid base salary bands that make negotiation difficult but more flexibility on equity or signing bonuses. Some companies resist equity grants but will negotiate base salary or benefits. By considering all components, you maximize your chances of improving the total package even when specific components are constrained.

The framing of your negotiation asks matters substantially. Rather than demanding higher compensation, you express appreciation for the offer while noting that based on your research of market rates for similar roles and given your specific experience and the value you will provide, you were expecting compensation in a higher range. You state that range specifically rather than asking what they can do or whether there is room for negotiation. This approach provides a specific target for them to respond to rather than leaving them uncertain about what would satisfy you. When they ask how you arrived at that range, you reference your market research and you connect your request to the value you will deliver rather than merely to your personal needs or preferences.

The acceptance of the offer should include written confirmation of all agreed terms including base salary, bonus structure, equity grants with vesting schedules, benefits, start date, and any special agreements about flexible work or other arrangements. The ninety-nine percent accept offers verbally and trust that written offer letters will match what was discussed. The one percent verify every detail in writing before resigning from current positions because verbal agreements that differ from written offers create conflicts that favor the employer rather than the employee. This attention to detail prevents misunderstandings and it establishes from the beginning that you are precise about contractual terms.

The follow-up after interviews determines whether you remain top-of-mind during decision-making or whether you are forgotten among numerous candidates who interviewed. You send thank-you emails within twenty-four hours to each person who interviewed you, personalizing each message by referencing specific topics you discussed. You use these messages not merely to express gratitude but to reinforce key points about your candidacy, to address any concerns that arose during interviews, and to reiterate your enthusiasm for the opportunity. These messages should be brief—

three to four paragraphs maximum—while being substantive rather than generic.

The mistakes most candidates make in interview follow-up are sending generic thank-you notes that could be sent to anyone, sending messages only to the hiring manager while ignoring other interviewers, or failing to send follow-up at all. Each of these errors reduces your chances of receiving offers because you have wasted an opportunity to strengthen your candidacy. The one percent treat follow-up as integral component of the interview process itself rather than as optional courtesy, and they invest time crafting messages that advance their case for being hired.

The learning from each interview regardless of outcome determines whether your interview performance improves over time. After every interview, you should document what went well, what you could have done better, which questions you struggled to answer, and what you learned about what employers in your field care about most. This documentation creates record you can review before future interviews and it allows you to identify patterns in your performance that need addressing. Most people conduct interviews, receive offers or rejections, and move on without systematic reflection that would improve future performance.

The rejection from positions you wanted provides particularly valuable learning if you can overcome the emotional response to focus on analysis. You should request feedback from recruiters or hiring managers about why you were not selected, acknowledging that many will decline to provide detailed feedback but that some will offer useful insights. Even vague feedback about concerns regarding your experience in certain areas or about cultural fit provides direction for how to position yourself differently in future interviews. The one percent view rejections as data points in continuous improvement process rather than as judgments of their worth.

The broader principle underlying interview mastery is understanding that career advancement and compensation growth over your working years determine your capacity to build wealth more than almost any other factor. You can be brilliant at investing and real estate but if your income remains modest because you never learned to interview effectively, your wealth-building capacity is fundamentally limited. Conversely, someone with average investment returns but exceptional ability to advance their career and negotiate compensation will accumulate substantial wealth simply through the high income their interview skills generate.

Sheryl Sandberg's trajectory from relatively junior policy roles to executive positions at Google and Facebook was not predetermined by her Harvard education or her Treasury experience. Many people with similar or superior credentials never achieve comparable success because they cannot demonstrate their value in high-stakes interviews where opportunities are won or lost. Sandberg mastered the art of understanding what employers needed, positioning herself as uniquely qualified to deliver those results, and negotiating compensation that reflected the value she would provide. These are learnable skills that anyone can develop through study, practice, and systematic application of the frameworks this chapter provides.

The one percent treat every interview as practice for future interviews even when they are not actively job searching. They maintain interview readiness through regular updating of their achievement stories, through staying current on industry trends that might arise in conversations, and through occasional interviews for positions that interest them even when they are satisfied with current roles. This continuous readiness means that when unexpected opportunities arise or when they decide to make moves, they are already operating at peak interview performance rather than trying to remember how to interview effectively after years of not practicing these skills.

We have now examined every major component of wealth building from foundations in stewardship and values through strategic decisions about money, investments, real estate, major spending categories, partner selection, and communication. This chapter addresses how to maximize the income component that provides the capital for all other wealth-building activities. Your ability to interview effectively determines whether you earn fifty thousand or eighty thousand, whether you advance to management or remain in individual contributor roles, whether you receive multiple offers that create negotiating leverage or whether you must accept whatever single offer you receive. These differences compound over forty-year careers into millions of dollars of differential wealth accumulation.

The frameworks for interview mastery are not secret or complex. Research thoroughly. Prepare specific stories demonstrating your capabilities. Ask strategic questions. Read the room and adapt dynamically. Address objections directly. Close actively. Negotiate compensation effectively. Follow up substantively. Learn from every interaction. These are practices that anyone can implement if they are willing to invest the time preparing and practicing rather than hoping that adequate performance and likability will suffice. The one percent implement these practices systematically. The ninety-nine percent wing it and wonder why they receive offers below market rates or no offers at all.

CHAPTER 17:
CLIMBING CORPORATE LADDER—STRATEGIC CAREER ADVANCEMENT

In 1994, a thirty-eight-year-old woman named Indra Nooyi joined PepsiCo as Senior Vice President of Corporate Strategy and Development. She had been recruited from ABB, a European industrial conglomerate, where she had earned a reputation for analytical brilliance and strategic thinking. PepsiCo was facing challenges—its restaurant division was underperforming, its core beverage business was losing ground to Coca-Cola, and the company needed transformation. Most executives in similar positions would have focused on executing their defined responsibilities competently while hoping for eventual recognition and promotion. Nooyi operated from an entirely different playbook.

She immediately began analyzing not just her division but the entire corporate portfolio. She identified that PepsiCo's restaurant businesses—Pizza Hut, Taco Bell, and KFC—were consuming capital without generating returns commensurate with their strategic value. She developed a comprehensive plan to spin off these restaurants into a separate public company, allowing PepsiCo to focus on its packaged food and beverage operations where it could compete more effectively. This was far beyond her job description. She was proposing that the company fundamentally restructure itself, eliminating billions in revenue to sharpen strategic focus.

The proposal was risky. If the spin-off failed or if senior leadership rejected her analysis, she would have identified herself as someone who overstepped boundaries and challenged core strategic assumptions. Nooyi presented her case anyway, backing it with rigorous financial analysis and strategic logic that was difficult to refute. The CEO, Roger Enrico, recognized both the validity of her analysis and her exceptional strategic capability. The spin-off occurred in 1997, creating what became Yum! Brands. Nooyi was promoted to Senior Vice President of Strategic Planning, then to Chief Financial Officer in 2001, and finally to CEO in 2006. She spent the next twelve years transforming PepsiCo into a company focused on healthier products while delivering exceptional shareholder returns.

Her ascent from senior vice president to CEO in twelve years was not predetermined by her credentials or her initial role. It resulted from a systematic approach to career advancement that made her indispensable, that positioned her as the obvious choice for increasing responsibility, and that demonstrated she thought about the entire enterprise rather than merely executing her assigned functions. This is how the one percent advance through corporate hierarchies while their equally talented peers stagnate in roles that fail to provide visibility or opportunity to demonstrate strategic capability.

Corporate advancement is not a meritocracy in any pure sense. The most competent technical performer does not automatically rise to leadership. The hardest worker does not necessarily receive promotions. The most likable colleague does not inevitably ascend to executive ranks. What appears from the outside as meritocracy is actually a complex political system where those who understand the rules advance while those who merely perform their jobs competently plateau regardless of their capabilities. The one percent study these rules as carefully as they study any other system affecting their wealth, because career advancement is the primary mechanism through which most people increase their earning capacity during their wealth-building years.

The foundation of strategic career advancement begins with understanding that your actual job responsibilities represent the minimum threshold for remaining employed, not the activities that drive promotion. The ninety-nine percent focus obsessively on executing their defined roles with excellence, believing that superior performance in current responsibilities will be noticed and rewarded. This belief is false. Superior performance in your current role demonstrates that you are excellent at your current level, not that you are ready for the next level. Companies promote people who demonstrate capability for the role being filled, not people who are merely excellent at their current roles.

The distinction matters enormously. To advance from individual contributor to management, you must demonstrate management capabilities before receiving the title. To advance from management to senior leadership, you must demonstrate strategic thinking and enterprise-wide perspective before being given responsibility for strategy. The one percent engineer opportunities to demonstrate next-level capabilities while still performing excellently in their current roles. They volunteer for projects that require management of others even when their role is individual contributor. They develop strategic analyses of business challenges even when their role is tactical execution. They make themselves visible to senior leaders even when their organizational position does not require such interaction.

This is work beyond your job description, which is precisely why it drives promotion while merely doing your job does not. The person who clocks in, executes assigned tasks excellently, and clocks out is valuable in their current role and the company has no incentive to promote them because they are already providing maximum value where they are. The person who executes assigned tasks excellently while simultaneously demonstrating capabilities beyond their current role creates pressure for promotion because their talents are being underutilized in their current position.

Nooyi's analysis of PepsiCo's portfolio was not part of her job description as Senior Vice President of Corporate Strategy and Development. Her role was implementing strategy, not recommending fundamental restructuring of the entire company. By choosing to analyze the portfolio comprehensively and by developing a recommendation that addressed CEO-level strategic questions, she demonstrated that she thought at a level several positions above her current role. This demonstration, backed by rigorous analysis that proved correct, made her the obvious candidate for increasing responsibility because she had already shown she could operate at those levels.

The management of your actual boss determines whether you advance or stagnate more directly than almost any other factor. The ninety-nine percent view their relationship with their manager as evaluative—the manager assesses their performance and determines their fate. This is backwards. Your relationship with your manager should be collaborative, with your success tied directly to your manager's success. When your manager succeeds in their goals, they advance or receive recognition. When they advance, they create vacancies that you might fill. When they receive recognition, they gain political capital that can be deployed to advocate for your advancement. Your job is making your boss successful, and the more instrumental you are in that success, the more invested they become in your advancement.

The practical implementation of managing up begins with understanding what your manager cares about most. Some managers prioritize hitting numerical targets and care primarily about whether your work contributes to those metrics. Some managers care about relationships with senior leadership and value employees who make them look good in those interactions. Some managers are overwhelmed by operational details and desperately need someone who can handle complexity without constant supervision. Some managers face resistance to their initiatives and need allies who can help build support. Each cares about different things, and you must identify what specifically your manager needs to be successful.

Once you understand what matters most to your manager, you align your efforts to address those priorities. If they care about metrics, you ensure that your work directly moves those metrics and that you report progress regularly so they have positive updates to share upward. If they care about senior leadership relationships, you make them look good by producing work that can be presented at executive meetings and by ensuring they never look uninformed when senior leaders ask about your area. If they are overwhelmed operationally, you take ownership of complex problems and solve them with minimal management attention required. If they face political resistance, you help build coalitions and communicate their initiatives positively to stakeholders.

This is not subservience or manipulation. This is recognition that organizational systems promote people who help others succeed, and that your most direct path to advancement runs through your immediate manager's success. The manager who depends on you for their own performance will advocate aggressively for your promotion because your advancement reflects well on their ability to develop talent and because they want to maintain access to your capabilities even as you take on broader responsibilities.

The management of people beneath you in hierarchy matters equally for advancement to leadership roles. Companies promote people to management based partly on evidence that they can develop others and build effective teams. If you have no direct reports in your current role, you create opportunities to demonstrate these capabilities through mentoring junior colleagues, leading cross-functional project teams, or organizing working groups that address specific challenges. The one percent engineer situations where they can demonstrate people development and team leadership long before they have formal management responsibilities.

When you do manage people directly, the approach that builds your reputation and prepares you for advancement focuses on developing talent rather than merely directing activities. You invest time coaching team members, you create opportunities for them to stretch beyond their current capabilities, you advocate for their advancement, and you document their growth under your leadership. When your team members advance, this reflects positively on your leadership capability. When they speak positively about your management, this creates organizational perception that you are effective developer of talent. When senior leaders see that people want to work for you, this signals that you possess leadership qualities that merit additional responsibility.

The volunteering for high-visibility projects represents perhaps the most direct mechanism for demonstrating capabilities beyond your current role while building relationships with senior leaders who control advancement decisions. High-visibility projects are initiatives that senior leadership cares about deeply, that involve multiple functions or divisions, that address strategic priorities, and that provide opportunities for exposure to executives who do not normally interact with people at your level. These projects invariably require significant additional work beyond your normal responsibilities, which is precisely why many people avoid them. The one percent seek them aggressively because they understand that these projects provide the visibility and relationship-building opportunities that drive promotion.

The identification of high-visibility opportunities requires attention to organizational priorities and awareness of which initiatives senior leadership discusses frequently in communications or meetings. When the CEO mentions strategic priorities in town halls or quarterly communications, those priorities represent areas where volunteer effort will be noticed. When your division president asks for volunteers to serve on task forces or working groups addressing specific challenges, these requests represent opportunities for visibility. When cross-functional initiatives are announced requiring collaboration across departments, these initiatives provide chances to build relationships outside your immediate area while demonstrating broader capability.

The execution of high-visibility projects determines whether the visibility helps or harms your advancement prospects. Taking on visible projects and failing to deliver destroys your reputation far more effectively than never volunteering at all. The one percent only volunteer for projects where they have genuine capability to contribute meaningfully and where they can commit the time required to deliver excellence. They understand that one excellent execution on a visible project advances their careers more than three mediocre executions that establish perception of overextension or inadequate capability.

The building of cross-functional relationships creates advancement opportunities that remaining siloed within your function cannot provide. The ninety-nine percent interact primarily with colleagues in their immediate team or function, developing deep expertise in their area while remaining unknown to leaders in other parts of the organization. This limits advancement because senior roles almost always require cross-functional collaboration and enterprise-wide perspective. The person who is known and respected only within their function appears as narrow specialist. The person who is known across multiple functions appears as potential leader who can operate at enterprise level.

The cultivation of cross-functional relationships begins with identifying whose work intersects with yours and reaching out to build collaborative relationships rather than transactional interactions. When you need something from another function, you invest time understanding their constraints and priorities rather than simply making requests. When they need something from your function, you respond with more than minimal cooperation required. You schedule periodic check-ins with key contacts in other functions to maintain relationships even when no immediate project requires interaction. These relationships accumulate into network that provides multiple benefits—easier collaboration when you need it, intelligence about opportunities and challenges in other areas, and people in other functions who can speak positively about you when advancement opportunities arise.

The documentation of your contributions determines whether your accomplishments are remembered and attributed to you or whether they disappear into collective organizational memory. The ninety-nine percent complete excellent work and assume that quality speaks for itself and that accomplishments will be remembered when promotion decisions are made. This is false. Organizations have short memories, managers change frequently, and the person who documented and communicated their contributions systematically has substantial advantage over equally accomplished person who simply did great work without ensuring it was visible and attributed correctly.

The practical documentation involves maintaining records of major projects completed, results achieved with specific metrics, recognition received from internal or external sources, and capabilities demonstrated through various assignments. This documentation should be updated quarterly at minimum, capturing accomplishments while they are fresh rather than attempting to reconstruct them from memory when performance reviews or promotion discussions occur. The one percent maintain this documentation as routine business practice rather than preperformance-review scramble.

The communication of accomplishments requires balance between self-promotion that appears boastful and silence that ensures you are forgotten. The approach that works is framing accomplishments as team successes while ensuring your specific contribution is clear, sharing results through regular updates to managers and stakeholders rather than waiting for formal reviews, and using objective metrics that speak for themselves rather than subjective claims about your excellence. When you led a project that increased efficiency by twenty-seven percent, stating this fact with the context of the project represents appropriate communication rather than boasting. When you helped a colleague solve a complex problem, mentioning this in your regular update to your manager provides visibility without appearing to seek credit inappropriately.

The asking for promotions and raises separates those who actively manage their careers from those who wait passively for recognition that may never arrive. The ninety-nine percent believe that excellent performance should be recognized and rewarded automatically, and they feel uncomfortable advocating for themselves. The one percent understand that promotion decisions involve budget constraints, political considerations, and competing priorities, and that their advancement interests them far more than they interest anyone else in the organization. They advocate for themselves systematically while providing clear justification based on their performance and market value.

The timing of advancement requests matters substantially. You should not ask for promotion immediately after receiving one, as this signals that you are never satisfied and that granting promotions will not retain you. You should not wait years after becoming qualified for the next level, as this signals that you do not value your own advancement enough to advocate for it. The appropriate timing is approximately eighteen to twenty-four months after your last significant advancement, assuming you have demonstrated capabilities justifying next-level responsibility during that period.

The framing of your request should focus on your readiness for increased responsibility based on capabilities you have demonstrated rather than on your tenure, your financial needs, or your feelings about deserving recognition. You prepare specific examples of how you have operated at the next level while in your current role, how you have delivered results that match or exceed expectations at that level, and how you have developed capabilities that prepare you for that level's responsibilities. You request a meeting with your manager specifically to discuss your career progression rather than raising the topic during routine one-on-one meetings where it will receive inadequate attention.

The response to being told you are not ready for promotion yet determines whether you eventually advance or whether you stagnate. When managers cite specific gaps or capabilities you need to develop, you should treat this as roadmap rather than as rejection. You clarify exactly what you need to demonstrate to be considered ready, you establish timeline for reassessing your readiness, and you document this conversation so that both parties have clear understanding of expectations. Then you systematically address the gaps identified while building evidence that you have developed the capabilities in question. This transforms a "not yet" into a "yes" within defined timeframe rather than allowing it to remain perpetual "not yet" that never resolves.

The decision about when to leave your current company for external opportunities represents perhaps the most significant career advancement choice most people face. The ninety-nine percent remain at companies far longer than optimal because they are comfortable, because they fear the unknown, or because they believe loyalty will be rewarded. The one percent recognize that external moves typically generate larger compensation increases and faster advancement than internal promotions, and they monitor market opportunities continuously even when they are satisfied with current roles.

The general principle is that after two to four years at a company, your compensation and advancement trajectory often lag what external market would offer. Internal promotion budgets are constrained by existing salary structures and by the fact that the company already has you and sees limited risk of losing you absent clear signals that you are actively looking. External offers are unconstrained by your current salary and they must be competitive with what other companies might offer to attract you. The difference often represents fifteen to thirty percent increases in compensation for lateral moves and thirty to fifty percent increases when moving to higher-level roles.

The strategic approach is remaining at companies long enough to build track record and reputation but not so long that you are typecast in particular role or level. The typical pattern for the one percent is two to four years at each company during the peak careerbuilding years from late twenties through early forties. This provides enough time to deliver meaningful accomplishments while maintaining momentum through regular moves to increasing responsibility. After reaching senior levels where opportunities are fewer and advancement is slower, this pattern may change to longer tenures, but during the critical building years, regular external moves accelerate advancement beyond what internal progression typically allows.

The exception to this pattern involves companies where you have unusually strong trajectory, where mentors actively champion your advancement, or where you are positioned to capture significant equity value through acquisition or public offering. The person who joins a startup with meaningful equity stake and clear path to senior leadership may benefit more from remaining through exit event than from moving for higher salary elsewhere. The person who has senior champion advocating aggressively for their advancement may progress faster internally than they could through external moves.

These situations are notable precisely because they are exceptions to the pattern that external moves typically accelerate advancement.

The reading of organizational politics determines whether you navigate reorganizations successfully or whether you find yourself marginalized or eliminated when structures change. The ninety-nine percent view politics as distasteful manipulation that they prefer to avoid through focusing solely on work quality. This is naive. Politics is simply the reality of how decisions get made when multiple stakeholders have competing interests and limited resources must be allocated among various priorities. The person who ignores politics does not avoid it—they simply ensure that others make political decisions affecting them without their input or influence.

The organizational politics you must understand include identifying who has real power versus formal authority, understanding which executives are ascending versus which are in decline, recognizing which initiatives have genuine senior support versus which are performative, and knowing which relationships matter for protection during reorganizations. These things are rarely explicit in organizational charts or official communications. They are revealed through careful observation of whose opinions carry weight in meetings, whose projects receive resources and attention, who gets assigned to high-visibility opportunities, and who has access to senior leaders.

The navigation of reorganizations requires having built relationships across multiple parts of the organization so that you have options and advocates regardless of how structures change. The person who is deeply embedded in a single function or who has strong relationship with only one executive is vulnerable to any change that affects that function or that executive's standing. The person who has built reputation and relationships across the enterprise has multiple parties who might want to retain them or who might advocate for them when decisions are being made about who stays and who goes.

Indra Nooyi's advancement at PepsiCo exemplified every principle discussed in this chapter. She demonstrated capabilities beyond her role by analyzing enterprise-wide strategy. She made her bosses successful by providing them with strategic insights that solved problems they faced. She built relationships across the organization by working on initiatives that spanned multiple functions. She documented and communicated her contributions through presentations to senior leadership. She asked for increasing responsibility explicitly rather than waiting to be noticed. She understood organizational politics well enough to know which executives supported her and which initiatives mattered most. The result was twelve-year progression from senior vice president to CEO of a Fortune 500 company.

This is not exceptional intelligence or rare capability. This is systematic application of career advancement principles that are knowable and learnable but that most people never discover or never implement. You have now been provided the complete framework. You understand that job performance is necessary but insufficient for advancement. You understand how to manage up by making your boss successful and how to manage down by developing people who advance under your leadership. You understand the value of high-visibility projects and cross-functional relationships. You understand how to document accomplishments and communicate them appropriately. You understand when to ask for promotion and when to seek external opportunities. You understand that politics is reality rather than distraction and that navigating it successfully is essential for advancement.

The implementation of this framework over twenty to thirty years of career development determines whether you increase your income from entry-level salary to multiple six figures or whether you plateau at some middle level where your earning capacity remains modest. The person who enters workforce at forty thousand and advances systematically to two hundred fifty thousand accumulates dramatically more wealth than equally capable person who enters at forty thousand and stagnates at eighty thousand despite competent performance. The income differential compounds over decades into millions of dollars in accumulated wealth difference.

The one percent understand that career advancement is not something that happens to them based on merit or luck. It is something they engineer systematically through strategic application of principles that govern how organizations actually make advancement decisions. They do not wait to be noticed. They create visibility. They do not hope that performance speaks for itself. They document and communicate accomplishments. They do not assume loyalty will be rewarded. They pursue external opportunities when internal advancement stalls. They do not avoid politics. They understand and navigate it effectively.

You have been provided education about every aspect of wealth building from foundations through strategies to execution. Career advancement is the mechanism that provides the income to fund all other wealth-building activities. Without advancing your income, you cannot build substantial wealth regardless of how well you invest or how disciplined your spending becomes. The frameworks for advancement exist. The principles are clear. The implementation requires consistent application over years rather than occasional effort. The one percent implement these principles systematically. The ninety-nine percent hope that competent performance and likability will suffice and then wonder why they remain stuck while less talented colleagues advance past them.

The choice here is whether to engineer your career advancement strategically using the frameworks provided or whether to rely on meritocracy that does not actually exist in any pure form. The former leads to income growth that funds substantial wealth accumulation. The latter leads to income stagnation that prevents wealth building regardless of other good decisions. You now understand how career advancement actually works versus how most people believe it works. The gap between these understandings explains most of the differential outcomes people experience in corporate environments.

CHAPTER 18:
HOUSE FLIPPING—TRADING LABOR FOR PROFIT

In 2008, a young couple in Orange County, California, faced financial catastrophe. Tarek El Moussa had been working as a real estate agent during the housing boom, earning substantial commissions by selling properties in the overheated Southern California market. When the market collapsed, his income disappeared almost overnight. He and his wife Christina found themselves with no income, mounting debts, and an uncertain future. Most people in their situation would have scrambled for any employment they could find, perhaps leaving real estate entirely for more stable industries. The El Moussas recognized something different in the crisis surrounding them.

Properties across Southern California were being foreclosed at unprecedented rates. Homes that had sold for six hundred thousand dollars in 2006 were being auctioned for three hundred thousand or less. Banks were desperate to clear inventory and were accepting offers far below pre-crash values. Tarek understood that while the retail real estate market had collapsed, an opportunity existed for those with the knowledge to identify undervalued properties, the skills to renovate them efficiently, and the nerve to operate in a market where most participants were fleeing in panic.

The couple scraped together enough capital to purchase their first foreclosed property for a fraction of its former value. They had minimal renovation experience and even less capital for extensive improvements. What they did have was Tarek's understanding of what buyers wanted based on his years showing properties, Christina's eye for design that could be implemented inexpensively, and their willingness to do much of the work themselves to minimize costs. They renovated the property over six weeks, sold it for a profit of thirty-four thousand dollars, and immediately deployed that profit into purchasing their next property.

They systematized the process over the following months. They developed relationships with wholesalers who brought them deals before properties reached the open market. They built a network of contractors who could execute renovations on predictable timelines and budgets. They created checklists and cost estimation spreadsheets that allowed them to evaluate properties rapidly and bid confidently. They established relationships with hard money lenders who would finance purchases when their own capital was deployed in other projects. Within three years, they had flipped dozens of properties and generated millions in profits. Their success eventually led to a television show documenting their business, though by that point they had already achieved financial security through the systematic application of house flipping principles during a period when opportunity was obvious to anyone willing to act while others were paralyzed by fear.

House flipping is not passive real estate investing. This distinction must be established clearly because the wealth-building frameworks we have discussed in previous chapters emphasized patient capital deployment, compound returns over decades, and minimal time commitment. Flipping houses is active business that trades your time, expertise, and risk tolerance for profits that can be generated in months rather than years or decades. The person who succeeds at flipping is operating a business that manufactures value through renovation and sells products in the form of improved properties. This requires completely different skills and mindset than buying rental properties and holding them for long-term appreciation and cash flow.

The economics of house flipping depend on identifying properties trading below their potential value, improving them through renovation, and selling them quickly for more than your total invested capital including purchase price, renovation costs, financing costs, and transaction expenses. The mathematics are straightforward but unforgiving. If you purchase a property for two hundred thousand dollars, invest fifty thousand in renovations, pay ten thousand in financing and holding costs, and incur twenty-five thousand in transaction costs for both purchase and sale, you need to sell for at least two hundred eighty-five thousand just to break even. Your profit exists only to the extent that you can sell for more than this break-even figure.

Most markets and most properties do not offer this spread between distressed purchase price and renovated sale price. The opportunities exist in specific circumstances where motivated sellers or unusual conditions create temporary dislocations between a property's current value and its potential value after improvements. The housing crisis of 2008 through 2012 created these circumstances systematically across much of the United States. Foreclosed properties flooded the market, banks were accepting discounts to clear inventory, and retail buyers were scarce due to tight lending standards. These conditions created ideal environment for flippers who could access capital and execute renovations while traditional homebuyers were largely absent from the market.

The subsequent years through the present have seen far fewer systematic opportunities because property prices have recovered and in many markets exceeded pre-crisis levels. The spreads that made flipping profitable during the crisis have compressed or disappeared in most markets. This does not mean flipping opportunities no longer exist, but it means you cannot succeed simply by buying any distressed property and renovating it. You must find the specific properties where the spread exists, and you must execute renovations efficiently enough to capture that spread without destroying it through cost overruns or extended timelines that increase holding costs.

The identification of properties suitable for flipping begins with understanding what creates the spread between current and potential value. Properties become undervalued relative to their potential through several mechanisms. Distress sales occur when owners face foreclosure, divorce, bankruptcy, or death and need to liquidate quickly without time for proper marketing. These sellers often accept below-market offers to achieve certainty and speed.

Deferred maintenance occurs when owners lack capital or motivation to maintain properties properly, allowing them to deteriorate until they present poorly to typical buyers but still possess sound structure underneath cosmetic problems. Poor design or outdated finishes reduce property appeal to modern buyers even when the home is structurally sound and located in desirable area.

The challenge is that these conditions are visible to everyone with access to Multiple Listing Service or foreclosure auction listings. The properties that represent obvious opportunities receive multiple competing bids from other flippers, driving prices upward until the spread compresses and the deal becomes marginal or unprofitable. The flippers who succeed consistently have developed mechanisms for finding properties before they reach broader market awareness. They build relationships with wholesalers who identify distressed properties and put them under contract, then assign those contracts to flippers for fees. They network with probate attorneys who represent estates that need to liquidate inherited properties. They contact divorce attorneys whose clients need to sell homes quickly. They mail letters directly to owners of properties showing signs of distress or neglect. These direct marketing approaches generate leads that face no competition because the properties never reach the open market.

The analysis of whether a specific property represents profitable flip opportunity requires disciplined estimation of both potential after-repair value and total renovation costs. The after-repair value is what the property should sell for once renovations are complete and it has been properly marketed. This figure is determined by examining comparable sales of similar properties in similar condition in the same neighborhood within the past three to six months. You must adjust these comparables for differences in square footage, bedroom and bathroom count, lot size, and features. Most novice flippers overestimate after-repair value by using comparables that are not truly comparable or by assuming their property will command premium pricing despite lacking features that justify such pricing.

The renovation cost estimation determines whether the deal works financially. This is where most novice flippers destroy their profits through systematic underestimation of costs and timelines. They walk through properties, make mental notes about needed repairs, develop rough cost estimates based on intuition or limited research, and convince themselves the property can be renovated for far less than it actually requires. Then reality arrives in the form of hidden structural issues discovered during renovation, permit requirements that were not anticipated, contractor delays that extend timelines, and material cost increases that exceed original estimates. The original fifty-thousand-dollar renovation budget becomes seventy-five thousand or more, and the profit margin that appeared comfortable when the property was purchased evaporates entirely.

The disciplined approach to cost estimation begins with comprehensive property inspection before purchase. You walk through the property systematically, documenting every issue requiring attention. You photograph conditions to ensure accurate memory later. You hire professional inspectors to identify structural, electrical, plumbing, and foundation issues that you might miss. You research permit requirements with the local building department to understand what work requires permits and inspections. You obtain bids from contractors for major work categories before finalizing your purchase decision rather than assuming you know what work will cost.

The cost estimation spreadsheet should break down every renovation category with specific line items. Roof replacement if needed, with separate entries for materials, labor, and disposal. HVAC system replacement or repair. Electrical updates required for code compliance. Plumbing repairs or replacements. Foundation work if inspection revealed issues. Structural repairs to framing or supports. Exterior work including siding, paint, landscaping, and hardscaping. Kitchen renovation broken down by cabinets, countertops, appliances, flooring, and fixtures. Bathroom renovations with similar detail. Flooring throughout the home. Interior paint. Lighting fixtures. Doors and hardware. Window replacement if required. The total from this detailed estimation should then be increased by twenty to thirty percent to account for items you missed, changes you make during renovation, and cost increases that occur during the project. This contingency appears excessive to novice flippers who are optimistic about their estimates, but it proves essential when reality does not match optimistic assumptions.

The final determination of whether to purchase requires calculating your maximum allowable offer based on after-repair value and estimated costs. The standard formula in the flipping industry is that your maximum offer should be seventy percent of after-repair value minus renovation costs. If a property should sell for three hundred thousand after renovation and requires fifty thousand in improvements, your maximum offer is one hundred sixty thousand. This formula provides margin for the transaction costs, financing costs, holding costs, and profit that must come from the spread between your total investment and the sale price.

Many properties fail this formula test, which is why successful flippers evaluate dozens or hundreds of properties before finding one that represents genuine opportunity. The ninety-nine percent become emotionally attached to properties, convince themselves that they can make deals work through superior execution, and purchase properties that never had adequate margin. The one percent walk away from deals that do not meet their criteria regardless of how much time they invested in analysis or how appealing the property appears. They understand that discipline in property selection prevents losses that cannot be recovered through superior renovation execution.

The financing of house flips typically involves hard money lenders rather than conventional mortgages because conventional financing requires owner occupancy and longer closing periods than most flip opportunities allow. Hard money lenders provide short-term loans secured by the property, typically with terms of six to twelve months, interest rates of eight to twelve percent, and origination fees of two to five percent of the loan amount. These costs seem high compared to conventional mortgage rates, but they provide speed and flexibility that conventional financing cannot match. You can close hard money loans in days rather than weeks, you can finance properties that need substantial renovation, and you can repay without penalty when you sell the property.

The mathematics of hard money financing must be incorporated into your deal analysis. If you borrow two hundred thousand at ten percent for six months plus three percent origination, your financing costs are ten thousand in interest plus six thousand in origination fees for a total of sixteen thousand. This amount must be covered by your spread between purchase price and sale price or your profit is reduced by the full financing cost. Many novice flippers fail to properly account for financing costs in their initial analysis, discovering only after purchase that these costs have consumed much of their projected profit.

The renovation management determines whether your cost and timeline estimates prove accurate or whether the project spirals into extended delays and cost overruns that destroy profitability. The fundamental choice is whether to serve as your own general contractor, managing all trades and suppliers directly, or whether to hire a general contractor who coordinates everything for a markup of ten to twenty percent. The tradeoff is between saving the general contractor's markup versus investing substantial time in project management and accepting risk that your inexperience causes delays or quality issues.

The person who chooses to serve as their own general contractor must develop systems for managing multiple simultaneous activities. You create detailed project schedules showing when each trade needs to perform their work and what dependencies exist between trades. You cannot install flooring until drywall is complete and painted. You cannot install countertops until cabinets are set. You cannot perform final plumbing connections until finishes are in place. Understanding and managing these sequences prevents trades from showing up for work before they can actually proceed, which wastes their time and damages relationships. You maintain regular communication with every trade, confirming schedules multiple times before their planned work dates and following up immediately when anyone fails to appear as scheduled.

The contractor relationships determine whether your renovations proceed smoothly or whether you face constant struggles with quality, reliability, and pricing. The one percent build networks of contractors who perform specific trades competently, reliably, and at fair prices. They develop these networks through trial and error over multiple projects, testing various contractors and eventually identifying those who consistently meet expectations. They maintain these relationships through fair treatment, prompt payment, regular work volume that makes them valuable customers, and clear communication about expectations. Once established, these contractor networks provide enormous competitive advantage because you can estimate costs accurately based on known pricing and you can schedule work confidently based on proven reliability.

The permit process receives insufficient attention from novice flippers who either ignore permit requirements entirely or underestimate the time and cost involved in obtaining permits. Operating without required permits is illegal and it creates problems when you attempt to sell the property. Buyers conducting inspections discover unpermitted work, which raises questions about work quality and code compliance. This can kill sales or force price reductions that exceed what the permits would have cost. The disciplined approach is researching permit requirements before purchase, incorporating permit costs into your renovation budget, and scheduling permit applications early in your project timeline to avoid delays when work requires inspection before proceeding.

The scope management during renovation separates profitable flips from money-losing disasters. The temptation during renovation is to upgrade beyond your original plan whenever you discover additional issues or whenever you convince yourself that additional improvements will increase sale price. This scope creep destroys budgets because the additional expenditures rarely generate proportional increases in sale price. The one percent define renovation scope based on what comparable properties in the neighborhood offer and what is required to bring the property to competitive standard. They resist the temptation to over-improve because they understand that luxury finishes in a modest neighborhood do not generate returns justifying their cost. They make changes during renovation only when they discover conditions that must be addressed for safety or code compliance, and they immediately adjust their profit projections to reflect these additional costs rather than pretending the overages will not affect their bottom line.

The timeline management matters as much as cost management because every month you hold the property costs money in financing charges, property taxes, insurance, utilities, and opportunity cost of capital tied up in this project rather than deployed in your next one. The property that requires three months to renovate and sell generates far better annualized return than the property that requires nine months despite similar dollar profit. The one percent create aggressive but realistic timelines based on their contractor network's typical performance. They monitor progress weekly and they address delays immediately rather than hoping schedules will self-correct. They understand that construction projects rarely finish early but they frequently run late, so they build modest time buffers into their plans while pushing to complete as quickly as possible.

The marketing and sale process begins before renovation is complete. The one percent hire photographers to create professional listing photos immediately upon completion. They stage properties with furniture and decor that helps buyers visualize living in the space. They price properties based on recent comparable sales rather than on what they need to achieve their target profit, understanding that the market determines price and that overpricing extends time on market while carrying costs accumulate. They work with real estate agents who have strong track records in their target neighborhoods and who can provide realistic pricing guidance rather than inflated estimates designed to win listings.

The common mistakes that destroy novice house flippers are predictable and entirely avoidable through discipline and education. The first mistake is purchasing properties without adequate margin because they convinced themselves they could find ways to make the numbers work. The second mistake is underestimating renovation costs through optimism or insufficient due diligence. The third mistake is overimproving properties beyond neighborhood standards in hopes of commanding premium prices. The fourth mistake is poor contractor management leading to delays and cost overruns. The fifth mistake is operating without required permits to save money, creating problems during sale. The sixth mistake is allowing emotional attachment to properties to cloud judgment about when to cut losses rather than continuing to pour money into unprofitable projects.

The psychology required for successful house flipping differs dramatically from the psychology required for long-term investing. Long-term investing rewards patience, emotional detachment from price fluctuations, and focus on decades-long horizons. House flipping rewards aggressive action, disciplined risk management, and willingness to walk away from situations not working as planned. The person who succeeds at flipping must be comfortable making rapid decisions with incomplete information, must tolerate the stress of managing complex projects with multiple moving parts, and must maintain emotional equilibrium when projects encounter inevitable problems that require immediate attention and additional capital to resolve.

The business structure for house flipping should be established formally through entity formation that provides liability protection and appropriate tax treatment. Most flippers operate through Limited Liability Companies that provide personal liability protection while allowing pass-through taxation where profits are taxed on personal returns rather than at entity level. The specific structure should be determined in consultation with attorneys and tax advisors who understand real estate business operations and can recommend optimal configuration for your circumstances.

The tax treatment of house flipping differs from long-term real estate investing in important ways. Properties you renovate and sell within one year generate ordinary income taxed at your marginal rate rather than long-term capital gains taxed at preferential rates. If you flip properties regularly, the IRS may classify you as a dealer rather than investor, which means all profits are ordinary income regardless of holding period and you cannot use 1031 exchanges to defer taxes. This classification also subjects your profits to self-employment taxes of approximately fifteen percent in addition to ordinary income taxes. The total tax burden on flipping profits can reach forty to fifty percent when combining federal, state, and self-employment taxes. This must be incorporated into your profitability calculations because after-tax profit is what actually matters for wealth building.

The scaling of house flipping business from individual projects to systematic operation requires building infrastructure that most people never develop. You need systems for generating deal flow consistently rather than finding properties opportunistically. You need networks of contractors who can execute multiple projects simultaneously rather than working with whatever contractors are available when you find a property. You need relationships with multiple capital sources so you can finance several projects at once rather than completing one before starting another. You need team members who can manage projects while you focus on deal analysis and business development rather than attempting to personally oversee every renovation detail.

Tarek and Christina El Moussa built exactly this infrastructure over their first several years of flipping. They systemized their property evaluation so they could rapidly determine whether opportunities merited detailed analysis. They developed contractor networks that allowed them to renovate multiple properties simultaneously. They established hard money lending relationships that provided capital for multiple projects. They eventually hired project managers who supervised renovations while they focused on finding deals and growing the business. This systematization allowed them to scale from flipping several properties annually to flipping dozens while maintaining quality and profitability.

The relationship between house flipping and long-term wealth building is complex. Flipping generates rapid profits that can be deployed into rental properties or other investments if you maintain discipline. The person who flips properties and spends the profits on consumption builds no lasting wealth despite generating substantial income. The person who flips properties and deploys profits into acquiring rental properties or into stock market investments builds wealth through both the immediate profits from flipping and the long-term compound returns from deploying those profits strategically. This is the optimal use of flipping—as mechanism for generating capital rapidly that can be deployed into assets that generate long-term passive income and appreciation.

The decision about whether to pursue house flipping depends entirely on your circumstances, risk tolerance, skill set, and wealth-building timeline. Flipping makes sense for people who have renovation knowledge or willingness to develop it quickly, who have access to initial capital either personally or through lending relationships, who can tolerate the stress of managing complex projects with uncertain outcomes, and who need to generate capital more rapidly than long-term investing typically allows. Flipping makes no sense for people who prefer passive investment approaches, who lack time to manage active projects, who cannot tolerate the possibility of losing capital when deals go wrong, or who have already established strong income streams that fund systematic long-term investing.

The opportunity landscape for house flipping changes continuously based on market conditions. The crisis years of 2008 through 2012 provided systematic opportunities that required only modest skill to capture profitably. The subsequent recovery years compressed margins and increased competition, requiring far greater skill and discipline to succeed. Future market cycles will create new opportunities during downturns when distressed inventory increases and competition decreases. The person who develops flipping expertise during normal markets positions themselves to capitalize on exceptional opportunities when the next crisis inevitably arrives.

We have now examined every major wealth-building strategy from stock market investing through real estate rental property acquisition, real estate tax optimization, and house flipping. Each strategy serves different purposes and suits different personality types.

Stock market investing through index funds is passive, requires minimal expertise, and produces wealth reliably over decades through compound returns. Rental property investing is less passive, requires more expertise in property selection and management, and produces wealth through multiple simultaneous sources including cash flow, appreciation, mortgage paydown, and tax benefits. House flipping is active business rather than investment, requires substantial expertise in renovation and project management, and produces wealth through rapid profit generation that must be deployed wisely to create lasting value.

The one percent often combine multiple strategies across their wealth-building years. They might begin with stock market investing while building income and learning about other options. They might add rental property investing once they have accumulated capital for down payments and developed real estate knowledge. They might pursue house flipping during periods when their time availability allows active project management and when market conditions provide opportunity. They deploy profits from active strategies like flipping into passive strategies like rental properties and stock investments, gradually building portfolios that generate increasing passive income requiring less ongoing management attention.

The ninety-nine percent typically commit to single strategies based on initial preference or accidental introduction to particular approaches, missing opportunities to combine strategies synergistically. Or they attempt multiple strategies simultaneously without adequate capital or expertise for any of them, spreading themselves too thin and failing to execute any strategy well. The optimal approach is mastering strategies sequentially while deploying profits from earlier successes into additional strategies as your capital, knowledge, and capacity allow.

You have now been educated about every major wealth-building strategy and every significant decision affecting wealth accumulation. House flipping represents one option among several, suitable for certain people in certain circumstances. It is not essential for wealth building, as the long-term strategies discussed previously can generate substantial wealth without ever flipping a single property. But for those with appropriate skill sets and circumstances, flipping provides mechanism for rapid profit generation that can accelerate wealth building beyond what passive strategies alone typically produce. Whether you pursue this approach depends on honest assessment of your capabilities, risk tolerance, and circumstances.

CHAPTER 19:
BUDGETING—PAY YOURSELF FIRST

In 1926, a insurance agent and businessman named George Clason published a slim volume titled "*The Richest Man in Babylon*" that would influence financial thinking for the next century. The book presented ancient Babylonian parables about wealth building, though Clason had in fact written the stories himself based on principles he had observed during his decades working in business and publishing. The central character, Arkad, began his life as a poor scribe in ancient Babylon and ended it as the wealthiest man in the city. When his childhood friends asked him to reveal the secret of wealth accumulation, he provided advice so simple that it seemed almost insulting: "A part of all you earn is yours to keep."

The friends protested that they already kept everything they earned. Arkad explained that this was false. They earned money and immediately spent it on housing, food, clothing, entertainment, and countless other expenses. By the time their spending was complete, nothing remained. What they kept was not their earnings but the brief satisfaction of consumption that faded almost immediately after purchase. Arkad's principle was that before paying anyone else, before buying anything, before any expense was incurred, a portion of earnings should be set aside and never touched for consumption. This portion belonged to your future self rather than to your present circumstances. Pay yourself first, Arkad advised, and then live on what remains.

This principle sounds obvious to the point of being simplistic, yet the vast majority of people violate it constantly throughout their entire working lives. They receive paychecks, pay their bills, spend on groceries and gas and entertainment and countless small purchases, and then save whatever remains at the end of the month. What remains is almost always nothing or nearly nothing because spending expands to consume available resources. This is Parkinson's Law applied to personal finance: expenses rise to meet income regardless of how much income increases. The person earning forty thousand annually and the person earning one hundred fifty thousand annually both somehow arrive at month's end with depleted accounts and vague uncertainty about where the money went.

The one percent invert this sequence entirely. They determine what percentage of income they will save and invest before receiving their paychecks. They establish automatic transfers that move this predetermined amount into investment accounts the moment income arrives. Only after this transfer occurs do they consider what remains available for living expenses. This forces them to live on less than they earn because the money designated for savings never exists as available funds for spending. The sequence is critical. Decide your savings rate, automate the transfer, then structure your life around what remains. Attempting to save what remains after spending ensures that nothing remains to be saved.

The determination of appropriate savings rate depends on income level, current expenses, wealth-building goals, and timeline to financial independence. Someone earning $40,000 annually with high fixed expenses might struggle to save 15% initially though they should work systematically toward this minimum threshold. Someone earning $100,000 annually should be saving 30 to 40 percent because their after-tax income substantially exceeds reasonable living expenses in most geographies. Someone earning $200,000 or more should be saving 50 to 60 percent or higher because the income at this level provides far more than necessary to maintain excellent quality of life while building substantial wealth.

These percentages seem extreme to most people because they are mentally allocating their income as it has always been allocated, with housing consuming thirty percent, transportation consuming fifteen percent, food consuming ten percent, and so forth until the entire income is consumed by some combination of fixed and discretionary expenses. The one percent design their lives around their target savings rate rather than designing their savings around their lifestyle. If your goal is saving forty percent of a one hundred thousand dollar income, you have sixty thousand dollars after tax to fund all living expenses. You choose housing, transportation, food, and entertainment that fit within this constraint rather than choosing these items first and hoping you can save from what remains.

This requires examining every major spending category with the explicit objective of minimizing costs without sacrificing fundamental quality of life. Housing receives first attention because it typically represents the largest single expense and because excessive housing costs destroy wealth-building capacity more reliably than any other category. We have addressed housing extensively in Chapter Nine regarding the rent versus buy decision. The principle here is that housing should consume no more than twenty-five to thirty percent of gross income maximum, and the one percent often keep it substantially below this threshold particularly during wealth-building years. Someone earning one hundred thousand annually should be spending no more than twenty-five to thirty thousand on housing costs annually. This is approximately two thousand to twenty-five hundred monthly for all housing expenses including rent or mortgage, insurance, property taxes, and utilities.

Achieving this housing cost target in expensive cities requires either accepting smaller or less conveniently located housing than cultural norms suggest you should have at your income level, or it requires house hacking approaches discussed in Chapter Seven where rental income from tenants offsets most or all of your housing costs. The person who insists on living alone in a one-bedroom apartment in an expensive neighborhood will pay three thousand monthly or more, consuming thirty-six thousand annually and destroying their capacity to save forty percent of one hundred thousand dollar income. The person who accepts roommates or who house hacks in a duplex where a tenant pays most of the housing costs saves twenty-four thousand annually in housing expenses. This difference of twenty-four thousand invested annually at ten percent returns becomes over six hundred twenty-five thousand in twenty years. Your insistence on living alone costs you more than half a million dollars in wealth over two decades.

Transportation receives second attention as the second-largest expense category for most people. We addressed vehicle acquisition and ownership in Chapter Eleven. The principle for budgeting purposes is that total transportation costs including vehicle depreciation, insurance, fuel, maintenance, and parking should not exceed ten to fifteen percent of gross income. Someone earning one hundred thousand annually should spend no more than ten to fifteen thousand annually on transportation. This is approximately eight hundred to twelve hundred fifty monthly for all transportation expenses. Achieving this target requires driving older paid-off vehicles, using public transportation where available, or combining these approaches. The person financing a new forty-thousand-dollar vehicle paying five hundred monthly for the loan, plus two hundred monthly for insurance, plus one hundred fifty monthly for fuel, plus one hundred monthly for maintenance and parking, is spending nine hundred fifty monthly or eleven thousand four hundred annually on transportation. This fits within the budget if barely. The person financing two new vehicles for a household is spending double this amount and has destroyed their capacity to save meaningful percentages of income.

Food represents the third major category where costs can be controlled substantially without sacrificing nutrition or reasonable quality of life. The average American household spends approximately ten to fifteen percent of gross income on food including both groceries and restaurant meals. The one percent reduce this to five to eight percent through systematic approaches to grocery shopping and severe limitation of restaurant meals. Someone earning one hundred thousand annually spending seven percent on food allocates seven thousand annually, which is approximately five hundred eighty monthly or one hundred thirty-five weekly for all food costs. This requires cooking most meals at home, shopping strategically for groceries, limiting expensive proteins and prepared foods, and treating restaurant meals as rare exceptions rather than regular occurrences. The next chapter will address grocery strategy in detail, but for budgeting purposes the key is recognizing that cutting food costs from fifteen percent to seven percent saves eight thousand annually on a one hundred thousand dollar income. This eight thousand invested annually at ten percent returns becomes over two hundred eight thousand in twenty years.

The elimination of all remaining budget categories into a single discretionary spending allocation prevents the micromanagement trap that causes most budgets to fail. The ninety-nine percent attempt detailed tracking of dozens of spending categories, recording every coffee purchase and clothing expense and entertainment cost. This becomes exhausting administrative burden that people abandon within weeks or months. The one percent establish targets for the three major categories of housing, transportation, and food, then create a single discretionary category for everything else. As long as they stay within their overall savings target and their major category limits, they can spend the discretionary funds however they choose without tracking every transaction.

The mathematics for someone earning one hundred thousand annually targeting forty percent savings might look as follows. Gross income of one hundred thousand becomes approximately seventy-five thousand after federal, state, and payroll taxes depending on location and filing status. Target savings of forty thousand means thirty-five thousand available for all living expenses. Housing consumes twenty-four thousand annually. Transportation consumes ten thousand annually. Food consumes seven thousand annually. The major categories total forty-one thousand, which exceeds the available thirty-five thousand by six thousand. This person must either reduce major expenses by six thousand through cheaper housing or transportation, or they must reduce their savings rate from forty percent to thirty-two percent to balance the budget.

This reveals the reality that aggressive savings rates require aggressive expense management. You cannot maintain typical American spending patterns while saving forty to fifty percent of income unless your income is extraordinarily high. The one percent accept this reality and design their lives accordingly. They live in smaller homes or share housing. They drive old vehicles or use public transportation. They cook their meals and pack lunches. They choose free entertainment over expensive activities. These choices are uncomfortable because they create visible differences between their lifestyles and their peers' lifestyles. Friends and family question why someone earning good income lives so modestly. The criticism and incomprehension are prices paid for wealth building that most people are unwilling to pay, which is precisely why most people never build substantial wealth.

The automation of savings prevents the decision from being made monthly based on how you feel about your spending that month or whether you feel you can afford to save. The ninety-nine percent intend to save but they evaluate this intention monthly when they review their account balances. Some months they saved because expenses happened to be lower. Other months they saved nothing because expenses were higher or because they decided they deserved to spend more given how hard they had worked. This approach guarantees minimal wealth accumulation because the decision to save or spend is made when spending is most tempting rather than when commitment to future self is clearest.

The one percent eliminate this monthly decision entirely through automatic transfers executed the day after paychecks deposit. Their checking accounts never contain their full paychecks. The money appears and immediately a predetermined percentage transfers to investment accounts, never to return except in genuine emergencies. What remains in the checking account is available for spending, but the savings portion is simply not accessible for spending temptations. This automation requires approximately one hour of setup time establishing automatic transfers from checking accounts to retirement accounts, taxable brokerage accounts, and other investment vehicles. Once established, the system operates indefinitely without requiring willpower or monthly decisions.

The psychological benefit of this automation exceeds even the financial benefit. You never feel deprived or like you are sacrificing because the money transferred to savings never registered as available for spending. You live on what remains without thinking about what could have been spent differently. Contrast this with the person who sees their full paycheck in their checking account, spends most of it during the month, then attempts to transfer what remains to savings at month end. They see exactly what they are giving up by saving that final five hundred or thousand dollars. They know the vacation or purchase or restaurant meals they could have enjoyed with that money. The psychological difficulty of this choice means they often choose immediate gratification over future wealth.

The emergency fund represents the one exception to the rule of automatically investing all savings. Before beginning aggressive investment in retirement accounts and taxable brokerage accounts, you must establish emergency fund covering three to six months of living expenses. This fund sits in high-yield savings account earning whatever interest rates such accounts currently offer. The purpose is providing resources to handle unexpected expenses or temporary income loss without disrupting long-term investments or accumulating high-interest debt. The person who loses their job and has no emergency fund must either sell investments at potentially unfavorable times or must rack up credit card debt at high interest rates to cover basic expenses while job searching. The person with adequate emergency fund handles the same job loss by drawing on the fund while maintaining all long-term investments and incurring no debt.

The appropriate emergency fund size depends on income stability and expense flexibility. Someone with volatile income or high fixed expenses should maintain six months or more in emergency funds. Someone with stable employment and flexible expenses might maintain three months. The calculation is monthly expenses multiplied by the target number of months. Someone spending three thousand monthly targeting six months of coverage needs eighteen thousand in emergency fund. This seems like substantial sum to keep in low-interest savings rather than invested for higher returns, but the insurance value of emergency funds justifies the opportunity cost. The alternative is being forced into catastrophically bad financial decisions during actual emergencies when you lack liquid resources.

The management of lifestyle inflation as income increases determines whether higher income translates into wealth accumulation or merely into higher spending that leaves you no better positioned financially despite earning substantially more. The ninety-nine percent experience income increases and immediately adjust spending upward. They move to more expensive housing, purchase nicer vehicles, eat at better restaurants, take more elaborate vacations, and generally spend whatever additional income arrives. Five years after doubling their income they find themselves no wealthier than before the increases because spending rose proportionally with earnings.

The one percent commit to saving all or most of income increases rather than allowing lifestyle to inflate with earnings. When they receive a five thousand dollar annual raise, they increase their automatic savings transfers by four thousand dollars annually and allow themselves perhaps one thousand dollars in increased annual spending if any increase at all. This means their lifestyle at one hundred thousand annual income differs only marginally from their lifestyle at seventy thousand annual income, but their wealth accumulation accelerates dramatically because the additional thirty thousand is deployed almost entirely into investments rather than consumed through lifestyle inflation.

This requires resisting enormous social and psychological pressure. Your peers who earn similar incomes are upgrading their lifestyles continuously. They drive nicer cars, live in bigger homes, vacation in more expensive destinations, and appear to be succeeding financially. You are driving the same old car, living in the same modest housing, taking inexpensive vacations, and appearing to be failing to keep pace financially despite earning as much or more than your peers. The psychological difficulty of maintaining this discipline while surrounded by lifestyle inflation cannot be overstated. You must develop genuine conviction that wealth building matters more than appearance of wealth, and you must maintain this conviction for decades while everyone around you makes different choices.

The periodic review of spending patterns identifies areas where costs have crept upward without conscious decision. The one percent review spending quarterly rather than tracking it daily or weekly. They export three months of transactions from their checking and credit card accounts. They sort these transactions by category to see where money is actually going rather than where they think it is going. They identify categories where spending has increased or where spending levels surprise them. They make conscious decisions about whether this spending serves their priorities or whether it represents drift toward convenience or habit rather than intentional choice.

These reviews typically reveal small recurring expenses that individually seem trivial but collectively consume thousands annually. The subscription services that auto-renew monthly despite being rarely used. The convenience purchases of prepared foods or takeout meals that happen more frequently than realized. The incremental upgrades in product choices that add dollars to every shopping trip. The one percent ruthlessly eliminate these expenditures because they understand that every dollar unnecessarily spent is a dollar not compounding in investment accounts. Five dollars daily on convenience purchases seems insignificant. Over a year this is eighteen hundred twenty-five dollars. Invested at ten percent returns for thirty years this becomes thirty-two thousand dollars. Your daily convenience habit costs you thirty-two thousand dollars in eventual wealth. Multiply this by the dozens of small wasteful expenditures most people maintain and you understand why spending patterns determine wealth outcomes as surely as investment returns do.

The integration of budgeting with tax-advantaged account strategies discussed in Chapter Four ensures that your savings rate generates maximum wealth accumulation. The sequence for deploying savings should prioritize accounts in order of their tax advantages and employer matches. First contributions go to employer retirement accounts to capture full company match because this is free money providing one hundred percent immediate returns. Second contributions fill Health Savings Accounts to maximum allowed amounts because HSAs provide triple tax advantages unavailable elsewhere. Third contributions maximize Roth IRA contributions because tax-free growth and withdrawals become increasingly valuable as wealth compounds over decades. Fourth contributions return to maxing out traditional 401k or 403b accounts for current tax deductions. Fifth contributions flow to taxable brokerage accounts for additional investment beyond retirement account limits.

This sequencing captures maximum tax advantages while maintaining appropriate balance between tax-deferred, tax-free, and taxable accounts. Someone earning one hundred thousand and saving forty thousand annually might allocate funds as follows: six thousand to employer 401k to capture a six percent company match that contributes another six thousand, eight thousand to family HSA, seven thousand to Roth IRA, nineteen thousand more to complete 401k maximum contribution of twenty-three thousand including the initial six thousand. This totals forty thousand in contributions generating fifty-two thousand when including employer match. If income were higher or savings rate lower, the sequence would determine which accounts to prioritize.

The relationship between budgeting discipline and the wealthbuilding strategies discussed in previous chapters should now be clear. You cannot systematically invest in index funds as described in Chapter Six without budget discipline that generates savings to invest. You cannot acquire rental properties as discussed in Chapter Seven without accumulated capital for down payments that comes from years of high savings rates. You cannot pursue house flipping as discussed in Chapter Eighteen without either accumulated capital or income sufficient to qualify for hard money loans. Every wealthbuilding strategy depends on generating surplus capital through the simple mechanism of spending less than you earn and deploying the difference systematically into assets that compound over time.

George Clason's principle of paying yourself first has survived a century because it captures the fundamental requirement for wealth building in a single sentence that anyone can understand and implement. You cannot build wealth by saving what remains after spending because nothing remains after spending. You can only build wealth by saving first and spending what remains. This requires designing your life around your savings target rather than designing your savings around your lifestyle. The ninety-nine percent will never accept this because it requires temporary discomfort and visible differences from how peers live. The one percent accept this fully because they understand that temporary discomfort during building years creates permanent financial freedom that their peers will never achieve.

The specific tactics for maintaining spending discipline during the decades required to build substantial wealth include environmental controls that make spending difficult rather than relying on willpower alone. You delete shopping apps from your phone so impulse purchases require intentional computer access rather than thumb swipes. You unsubscribe from marketing emails that create desire for unnecessary purchases. You avoid shopping as entertainment activity. You implement waiting periods for any purchase over some threshold amount, perhaps one hundred dollars, requiring a week of consideration before completing purchases to ensure you actually need or want the item rather than merely experiencing temporary desire. You remove stored payment information from websites to create friction in purchasing processes. You freeze credit cards in blocks of ice if necessary to prevent impulse use.

These tactics seem extreme to people who trust their discipline to resist spending temptation. The one percent recognize that discipline is limited resource that gets depleted through use and that environmental design preventing temptation is far more reliable than willpower resisting temptation. They make good financial decisions easy and bad financial decisions difficult through these environmental controls rather than depending on making correct choices in every moment when temptation arises.

The communication about your financial choices with family and friends determines whether your social environment supports or undermines your budgeting discipline. The ninety-nine percent either hide their frugality out of embarrassment or they explain it apologetically as if temporary hardship rather than deliberate wealthbuilding strategy. This creates social pressure to abandon the approach whenever peers question why you are living so modestly despite good income. The one percent are direct about their financial priorities without apology. When friends suggest expensive activities, they propose less expensive alternatives or they decline without elaborate justification. When family questions their housing or vehicle choices, they explain briefly that they are building wealth and that lifestyle consumption is not their priority. This directness prevents ongoing pressure to justify choices while establishing clear boundaries about what you will and will not spend money on regardless of social expectations.

The timeline from beginning aggressive budgeting discipline to achieving financial independence varies based on income level and savings rate but follows predictable mathematical patterns. Someone saving fifteen percent of income requires approximately forty-three years to accumulate sufficient wealth to retire if starting from zero. Someone saving thirty percent requires approximately twenty-eight years. Someone saving fifty percent requires approximately seventeen years. Someone saving sixty-five percent requires approximately ten years. These calculations assume your savings earn returns matching inflation plus seven percent and that you need to accumulate twenty-five times your annual expenses to fund retirement based on the four percent withdrawal rate. The mathematics are available in any financial independence calculator, but the principle is that your savings rate determines your working years far more than your investment returns do.

This reveals why budgeting discipline matters more for wealth building than investment genius. The person who saves twenty percent of income and earns eight percent returns reaches financial independence faster than the person who saves ten percent and earns twelve percent returns. Savings rate is completely within your control while investment returns are largely outside your control beyond choosing appropriate asset allocation and maintaining low costs. The one percent recognize this and focus their optimization efforts on the factor they control rather than on the factor they do not.

You have now been provided comprehensive education about wealth building from proper foundations through specific strategies to the budgeting discipline that makes all strategies possible. Budgeting is not the exciting component of wealth building. It is the unglamorous foundation that determines whether any other strategy can be implemented successfully. You can learn everything about stock market investing, real estate acquisition, business building, and tax optimization, but without the discipline to spend substantially less than you earn and deploy the difference systematically, none of that knowledge generates wealth. The knowledge might allow you to deploy capital more effectively once you have it, but the budgeting discipline is what creates the capital to deploy.

George Clason's advice to pay yourself first is not complicated. The complication lies, again, not in understanding the principle, but in implementing it for decades while surrounded by people making different choices and while facing constant temptation to spend rather than save. The one percent implement this principle through automation that removes decision-making from the process, through environmental design that makes spending difficult, through conscious choice to live below their means regardless of income level, and through complete clarity that wealth building requires different choices than the ninety-nine percent make.

CHAPTER 20:
GROCERY STRATEGY—NUTRITION AND EFFICIENCY

In 2011, billionaire entrepreneur Mark Cuban sat for an interview where the conversation turned to his daily routines and personal habits. The interviewer expected to hear about elaborate morning rituals, personal chefs preparing customized meals, or sophisticated dietary protocols managed by nutritionists. Instead, Cuban described something far simpler and more deliberate. He ate the same breakfast every single day without variation. He had identified the combination of foods that provided the nutrition and energy he needed to perform optimally, and he saw no reason to waste mental energy making breakfast decisions when a proven solution already existed. His lunch and dinner choices rotated through a limited set of options he had similarly tested and validated. This systematic approach to eating struck the interviewer as unusual for someone with unlimited resources to explore any culinary possibility.

Cuban explained that decision fatigue is real and cumulative. Every choice you make throughout the day depletes the mental resources available for subsequent decisions. Successful people understand this and ruthlessly eliminate unnecessary decisions from their lives to preserve cognitive capacity for choices that actually matter. What to eat for breakfast does not matter beyond meeting basic nutritional requirements. Whether to invest in a particular company, how to structure a business deal, or which strategic direction to pursue with an existing venture matters enormously. Cuban refuses to waste decision-making capacity on the former so that he has maximum capacity available for the latter. His systematic approach to food is not about restriction or deprivation. It is about optimization and efficiency.

This principle applies with even greater force to people building wealth who lack Cuban's resources and who cannot delegate as many decisions as billionaires can. When you are managing limited income, working full time while building side businesses or investment portfolios, and attempting to maintain relationships and health simultaneously, every unnecessary decision represents cognitive load you can eliminate through systems. Food represents the third-largest expense category for most households after housing and transportation, consuming ten to fifteen percent of gross income for the average American family. More importantly, food decisions occur multiple times daily, creating dozens of opportunities weekly to either advance your wealth-building goals through disciplined choices or undermine those goals through convenience-driven spending.

The one percent approach food strategically as they approach every other domain affecting wealth accumulation. They recognize that food serves functional purposes of providing nutrition and energy while avoiding negative health consequences that impair earning capacity. Everything beyond these functional purposes is entertainment or social signaling that may or may not justify its cost. They establish systems for acquiring and preparing food efficiently while meeting nutritional requirements, and they execute these systems with minimal variation or decision-making. This approach seems joyless to those who view food as primary source of pleasure or who use meals as entertainment. To those focused on wealth building, this approach represents practical efficiency that frees resources for deployment into assets while freeing mental capacity for decisions that actually affect outcomes.

The mathematics of food spending reveal substantial opportunity for wealth building through modest discipline. The average American household earning seventy-five thousand annually spends approximately ten thousand dollars on food, split roughly evenly between groceries and restaurant meals. This represents thirteen percent of gross income. The one percent reduce total food spending to five to seven percent of gross income through systematic grocery shopping and severe limitation of restaurant expenditures. A household earning seventy-five thousand reducing food costs from thirteen percent to seven percent saves forty-five hundred dollars annually. This amount invested at ten percent returns becomes approximately one hundred seventeen thousand dollars over twenty years. Your food spending patterns determine whether you build one hundred seventeen thousand in investment wealth or consume it through restaurant meals and inefficient grocery shopping.

The foundation of food cost optimization begins with near-total elimination of restaurant meals except for genuine social occasions that provide relationship value justifying the expense. The ninety-nine percent eat restaurant meals regularly because cooking seems inconvenient or because they view eating out as normal reward for working hard or because they have not developed cooking skills that make home meal preparation efficient. These justifications create spending patterns that destroy thousands annually in wealth-building capacity. A meal at a casual restaurant costs fifteen to twenty-five dollars per person after tax and tip. The same meal prepared at home costs three to five dollars per person using grocery store ingredients. The restaurant meal markup is three hundred to five hundred percent over home cooking costs.

Someone eating restaurant lunch five days weekly at twelve dollars per meal spends sixty dollars weekly or three thousand one hundred twenty dollars annually just on work lunches. The same person could prepare lunches at home for approximately fifteen dollars weekly or seven hundred eighty dollars annually, saving twenty-three hundred forty dollars annually through this single change. Dinner restaurant meals cost more and create larger savings opportunities. A family of four eating dinner at restaurants twice weekly at seventy-five dollars per meal spends fifteen hundred dollars monthly or eighteen thousand dollars annually on restaurant dinners. The same family preparing equivalent meals at home would spend approximately three hundred dollars monthly or thirty-six hundred dollars annually, saving fourteen thousand four hundred dollars annually through home cooking.

These are not hypothetical numbers constructed to make a point. These are typical spending patterns for middle-income

American families who wonder why they cannot save meaningful amounts despite reasonable incomes. The difference between restaurant meal costs and home-cooked meal costs represents pure waste of capital that could be building wealth through compound returns. The person who maintains these spending patterns for thirty years while earning eight percent returns on savings consumes approximately one million six hundred thousand dollars in eventual wealth through restaurant meal expenditures that could have been reduced by eighty percent through basic home cooking.

The grocery shopping strategy that minimizes costs while maintaining nutrition begins with meal planning that eliminates impulse purchases and reduces food waste. The ninety-nine percent shop without plans, wandering grocery aisles and selecting items that appeal in the moment or that they believe they might use. This approach guarantees impulse purchases of expensive prepared foods, creation of a pantry full of ingredients that never combine into actual meals, and waste of fresh foods that spoil before being used. The one percent plan meals for the coming week before entering any grocery store, creating shopping lists that include only the specific ingredients required for planned meals plus stable staples that need replenishing.

The meal planning process requires perhaps thirty minutes weekly to review recipes, identify meals for the week, and create comprehensive shopping lists. This time investment seems like burden to those who prefer spontaneity in food choices, but it generates enormous returns through reduced costs, eliminated food waste, and removal of daily decision-making about what to eat. You decide once weekly what meals you will prepare, you shop once for all required ingredients, and you execute the meal plan throughout the week without additional decisions beyond which planned meal to prepare on which day.

The meal rotation should be limited to perhaps ten to fifteen reliable meals that you prepare repeatedly rather than constantly seeking new recipes that require unusual ingredients and extended preparation. Mark Cuban's approach of eating the same breakfast daily represents the extreme end of this principle, but even rotating through fifteen dinner options provides sufficient variety for most people while maintaining efficiency through repetition. When you prepare the same meals regularly, you become efficient at preparation, you maintain required ingredients as stable pantry items, and you eliminate the need to learn new techniques or acquire new equipment for each meal. The person who attempts thirty different recipes monthly spends far more time cooking, wastes money on ingredients used once and then discarded, and generally experiences home cooking as burdensome rather than efficient.

The selection of meals to include in your regular rotation should prioritize nutrition density, cost efficiency, and preparation simplicity. The optimal meals provide substantial protein, adequate vegetables, reasonable complex carbohydrates, and healthy fats while requiring minimal preparation time and using inexpensive ingredients. Examples might include grilled chicken with roasted vegetables and rice, simple pasta with tomato sauce and ground turkey, bean-based chili with cornbread, stir-fried vegetables with tofu or chicken over rice, baked fish with steamed vegetables and quinoa, simple tacos using seasoned ground meat and standard toppings, large batch soups or stews that provide multiple meals, and basic protein and vegetable combinations using whatever is on sale seasonally.

These meals are not elaborate or Instagram-worthy. They are functional nutrition that meets your body's requirements while minimizing cost and preparation time. The ninety-nine percent reject this approach as boring or unsophisticated, preferring varied meals that demonstrate their culinary appreciation or their cultural awareness. The one percent recognize that food sophistication is expensive entertainment that they can pursue once wealthy if they choose, but that during wealth-building years food should serve its functional purpose with maximum efficiency and minimum cost. There will be decades after reaching financial independence to explore elaborate cooking or expensive restaurants if that interests you. During the building years, systematic efficiency in food preparation preserves both capital and time for wealth creation.

The grocery shopping execution requires discipline to purchase only items on your planned list regardless of what promotional displays or strategic product placements tempt you to buy. Grocery stores are designed with sophisticated understanding of consumer psychology. High-margin impulse items are positioned at eye level and near checkout areas. Essential items like milk and eggs are placed in back corners forcing you to walk past hundreds of products to reach them. Promotional displays create perception of bargains even when prices are not particularly favorable. The bakery section is positioned near the entrance so fresh bread aromas trigger hunger that increases purchase quantities. These design features exist specifically to increase your spending beyond what you intended when you entered the store.

The defense against these manipulations is simple but requires discipline: shop with a list, purchase only items on the list, and exit immediately upon completing the list. Do not browse aisles for interesting products. Do not respond to promotional displays unless the promoted item is already on your list. Do not shop while hungry because hunger dramatically increases impulse purchases of prepared foods and snacks. Do not bring children if possible because they create pressure for expensive convenience foods and treats. These rules seem restrictive but they prevent the typical twenty to thirty percent spending increase that occurs when people shop without lists or when they browse rather than executing planned purchases efficiently.

The selection of store matters substantially for total costs. Discount grocers like Aldi, Lidl, or regional equivalents offer prices twenty-five to thirty-five percent below conventional supermarkets for equivalent products. The shopping experience is less pleasant because these stores maintain minimal staff, require you to bag your own groceries, offer limited brand selection, and generally lack the amenities of conventional supermarkets. The one percent accept these inconveniences cheerfully because twenty-five percent savings on five thousand dollars annual grocery spending saves twelve hundred fifty dollars annually. This amount invested at ten percent returns becomes approximately thirty-two thousand five hundred dollars over twenty years. Whether you prefer pleasant shopping experience or thirty-two thousand five hundred dollars in wealth is a choice, but understand that you are actually making this choice rather than pretending the difference does not matter.

The bulk purchasing of stable staples through warehouse clubs like Costco or Sam's Club provides additional savings for items you use regularly. Rice, beans, pasta, canned goods, frozen vegetables, cooking oils, and similar products cost thirty to fifty percent less in bulk formats than in conventional grocery quantities. The limitation is that bulk purchasing requires storage space and upfront capital to buy large quantities. You must also verify that bulk pricing actually provides savings because some items at warehouse clubs cost more per unit than conventional grocery sale prices. The one percent comparison shop systematically rather than assuming bulk always means savings, and they limit warehouse club purchases to items they will definitely use before expiration.

The fresh produce strategy should prioritize seasonal vegetables and fruits rather than purchasing whatever appeals regardless of price. Produce prices fluctuate wildly based on seasonal availability, with items costing three to four times more out of season than during peak harvest. The person who insists on berries and asparagus year-round pays premium prices most of the year. The person who eats whatever vegetables are currently in season and cheap pays one-quarter to one-third the amount for equivalent nutrition. Learning which produce is seasonal in your region and adjusting your meal planning accordingly saves hundreds to thousands annually while generally improving quality because seasonal produce is fresher and tastes better than out-of-season items shipped from distant locations.

The protein selection should focus on the most cost-effective options relative to nutritional value. Chicken is substantially cheaper per serving than beef and provides equivalent protein. Eggs provide excellent protein at minimal cost. Beans and lentils provide plantbased protein at costs far below meat. Fish prices vary enormously with frozen fish often providing better value than fresh. The one percent build their meal planning around whichever proteins are currently on sale or most cost-effective rather than selecting proteins based on preference independent of cost. They might prefer steak, but they eat chicken during wealth-building years because the cost difference accumulates to tens of thousands over decades when invested rather than consumed.

The processed and prepared food avoidance represents perhaps the largest single opportunity for cost reduction in grocery spending. Prepared foods command two hundred to four hundred percent markups over the cost of raw ingredients. Pre-cut vegetables, pre-marinated meats, ready-to-heat meals, and similar convenience products save perhaps five to ten minutes of preparation time while doubling or tripling costs. A family spending thirty percent of their grocery budget on convenience prepared foods is wasting approximately fifteen hundred dollars annually that could be saved through ten additional minutes daily of basic preparation like washing and cutting vegetables or marinating proteins.

The brand selection between name brands and store brands affects costs materially across most product categories. Store brand products typically cost twenty to forty percent less than name brand equivalents while being manufactured in the same facilities using similar or identical formulations. The loyalty to name brands is primarily result of marketing rather than quality differences. The one percent purchase store brands for virtually all commodity products like dairy, canned goods, frozen vegetables, pasta, rice, and basic ingredients. They purchase name brands only when genuine quality differences exist or when extreme couponing or sales make name brands cheaper than store brand regular prices. This systematic selection of lower-cost equivalent products saves three hundred to five hundred dollars annually on typical grocery budgets.

The meal preparation efficiency determines whether home cooking remains sustainable or whether time burden drives reversion to expensive restaurant habits. The ninety-nine percent approach each meal as individual cooking event requiring separate preparation and cleanup. This creates perception that cooking is time-intensive burden rather than efficient system. The one percent use batch cooking strategies that prepare multiple servings or multiple meals simultaneously, dramatically reducing per-meal time requirements. They prepare large batches of staples like rice or beans that serve as base for multiple meals throughout the week. They prepare proteins in bulk quantities that can be reheated for various meals. They cook complete meals in large quantities that provide leftovers for several days.

The Sunday meal preparation session where you cook large quantities of several dishes that provide meals throughout the week represents perhaps the most efficient approach to home cooking. Two to three hours on Sunday cooking chicken breasts, preparing a large pot of beans, cooking rice or quinoa in bulk, chopping vegetables for the week, and assembling complete meals in containers produces twelve to fifteen servings ready for reheating throughout the week. The daily time requirement becomes five to ten minutes reheating meals rather than thirty to sixty minutes cooking from scratch. This efficiency makes home cooking sustainable even for people with demanding work schedules who otherwise claim they lack time to cook.

The kitchen equipment required for efficient meal preparation is minimal despite what cooking shows and equipment marketing suggests. You need quality knife, cutting board, a few pots and pans, baking sheets, basic cooking utensils, and storage containers. This equipment costs perhaps two to three hundred dollars purchased wisely and lasts many years. The elaborate equipment that most people accumulate through wedding registries or aspirational purchases sits unused while occupying storage space. The one percent own minimal kitchen equipment that they actually use regularly rather than collections of specialized items that make cooking seem more complicated than it is.

The nutrition framework that guides meal selection should prioritize protein adequacy, vegetable consumption, and avoidance of excessive processed carbohydrates and added sugars. The specific macronutrient ratios and dietary philosophies that generate endless debate matter far less than these basic principles that are universally accepted across nearly all dietary approaches. You need adequate protein to maintain muscle mass and support metabolic functions. You need substantial vegetables for micronutrients and fiber. You need to avoid excessive refined carbohydrates and added sugars that provide calories without nutrition and that create blood sugar instability affecting energy and cognitive function. Meeting these basic requirements through the simple meals described previously provides completely adequate nutrition for optimal health and performance without requiring sophisticated nutritional knowledge or elaborate meal planning.

The specific protein target for active adults should be approximately 0.7 to 1.0 grams per pound of body weight daily. Someone weighing one hundred fifty pounds needs approximately one hundred to one hundred fifty grams of protein daily. This is achievable through combination of animal proteins like chicken, fish, eggs, and dairy, or through plant proteins like beans, lentils, tofu, and protein powders if following plant-based approach. Most people underconsume protein relative to optimal amounts, leading to muscle loss with age, inadequate satiety after meals that drives snacking, and suboptimal metabolic function. The one percent prioritize protein at every meal to ensure they meet daily requirements without conscious calculation.

The vegetable consumption target should be substantial servings at lunch and dinner minimum. The specific quantity matters less than ensuring that vegetables comprise half or more of lunch and dinner plate volume. This approach provides fiber that supports digestion and satiety, micronutrients that support cellular function, and displacement of less nutritious foods from meals. The person who fills half their plate with vegetables inevitably eats less of higher-calorie foods that provide minimal nutritional value. The one percent achieve this through frozen vegetables that require minimal preparation, through bulk roasting of seasonal vegetables on Sunday for use throughout the week, or through simple preparations like steaming that require almost no skill or time.

The hydration through water rather than caloric beverages saves money while supporting health and cognitive function. The average American consumes substantial calories through sodas, juices, coffee drinks, and alcohol. These beverages cost money, provide minimal or negative nutritional value, and add calories that impair weight management without providing satiety. Water costs nearly nothing, provides the hydration your body requires, and contributes zero calories. The one percent drink almost exclusively water, black coffee, and unsweetened tea, reserving caloric beverages for rare social occasions if at all. This single change saves hundreds annually in beverage costs while eliminating thousands of empty calories that most people consume without conscious awareness.

The relationship between food quality and earning capacity deserves attention because poor nutrition impairs cognitive function, energy levels, and health in ways that reduce your capacity to earn income and build wealth. The person who eats processed foods high in refined carbohydrates and added sugars experiences blood sugar fluctuations that create energy crashes, difficulty concentrating, and mood instability. These effects impair work performance directly through reduced productivity and focus. Over years and decades, poor nutrition contributes to obesity, type two diabetes, cardiovascular disease, and other conditions that increase healthcare costs and potentially force early retirement or disability. The one percent understand that food quality affects earning capacity and they prioritize nutrition accordingly even when this costs slightly more than the absolute cheapest options.

This does not require expensive organic products, grass-fed meats, or sophisticated supplements. Basic nutrition built around whole foods, adequate protein, substantial vegetables, and limited processed foods provides the foundation for optimal health and performance at modest cost. The person eating chicken, rice, beans, frozen vegetables, eggs, and basic fruits spends far less than the person eating processed convenience foods while achieving superior nutrition that supports health and productivity. The marginal cost differences between adequate nutrition and optimal nutrition are small, while the performance differences are substantial enough to affect earning capacity measurably.

The social pressure around food choices creates challenges for those attempting to minimize food costs while peers spend freely on restaurants and expensive grocery items. Friends suggest eating out regularly. Family gatherings involve expensive restaurants. Colleagues discuss their latest culinary discoveries and food experiences. You are choosing different path that involves basic home-cooked meals and rare restaurant visits. This makes you conspicuous and subject to questions or criticism about why you are being so frugal when you earn reasonable income. The one percent develop comfort with being different and with explaining when necessary that their priorities involve building wealth rather than experiencing every food opportunity that presents itself.

The alternative to direct explanation is participating in social food events selectively while maintaining your core discipline. You might agree to monthly social meals at restaurants with important relationships while declining the weekly casual meals that provide minimal social value. You might host gatherings at your home where you prepare simple meals rather than meeting at expensive restaurants. You might suggest specific less expensive restaurants when the social connection matters but the expense does not. These approaches maintain relationships while preventing food spending from consuming wealth-building capacity through undisciplined frequency of expensive meals.

The coffee spending deserves specific attention as a category where small daily expenditures accumulate to substantial annual costs. The person spending five dollars daily on coffee shop drinks spends eighteen hundred twenty-five dollars annually. This invested at ten percent returns becomes approximately forty-seven thousand five hundred dollars over twenty years. Your coffee habit costs you forty-seven thousand five hundred dollars in eventual wealth. Making coffee at home costs approximately twenty-five cents per cup or ninety-one dollars annually for daily consumption, saving seventeen hundred thirty-four dollars annually. This single change implemented consistently creates nearly fifty thousand in wealth over two decades compared to maintaining coffee shop habits.

The one percent prepare coffee at home using basic equipment that costs fifty to one hundred dollars and lasts years. They view daily coffee shop purchases as wealth destruction similar to any other unnecessary recurring expense. They understand that the coffee shop visit is partly about convenience and partly about social signaling—being seen with the branded cup suggests you have disposable income and cultivated taste. They reject this signaling as expensive irrelevance and make coffee at home without apology or embarrassment about carrying home-brewed coffee in a reusable container.

The alcohol consumption for those who drink represents another category where costs accumulate substantially without conscious awareness. The person drinking three drinks weekly at bars or restaurants at eight dollars per drink spends one thousand two hundred forty-eight dollars annually. The person drinking equivalent amounts at home using liquor or wine purchased at retail costs approximately three hundred dollars annually, saving nine hundred forty-eight dollars through home consumption rather than bar prices. The one percent either eliminate alcohol entirely or restrict consumption to home where costs are minimal and where quantity naturally limits itself through unavailability rather than through willpower required to decline another round at a bar.

The elimination of food waste through proper storage and systematic use of leftovers saves hundreds annually for typical households. The average American household wastes approximately thirty percent of food purchased, with most waste resulting from fresh foods spoiling before use or leftovers being forgotten in refrigerators until they become inedible. This represents pure waste of approximately fifteen hundred dollars annually for households spending five thousand on groceries. The one percent prevent this waste through meal planning that uses ingredients across multiple meals, through proper food storage that extends freshness, through prominent positioning of leftovers in refrigerators where they are visible and likely to be consumed, and through ruthless discipline about using foods before they spoil rather than allowing them to sit unused until disposal becomes necessary.

The integration of food strategy with overall wealth-building approach should be clear. We have established in previous chapters that you must save thirty to fifty percent of income to build substantial wealth within reasonable timeframes. We have established that major spending categories of housing, transportation, and food determine whether these savings rates are achievable. Food represents approximately ten percent of gross income for typical American households. Reducing this to five to seven percent through the strategies described saves three to five percent of income annually. On seventy-five thousand dollar income, this is twenty-two hundred fifty to thirty-seven hundred fifty dollars annually. Invested at ten percent returns for thirty years, this becomes one hundred eighty-four thousand to three hundred seven thousand dollars in accumulated wealth. Your grocery and restaurant choices determine whether you build nearly two hundred thousand to three hundred thousand dollars in investment assets or whether you consume it through food spending that provides minimal lasting value.

Mark Cuban's systematic approach to eating represents the extreme end of food efficiency where the same meals repeat with no variation. Most people need not go this far to capture the majority of benefits from strategic food management. The principles that matter are planning meals rather than shopping impulsively, cooking at home rather than eating at restaurants, buying cost-effective ingredients rather than premium brands or convenience products, preparing simple reliable meals rather than attempting elaborate recipes, and eliminating waste through systematic use of purchased foods. These principles implemented consistently reduce food costs by thirty to forty percent while potentially improving nutrition through increased whole food consumption and reduced processed food intake.

The time investment required for this approach is approximately thirty minutes weekly for meal planning and two to three hours weekly for grocery shopping and meal preparation. This totals three to four hours weekly compared to perhaps one hour weekly for someone who shops without planning and who eats restaurant meals regularly. The additional two to three hours weekly generates savings of forty-five hundred dollars annually on seventy-five thousand-dollar household income, which means you earn approximately one thousand five hundred dollars per hour for time invested in systematic food management. This is among the highest return activities available to anyone building wealth because the returns are guaranteed and risk-free unlike investment returns which fluctuate based on market conditions.

We have now addressed every major spending category that determines whether you can maintain the savings rates required for wealth building. Housing in Chapter Nine, insurance in Chapter Ten, vehicles in Chapter Eleven, and food in this chapter represent approximately sixty-five to seventy-five percent of gross income for typical American households. The one percent systematically minimize costs in each category through strategies that the ninety-nine percent reject as excessive or unnecessarily restrictive. The cumulative effect of optimization across all major categories creates savings rates of forty to sixty percent that build substantial wealth within fifteen to twenty-five years. The ninety-nine percent optimize none of these categories and accumulate minimal wealth over entire working lifetimes despite often earning comparable or higher incomes than their wealthier peers.

The choice about food strategy is yours to make. You can maintain typical American eating patterns with regular restaurant meals, convenience grocery products, and impulse purchases that feel normal and that create no social friction. This path leads to food costs consuming ten to fifteen percent of income and it prevents wealth accumulation through compounding over decades. Or you can implement systematic food management through meal planning, home cooking, strategic grocery shopping, and discipline around restaurant spending. This path leads to food costs consuming five to seven percent of income and it creates investment capital that compounds into hundreds of thousands of additional wealth over working years. The meals in both scenarios provide adequate nutrition. The wealth outcomes diverge by amounts that determine whether you achieve financial independence or work until forced retirement.

CHAPTER 21:
HEALTH AND EXERCISE—THE IRREPLACEABLE ASSET

In 1975, a twenty-six-year-old commodities trader named Ray Dalio founded an investment advisory firm from his two-bedroom apartment in New York City. Over the following decades, he built Bridgewater Associates into the largest hedge fund in the world, managing over one hundred fifty billion dollars in assets and generating billions in personal wealth. Throughout this journey, Dalio maintained practices that most of his Wall Street peers dismissed as distractions from wealth building. He meditated daily for twenty minutes regardless of market conditions or business demands. He exercised consistently every morning before market open. He tracked his sleep patterns and adjusted his schedule to ensure seven to eight hours nightly. He approached physical maintenance with the same systematic rigor he applied to investment analysis, treating his body as the infrastructure upon which everything else depended.

When colleagues questioned why someone so focused on performance would spend ninety minutes daily on meditation and exercise rather than working additional hours, Dalio explained that the ninety minutes invested in physical and mental maintenance produced far better decision-making during the remaining hours than those ninety minutes possibly could if spent working. His cognitive clarity, emotional stability, and sustained energy throughout trading days provided competitive advantages that no amount of additional work hours could replicate. More importantly, his systematic health maintenance allowed him to sustain peak performance for decades rather than burning out after several intense years as many of his peers did.

By his seventies, Dalio remained actively engaged in managing his firm and pursuing new ventures while many contemporaries had retired due to health problems or cognitive decline. His systematic investment in physical maintenance had compounded across decades into the capacity to continue generating wealth and impact long after most people exit productive work. This is the reality that separates the one percent from the ninety-nine percent in their approach to health: the understanding that your body is your only truly irreplaceable asset, and that every other form of wealth becomes meaningless if you lack the health to enjoy it or the longevity to benefit from its compound growth.

This chapter addresses what may be the most overlooked component of wealth building. We have discussed how to earn income, how to invest capital, how to minimize expenses, and how to structure your life for maximum wealth accumulation. All of these strategies depend completely on your continued capacity to work, to think clearly, to make sound decisions, and to sustain effort over decades. Poor health destroys this capacity. Chronic disease forces early retirement. Cognitive decline impairs judgment. Low energy reduces productivity. Death eliminates all opportunity to benefit from wealth you spent decades accumulating. The person who optimizes every financial decision while neglecting physical health has built their wealth on a foundation that will eventually collapse regardless of how sound the financial structure appears.

The one percent understand that health is not separate from wealth building but rather is the foundation upon which all wealth building occurs. They invest in physical maintenance not because they enjoy exercise or because they are health enthusiasts, but because they recognize that sustained high performance requires physical infrastructure that supports rather than undermines their capabilities. They view time spent on exercise, sleep, and nutrition as non-negotiable investments rather than as optional activities to be squeezed in when convenient. They understand that the short-term cost of this investment in time and attention produces long-term returns in sustained earning capacity, avoided healthcare costs, extended productive years, and quality of life that makes wealth meaningful rather than merely numerical.

The mathematics of health investment versus health neglect demonstrate why this matters for wealth building specifically rather than merely for general wellbeing. The person who maintains excellent health throughout their working years works productively for forty to fifty years, experiences minimal lost work time due to illness, avoids major medical expenses beyond routine preventive care, maintains cognitive function that allows sound decision-making through their sixties and beyond, and potentially continues generating income or managing investments actively into their seventies and eighties. The person who neglects health experiences declining productivity during their forties and fifties as energy diminishes and chronic conditions develop, loses weeks or months of productive time to illness and medical treatments, incurs tens or hundreds of thousands in medical expenses that drain accumulated wealth, experiences cognitive decline that impairs investment judgment during critical years, and often faces forced retirement in their early sixties or even fifties due to inability to continue working.

The difference in lifetime earnings and wealth accumulation between these paths easily exceeds one million dollars for high earners. The person who maintains health and works productively until seventy rather than retiring due to health problems at fifty-five generates fifteen additional years of peak earning and wealth accumulation. At two hundred thousand annual income, this is three million in additional earnings before accounting for investment returns on that income. The person who avoids major health expenses by preventing chronic disease through lifestyle maintenance saves one hundred thousand to five hundred thousand in medical costs that would otherwise drain retirement accounts. The person who maintains cognitive function through their sixties and seventies makes better investment decisions that generate superior returns during decades when their portfolios are largest and when good decisions matter most.

These are not abstract benefits disconnected from the wealth-building focus of this book. These are direct financial impacts that dwarf the returns from clever investment strategies or tax optimization. Yet most people invest enormous time analyzing investment options while investing zero time in physical maintenance that would generate far larger returns. They will spend hours researching which index funds to purchase while refusing to spend thirty minutes exercising because they claim they lack time. This is irrational prioritization driven by the fact that investment returns seem obviously connected to wealth while health maintenance seems like separate domain unrelated to financial outcomes.

The framework for health maintenance that produces optimal results without requiring excessive time commitment or unsustainable lifestyle changes begins with understanding the concept of minimum effective dose. This principle from pharmacology states that for any intervention, there exists a dosage that produces the desired effect, and that exceeding this dosage produces minimal additional benefit while increasing cost or side effects. Applied to exercise and health maintenance, minimum effective dose means identifying the smallest input that produces the outcomes you need—sustained energy, cognitive function, disease prevention, and longevity—without requiring time commitment or intensity level that proves unsustainable over decades.

The minimum effective dose for exercise that produces meaningful health and performance benefits involves approximately thirty minutes of resistance training three times weekly and consistent achievement of ten thousand steps daily through walking or equivalent low-intensity movement. This represents roughly two and a half hours weekly of deliberate exercise plus the walking that should occur naturally through active lifestyle rather than sedentary patterns. This amount of exercise provides sufficient stimulus to maintain muscle mass and strength, supports cardiovascular health, promotes insulin sensitivity that prevents metabolic disease, enhances cognitive function, and contributes to longevity. Exceeding this amount produces marginal additional benefits while requiring substantially more time that could be allocated to wealth-building activities.

The resistance training component is non-negotiable because muscle mass is the primary metabolic tissue that determines your metabolic rate, physical capability, and resilience against age-related decline. Adults who do not engage in resistance training lose approximately eight percent of muscle mass per decade after age thirty. By age seventy, the sedentary person has lost thirty-two percent of their muscle mass, becoming frail and incapable of physical activities that were effortless in youth. This muscle loss reduces metabolic rate, making weight management progressively more difficult. It impairs glucose disposal, contributing to diabetes risk. It reduces physical capacity in ways that force retirement from physically demanding work earlier than necessary. It increases fall risk and injury susceptibility that can trigger cascades of health decline in later years.

The person who maintains resistance training three times weekly throughout their working years preserves muscle mass and strength essentially unchanged from their thirties through their seventies. They maintain physical capacity to perform any work their careers require. They sustain metabolic health that prevents the chronic diseases that disable many of their peers. They remain independent and capable in their seventies and eighties rather than requiring assistance with basic activities. The time investment is ninety minutes weekly. The return is decades of sustained physical capacity and avoided disability. The person who cannot find ninety minutes weekly for resistance training will eventually find years or decades for managing chronic disease and disability that result from neglecting this fundamental maintenance.

The resistance training approach should be simple and efficient rather than elaborate. You need access to basic equipment—dumbbells, resistance bands, or a gym with standard equipment—and you need to perform compound movements that work multiple muscle groups simultaneously rather than isolation exercises that work single muscles. The fundamental movements are variations of squatting, hinging, pushing, and pulling. Squats or leg presses work all leg muscles. Deadlifts or similar hip hinge movements work the posterior chain. Bench presses, overhead presses, or pushups work all pressing muscles. Rows and pulldowns work all pulling muscles. Performing two to three exercises from these categories for three sets of eight to twelve repetitions provides sufficient stimulus when performed with progressive overload where you gradually increase weight or difficulty over time.

This is not complicated training requiring specialized knowledge or coaching for most people. The basic movements are intuitive and can be learned from books, videos, or brief instruction from competent trainers. The time requirement per session is thirty minutes including warm-up. The person who claims this is too complicated or time-consuming to implement is revealing that they have not seriously considered the alternative of declining physical capacity and eventual disability. The one percent view resistance training as non-negotiable infrastructure maintenance rather than as optional hobby requiring motivation or interest.

The walking or general movement target of ten thousand steps daily represents approximately five miles of walking or equivalent activity. For sedentary office workers, this requires deliberate effort because typical office work generates perhaps two thousand to four thousand steps daily, leaving a deficit of six thousand to eight thousand steps that must be added through intentional walking. This might be achieved through walking during lunch breaks, taking stairs rather than elevators, parking at distant locations rather than near entrances, walking while taking phone calls when possible, or dedicated evening walks. The time requirement varies based on walking speed but approximates sixty to ninety minutes daily of walking spread across multiple short periods rather than requiring a single dedicated block.

This seems like substantial time investment until you understand what this movement provides. Regular walking reduces all-cause mortality by approximately thirty percent independent of other exercise. It supports cardiovascular health without the joint stress of running. It provides opportunity for mental processing that often produces insights unavailable during focused desk work. It breaks up prolonged sitting that contributes to metabolic dysfunction regardless of whether you exercise separately. The person who walks ten thousand steps daily while maintaining sedentary job experiences metabolic health similar to someone with moderately active job rather than experiencing the metabolic dysfunction that accompanies purely sedentary lifestyle.

The nutrition framework that supports health and performance without requiring elaborate meal planning or unsustainable restriction emphasizes three principles that are universally accepted across nearly all dietary philosophies despite their disagreement on specifics. First, protein consumption should be adequate to support muscle maintenance and metabolic function. Second, vegetable consumption should be substantial to provide micronutrients and fiber. Third, refined carbohydrates and added sugars should be limited because they provide calories without nutritional value while promoting metabolic dysfunction. Following these three principles while otherwise eating according to preference produces dramatically better health outcomes than the typical American diet regardless of which specific dietary approach you favor.

The protein target for adults maintaining muscle mass should approximate 0.7 to 1.0 grams per pound of body weight daily. Someone weighing one hundred sixty pounds needs approximately one hundred twelve to one hundred sixty grams of protein daily. This is substantially more than most people consume because protein is generally more expensive and requires more preparation than carbohydrate-based foods. The person who prioritizes protein at every meal through combination of animal proteins like chicken, fish, eggs, and dairy, or through plant proteins like beans, lentils, and tofu, meets this target without conscious calculation. The person who eats carbohydrate-focused meals with protein as afterthought consistently underfeeds protein requirements and experiences muscle loss, poor satiety leading to excessive calorie consumption, and suboptimal metabolic function.

The vegetable target should be substantial servings with lunch and dinner at minimum. The specific quantity matters less than ensuring vegetables comprise at least half of your plate volume at major meals. This approach automatically provides the fiber and micronutrients your body requires while displacing less nutritious foods from your meals. The person who fills half their plate with vegetables at lunch and dinner consumes perhaps six to eight servings daily, far exceeding the pathetically low vegetable consumption of typical Americans who average one to two servings daily. This single change produces measurable improvements in markers of metabolic health, digestive function, and disease risk independent of any other dietary modifications.

The limitation of refined carbohydrates and added sugars means minimizing consumption of breads, pastas, white rice, sugary beverages, desserts, and snack foods that comprise the majority of calories in typical American diets. These foods provide rapid glucose spikes followed by crashes that create energy fluctuations, impair cognitive function, and drive hunger shortly after consumption despite high calorie content. They contribute to insulin resistance that progresses to type two diabetes affecting nearly half of American adults. They provide essentially zero nutritional value beyond calories that most people already consume in excess. The person who eliminates or drastically reduces these foods while maintaining adequate protein and vegetables experiences stable energy, improved cognitive function, better weight management, and substantially reduced disease risk.

This nutrition framework requires no special foods, no complicated meal plans, no calorie counting, and no elimination of entire food groups. It simply means prioritizing protein and vegetables while limiting foods that everyone knows are nutritionally poor despite consuming them regularly out of habit and convenience. The person who implements this framework while otherwise eating flexibly according to preference achieves the vast majority of benefits available from any dietary approach without the restrictions or complexity that make most diets unsustainable over decades.

The sleep component of health maintenance deserves attention equal to exercise and nutrition because sleep deprivation impairs cognitive function, emotional regulation, and metabolic health in ways that directly undermine wealth-building capacity. The person who consistently sleeps fewer than seven hours nightly experiences cognitive impairment equivalent to moderate alcohol intoxication. Their decision-making quality declines, their ability to focus diminishes, their emotional responses become less controlled, and their physical health suffers through disrupted hormonal regulation and impaired immune function. The person who maintains seven to eight hours of consistent sleep maintains cognitive function, emotional stability, and physical health that support peak performance.

The one percent prioritize sleep as non-negotiable foundation for performance rather than as luxury to be sacrificed when busy. They establish consistent sleep schedules even when this requires declining evening activities or structuring work to accommodate adequate sleep. They create sleep environments that support quality rest through darkness, quiet, cool temperatures, and comfortable bedding. They avoid caffeine in afternoon and evening hours because it impairs sleep quality even when you successfully fall asleep. They limit alcohol because while it may facilitate falling asleep, it disrupts sleep architecture and prevents the deep sleep stages necessary for physical recovery and cognitive restoration.

The practical implementation of these health maintenance principles requires systems that make good choices automatic rather than depending on daily motivation or willpower. You schedule exercise sessions in your calendar as non-negotiable appointments that receive the same priority as important business meetings. You prepare simple meals in bulk during weekend cooking sessions so that eating well requires no more time or effort than eating poorly during busy weekdays. You establish bedtime routines that begin ninety minutes before target sleep time, creating wind-down period that facilitates quality sleep rather than attempting to transition directly from high-intensity work to sleep. These systems remove decision-making from the process, making health maintenance as automatic as other routines you maintain without conscious effort.

The cost of implementing these health maintenance practices is minimal compared to the costs of neglecting health. Resistance training requires either minimal home equipment costing one hundred to three hundred dollars or gym membership costing three hundred to six hundred dollars annually. Walking requires no equipment beyond appropriate shoes. The nutrition principles described add no cost and likely reduce food spending by eliminating expensive processed foods and restaurant meals. Sleep requires no expenditure beyond potentially upgrading mattress or bedding if current items impair sleep quality. The total annual cost of implementing comprehensive health maintenance is perhaps five hundred to one thousand dollars plus approximately five to seven hours weekly of time investment.

The return on this investment dwarfs returns from any financial investment available to ordinary investors. The person who maintains health adds years or decades to their productive working life, generating hundreds of thousands to millions in additional earnings. They avoid tens or hundreds of thousands in medical expenses treating preventable chronic diseases. They maintain cognitive function that allows superior investment decisions during decades when their portfolios are largest. They preserve quality of life that makes wealth meaningful rather than merely supporting existence during years of disability. The financial impact of health maintenance versus health neglect easily exceeds one million dollars over a lifetime for anyone earning reasonable income.

The comparison to financial investments clarifies the priority that health maintenance deserves. Someone who invests ten thousand dollars at age thirty at ten percent returns accumulates one hundred seventy-four thousand dollars by age sixty-five. This seems like excellent return and motivates people to prioritize investing despite requiring discipline to save rather than spend the capital. The same person who invests five hours weekly in health maintenance from age thirty to sixty-five adds perhaps ten productive working years extending career to seventy-five, generates three million in additional earnings at one hundred thousand annually after sixty-five, avoids two hundred thousand in medical expenses treating diabetes and cardiovascular disease, and makes better investment decisions through sustained cognitive function that add perhaps five hundred thousand to portfolio value through superior returns during peak wealth years. The total financial impact exceeds three million seven hundred thousand dollars. The time invested is approximately nine thousand hours over thirty-five years. The return is over four hundred dollars per hour invested in health maintenance. No financial investment available to ordinary investors produces comparable returns with such reliability.

Yet people invest countless hours optimizing financial decisions while investing zero hours in health maintenance that would generate returns ten times larger. This is not rational behavior but rather is result of disconnection between health choices and financial outcomes in most people's minds. They view health as separate domain from wealth building rather than recognizing that health is the foundation upon which all wealth building depends. The one percent make this connection explicitly and prioritize health maintenance accordingly because they understand the mathematics and because they have observed peers whose wealth building was cut short or made meaningless by health neglect.

The sustainability of health maintenance approaches matters more than their theoretical optimality because the benefits accrue through decades of consistent implementation rather than through intensity during brief periods. The person who trains intensely for six months then stops due to injury or burnout receives minimal lasting benefit. The person who maintains modest consistent exercise for forty years transforms their health trajectory and extends their productive years substantially. The one percent choose approaches they can sustain indefinitely rather than pursuing optimal protocols that prove unsustainable and lead to abandonment.

This means choosing exercises you tolerate even if they are not your favorites, because tolerability matters more than enthusiasm when the requirement is decades of consistency. It means establishing nutrition patterns that feel normal and sustainable rather than following restrictive diets that require constant willpower to maintain. It means creating sleep routines that fit within your life constraints rather than adopting idealized sleep schedules that cannot be maintained given work and family obligations. The perfect program that you abandon after six months produces worse results than the adequate program you maintain for forty years.

The preventive care component of health maintenance includes regular medical checkups and age-appropriate screening that allows early detection and treatment of problems before they become serious. The one percent view preventive care as essential maintenance rather than as optional when they happen to feel sick. They establish relationships with primary care physicians who know their medical histories and who can provide continuity of care over decades. They complete recommended screenings for cancer, cardiovascular disease, and metabolic conditions at appropriate ages and intervals. They address small problems promptly rather than ignoring them until they become large problems requiring major interventions.

The cost of preventive care is minimal and often fully covered by insurance. Annual checkups, basic blood work, and age-appropriate screenings typically cost little or nothing out of pocket while potentially detecting problems early when treatment is far less expensive and more effective than treatment after symptoms develop. The person who skips preventive care because they feel fine often discovers serious problems only after they have progressed to stages requiring major treatment or after they have caused irreversible damage. This penny-wise pound-foolish approach to medical care destroys wealth through medical expenses that could have been prevented or minimized through early detection and intervention.

The stress management and recovery practices that support sustained high performance include activities that allow mental and physical recovery from work demands. The one percent understand that peak performance requires both intense effort during work periods and adequate recovery between efforts. They schedule activities that provide mental breaks from work-related thinking, whether this involves exercise, hobbies, time with family and friends, or simply periods of doing nothing without obligation or stimulation. They take vacations not as rewards for hard work but as necessary recovery periods that allow sustained performance across years and decades. They recognize warning signs of burnout or excessive stress and they respond by adjusting workload or implementing additional recovery practices rather than pushing through until performance collapses.

The relationship between physical health and earning capacity operates through multiple mechanisms that compound over working years. The person who maintains high energy through proper nutrition, adequate sleep, and regular exercise produces more and better work than equally skilled person who experiences low energy from poor health habits. This productivity difference affects income through promotions, opportunities, and business success that favor those who consistently deliver excellent performance. The person who maintains cognitive function through health practices makes better decisions about career moves, investment opportunities, and business strategies than person whose judgment is impaired by poor metabolic health or inadequate sleep. These better decisions compound into substantially superior financial outcomes across decades. The person who maintains physical health works additional years beyond typical retirement age when their skills are most valuable and when their portfolios are largest, generating enormous additional wealth compared to person forced into early retirement by preventable health problems.

The integration of health maintenance with wealth-building strategy should be explicit rather than hoping health somehow takes care of itself while you focus on financial matters. You schedule exercise sessions and protect them with the same discipline you apply to important business meetings. You structure your food shopping and preparation with the same systematic approach you use for budgeting and investing. You track your sleep with the same attention you give to tracking expenses or investment returns. You view time invested in health maintenance as essential infrastructure spending rather than as optional activity competing with wealth-building priorities. This integration ensures that health receives appropriate attention rather than being consistently sacrificed to short-term work demands that seem urgent but that ultimately undermine the long-term performance health would have supported.

Ray Dalio's systematic approach to health maintenance exemplifies how the one percent integrate physical infrastructure maintenance with their wealth-building activities. He did not wait until health problems forced attention to these issues. He established health practices early in his career and maintained them through decades regardless of business demands or market conditions. This proactive approach allowed sustained peak performance across five decades of building and managing his investment firm. The meditation practice provided emotional regulation and cognitive clarity that supported better decision-making during stressful market conditions. The exercise routine sustained energy and physical health that allowed decades of intense work without burnout or decline. The sleep prioritization maintained cognitive function necessary for analyzing complex investment opportunities and managing billions in assets.

The broader principle is that your body is infrastructure that either supports or limits everything else you attempt to accomplish. Financial wealth matters only if you have the health to enjoy it and the longevity to benefit from its compound growth. Career success matters only if you can sustain performance long enough to build meaningful achievements. Investment knowledge matters only if you maintain cognitive function to apply it effectively during decades when your portfolios are largest. All of these depend completely on physical health that results from consistent maintenance rather than from hoping good health persists without investment in the practices that create it.

We have now addressed every major component of wealth building from mindset and values through strategies for earning, investing, and preserving capital, through management of major expense categories, through optimization of career advancement and communication, through systematic approaches to food and now to health. The pattern across all domains is that the one percent make decisions based on long-term outcomes rather than short-term convenience, they establish systems that make optimal choices automatic rather than depending on daily motivation, and they prioritize fundamentals that matter rather than being distracted by complexity or optimization at the margins.

Health maintenance represents perhaps the clearest example of this pattern because the benefits of good practices and the costs of neglect compound so dramatically across decades. The thirty-year-old who establishes excellent health habits experiences minimal immediate benefit because they likely feel fine regardless of their choices at that age. The seventy-year-old who maintained those habits for forty years experiences profound benefits through sustained physical capability, cognitive function, independence, and quality of life that their peers who neglected health do not enjoy. The choice is whether to invest modest time and attention in health practices whose benefits compound across decades, or whether to focus exclusively on financial wealth that becomes meaningless without the health to enjoy it or the longevity to benefit from its growth.

The one percent make this choice consciously by prioritizing health maintenance as essential infrastructure supporting all other wealth-building activities. The ninety-nine percent ignore health maintenance while focusing on financial optimization, then discover during their fifties and sixties that poor health undermines or destroys the wealth they spent decades building. You now understand why health maintenance matters for wealth building specifically and how to implement sustainable practices that provide the benefits without requiring unsustainable time investment or lifestyle restrictions. Whether you implement these practices or continue neglecting the physical infrastructure upon which everything else depends on will lead to consequences which will compound across your remaining years in ways that determine whether your wealth building produces the freedom and quality of life you imagine or whether health problems consume the wealth you built while preventing you from enjoying the life that wealth was supposed to enable.

CHAPTER 22:
HIGH-YIELD SAVINGS AND CASH MANAGEMENT

In March 2009, a portfolio manager named David Swensen sat in his office at Yale University watching global financial markets implode around him. The endowment he managed had declined by nearly thirty percent during the previous year as stocks, real estate, and nearly every asset class experienced simultaneous collapse. Most institutional investors were paralyzed with fear, holding positions that continued deteriorating while hoping for eventual recovery. Swensen had a different problem. He had maintained substantial cash positions throughout the preceding years despite criticism from board members who questioned why Yale was holding billions in cash earning minimal returns while markets rose. That cash, which had seemed like drag on performance during the boom years, suddenly represented the most valuable asset in Yale's portfolio.

While other institutions faced margin calls, forced liquidations, and desperate searches for liquidity, Swensen deployed Yale's cash reserves into assets that had declined seventy to eighty percent from peak values. He purchased distressed debt, acquired positions in companies trading at fraction of intrinsic value, and negotiated favorable terms with managers desperate for capital. These investments, made possible only because Yale had maintained disciplined cash reserves during years when holding cash seemed foolish, generated returns over the following decade that transformed what appeared to be Yale's worst endowment performance into one of its best strategic decisions. The cash that critics had derided as wasted opportunity during rising markets proved to be the dry powder that allowed Yale to capitalize on the greatest buying opportunity in generations.

This example demonstrates the principle that separates sophisticated investors from those who merely follow conventional wisdom. Cash is not dead money earning nothing while inflation erodes its value. Cash is optionality. It is the capacity to act when opportunities arise. It is the insurance that prevents forced selling during downturns. It is the foundation that allows you to sleep well regardless of what other assets in your portfolio are experiencing. The question is not whether to hold cash but rather how much to hold, where to hold it, and how to ensure that while it sits waiting for deployment or emergency use, it generates reasonable returns rather than being genuinely idle.

The framework for understanding cash management begins with recognizing that cash serves multiple distinct purposes in a wealth-building portfolio, each requiring different treatment and optimization. Transaction cash funds daily living expenses and must be immediately accessible without any risk of loss or delay. This money sits in checking accounts where it earns essentially nothing because the purpose is facilitating transactions rather than generating returns. Emergency reserves protect against unexpected expenses or temporary income loss and must be accessible within days without risk of loss. These funds belong in savings vehicles that offer higher interest than checking accounts while maintaining complete safety and reasonable access. Opportunity reserves position you to act on investments or business opportunities when they arise and can tolerate slightly longer access timeframes in exchange for modestly higher returns. Strategic cash positions in overall portfolio provide both downside protection during market volatility and capital for deployment during market dislocations. These larger cash positions might be optimized through vehicles offering highest safe returns even if access requires several days or weeks.

The checking account serves transaction purposes exclusively and should contain approximately one month of living expenses. This provides sufficient buffer to handle normal monthly expenses while avoiding the need to monitor account balances constantly or worry about overdrafts. Anything beyond this amount represents capital earning zero return while inflation slowly erodes its purchasing power. The ninety-nine percent maintain checking account balances far exceeding their transaction needs because they view their checking account as general holding location for money rather than as specifically designated transaction vehicle. They might maintain five thousand or ten thousand dollars in checking accounts earning nothing despite needing only two thousand for actual transactions. The excess three to eight thousand dollars earning zero return costs them one hundred fifty to four hundred dollars annually in foregone interest at five percent rates that high-yield savings accounts currently offer. Over twenty years, this seemingly small optimization failure costs ten thousand to twenty-five thousand dollars in accumulated wealth.

The one percent maintain minimal checking balances sufficient for transactions plus small buffer, then sweep everything else into higher-yielding vehicles. They establish automatic transfers that move excess checking balance to savings or money market accounts weekly or even daily. This ensures that capital never sits idle in checking accounts when it could be earning meaningful returns in equally safe vehicles. The automation requires perhaps fifteen minutes to establish and operates indefinitely without attention. The return is hundreds to thousands annually depending on account balances. This represents guaranteed risk-free return available to anyone with internet access and basic ability to open accounts at online financial institutions.

The emergency fund represents the next tier of cash positioning and should cover three to six months of living expenses in accounts offering high interest rates while maintaining complete safety and reasonable access. We discussed emergency fund sizing in Chapter Nineteen during budgeting discussion, but the question here is where to hold these funds for optimal returns while meeting accessibility requirements. The traditional answer has been savings accounts at major banks offering interest rates of approximately 0.01 to 0.1 percent annually. These rates are effectively zero, providing no meaningful compensation for your deposits while the banks use your capital to generate their own returns through lending and investment activities. This arrangement benefits banks enormously while providing depositors essentially nothing.

The emergence of online banks without physical branch infrastructure has disrupted this exploitative dynamic by offering savings accounts paying competitive interest rates that actually compensate depositors fairly for use of their capital. As of late 2024 and into 2025, high-yield savings accounts at institutions like Marcus by Goldman Sachs, Ally Bank, American Express Personal Savings, and numerous other online banks are offering rates between four and five percent annually. These rates fluctuate based on Federal Reserve policy and competitive dynamics, but they consistently exceed rates at traditional brick-and-mortar banks by four to five percentage points. The difference represents real money at any meaningful account balance.

Someone maintaining a twenty-thousand-dollar emergency fund in traditional savings account earning 0.05 percent annually receives ten dollars in interest. The same person moving that emergency fund to high-yield savings account earning 4.5 percent receives nine hundred dollars annually. The difference of eight hundred ninety dollars represents guaranteed risk-free additional return captured simply by opening an account at different institution and transferring funds electronically. Over ten years, this single optimization generates nine thousand dollars in additional wealth compared to leaving funds in traditional savings account. The time required is perhaps thirty minutes to research high-yield savings accounts, open an account, and initiate transfer. The return is approximately eighteen thousand dollars per hour for that time investment.

The objections to high-yield savings accounts typically involve concerns about safety, accessibility, or legitimacy of online institutions most people have never heard of. These concerns are misplaced. High-yield savings accounts at reputable online banks are insured by the Federal Deposit Insurance Corporation exactly like accounts at traditional banks, providing protection up to two hundred fifty thousand dollars per depositor per institution. The funds are accessible through electronic transfer to your checking account, typically arriving within one to three business days. This represents reasonable accessibility for emergency funds where the definition of emergency is unexpected major expense or temporary income loss rather than needing cash within hours. For genuine same-day emergencies, you can use credit cards and pay them off when savings transfers arrive.

The legitimacy concern about online banks unfamiliar to most people fails to recognize that many of these institutions are backed by major financial companies with decades of history. Marcus is operated by Goldman Sachs, one of the most established financial institutions in America. American Express has operated financial services for over a century. Ally Bank emerged from GMAC, the financing arm of General Motors that operated for nearly a century before rebranding. These are not fly-by-night operations but rather are major financial institutions that happen to operate online rather than through physical branches. Their lack of branch infrastructure is precisely what allows them to offer higher interest rates because they avoid the enormous costs of maintaining thousands of physical locations and the staff to operate them.

The selection of specific high-yield savings accounts should consider current interest rates, account minimums, ease of transferring funds to and from the account, customer service reputation, and any fees or restrictions. The interest rates at various online banks cluster within narrow ranges because they compete directly with each other for deposits. You need not optimize for the absolute highest rate if that requires using less established institution with poor customer service or difficult account management. The difference between 4.3 percent and 4.5 percent on twenty thousand dollars is forty dollars annually. This matters, but it matters less than whether you can easily transfer funds when needed or whether you can reach competent customer service if problems arise.

The maintenance of emergency funds at multiple institutions provides additional FDIC insurance coverage and reduces concentration risk from having all emergency funds at single institution. If you maintain fifty thousand in emergency reserves, holding twenty-five thousand at two different high-yield savings accounts provides five hundred thousand in total FDIC coverage rather than the two hundred fifty thousand maximum per institution. This becomes relevant for anyone maintaining emergency funds exceeding FDIC limits at single institution. The additional benefit is that you maintain redundancy in access if one institution experiences technical problems or other issues that temporarily impair your ability to transfer funds. The person with emergency funds at two institutions can access funds from either account if one experiences problems.

The money market funds represent alternative vehicle for holding cash that offers competitive yields while providing additional flexibility for larger balances. Money market funds are mutual funds that invest exclusively in short-term high-quality debt instruments like Treasury bills, commercial paper, and certificates of deposit. They aim to maintain stable one-dollar net asset value per share while generating returns through the underlying securities. The returns typically approximate or slightly exceed high-yield savings account rates depending on current market conditions. Money market funds are not FDIC insured because they are investment vehicles rather than bank deposits, but they invest in securities considered extremely safe and the stable NAV structure means your balance does not fluctuate from day to day.

The advantages of money market funds include typically higher yields than even high-yield savings accounts, ease of transferring large amounts without transaction limits or fees, and availability within brokerage accounts where you may already maintain investment portfolios. If you hold stocks and bonds in a Vanguard or Fidelity account, you can hold cash in their money market funds and transfer between money market funds and investment positions instantly without moving money between institutions. This convenience matters for opportunity capital that you might deploy into investment opportunities when they arise. The disadvantage is that money market funds lack FDIC insurance and technically carry minimal credit risk from underlying securities, though this risk is extremely low for funds investing in Treasury securities or high-quality commercial paper.

The Treasury bill laddering provides alternative cash management strategy offering yields that typically exceed both high-yield savings accounts and money market funds while maintaining complete safety through direct investment in U.S. government obligations. Treasury bills are short-term government securities with maturities ranging from four weeks to fifty-two weeks. They are sold at discount to face value and mature at face value, with the difference representing your interest return. As of late 2024 and into 2025, Treasury bill yields have ranged from approximately 4.5 to 5.5 percent depending on maturity, offering attractive returns on completely safe capital.

The laddering strategy involves purchasing Treasury bills with staggered maturities so that portions of your cash position mature at regular intervals. For example, you might divide sixty thousand dollars in opportunity capital into twelve equal portions of five thousand dollars each, purchasing one Treasury bill maturing in each of the next twelve months. Every month, one bill matures and provides five thousand dollars that you can either deploy into opportunities or roll into a new twelve-month bill if no opportunities have emerged. This provides both superior yields on your cash and regular liquidity at monthly intervals without requiring you to sell securities before maturity.

The Treasury bill purchasing process has been simplified through TreasuryDirect, the government website that allows direct purchase of Treasury securities without using brokers. You establish an account, link your bank account, and purchase bills at weekly auctions. The process requires perhaps an hour initially to set up the account and understand the mechanics, then perhaps fifteen minutes monthly to maintain the ladder by purchasing new bills as old bills mature. The alternative is purchasing Treasury bills through your brokerage account, which many major brokers now support with even simpler interfaces than TreasuryDirect but potentially with small transaction fees that slightly reduce your net returns.

The decision among high-yield savings accounts, money market funds, and Treasury bill ladders depends on your total cash position, your need for immediate versus delayed accessibility, your comfort with different vehicles, and current rate differentials. For emergency funds requiring maximum accessibility and complete safety, high-yield savings accounts represent the optimal choice. For larger opportunity capital that might remain uninvested for months or longer, Treasury bill ladders offer superior yields while maintaining safety. For cash within brokerage accounts that you might deploy into investment opportunities, money market funds provide convenience while generating competitive returns. The one percent use all three vehicles appropriately for different purposes rather than treating all cash as identical and holding it all in single location.

The avoidance of bank fees represents another dimension of cash management that most people neglect despite these fees consuming hundreds of dollars annually. Major banks charge maintenance fees for checking and savings accounts unless you maintain minimum balances or establish direct deposits. They charge overdraft fees when account balances go negative. They charge ATM fees when you use machines outside their network. They charge wire transfer fees, stop payment fees, and various other fees for routine banking activities. These fees aggregate to substantial amounts over years while providing essentially no value to account holders. The banks profit enormously from fee income extracted from customers who tolerate these charges because they have always banked at these institutions and never considered alternatives.

The one percent pay essentially zero banking fees by using online banks and credit unions that compete on service rather than on fees. Online banks typically charge no monthly maintenance fees, provide unlimited ATM fee reimbursements, charge no overdraft fees if you maintain minimal balances, and generally avoid the fee structures that traditional banks use to extract revenue from deposit accounts. Credit unions similarly operate with lower fee structures than major banks because they are member-owned rather than profit-maximizing corporations. Moving from a major bank charging two hundred dollars annually in various fees to an online bank charging zero fees saves two hundred dollars annually guaranteed. Over thirty years, this is six thousand dollars in fees avoided, which compounds to approximately seventeen thousand dollars at ten percent returns if the saved fees are invested rather than consumed.

The monitoring of interest rates and willingness to move capital when better opportunities emerge separates those who optimize cash management from those who establish accounts once and then ignore rates for years. Interest rates fluctuate based on Federal Reserve policy and competitive dynamics among financial institutions. The high-yield savings account offering competitive 4.5 percent rate today might offer only 2 percent if Federal Reserve lowers rates while new competitors emerge offering 3 percent. The person who established their account when rates were competitive and never reviews current offerings misses opportunities to capture higher returns through moving capital to better-paying institutions.

The one percent review their cash positioning annually at minimum, checking current rates at their existing institutions against rates available at competitors. When meaningful rate differentials exist and persist, they transfer funds to institutions offering superior rates. This requires perhaps thirty minutes annually to research current rates and potentially another thirty minutes to open new accounts and transfer funds if better options exist. The return depends on the rate differential and account balances but can easily represent several hundred dollars annually in additional interest captured through active management rather than passive neglect. The monitoring and occasional account movement prevent the gradual decay that occurs when you establish competitive positioning initially but then allow it to become uncompetitive through years of neglect.

The integration of cash management with broader investment strategy requires understanding cash as one component of overall asset allocation rather than treating it as separate category unconnected to your stocks, bonds, and real estate positions. The appropriate cash allocation depends on your current life stage, upcoming needs for capital, risk tolerance, and market conditions.

Someone in their twenties with stable employment and no major expenses on the horizon might maintain minimal cash beyond three months of emergency funds, deploying essentially all other capital into stock market investments that offer higher expected returns over the decades until retirement. Someone in their fifties approaching retirement might maintain twelve to twenty-four months of living expenses in cash to provide buffer against being forced to sell stocks during market downturns that often occur near retirement. Someone who has identified specific investment opportunity that will require capital deployment in coming months holds that capital in cash rather than in stocks where it might decline in value before needed.

This dynamic cash management based on circumstances and opportunities requires judgment and regular reassessment rather than establishing some fixed cash percentage and maintaining it regardless of changing situations. The rigid approach that maintains exactly ten percent cash allocation while other assets fluctuate forces you to sell stocks when they rise to replenish cash and to buy stocks with cash when markets fall. This sounds like disciplined rebalancing but it actually costs you returns because you are maintaining fixed cash allocation during periods when holding more stocks would serve you better. The flexible approach adjusts cash levels based on whether you anticipate needing capital soon, whether market conditions suggest heightened risk that makes additional cash positioning prudent, or whether opportunities exist that justify holding cash temporarily awaiting deployment.

David Swensen's maintenance of substantial cash positions at Yale during the mid-2000s while markets rose exemplifies this flexible approach. He recognized that valuations across most asset classes had become extended, that opportunities to deploy capital into attractive investments had become scarce, and that maintaining higher-than-normal cash positions provided both protection if markets declined and capacity to invest aggressively if opportunities emerged. The opportunity cost during rising markets was real but acceptable given the protection and optionality the cash provided. When markets collapsed and opportunities emerged exactly as his positioning anticipated, the cash reserves proved invaluable and generated returns that more than compensated for the opportunity cost during preceding years.

Most people lack the sophistication or conviction to position their portfolios this way. They follow fixed allocation rules because these rules provide certainty and remove decision-making burden. This is acceptable if you understand what you are giving up through this simplified approach. The fixed allocation to cash provides some protection and optionality but less than dynamic allocation would provide. The fixed allocation might maintain more cash than optimal during periods when deploying that cash into investments would generate superior returns. These are prices paid for simplicity and for avoiding the judgment calls required by dynamic allocation approaches.

The tax treatment of interest income from cash holdings matters for high earners who might be in substantial tax brackets. Interest from savings accounts, money market funds, and Treasury bills is taxed as ordinary income at your marginal rate. Someone in the thirty-five percent combined federal and state tax bracket earning 4.5 percent interest receives 2.9 percent after-tax return. This is still superior to earning nothing on cash sitting in checking accounts, but it reduces the real return materially. Treasury bills offer modest tax advantage because they are exempt from state and local taxes though still subject to federal tax. In states with high income taxes, this state tax exemption can represent meaningful advantage over savings accounts and money market funds that are fully taxable.

The municipal money market funds invest in short-term municipal securities and generate income exempt from federal taxes and potentially from state taxes if you purchase funds investing in securities from your state of residence. These funds typically offer lower nominal yields than taxable money market funds but higher after-tax yields for investors in high tax brackets. Someone in thirty-five percent federal bracket earning 3 percent tax-exempt yield receives equivalent of 4.6 percent taxable yield. This makes municipal money market funds potentially attractive for high earners holding substantial cash balances, though you must verify that your specific tax situation and the fund's yield justify the additional complexity compared to simply using taxable money market funds or Treasury bills.

The cash management within retirement accounts follows different considerations because these accounts already provide tax advantages that eliminate or reduce the importance of tax-efficient cash vehicles. Money held in traditional IRAs or 401k accounts generates no current tax on interest regardless of source. Money held in Roth IRAs generates no tax ever on interest. This means you should prioritize highest-yielding safe cash vehicles within retirement accounts without concern about tax treatment. You might use Treasury bills or corporate bond funds offering higher yields than savings accounts, accepting that these generate ordinary income that would be heavily taxed in taxable accounts but that generates no current tax within retirement accounts.

The broader principle connecting cash management to wealth building is that wealth is built through systematic deployment of capital into assets that generate returns above inflation and taxes. Cash is necessary for transaction purposes, for emergency protection, for opportunity positioning, and for portfolio stability. Cash is not where you build wealth because cash returns barely exceed or potentially fall below inflation after taxes. The goal of cash management is ensuring that cash serves its necessary purposes efficiently while generating best available returns given safety and accessibility requirements, and then ensuring that all capital beyond these cash needs is deployed into higher-returning assets like stocks, real estate, or businesses.

The person who maintains twenty percent of their net worth in cash earning four percent when they have no need for that much liquidity is building wealth approximately six percent more slowly than the person who maintains appropriate cash reserves and deploys everything else into stocks earning ten percent. Over thirty years, this six percentage point difference in returns on twenty percent of portfolio compounds into enormous wealth differential. Someone with five hundred thousand in assets maintaining one hundred thousand in unnecessary cash rather than deploying eighty thousand of it into stocks generates approximately five hundred thousand dollars less wealth over thirty years through this single suboptimal allocation decision.

The one percent recognize that while cash management matters, it matters far less than the major decisions about earning income, maintaining high savings rates, choosing appropriate investment vehicles, and avoiding major spending mistakes. Optimizing cash management by moving from zero percent to four percent returns on cash balances generates measurable benefit worth capturing through modest effort. But if you are maintaining checking balances earning nothing while carrying credit card debt at twenty percent interest, optimizing your cash accounts is rearranging deck chairs while your ship sinks. The hierarchy of financial optimization should always address the largest problems first before moving to smaller optimizations.

This does not mean ignoring cash management. It means addressing cash management in its proper sequence after you have established appropriate spending discipline that generates high savings rate, after you have eliminated high-interest debt, after you have established automatic contributions to tax-advantaged investment accounts, and after you have structured major spending categories rationally. Cash management represents the refinement that ensures your emergency funds and transaction capital generate reasonable returns while maintaining appropriate safety and accessibility. This refinement is worth implementing because it costs minimal time and generates guaranteed returns. It simply should not distract you from larger wealth-building priorities if those remain unaddressed.

We have now examined every component of the wealth-building framework from foundational principles through earning strategies, investment vehicles, spending optimization, and now cash management. The pattern is that wealth is built through systematic deployment of capital generated by high savings rates into assets that compound over decades. Cash facilitates this process by providing transaction capability, emergency protection, and opportunity positioning. Cash management ensures these necessary cash holdings generate optimal returns given their constraints. The framework is comprehensive. The principles are clear. The implementation requires discipline sustained over decades.

David Swensen demonstrated through Yale's endowment management that strategic cash positioning combined with willingness to deploy that cash aggressively during market dislocations generates returns that seemingly smarter strategies cannot match. His approach was not complex. He maintained appropriate cash reserves in safe liquid vehicles. He waited for opportunities rather than forcing deployment when valuations were unattractive. He acted decisively when opportunities emerged. This simple framework applied consistently over decades built Yale's endowment into one of the most successful institutional investment portfolios in history. The principles that worked for managing billions at Yale work equally well for managing thousands or millions in personal wealth building. The question is whether you will implement these principles or whether you will leave cash sitting idle while opportunities compound for those who position themselves properly to act when circumstances warrant.

You now understand how to manage cash efficiently while maintaining appropriate safety and accessibility for different purposes. You understand that emergency funds belong in high-yield savings accounts offering competitive rates and FDIC insurance. You understand that larger cash positions might be optimized through money market funds or Treasury bill ladders offering superior yields. You understand that opportunity capital should be positioned for deployment while generating returns during waiting periods. You understand that cash allocation should be flexible based on circumstances rather than rigidly fixed regardless of changing needs or market conditions. The implementation of these principles requires perhaps two hours initially to establish appropriate accounts and another hour annually to review positioning and rates. The returns generated through this modest effort accumulate over decades into thousands or tens of thousands in additional wealth compared to leaving cash idle or suboptimally positioned.

CHAPTER 23:
CREDIT CARDS—LEVERAGE AND REWARDS

In 2003, a young writer named Chris Guillebeau faced a decision that most people would consider reckless. He had been reading about a strategy that seemed too good to be true: certain credit cards offered signup bonuses so generous that if you could meet their spending requirements, you could accumulate enough points to fly around the world essentially for free. The catch was that executing this strategy required opening multiple credit cards, managing various spending thresholds and payment deadlines, and maintaining perfect discipline to never carry balances or miss payments. Most financial advisors would have counseled against this approach, warning that multiple credit applications would damage his credit score and that juggling numerous cards would inevitably lead to missed payments and accumulating debt.

Guillebeau ignored this conventional wisdom and proceeded methodically. He researched which credit cards offered the most valuable signup bonuses relative to their spending requirements. He established systems for tracking every card's billing cycle, payment deadline, and spending progress toward bonus thresholds. He set up automatic payments ensuring that every card received full payment of its statement balance monthly regardless of whether he remembered to pay manually. He never purchased anything on credit cards that he would not have purchased with cash. The cards were simply payment mechanisms that happened to generate rewards, not licenses to spend money he did not have.

Over the following decade, Guillebeau used this systematic approach to accumulate millions of airline miles and hotel points. He traveled to every country in the world, visiting all one hundred ninety-three United Nations member states, while spending a fraction of what such travel would have cost paying cash for flights and accommodations. His credit score, rather than being destroyed by multiple applications as conventional wisdom predicted, remained excellent throughout because he maintained perfect payment history and low utilization across all accounts. He documented his strategies in articles and books that taught others how to replicate his success, helping thousands of people travel extensively using rewards generated from credit cards that most people viewed as dangerous financial instruments to be avoided.

This example reveals the fundamental truth about credit cards that separates the one percent from the ninety-nine percent in their approach to these financial tools. Credit cards are neither inherently good nor inherently bad. They are leverage that amplifies whatever financial discipline or dysfunction you bring to them. The person with excellent financial discipline uses credit cards to generate substantial rewards while building credit history that provides access to favorable financing for major purchases. The person with poor financial discipline uses credit cards to finance consumption they cannot afford, accumulates debt at interest rates that make wealth building impossible, and destroys their credit scores in ways that haunt them for years. The tool is identical. The outcomes diverge completely based on how it is wielded.

The foundation of credit card wisdom begins with understanding how these instruments generate profit for issuing banks and how those profit mechanisms create opportunity for disciplined users while creating catastrophe for undisciplined users. Credit card companies earn revenue from three primary sources. First, they collect interchange fees from merchants every time you use the card, typically two to three percent of transaction value. Second, they charge interest on any balances you carry from month to month, typically at rates between fifteen and twenty-five percent annually. Third, they collect various fees including annual fees for premium cards, late payment fees, over-limit fees, foreign transaction fees, and balance transfer fees.

The disciplined user who pays their balance in full monthly generates revenue for the card company only through interchange fees. The card company must pay you rewards from their interchange revenue and still profit from your account. This is possible because interchange fees on your spending exceed the cost of rewards provided. A card offering two percent cash back on purchases collects approximately 2.5 percent in interchange fees, leaving 0.5 percent margin for the card company. This slim margin is acceptable to card companies because they profit enormously from the majority of cardholders who carry balances and pay interest. Your disciplined use is subsidized by the undisciplined majority who destroy themselves through interest payments and fees.

The undisciplined user who carries balances from month to month generates massive revenue for the card company through interest charges that dwarf interchange fees and rewards. Someone carrying a five thousand dollar balance at twenty percent annual interest pays one thousand dollars annually in interest alone. This single account generating one thousand dollars in annual interest profit subsidizes perhaps fifty accounts used by disciplined users who pay no interest and who collect rewards. The credit card business model depends on this dynamic where a minority of disciplined users extract value while the majority of undisciplined users provide the profits that make the entire system viable.

This understanding should shape your entire approach to credit cards. You are either in the minority extracting value from the system or you are in the majority being exploited by the system. There is no middle ground where you carry small balances occasionally and somehow come out ahead. The mathematics are inexorable. Any interest you pay overwhelms any rewards you receive. The credit card offering two percent cash back that charges twenty percent interest on carried balances requires that you pay full balances every single month without exception. Carrying even small balances even occasionally transforms you from value extractor to exploitation victim because the interest charges exceed the rewards earned.

The cardinal rule of credit card use that determines whether you benefit or suffer from these instruments is this: never carry a balance. Pay the full statement balance every month before the due date. If you cannot afford to pay the full statement balance, you cannot afford to use credit cards and you should stop using them immediately until you have established financial discipline that makes full monthly payment automatic and non-negotiable. This rule has no exceptions. The person who carries balances believing they will pay them off next month or believing that small balances are manageable is already on the path to credit card debt that will take years to eliminate and that will destroy thousands or tens of thousands in wealth through interest payments and foregone investment returns.

The practical implementation of this rule requires treating credit cards as debit cards that happen to provide rewards. Before making any purchase on a credit card, you ask whether you would make this same purchase if you had to pay cash immediately. If the answer is no, you do not make the purchase regardless of available credit on the card. The available credit on your cards is not your money. It is the bank's money that they will lend you at twenty percent interest if you are foolish enough to accept the loan. The disciplined user views available credit as emergency resource to be used only in genuine emergencies where the alternative would be worse than paying high interest temporarily. They never view available credit as license to purchase things they cannot afford with cash.

The automation of full payment eliminates the risk of missed payments that generate late fees and damage credit scores. You establish automatic payments with your credit card companies to withdraw full statement balance from your checking account on the due date every month. This removes human decision-making and the possibility of forgetting to pay. The ninety-nine percent resist automatic full payment because they fear overdrawing checking accounts if the payment is larger than expected. This fear reveals that they are spending more on credit cards than they can actually afford, which is precisely the problem automatic payment prevents by making overspending immediately visible through insufficient checking account funds. The one percent maintain sufficient checking account balances that automatic full payment never risks overdraft, and they review credit card statements before payment dates to verify that charges are legitimate and that they have sufficient checking funds to cover the payment.

The building of credit history and credit scores provides the primary non-reward benefit of credit card use. Your credit score is a numerical representation of your creditworthiness based on your borrowing and repayment history. The score ranges from three hundred to eight hundred fifty, with scores above seven hundred forty considered excellent. This score determines whether you can obtain mortgages, auto loans, and other financing, and it determines the interest rates you pay on any debt you do incur. The difference between excellent credit and poor credit represents hundreds of thousands of dollars in lifetime costs through interest rate differentials on major purchases like homes and vehicles.

The credit score calculation depends on five factors weighted differently in importance. Payment history comprises thirty-five percent of your score and reflects whether you pay all debts on time. A single missed payment can reduce your score by fifty to one hundred points and remains on your credit report for seven years. This makes payment reliability the single most important factor in credit score maintenance. Credit utilization comprises thirty percent and measures how much of your available credit you are using at any given time. Using ten percent of available credit is better than using fifty percent, and using zero to one percent is better still. Length of credit history comprises fifteen percent and measures the average age of your credit accounts and the age of your oldest account. Longer credit history improves scores. Credit mix comprises ten percent and reflects whether you have experience with different types of credit including revolving credit like credit cards and installment loans like mortgages or auto loans. New credit comprises ten percent and measures how many new accounts you have opened recently and how many hard inquiries appear on your credit report from applications for credit.

The strategy for building excellent credit scores involves maximizing the factors you can control. You establish perfect payment history by never missing any payment on any debt ever. You maintain low credit utilization by paying balances in full monthly and by requesting credit limit increases that raise your total available credit. You build length of credit history by opening credit accounts early and keeping old accounts open even if you stop using them actively. You develop credit mix by eventually having both revolving credit and installment loans when you purchase homes or vehicles. You minimize new credit impact by spacing credit applications over time rather than opening multiple accounts simultaneously.

The person with no credit history faces the challenge that they cannot obtain credit because they have no history, but they cannot build history without obtaining credit. This catch-twenty-two is resolved through secured credit cards designed specifically for people building credit from zero. A secured card requires you to deposit money as collateral, typically five hundred to one thousand dollars, and provides a credit limit equal to your deposit. You use this card for small purchases and pay the balance in full monthly. After six to twelve months of perfect payment history, the card company refunds your deposit and converts the account to unsecured status or you qualify for traditional unsecured cards. This allows you to establish payment history that enables access to standard credit cards and eventually to other forms of credit.

The person who damaged their credit through previous mistakes faces similar challenges requiring deliberate rehabilitation. They begin by obtaining a secured card if necessary, make perfect payments for extended periods to establish new positive history, pay down existing debts to reduce utilization, avoid new credit applications that would generate additional hard inquiries, and wait for negative items to age off their credit reports after seven years. Rebuilding credit requires patience and discipline sustained over years, but the payoff is access to financing at reasonable rates rather than being locked into subprime interest rates or denied credit entirely.

The selection of which credit cards to obtain depends on your spending patterns, your willingness to manage complexity, and your goals for rewards. The basic categories are cash back cards that provide percentage rebates on purchases, travel rewards cards that provide points or miles usable for flights and hotels, and co-branded cards affiliated with specific airlines or hotel chains. Cash back cards offer simplicity because the rewards are straightforward percentages of spending that arrive as statement credits or deposits. Travel rewards cards offer potentially higher value if you use points strategically for travel redemptions that exceed the cash value of the points. Co-branded cards offer the highest rewards for spending with specific merchants but lower rewards for other spending.

The one percent select cards based on where they spend money most frequently. If you spend substantially on groceries, a card offering three to four percent cash back on groceries provides better returns than a card offering two percent on everything. If you spend substantially on dining and travel, a card offering three percent on those categories beats a general two percent card. If you spend relatively evenly across categories, a simple two percent cash back card on all purchases provides excellent returns without requiring tracking of category bonuses or rotating categories. The optimal strategy for most people is holding one or two cards that cover their major spending categories well rather than holding dozens of cards requiring complex tracking to optimize rewards across numerous programs.

Chris Guillebeau's approach of holding numerous cards to maximize signup bonuses represents advanced strategy appropriate for people who have demonstrated perfect discipline with credit cards and who have systems for managing complexity. The average person attempting to replicate this strategy will likely miss payments, fail to track spending across multiple cards, and accumulate fees that exceed any rewards earned. The signup bonuses are substantial, often worth five hundred to one thousand dollars or more per card, but capturing these bonuses requires meeting spending thresholds within specific timeframes, tracking which cards you have already obtained from which banks, spacing applications to avoid having too many hard inquiries concentrated in short periods, and maintaining perfect payment across all accounts. This is sophisticated financial management that should not be attempted by anyone who has ever carried credit card balances or missed payments.

The cash back redemption strategies maximize the value of rewards earned. Some cards provide statement credits that directly reduce your balance, which is simple but provides no additional benefit beyond the cash value. Other cards allow you to redeem cash back for deposits to investment accounts, which provides the same cash value but makes it easier to ensure that rewards are invested rather than spent. Some cards provide bonuses for redeeming rewards for specific purposes like travel booked through their portals or for gift cards, which might provide value exceeding straight cash if you would purchase those items anyway. The one percent systematically redeem rewards and either invest them or use them for planned spending that they would incur regardless, ensuring that rewards enhance wealth rather than generating additional consumption.

The travel rewards optimization requires more sophisticated understanding because point values vary dramatically based on how they are redeemed. Points might be worth one cent each when redeemed for cash or for economy flights, but worth five to ten cents each when redeemed for first-class international flights or luxury hotel rooms. The person who uses points casually without understanding redemption values receives a fraction of the value that someone who studies award charts and books strategically receives. This complexity is why many people should simply use cash back cards rather than travel rewards cards unless they are willing to invest time learning optimal redemption strategies.

The credit card churning strategy that Guillebeau employed involves repeatedly opening cards to capture signup bonuses, then closing or downgrading cards after the bonus is earned or after annual fees outweigh benefits. This strategy generates substantial rewards but requires careful tracking because banks have implemented rules limiting signup bonuses to once per cardholder or once per twenty-four months. Opening cards from different banks in strategic sequence allows you to continue earning bonuses over time without violating these restrictions. The risk is that multiple hard inquiries from applications and the reduction in average credit age from opening new accounts can temporarily reduce credit scores. For someone planning to apply for a mortgage or auto loan in the near future, churning should be avoided because the temporary score reduction might affect interest rates offered. For someone with no immediate need for major loans, the temporary score impact is acceptable cost of generating substantial rewards.

The annual fee calculation determines whether premium cards offering enhanced rewards justify their costs. Cards charging annual fees of ninety-five to five hundred ninety-five dollars provide rewards or benefits that supposedly offset the fees for people who spend sufficiently or who use the travel credits and other perks these cards provide. The analysis requires calculating whether your spending in bonus categories generates rewards exceeding the annual fee compared to no-fee cards. A card charging ninety-five dollars annually and providing three percent on dining and travel breaks even compared to a no-fee card providing two percent on everything if you spend ninety-five hundred dollars annually on dining and travel. If your spending exceeds this breakeven, the annual fee card provides better value. If not, you should use the no-fee card.

The premium cards charging five hundred dollars or more in annual fees justify their costs only for people with very specific spending patterns or who extract substantial value from perks like airport lounge access, travel statement credits, or hotel elite status. Most people cannot justify these cards because their spending and travel patterns do not generate rewards exceeding the fees. The one percent analyze these cards dispassionately based on mathematics rather than being seduced by prestige or by marketing suggesting that premium cards indicate status. The card that provides the best return on your specific spending is the correct card regardless of whether it carries annual fee or whether it is made of metal rather than plastic.

The credit card fees beyond annual fees should be avoided entirely through proper card selection and use. Foreign transaction fees of three percent apply to purchases made outside your home country or in foreign currencies. These fees are completely avoidable by using cards that charge no foreign transaction fees, which are now widely available from most major issuers. If you travel internationally even occasionally, you should hold at least one card charging no foreign transaction fees and use it for all international spending. Late payment fees of twenty-five to forty dollars result from missing payment deadlines. These are avoidable through automatic payment. Over-limit fees result from exceeding credit limits. These are avoidable by monitoring spending and keeping utilization well below limits. Balance transfer fees of three to five percent of transferred amount might be worthwhile if you are paying down high-interest debt by transferring it to a card offering zero percent promotional rate, but ideally you never carry balances that require transfer.

The credit limit management involves requesting increases periodically to maintain low utilization and to demonstrate creditworthiness. Credit card companies allow you to request limit increases online or by phone, and they typically evaluate these requests based on your payment history, income, and credit score. Requesting increases every six to twelve months once you have established positive payment history results in gradual increases that raise your total available credit. Higher total credit lowers your utilization ratio for any given spending level, which improves your credit score. It also provides larger emergency buffer if you face unexpected major expenses. The one percent request limit increases routinely while maintaining spending discipline that ensures the higher limits never tempt overspending.

The number of credit cards to hold depends on your spending patterns and your ability to manage multiple accounts without confusion or missed payments. The person with simple spending patterns and no interest in optimizing rewards might hold one or two cards total, using one card for everything and holding a second as backup if the first is lost or compromised. The person pursuing signup bonuses or optimizing category rewards might hold five to ten cards, using each card for specific spending categories where it provides best rewards. The person actively churning cards for signup bonuses might have fifteen to twenty-five cards or more open at various times. There is no universally correct answer except that you should hold only as many cards as you can manage with perfect payment discipline and accurate tracking.

The closing of credit card accounts should be done thoughtfully because closing accounts reduces your total available credit and potentially reduces your average age of accounts, both of which can lower your credit score. The general principle is never closing your oldest card because age of oldest account significantly affects credit scores. For newer cards, you might close accounts if they charge annual fees that you can no longer justify, if you are not using them and prefer simplicity, or if you have accumulated so many cards that tracking them has become burdensome. Before closing any card with available balance, pay it to zero because closing a card with a balance harms your credit more than closing a card with no balance. Some cards allow you to downgrade from annual fee versions to no-fee versions, which preserves the account age and available credit while eliminating the fee.

The credit card fraud protection represents significant benefit beyond rewards that makes credit cards superior to debit cards for most purchases. When you use a credit card and fraudulent charges appear, you dispute them with the card company and you are not liable for the charges. When you use a debit card and fraudulent charges drain your checking account, the money is gone from your account immediately and you must wait for the bank to investigate and potentially restore the funds, which can take weeks. During this time, legitimate payments from your checking account might bounce, creating cascade of problems. For this reason, you should use credit cards rather than debit cards for all purchases where credit cards are accepted, reserving debit card use for ATM withdrawals where credit cards are not practical.

The credit monitoring services track your credit reports and scores, alerting you to changes that might indicate fraud or errors. Many credit card companies now provide free credit score monitoring to cardholders, eliminating the need for paid services that charge monthly fees for the same information. You should review your credit reports from all three major credit bureaus annually through AnnualCreditReport.com, which provides free reports that you are entitled to by federal law. Review these reports for accuracy, disputing any errors with the bureaus because errors can significantly harm your scores. Common errors include accounts that do not belong to you, payments incorrectly marked as late when they were paid on time, and accounts showing open when they have been closed.

The relationship between credit card debt and wealth destruction deserves emphasis because this is where most people fail in their use of these instruments. The average American household carrying credit card balances owes approximately six thousand dollars at interest rates averaging eighteen percent. This costs approximately one thousand eighty dollars annually in interest that provides no value and that could otherwise be invested. Over twenty years, eliminating this interest cost and investing the one thousand eighty dollars annually instead generates approximately sixty-eight thousand dollars at ten percent returns. This is wealth destroyed through credit card interest that represents pure waste benefiting only the credit card companies collecting the interest.

The person carrying larger balances experiences even more catastrophic wealth destruction. Someone carrying fifteen thousand dollars in credit card debt at twenty percent interest pays three thousand dollars annually in interest. Over twenty years, this costs sixty thousand in direct interest payments plus another two hundred forty-eight thousand in investment returns foregone if the three thousand annually were invested instead of paid as interest. The total wealth impact is three hundred eight thousand dollars destroyed through credit card debt that could have been avoided through spending discipline. This is not abstract cost but real money that determines whether you achieve financial independence or work until forced retirement.

The escape from credit card debt for those currently carrying balances requires systematic approach prioritizing either highest-interest-rate debt first for mathematical optimality or smallest-balance debt first for psychological momentum. The mathematically optimal approach pays minimum payments on all debts except the highest-interest-rate debt, which receives all available extra payment until eliminated, then repeats with the next-highest-rate debt. This minimizes total interest paid. The psychologically motivated approach pays minimum payments on all debts except the smallest-balance debt, which receives all available extra payment until eliminated, then repeats with the next-smallest balance. This provides quicker wins that maintain motivation despite paying slightly more total interest. Either approach works if executed consistently. What does not work is making only minimum payments on all debts, which ensures you remain in debt for years or decades while paying maximum interest.

The prevention of credit card debt is simpler than escape from it and requires only the discipline to never spend more on credit cards than you can pay in full monthly. If you lack this discipline currently, you stop using credit cards entirely and switch to debit cards or cash until you have established budgeting discipline that makes full payment automatic. The person who cannot control their spending with credit cards will destroy more wealth through interest payments than they could ever generate through rewards. The rewards are irrelevant compared to the damage from carried balances. Credit cards are advanced financial tools appropriate only for those who have demonstrated basic financial discipline through maintaining budgets and spending less than they earn consistently.

The teaching of credit card discipline to children or young adults should emphasize the dangers before discussing the benefits. Young people should understand that credit cards are not free money but loans that must be repaid with interest if not paid in full immediately. They should practice with secured cards or with authorized user status on parents' cards where spending is monitored and controlled before obtaining their own unsecured cards with substantial limits. They should experience the discipline of tracking all purchases, reconciling statements, and paying in full monthly in controlled environment before being exposed to the risk of unsupervised credit card use. Too many young adults receive credit cards with substantial limits and no education about their proper use, leading to debt accumulation that takes years to resolve and that permanently impairs their wealth-building capacity during critical early career years.

The broader principle is that credit cards represent leverage that amplifies whatever financial discipline or dysfunction you bring to them. Leverage always works this way regardless of domain. In investing, leverage magnifies returns when you are correct and magnifies losses when you are wrong. In business, leverage through debt financing accelerates growth when the business succeeds and accelerates failure when the business struggles. In credit card use, leverage through available credit generates valuable rewards when you pay in full monthly and generates catastrophic interest costs when you carry balances. The tool is neutral. Your use determines whether it helps or harms.

Chris Guillebeau's systematic extraction of value from credit cards through signup bonuses and rewards demonstrates what becomes possible when you master these instruments through perfect discipline and strategic thinking. His success was not luck or exploitation of loopholes. It was the natural result of treating credit cards as the sophisticated financial tools they are, learning how they work, establishing systems to use them optimally, and maintaining discipline that prevented the mistakes that destroy most users. Anyone can replicate his approach if they bring the same discipline and systematic thinking. Most people will not because they either lack discipline to pay full balances or they lack interest in the complexity required to optimize across numerous cards.

For most wealth builders, the optimal approach is simpler than Guillebeau's. You obtain one or two quality cash back cards with no annual fees offering two percent on all purchases or offering higher percentages on your major spending categories. You use these cards for all purchases where credit cards are accepted. You establish automatic full payment monthly from your checking account. You accumulate rewards and invest them rather than spending them on additional consumption. You build perfect payment history and excellent credit scores that provide access to favorable financing for major purchases. You never carry balances under any circumstances. This approach generates thousands in rewards over decades while building credit that saves tens of thousands in interest costs on mortgages and other major loans. The benefit is substantial despite being less dramatic than the six-figure travel rewards that advanced churning strategies can generate.

The decision about whether to use credit cards at all versus using only debit cards or cash depends entirely on your honest assessment of your own discipline. If you have ever carried credit card balances, if you have ever missed payments, if you have ever spent more on credit cards than you had in your checking account to pay off, or if you have any doubt about your ability to pay full balances every month, you should not use credit cards currently. You need to establish basic financial discipline through budgeting and living below your means before you are ready for the leverage that credit cards provide. If you have demonstrated consistent financial discipline through maintaining emergency funds, living below your means, and paying all debts on time, you are ready to use credit cards as the valuable tools they can be for generating rewards and building credit.

We have now addressed every major aspect of personal financial management from earning income through investing capital through managing spending through optimizing the tools like credit cards that facilitate all these activities. Credit cards represent the final major tool requiring specific instruction because they are uniquely dangerous for the undisciplined while being uniquely valuable for the disciplined. The patterns are consistent across all domains we have examined.

The one percent study tools carefully, develop systems for using them optimally, maintain discipline that prevents mistakes, and extract value that the ninety-nine percent never capture because they either avoid tools entirely out of fear or they misuse tools through lack of discipline or understanding.

Now, you understand how credit cards work, how they generate profit for issuers, how that profit mechanism creates opportunity for disciplined users, how to build and maintain excellent credit scores through proper use, how to select cards appropriate for your spending patterns, how to extract maximum rewards, and most importantly how to avoid the catastrophic debt that destroys wealth for millions who use these instruments without proper discipline or respect for their dangers. What you cannot do while claiming to understand wealth building is use credit cards improperly by carrying balances, paying interest, or accumulating debt that prevents the systematic investment and compound growth upon which all wealth building depends.

CHAPTER 24:

TAX PREPARATION—UNDERSTANDING THE SYSTEM

In 1977, a young accountant named Ed Slott began his career preparing tax returns for individuals and small businesses in Rockville Centre, New York. He performed the same work that thousands of other accountants performed each spring, translating financial information into forms required by the Internal Revenue Service and calculating the amounts his clients owed or would receive as refunds. The work was technical and detailed but fundamentally routine. Most accountants in his position would have continued this pattern for decades, preparing returns during tax season and perhaps handling bookkeeping or business consulting during the remaining months. Slott recognized something different in the questions his clients asked and the mistakes they made consistently.

His clients arrived each April with completed transactions, asking him to calculate taxes owed on those transactions. They had sold appreciated stock without considering tax implications. They had withdrawn money from retirement accounts in ways that triggered unnecessary penalties. They had made charitable contributions without documentation that would allow them to claim deductions. They had structured their businesses in ways that created higher tax burdens than necessary. In every case, by the time Slott saw their paperwork, the opportunities for tax optimization had passed. The transactions were complete. The taxes were determined. His role was recording what had happened rather than influencing what should happen.

Slott began scheduling meetings with clients in January rather than April, discussing tax planning for the coming year rather than merely preparing returns for the previous year. He explained which transactions they should consider before year end, which

345

documentation they needed to maintain throughout the year, and which opportunities existed to reduce taxes through legal means the tax code specifically created for these purposes. His clients' tax liabilities declined substantially despite no change in their income or spending levels. The difference was that they made decisions with tax consequences in mind rather than discovering those consequences only after transactions were complete.

This proactive approach transformed Slott's practice and eventually his career. He realized that most people paid far more in taxes than necessary not because they lacked knowledge of obscure loopholes but because they failed to understand basic tax principles and failed to plan transactions with tax consequences in mind. He began teaching other financial professionals how to provide tax guidance to their clients. He wrote dozens of books and created educational programs focused on retirement account taxation, which represents the most complex and consequential tax area for most people building wealth. He built a national reputation as a tax educator, eventually becoming one of the most recognized experts in retirement account taxation in America.

The principle Slott demonstrated through his career applies to anyone building wealth regardless of income level or financial sophistication. The tax code contains sixty thousand pages of regulations, but you do not need to understand all sixty thousand pages to minimize your tax burden legally. You need to understand several dozen provisions that affect ordinary wealth builders, and you need to think about tax consequences before rather than after completing financial transactions. The one percent do this systematically. The ninety-nine percent treat taxes as something that happens to them in April rather than as something they can influence through planning throughout the year.

The difference in lifetime tax payments between these approaches easily exceeds one hundred thousand dollars for middle-income households and exceeds one million dollars for high-income households. This is not money saved through aggressive tax avoidance or questionable strategies. This is money saved through understanding what the tax code allows, through structuring transactions to take advantage of those provisions, through maintaining proper documentation, and through making decisions with tax consequences in mind before those decisions are made. The money is available to anyone who invests modest time learning basic tax principles and who maintains discipline to apply those principles throughout the year rather than merely during tax season.

The framework for understanding when to prepare taxes yourself versus when to hire professionals depends on the complexity of your financial situation and the value of your time. Tax preparation software from companies like TurboTax, H&R Block, and TaxAct has become sophisticated enough that anyone with straightforward W2 income, standard deductions, and basic investment accounts can prepare accurate returns without professional assistance. The software interviews you about your situation, asks questions in plain language, and generates the appropriate forms based on your answers. For someone earning salary income with no side businesses, no rental properties, no complex investment transactions, and no unusual deductions or credits, the software suffices and costs perhaps sixty to one hundred twenty dollars for federal and state returns.

The situations requiring professional assistance include operating businesses as sole proprietors or through entities like LLCs or S corporations, owning rental properties with depreciation and expense tracking, having complex investment situations involving options, partnerships, or international holdings, facing major life events like inheritance or divorce that create tax complications, or earning income high enough that modest tax optimization generates savings exceeding professional fees. Someone earning two hundred thousand annually who pays a CPA one thousand dollars for tax preparation and planning that saves three thousand in taxes has generated two thousand in value from professional assistance. Someone earning fifty thousand annually with simple W2 income who pays a CPA three hundred dollars for preparation that provides no planning or optimization has wasted three hundred dollars compared to preparing the return themselves with software.

The selection of tax professionals requires understanding the difference between tax preparers who provide compliance services and tax advisors who provide strategic planning. Tax preparers translate your financial information into completed returns. They ensure forms are filled correctly and filed on time. They calculate what you owe or what refund you should receive. This is valuable service if your situation is complex enough that software becomes difficult to navigate, but it provides no optimization beyond correct calculation based on transactions you have already completed. Tax advisors provide planning that affects which transactions you complete and how you structure them. They recommend timing of income and deductions to minimize taxes. They suggest entity structures that reduce tax burdens for business owners. They identify credits and deductions you qualify for but might not know exist. They help you make decisions throughout the year with tax consequences in mind.

The distinction matters because fees for these services differ substantially and because the value they provide differs even more substantially. A tax preparer might charge two hundred to five hundred dollars to prepare returns based on information you provide. A tax advisor might charge one thousand to five thousand dollars or more for comprehensive planning that includes return preparation. The preparer saves you time compared to self-preparation. The advisor potentially saves you thousands in taxes compared to making decisions without tax planning input. For someone with simple finances, the preparer or software suffices. For someone with business income, rental properties, significant investment activity, or high earnings, the advisor generates returns far exceeding their fees if they are competent at their work.

The identification of competent tax advisors begins with understanding their credentials and asking questions about their approach. Certified Public Accountants have passed rigorous examinations and maintain continuing education requirements that ensure minimum competence in tax matters. Enrolled Agents are federally licensed tax practitioners who specialize in taxation and who have either passed comprehensive IRS examinations or worked for the IRS for sufficient years. Tax attorneys understand tax law at depth that accountants might not match but typically charge rates that make them cost-effective only for complex situations involving tax disputes or sophisticated entity structures. The credential matters less than the person's experience with situations similar to yours and their willingness to provide proactive guidance rather than merely reactive compliance.

The questions to ask prospective tax advisors include how many clients they serve with situations similar to yours, whether they provide year-round planning or only seasonal preparation, how they stay current on tax law changes, whether they will represent you if the IRS audits your return, and whether they provide written advice documenting their recommendations. The advisor who serves mostly W2 employees may lack experience with business taxation that you need if you operate a company. The advisor who will only communicate during tax season cannot provide the year-round planning that generates maximum value. The advisor who does not commit to audit representation may not stand behind their work if questions arise. The advisor who will not provide written documentation of their recommendations leaves you without proof of the advice you received if disputes arise later.

The cost of competent tax advice is investment that generates returns through reduced tax payments rather than expense that provides no return. Someone paying three thousand dollars for comprehensive tax planning that identifies ten thousand in legal deductions or optimizations they would have missed has generated seven thousand in value from a three-thousand-dollar investment. This is seventy percent return in a single year, far exceeding returns from most investments. The person who refuses to pay for advice and instead makes decisions without tax planning input often pays thousands more in taxes than necessary because they structured transactions suboptimally or missed deductions they qualified for but did not know existed.

The year-round tax thinking that characterizes the one percent involves considering tax consequences before completing any significant financial transaction. You do not sell appreciated stock without considering whether waiting a few more days or weeks would qualify for long-term capital gains treatment at lower rates. You do not withdraw money from retirement accounts without understanding the tax and penalty implications of various withdrawal strategies. You do not make large charitable contributions without determining whether bunching multiple years of contributions into single years might allow you to itemize deductions when standard deduction would otherwise be optimal. You do not start businesses without analyzing entity structure options and their tax implications. These decisions are made throughout the year when the opportunities exist, not in April when transactions are complete and options have closed.

The documentation of deductible expenses throughout the year determines whether you can claim deductions you actually qualify for or whether you must forfeit them because you lack required records. The IRS requires substantiation of expenses through receipts, bank statements, or other contemporaneous records. The verbal claim that you spent five thousand dollars on deductible business expenses without receipts to prove those expenses will be disallowed in an audit regardless of whether you actually spent the money. The one percent maintain organized records of all potentially deductible expenses throughout the year using systems ranging from simple folders where receipts are filed monthly to sophisticated software that captures expense information automatically from credit card transactions and bank accounts.

The categories of commonly missed deductions include home office expenses for those who work from home regularly and exclusively in dedicated space, mileage for business use of personal vehicles tracked with logs showing dates and business purposes, professional education and licensing fees required to maintain your employment or improve your skills, job search expenses when seeking employment in your current field, union dues and professional organization memberships, and unreimbursed employee expenses for tools or supplies required for your work. The Tax Cuts and Jobs Act of 2017 eliminated many of these deductions for W2 employees, but they remain available for self-employed individuals and business owners. Understanding which expenses remain deductible under current law prevents either claiming deductions you are not entitled to or missing deductions you are entitled to because you assume they were eliminated when they were not.

The charitable contribution documentation requires specific records depending on contribution size. Contributions under two hundred fifty dollars require receipts from the charity or bank records showing the contribution. Contributions of two hundred fifty dollars or more require written acknowledgment from the charity stating the amount and whether you received any goods or services in exchange. Contributions of non-cash property worth more than five hundred dollars require detailed descriptions of donated items and their estimated values. Contributions of property worth more than five thousand dollars require professional appraisals. The person who makes contributions without obtaining proper documentation cannot claim deductions regardless of how generous their giving was. The one percent obtain required documentation at the time of contribution rather than scrambling to reconstruct records during tax preparation.

The decision between itemizing deductions and claiming the standard deduction is made annually based on which provides greater tax benefit. The standard deduction for 2024 is approximately fourteen thousand six hundred dollars for single filers and twenty-nine thousand two hundred dollars for married couples filing jointly. You itemize only if your total itemizable deductions exceed these thresholds. Itemizable deductions include mortgage interest, state and local taxes up to ten thousand dollars, charitable contributions, and medical expenses exceeding 7.5 percent of adjusted gross income. The Tax Cuts and Jobs Act substantially increased standard deductions while limiting state and local tax deductions, which means many households who previously itemized now benefit more from standard deductions.

The bunching strategy optimizes deductions by concentrating itemizable expenses into alternating years rather than spreading them evenly. If your itemizable deductions typically approximate seventeen thousand dollars annually, you might bunch two years of charitable contributions into single years, creating thirty thousand dollars in deductions in bunching years when you itemize and four thousand in other years when you claim standard deduction of twenty-nine thousand two hundred dollars. Over two years, bunching generates total deductions of fifty-nine thousand two hundred dollars compared to forty-seven thousand two hundred dollars from steady contributions with itemizing both years. This saves taxes without changing total giving, merely changing timing. The strategy requires planning contributions in advance and potentially using donor-advised funds to make contributions in bunching years while distributing to charities over multiple years.

The tax-loss harvesting in investment accounts reduces taxes on investment gains by selling positions with losses to offset gains realized elsewhere in the portfolio. If you sold stock for twenty thousand dollar gain during the year and you hold other stocks with unrealized ten thousand dollar losses, selling the loss positions before year end allows you to offset the gains with losses, reducing your taxable gain to ten thousand dollars. At twenty percent capital gains rates, this saves two thousand dollars in taxes. The wash sale rule prohibits claiming losses if you repurchase substantially identical securities within thirty days before or after the sale, but you can either wait thirty-one days to repurchase the same security or immediately purchase similar but not identical securities that provide equivalent market exposure. The one percent harvest losses systematically in taxable brokerage accounts whenever positions with losses exist and whenever they have gains to offset elsewhere.

The entity structure decisions for business owners determine how business income is taxed and how much self-employment tax is owed. Sole proprietorships report business income on Schedule C of personal returns and pay both income taxes and self-employment taxes of approximately fifteen percent on all net profit. Single-member LLCs are taxed identically to sole proprietorships by default but provide liability protection that sole proprietorships do not. S corporations split business income between wages paid to the owner-employee and distributions of remaining profits to shareholders. The wages face both income and employment taxes, but the distributions face only income taxes without employment taxes. This structure potentially saves substantial self-employment taxes for businesses generating significant profits.

The determination of when S corporation status becomes worthwhile depends on net business income levels and administrative complexity tolerance. The S corporation requires filing separate business tax returns, maintaining corporate formalities, and paying reasonable wages through payroll systems that generate quarterly tax filings and annual forms. This complexity costs approximately one thousand to three thousand dollars annually in accounting and payroll processing fees. The employment tax savings must exceed these costs plus the time burden of maintaining corporate compliance for S corporation status to provide net benefit. For businesses generating less than sixty to eighty thousand dollars in net profit, the savings typically do not justify the complexity. For businesses generating substantially more, the savings often exceed ten thousand dollars annually, making the complexity clearly worthwhile.

The retirement account contribution strategies reduce current taxes while building wealth for future. Traditional IRA and 401k contributions reduce current taxable income dollar for dollar up to contribution limits, providing immediate tax savings at your marginal rate. Someone in twenty-four percent marginal tax bracket contributing twenty-three thousand dollars to 401k saves approximately five thousand five hundred twenty dollars in current taxes. These contributions make particular sense for high earners currently in high tax brackets who expect to be in lower brackets during retirement when withdrawals are taxed. Roth IRA and Roth 401k contributions provide no current deduction but eliminate all future taxes on growth and withdrawals. These make particular sense for those currently in low tax brackets who expect higher earnings and

THINK LIKE A ONE PERCENTER

tax rates in the future. We discussed these vehicles extensively in Chapter Four, but the tax planning element involves consciously choosing between traditional and Roth contributions based on current and expected future tax situations rather than making the choice arbitrarily.

The health savings account contributions provide triple tax advantages superior to any retirement account. Contributions reduce current taxable income, growth is tax-free, and withdrawals for qualified medical expenses are tax-free. For 2024, contribution limits are approximately four thousand one hundred dollars for individuals and eighty-three hundred dollars for families. These contributions make sense for essentially anyone with access to HSAs through high-deductible health plans because the tax benefits are unavailable elsewhere. The strategic error most people make is failing to invest HSA funds and instead treating them as spending accounts for current medical expenses. The optimal strategy is maximizing contributions, investing the funds for decades of growth, paying current medical expenses out of pocket, and allowing the HSA to compound tax-free until retirement when medical expenses are substantial and when tax-free withdrawals provide maximum value.

The estimated tax payment requirements apply to anyone with income not subject to withholding, including business owners, freelancers, and those with substantial investment income. The IRS requires quarterly estimated payments if you expect to owe more than one thousand dollars in taxes for the year. Failure to make adequate estimated payments results in penalties that are effectively interest charges on the underpaid amounts. The safe harbor rule states that if you pay at least ninety percent of current year taxes or one hundred percent of prior year taxes through withholding and estimated payments, you avoid penalties regardless of how much you ultimately owe. For high earners with income exceeding one hundred fifty thousand dollars, the safe harbor is one hundred ten percent of prior year taxes. The one percent make estimated payments quarterly to avoid penalties while keeping their money as long as possible rather than overpaying through excessive withholding that provides interest-free loans to the government.

The tax filing extensions provide additional time to prepare returns without additional time to pay taxes owed. Filing Form 4868 extends the filing deadline from April 15 to October 15, giving you six additional months to prepare and file your return. However, any taxes owed are still due on April 15. If you file an extension and later determine you owed taxes, you will owe interest and potentially penalties on the amount owed from April 15 forward regardless of the extension. Extensions are appropriate when you need additional time to gather documentation or to make complex tax planning decisions, but they do not eliminate the requirement to pay taxes on time. The one percent use extensions when appropriate to ensure accurate filing rather than rushing to meet the April deadline and making errors that cost more than the modest interest charges from delayed payment.

The audit risk and audit defense understanding provides context for how aggressive to be with tax positions. The IRS audits less than one percent of individual tax returns annually, with audit rates higher for high-income taxpayers and for returns claiming certain deductions or credits that frequently contain errors or fraud. The positions you take on your return should be supportable based on reasonable interpretation of tax law and proper documentation. Aggressive positions that lack support or documentation create audit risk and potential penalties if disallowed. Conservative positions that forfeit legitimate deductions and credits cost you money unnecessarily. The appropriate balance is claiming everything you are clearly entitled to with proper documentation while avoiding positions that stretch beyond reasonable interpretation of law. If your tax advisor recommends positions you are uncomfortable with or that lack clear legal support, you should seek a second opinion because you are legally responsible for what appears on your return even when a professional prepared it.

The state and local tax considerations add complexity because you must comply with tax rules in every jurisdiction where you have income or property. Someone living in one state while working remotely for a company in another state may owe taxes to both states on the income earned. Someone owning rental property in multiple states must file returns in each state where properties are located. Someone selling a business or investment property pays state capital gains taxes based on where the business or property was located. The rules vary by state and require professional guidance to navigate correctly. The one percent work with advisors who understand multi-state taxation when their situations involve income or property in multiple jurisdictions rather than attempting to navigate these rules themselves.

The retirement account withdrawal strategies minimize taxes during the years when you are drawing down accumulated wealth. The conventional wisdom of withdrawing from taxable accounts first, then tax-deferred accounts, then Roth accounts last may or may not be optimal depending on your tax situation in specific years. Someone with low income in early retirement before Social Security and required minimum distributions begin might accelerate withdrawals from tax-deferred accounts to fill low tax brackets while deferring Social Security and Roth withdrawals. Someone with high income from pensions or rental properties might reverse this sequence. The optimal withdrawal strategy requires analysis of your complete tax picture across multiple years rather than following simple rules that may not fit your situation. This is planning work that occurs before you begin taking withdrawals rather than reactive decisions made each year based on immediate needs.

The required minimum distributions from traditional retirement accounts beginning at age seventy-three force withdrawals and tax payments whether you need the money or not. The RMD amounts are calculated based on account balances and life expectancy tables that IRS publishes. Failure to take RMDs or taking less than the required amount results in penalties of twenty-five percent of the shortfall amount. These penalties are severe enough that you must ensure RMDs are taken correctly and on time. The one percent begin planning for RMDs years before reaching age seventy-three by considering whether Roth conversions in earlier years might reduce future RMD amounts and the taxes those RMDs generate. Converting traditional IRA assets to Roth IRA assets in years when income is low and tax brackets are favorable eliminates those assets from future RMD calculations while paying taxes at potentially lower rates than would apply during RMD years.

The qualified charitable distributions from IRAs after age seventy and a half allow direct transfers from traditional IRAs to qualified charities that count toward RMD requirements without generating taxable income. This is often superior to taking distributions as income, paying taxes, and then donating the after-tax proceeds to charity. The QCD bypasses income entirely, providing tax benefit even to those who do not itemize deductions. The annual limit is one hundred thousand dollars per person, which covers the charitable giving for most people making substantial donations. The one percent who give charitably from retirement assets use QCDs systematically rather than taking distributions and donating separately, saving taxes through the direct transfer mechanism.

The estate planning and gift tax considerations become relevant for those accumulating wealth exceeding federal estate tax exemptions of approximately thirteen million six hundred thousand dollars per individual or twenty-seven million two hundred thousand dollars per married couple as of 2024. These exemptions are scheduled to be cut roughly in half after 2025 unless Congress extends current law. For those approaching these thresholds, gifting strategies during life and proper estate planning documents become essential to minimize estate taxes that can claim forty percent of assets exceeding exemption amounts. This is specialized planning requiring estate planning attorneys rather than general tax preparers, but the one percent address these issues proactively during their working years rather than waiting until estate tax problems are imminent.

The software versus professional decision for most people evolves over time as financial situations change. Someone beginning their career with simple W2 income uses software for years until they start businesses, acquire rental properties, or reach income levels where professional planning generates clear value. At that transition point, they hire professionals for several years while their situations are complex. Later in retirement, if their situations simplify to Social Security income and retirement account withdrawals, they might return to software if they are comfortable preparing returns themselves. The one percent make these decisions based on complexity and value rather than based on habit or resistance to paying professional fees when those fees generate multiple times their cost in tax savings.

The relationship with your tax advisor should involve regular communication throughout the year rather than a single meeting during tax season. You contact them before making major financial decisions to understand tax implications. You share information about income changes, investment transactions, or business developments that might affect tax planning. You meet at least quarterly to review year-to-date tax situation and to discuss planning opportunities while time remains to implement them. This proactive relationship prevents the situation where your advisor learns about major transactions after they are complete and can only tell you what tax bill resulted rather than helping you structure transactions to minimize that bill. The one percent treat tax advisors as strategic partners involved throughout the year rather than as service providers used only when returns must be filed.

The cost of tax preparation and planning is itself tax deductible for business owners as business expense, though no longer deductible for W2 employees under current law. This means the true after-tax cost of tax advice for business owners is reduced by their marginal tax rate. Someone paying three thousand dollars for tax planning who is in thirty-five percent marginal tax bracket pays true cost of one thousand nine hundred fifty dollars after the deduction reduces taxes. This makes professional advice even more economically attractive for business owners because the government effectively subsidizes one-third or more of the cost through tax deductions.

Ed Slott's career demonstrates that the gap between what people actually pay in taxes and what they could legally pay through proper planning is enormous and that most of that gap results from lack of knowledge and lack of planning rather than from unwillingness to pay taxes. His clients were not tax cheats seeking aggressive strategies. They were ordinary people who made financial decisions without understanding tax consequences and who missed legitimate deductions because they did not know those deductions existed. His teaching emphasized that the tax code is not mysterious document requiring genius to navigate but rather is set of rules that reward specific behaviors Congress wants to encourage. Understanding those rules and planning around them is not tax avoidance but tax intelligence.

The pattern we have seen throughout this book applies to taxation exactly as it applies to every other domain. The one percent study the systems that govern outcomes, they make decisions with full understanding of how those systems work, and they position themselves to benefit from provisions others ignore or misunderstand. The ninety-nine percent react to systems after decisions are made, they pay whatever bills result from those decisions, and they never invest time understanding how different choices would generate different outcomes. This pattern in taxation costs people tens or hundreds of thousands of dollars over working lifetimes through nothing more than ignorance of rules that are publicly available and through failure to plan before rather than after completing transactions.

The time investment required to understand basic tax planning principles is perhaps ten to twenty hours initially plus several hours annually to maintain currency as laws change and as your situation evolves. This knowledge provides returns through reduced lifetime tax payments that easily exceed fifty thousand to one hundred thousand dollars for middle-income households and that exceed one million dollars for high-income households. The return per hour invested in tax education exceeds returns from nearly any other activity available to wealth builders because the savings are guaranteed and risk-free once you understand what the law allows and implement proper planning.

You have now been provided education about every major component of wealth building from earning income through investing capital through managing spending through understanding the tools and systems that facilitate or impede accumulation. Tax preparation and planning represents the final major technical skill that determines whether you keep the wealth you build or whether you unnecessarily surrender large portions to taxes you could have legally avoided through knowledge and planning. The one percent treat taxes as manageable cost that can be minimized through planning rather than as immutable burden that must be accepted. The ninety-nine percent treat taxes as something that happens to them rather than as something they influence through their choices. The difference in these approaches compounds over working careers into wealth differentials that determine whether financial independence is achievable or whether you work until forced retirement. You now understand the framework for thinking about taxes strategically and for engaging with professionals who can help you minimize legal tax burdens. Take advantage of tax advantages.

CHAPTER 25:
SIDE BUSINESSES—THE WEALTH ACCELERATOR

In 1998, a programmer named Pierre Omidyar was working full-time at General Magic, a technology company developing mobile operating systems, when he spent a Labor Day weekend writing code for a simple website. The concept was straightforward: allow people to auction items to each other online, with the website facilitating the transactions and taking a small percentage of each sale. He called the site AuctionWeb and launched it as a personal project, maintaining his full-time employment while spending evenings and weekends improving the functionality. The site attracted users slowly at first, with trading volume reaching approximately one thousand dollars monthly after the first year.

Omidyar continued working his full-time job while the side project grew. By the second year, auction volume had increased to the point where he needed to hire part-time help to manage customer service and technical infrastructure. By the third year, the revenue from what he had renamed eBay exceeded his full-time salary substantially. Only then did he leave his employment to focus on the business exclusively. By the time eBay went public in 1998, four years after its launch as a side project, Omidyar's stake was worth over seven billion dollars. The side business built during evenings and weekends while maintaining stable employment had become one of the most valuable companies created in the 1990s.

This example demonstrates the principle that separates side businesses from the speculation and gambling we criticized in Chapter Eight. Omidyar was not quitting stable employment to chase uncertain business dreams. He was building a business systematically while maintaining his income and lifestyle through employment. He deployed his time and modest amounts of capital into an entrepreneurial venture without risking his financial stability. When the business demonstrated clear success through growing revenue, he transitioned to full-time focus. This sequence—build while employed, prove the model through actual revenue, transition only after success is demonstrated—represents the rational approach to entrepreneurship that builds wealth without risking financial destruction through premature commitment to unproven ventures.

The framework for understanding side businesses as wealth-building tools begins with recognizing that employment income, while essential, creates inherent limitations on wealth accumulation. You exchange time for money at rates determined by employers and labor markets rather than by value you create directly. Your income is capped by how much one person can work and by what employers will pay for your type of work. You build no equity in your employment—when you stop working, the income stops immediately. You have minimal control over your income stability because employers can terminate your position based on business conditions or their preferences. These limitations mean that employment alone rarely creates substantial wealth unless you reach executive levels where equity compensation becomes significant.

Side businesses remove or reduce these limitations. You create value directly and capture that value rather than having an employer capture most of the value while paying you a fraction. Your income is determined by how much value you create and how effectively you monetize that value rather than by labor market rates for your type of work. You build equity in the business that continues generating income even when you are not actively working if you structure it properly. You control the business's existence and direction rather than depending on an employer's decisions. These characteristics mean that successful side businesses can generate wealth far exceeding what employment produces, particularly when you reinvest business profits into investments that compound over decades.

The distinction between side businesses and hobbies or gigs matters because only actual businesses build equity and produce enterprise value beyond immediate income. A hobby generates no income and is purely cost to be funded from other sources. A gig like driving for rideshare services or delivering food generates immediate income by trading your time for money, but it builds no enterprise value and stops generating income when you stop working. A business generates income through systems and processes that can eventually operate without your direct time input, building enterprise value that you could potentially sell or that can generate income for years with minimal ongoing effort.

The person who spends ten hours weekly driving for Uber earns perhaps two hundred to three hundred dollars weekly or ten to fifteen thousand dollars annually. This is gig income that disappears the moment they stop driving. The person who spends ten hours weekly building and operating an online business selling products or services might earn nothing initially, then modest amounts as they learn and improve, then eventually ten to fifteen thousand dollars annually or more from a business that operates systematically without requiring ten hours weekly once systems are established. The long-term value differs enormously even when short-term income might favor the gig initially.

The selection of which side business to pursue should be based on intersection of your existing skills or interests, market demand for solutions you can provide, and business models that require minimal capital to start and that can be operated efficiently alongside full-time employment. The one percent do not pursue side businesses based solely on passion or interest without considering whether customers exist who will pay for what they want to create. They do not chase elaborate business concepts requiring substantial capital investment before generating revenue. They identify problems people face, develop solutions they are capable of creating, validate that customers will pay for those solutions, and build businesses systematically while maintaining employment income and stability.

The service business model represents perhaps the most accessible entry point for most people because service businesses require minimal capital to start, generate revenue immediately when you acquire customers, and allow you to leverage skills you may already possess through your employment or education. Someone with marketing expertise gained through corporate employment can offer freelance marketing services to small businesses. Someone with design skills can offer graphic design or web design services. Someone with writing ability can offer content creation services. Someone with technical skills can offer programming, database management, or IT consulting. These businesses require essentially no capital beyond basic computer equipment most people already own, and they generate revenue from the first customer served.

The productized service approach creates more scalable service businesses by standardizing offerings and pricing rather than custom-quoting every engagement. Rather than offering general marketing services with custom proposals for each client, you offer a specific package like "social media management for dental practices—five posts per week plus monthly analytics report for twelve hundred dollars monthly." The specificity makes sales easier because prospects understand exactly what they receive and what it costs. The standardization makes delivery more efficient because you are executing the same processes repeatedly rather than reinventing approaches for each client. The focus on a niche like dental practices makes marketing more efficient because you can target prospects precisely rather than competing for attention in broad markets.

The digital product business model offers even greater scalability because products can be sold unlimited times with no additional production cost after initial creation. An online course teaching specific skills can be sold to hundreds or thousands of customers with no additional work beyond the initial course creation and periodic updates. An e-book providing specialized knowledge can be sold indefinitely with zero marginal cost per sale. Software tools or applications can be sold as subscriptions generating recurring revenue. Templates, spreadsheets, or other digital tools can be packaged and sold repeatedly. These products require substantial upfront work to create but generate revenue with minimal ongoing time investment once created and properly marketed.

The challenge with digital products is that most fail not due to quality problems but due to nonexistent marketing and customer acquisition. The person who creates an excellent course on a topic they understand deeply but who has no audience and no marketing channels will sell essentially nothing despite the product's quality. The person who has built an audience through content creation, who understands their audience's problems, and who creates products solving those problems will sell substantially regardless of whether their products are objectively superior to competitors. This means you cannot simply create digital products and expect sales to materialize. You must build audiences and develop marketing capabilities or your products will sit unsold.

The content creation approach to audience building involves producing valuable free content consistently over extended periods through blogs, YouTube videos, podcasts, social media posts, or newsletters. This content attracts people interested in your topic, demonstrates your expertise, and creates relationship with audience members who come to trust you through repeated exposure to your material. After building sufficient audience size—typically several thousand followers or subscribers minimum—you can launch products or services to that audience and achieve meaningful sales because you have established credibility and because audience members already understand the value you provide through the free content you have produced.

The content creation path requires patience because audience growth is slow, particularly in the beginning when you lack social proof and when your content creation skills are still developing. Most people start producing content, see minimal initial response, and quit within weeks or months before their content can attract meaningful audiences. The one percent who succeed with content-driven businesses maintain consistency for one to three years before achieving substantial audiences, understanding that the content they produce early in this period is both practice to improve their skills and seeds that may attract audience members months or years after publication.

The e-commerce business model involves sourcing or creating physical products and selling them online through platforms like Amazon, Shopify, or Etsy. The capital requirements vary enormously depending on your approach. Dropshipping involves listing products for sale that you do not own, then purchasing from suppliers and having them ship directly to customers after sales occur. This requires minimal capital but offers thin profit margins and lacks control over inventory and shipping. Private labeling involves finding existing products, applying your own branding, and selling them under your brand name. This requires thousands in initial inventory investment but offers better margins and more control. Manufacturing your own products offers maximum control and margins but requires tens of thousands in capital and substantial complexity in production management.

The e-commerce path has become substantially more competitive than when it emerged in the 2000s because barriers to entry are low and because successful products attract competitors rapidly. The person who identifies a product opportunity and launches quickly might generate substantial profits for months or years until competitors emerge. The person who enters markets that are already competitive without unique products or substantial marketing budgets will struggle to generate profits after accounting for product costs, platform fees, advertising expenses, and their own time. This is not to say e-commerce businesses cannot succeed, but rather that success requires either unique product angles, superior marketing, or willingness to accept modest margins while building businesses to substantial scale.

The local service business model serves local customers through businesses like lawn care, cleaning services, handyman services, pet sitting, tutoring, or other services that must be delivered in person within your geographic area. These businesses face limited competition compared to online businesses because you compete only with other providers in your area rather than with everyone globally. They generate revenue from day one if you can acquire customers. They require minimal capital beyond basic tools and transportation. They allow you to start solo and potentially build to teams of employees if you choose to scale. The limitations are that income is tied to your geographic area and that scaling typically requires hiring and managing employees, which introduces complexity many people prefer to avoid.

The validation of business ideas before investing substantial time or capital distinguishes those who build successful businesses from those who waste years on ventures with no market demand. Validation means determining whether customers actually exist who will pay for what you want to sell, and determining this through actual paying customers rather than through opinions from friends or through hypothetical survey responses. The person who spends six months building an elaborate product before attempting to sell it might discover that no one will pay for what they built regardless of its quality. The person who creates a minimum viable version of their offering, attempts to sell it immediately, and refines based on actual customer response discovers quickly whether viable business exists.

The practical validation approach involves creating the simplest possible version of your offering, identifying where your target customers gather, offering the basic version for sale, and seeing whether anyone buys. If you want to offer social media management services to dentists, you do not build elaborate website and marketing materials first. You identify ten dental practices in your area, call them directly, describe your service, and ask if they are interested in a trial period at discounted rates. If five of ten express interest and two become paying customers, you have validated that demand exists. If zero of ten express interest after you contact dozens, you have learned that either your offer does not match market needs or your target market is wrong, and you adjust before wasting months building something no one wants.

The capital requirements for side businesses should be minimal until you have validated that customers will buy and that unit economics work profitably. The ninety-nine percent invest thousands into business ideas before generating first dollar of revenue, gambling that customers will materialize once they build what they envision.

The one percent operate on minimum budgets until customers and revenue validate their concepts, then deploy capital to scale what has been proven to work. Starting a service business might require zero capital beyond a basic website built using free or cheap website builders. Starting a digital product business might require a few hundred dollars for hosting and software tools to create and deliver the products. Starting a local service business might require a few hundred to a few thousand dollars for basic equipment. Any business requiring tens of thousands in capital before generating revenue should be viewed with extreme skepticism unless you have exceptional domain expertise and specific competitive advantages.

The time allocation to side businesses must be sustainable alongside full-time employment without destroying your health or your performance in your primary job. The person who spends forty hours weekly at employment plus thirty hours weekly on side business while sleeping five hours nightly will burn out within months and will likely perform poorly in both domains. The sustainable approach is allocating five to fifteen hours weekly to side business consistently over extended periods, accepting that progress will be slow but that consistent effort compounds. Someone allocating ten hours weekly to side business accumulates five hundred twenty hours annually, which is substantial capacity if focused on high-value activities rather than scattered across low-impact busywork.

The high-value activities that build businesses include activities that acquire customers, that deliver services or products to existing customers, or that create systems allowing the business to operate more efficiently. Low-value activities that do not build businesses include obsessing over perfect branding, endlessly researching without taking action, attending networking events that generate no actual business, and engaging in activities that feel productive but that contribute nothing to revenue or customer acquisition. The one percent ruthlessly prioritize the former and eliminate the latter. They recognize that businesses are built through customers and revenue, not through perfect business cards or elaborate planning documents.

The pricing strategies for side businesses determine whether you generate meaningful profit or whether you waste time delivering services for compensation that does not justify your effort. The ninety-nine percent underprice their offerings because they lack confidence, because they fear losing customers to lower-priced competitors, or because they fail to calculate what their time is actually worth. Someone earning sixty thousand dollars annually in employment earns approximately thirty dollars per hour. If they provide freelance services for twenty-five dollars per hour, they are earning less than their employment rate while bearing additional complexity and risk from self-employment. This is wealth-destroying activity disguised as entrepreneurship.

The one percent price based on value delivered to customers rather than based on hours required. If you solve a problem that saves a business ten thousand dollars or that generates ten thousand dollars in additional revenue, charging two thousand dollars for the solution is reasonable regardless of whether the solution required five hours or fifty hours to deliver. The customer receives eight thousand dollars in value beyond what they paid. You receive compensation that justifies your effort and expertise. Both parties benefit from the exchange. This value-based pricing requires confidence and willingness to clearly articulate the value you provide, but it separates profitable businesses from time-wasting activities that generate minimal returns.

The client acquisition through direct outreach generates revenue faster than waiting for inbound inquiries from marketing activities that take months to produce results. Someone starting a freelance business can identify fifty target clients, research what challenges those businesses likely face, craft personalized outreach explaining how they can solve those challenges, and contact each prospect directly via email or phone. If these outreach efforts generate even two or three clients willing to pay for an initial engagement, the business has revenue and validation within weeks rather than waiting months for content marketing or advertising to generate leads.

The retention of existing clients generates more revenue with less effort than constantly acquiring new clients because existing clients already understand your value and already trust you based on previous positive experiences. The person who delivers excellent work to initial clients, stays in communication after projects complete, and proactively offers additional services or identifies additional problems to solve converts one-time engagements into ongoing relationships that generate recurring revenue. The person who treats each client as one-time transaction must constantly find new clients to maintain income, creating exhausting cycle of perpetual business development. The one percent build businesses around retained clients who provide steady revenue with minimal acquisition cost, freeing time to pursue selected new clients for growth rather than for survival.

The systemization of business processes determines whether side businesses remain demanding time obligations or whether they become efficient operations generating income with minimal ongoing involvement. The person who recreates processes for every client wastes time and makes errors through inconsistency. The person who documents standard operating procedures, creates templates and checklists, and establishes workflows that execute reliably operates far more efficiently while delivering consistent quality. This systemization allows you to eventually delegate tasks to contractors or employees if you choose to scale, because documented systems can be followed by others whereas undocumented processes that exist only in your head cannot be transferred.

The transition from side business to full-time focus should occur only after the business demonstrates clear financial viability through sustained revenue that matches or exceeds your employment income. The person who quits stable employment when side business generates twenty-five percent of their employment income is gambling recklessly on uncertain growth. The person who maintains employment until side business generates one hundred twenty-five to one hundred fifty percent of employment income for at least six to twelve consecutive months has validated that the business can support their lifestyle while providing buffer for inevitable revenue fluctuations. The premature transition from employment to full-time entrepreneurship creates financial stress that impairs decision-making and that often leads to business failure or return to employment under worse conditions than when you left.

The alternative to full transition is maintaining employment indefinitely while building side business to generate additional income that accelerates wealth building without replacing employment income. Someone earning eighty thousand annually from employment while generating thirty thousand annually from side business has increased their income by thirty-seven percent without sacrificing the stability and benefits employment provides. If they maintain their previous lifestyle on employment income while investing the entire side business income, they have increased their savings rate massively and accelerated their path to financial independence. This approach provides the benefits of entrepreneurship without the risks of depending entirely on business income.

The tax advantages of business ownership provide additional returns beyond the direct income businesses generate. Business owners deduct ordinary and necessary expenses from revenue before calculating taxable income. Home office expenses, vehicle expenses for business use, equipment purchases, software and subscriptions, professional development, travel for business purposes, and countless other legitimate business expenses reduce taxable income dollar for dollar. These deductions generate tax savings at your marginal rate, effectively making the government subsidize a portion of your business expenses through tax reductions. Someone in twenty-four percent marginal tax bracket who incurs ten thousand dollars in legitimate business expenses saves twenty-four hundred dollars in taxes compared to earning the same income as a W2 employee who cannot deduct those expenses.

The retirement account contributions for business owners potentially exceed the limits for employees significantly. Someone with side business income can establish Solo 401k allowing contributions up to sixty-nine thousand dollars annually compared to twenty-three thousand dollar limits for employee 401k contributions. The additional contribution capacity provides enormous wealth-building advantage over decades through compounding of these additional tax-advantaged contributions. This benefit alone can justify maintaining side businesses generating even modest profits because the retirement account benefits exceed what would be available through employment income alone.

The business structure decisions between sole proprietorships, LLCs, S corporations, and C corporations affect liability protection, tax treatment, and administrative complexity. We addressed these issues in Chapter Twenty-Four regarding taxes, but the side business context requires emphasis on simplicity during early stages. Starting as sole proprietorship or single-member LLC provides adequate structure for most service and digital businesses generating initial revenue. These structures require minimal administrative burden and provide appropriate tax treatment. As businesses grow and generate substantial profit, transitioning to S corporation status might reduce self-employment taxes significantly. But premature focus on entity structure before validating business viability wastes time and money on legal and accounting complexity that provides no benefit when the business is not yet generating meaningful revenue.

The failure rate of new businesses within five years exceeds fifty percent according to most studies, but these statistics combine people pursuing side businesses rationally alongside employment with people quitting jobs to chase uncertain dreams. The side business approach where you maintain employment while building systematically reduces your personal failure cost to the time invested rather than to financial catastrophe from lost employment income. If your side business fails to gain traction after a year of evenings and weekends, you have lost perhaps five hundred hours of time but you have maintained your income, your lifestyle, and your wealth-building trajectory. This is acceptable failure cost that allows you to try multiple business ideas over your working years without risking your financial security.

Pierre Omidyar's development of eBay while employed at technology companies exemplifies the rational entrepreneurship approach that builds wealth without reckless risk. He did not quit stable employment to pursue an uncertain business idea. He tested the concept using weekends and evenings while his income and benefits remained secure through employment. He allowed the business to prove itself through growing revenue before transitioning to full-time focus. He maintained rational perspective about whether the business justified his time or whether he should shut it down and try different approaches. This methodical approach to entrepreneurship looks boring compared to the dramatic stories of people quitting jobs and betting everything on business dreams, but it produces vastly superior outcomes for those without trust funds or family wealth to sustain them through years of unprofitable business experimentation.

The teaching of entrepreneurship to young people should emphasize this rational approach rather than romanticizing the entrepreneur who risks everything pursuing passion. Young people should be encouraged to develop skills through employment that provide both income and learning about how businesses operate. They should be encouraged to identify problems they observe in work or life and to experiment with solutions during time outside employment. They should be taught to validate ideas through actual paying customers before investing substantial time or capital. They should understand that successful entrepreneurship is typically built on foundation of employment income that provides stability while experiments proceed. The dramatic stories of college students building billion-dollar companies in dorm rooms are extreme outliers that do not represent paths available to or appropriate for typical people building wealth.

The integration of side business income with overall wealth-building strategy requires discipline to invest business profits rather than allowing lifestyle to inflate with business income. The person who generates thirty thousand annually from side business and spends it all on upgraded lifestyle has increased their income without building wealth. The person who generates thirty thousand annually from side business and invests the entire amount while living on employment income has accelerated their wealth building dramatically. At ten percent returns, investing thirty thousand annually becomes approximately five million dollars over thirty years. Your side business income determines whether you reach financial independence fifteen years earlier than you would through employment income alone, or whether you simply consume more without changing your long-term financial trajectory.

The selection of business pursuits should consider scalability and exit potential in addition to immediate income generation. Service businesses providing your personal time and expertise generate good income but have limited scalability and typically have zero exit value because the business depends entirely on your continued involvement. Product businesses or service businesses with documented systems that others can operate have potential to scale beyond your personal capacity and potentially have sale value to buyers who can operate the systems you have built. Someone building business with eventual exit in mind creates something fundamentally different than someone merely creating self-employment. Both are valid but they serve different purposes in wealth building.

The mistakes that destroy side businesses before they can succeed are predictable and avoidable. The first mistake is pursuing business ideas based solely on passion or interest without validating market demand. The second mistake is investing substantial capital before proving customers will buy. The third mistake is underpricing offerings to the point where the business generates no meaningful profit. The fourth mistake is failing to systematically track expenses and revenue so you do not know whether the business is actually profitable. The fifth mistake is allowing the business to consume time disproportionate to results because you cannot objectively assess whether continued effort is justified. The sixth mistake is quitting employment prematurely before business income provides adequate safety margin. These mistakes are avoidable through discipline and rational analysis rather than through passion and optimism.

The broader principle is that employment income alone rarely creates substantial wealth unless you reach exceptional compensation levels. Side businesses provide mechanism to increase income beyond employment limits while building equity that employment never provides. The question is whether you approach business building rationally by maintaining employment stability while validating concepts systematically, or whether you pursue entrepreneurship through the reckless approaches that create dramatic stories but that destroy wealth more often than they create it. The one percent build businesses methodically as supplements to employment that accelerate wealth building. The ninety-nine percent either never attempt entrepreneurship because they view it as too risky, or they attempt it recklessly by quitting employment to chase uncertain dreams. Both approaches forfeit the wealth-building acceleration that rational side business development provides.

You now understand how to identify business opportunities, how to validate concepts before major investment, how to acquire initial customers, how to price offerings profitably, how to operate businesses alongside employment sustainably, and when transition to full-time focus becomes rational rather than reckless. The implementation requires initiative that many people lack because employment provides comfortable certainty while business building requires embracing uncertainty and risking failure. But the wealth-building potential from successful side businesses exceeds what employment typically provides, making the effort worthwhile for those willing to act systematically rather than hoping that employment alone will generate the wealth they seek.

CHAPTER 26:
VACATION STRATEGY—REST WITHOUT FINANCIAL REGRESSION

In 2010, a software engineer named Matt Kepnes quit his corporate job with the intention of traveling for a few months before returning to the workforce. He had saved fifteen thousand dollars and planned to stretch it as far as possible through Southeast Asia and Europe before his money ran out and reality forced him home. Most people embarking on extended travel either drain trust funds their parents established, accumulate credit card debt that haunts them for years afterward, or return broke after a few months of experiences they can barely afford.

Kepnes took a different approach. He studied how long-term travelers and expatriates lived abroad for fractions of what tourists spent. He learned to book accommodations through local sites rather than international hotel chains. He ate where locals ate rather than at restaurants catering to tourists. He traveled during shoulder seasons when prices dropped by fifty percent or more. He used credit card rewards to eliminate flight costs entirely. He stayed in cities long enough to negotiate monthly apartment rentals at one-third the cost of nightly hotel rates.

His fifteen thousand dollars lasted not three months but eighteen months of continuous travel through forty countries. The experience taught him that the relationship between money spent and travel quality was not linear. Often the cheapest options provided the most authentic experiences while expensive tourist infrastructure delivered sanitized versions of culture designed for mass consumption. He returned to the United States not broke but with money remaining and with a revelation that would transform his life.

Kepnes launched a blog called "Nomadic Matt" documenting the strategies that had allowed him to travel so extensively for so little. The blog grew into a business generating multiple six figures annually while he continued traveling full-time. A decade after that initial trip, he had visited over ninety countries, written multiple bestselling books, and built a company that taught hundreds of thousands of people how to travel extensively without destroying their financial futures. His success was not built on exceptional income or inheritance but on understanding that travel, like every other expense category, could be optimized dramatically through knowledge and systematic implementation of strategies that most people never discover.

This chapter addresses what many consider the most difficult aspect of wealth building to reconcile with actual living: how do you experience life, maintain relationships, rest from work demands, and expose yourself and your family to the broader world without undermining the very wealth-building discipline that makes financial independence possible? The answer is not eliminating travel or accepting that vacations require financial regression. The answer is approaching travel with the same strategic thinking you apply to every other domain we have examined throughout this book.

The fundamental framework for vacation strategy begins with understanding that vacations serve legitimate purposes that justify their costs when those costs are reasonable and when the vacations are funded appropriately. Extended periods of work without rest reduce productivity, impair decision-making, and damage health in ways that cost far more than reasonable vacation spending. Relationships require focused time away from work demands where connection can deepen without the constant pull of professional obligations. Children benefit from exposure to different cultures, geographies, and experiences that broaden their understanding of the world beyond their immediate environment. Rest and recovery are not luxuries to be eliminated during wealth-building years but necessities that sustain the capacity for sustained high performance across decades.

The error most people make is not taking vacations but rather how they fund them and how much they spend on experiences that provide minimal lasting value. The ninety-nine percent treat vacations as rewards for hard work that justify unlimited spending because "you only live once" and because they "deserve" expensive experiences after months of labor. They book trips impulsively when they feel burned out rather than planning systematically months in advance when prices are lowest and best options remain available. They finance vacations through credit cards, paying twenty percent interest on experiences that provided a week of pleasure followed by months or years of payment obligation. They visit expensive tourist destinations during peak seasons, paying premium prices for overcrowded experiences. They stay in chain hotels that could be anywhere rather than in local neighborhoods where authentic culture exists at fraction of the cost.

The one percent approach vacation spending as they approach every expense category—by determining what purposes they need to serve, identifying the minimum effective cost to serve those purposes well, and structuring their financial lives to fund those costs without debt or without sacrificing systematic investment contributions. They establish separate vacation funds that accumulate throughout the year specifically for travel, ensuring that trips are paid in cash and that vacation spending never competes with investment contributions for the same dollars. They plan trips months in advance, capturing early-booking discounts and better availability while having time to optimize every component. They travel during shoulder seasons when prices drop by thirty to fifty percent while weather remains excellent and crowds thin dramatically. They prioritize experiences and relationships over luxury accommodations and expensive tourist activities.

The vacation fund represents the foundational structure that prevents vacation debt while ensuring that travel remains possible during wealth-building years. You establish a separate savings account designated exclusively for vacation expenses. You determine how much you want to spend annually on travel based on your income, your savings rate goals, and your priorities. You divide this annual amount by twelve and establish automatic monthly transfers from your checking account to your vacation fund. When planning trips, you spend only what has accumulated in the fund, ensuring that every vacation is fully funded before you depart.

The mathematics of vacation funding separate those who travel sustainably from those who destroy their financial futures through trip financing. Someone earning seventy-five thousand annually and targeting a forty percent savings rate has forty-five thousand available for all expenses after thirty thousand is saved and invested. If they allocate five thousand annually to vacation spending, this is approximately eleven percent of their available spending budget or approximately four hundred seventeen dollars monthly accumulating in their vacation fund. This amount funds substantial travel when deployed strategically. Someone earning one hundred fifty thousand and maintaining fifty percent savings rate has seventy-five thousand available for expenses and might reasonably allocate ten thousand annually to travel, or approximately eight hundred thirty-three dollars monthly.

The credit card rewards optimization provides the first major opportunity to reduce vacation costs while maintaining or improving experience quality. We discussed credit cards in Chapter Twenty-Three regarding building credit and avoiding debt, but the travel rewards component deserves specific attention for vacation planning. Credit cards offering travel rewards typically provide two to three points per dollar spent on travel purchases, one to two points per dollar on dining and other categories, and one point per dollar on everything else. These points can be redeemed for flights, hotels, and other travel expenses at values ranging from one cent per point for cash-back redemptions to two cents per point or more for strategic travel bookings.

The systematic approach involves obtaining credit cards offering substantial signup bonuses, meeting minimum spending requirements through normal expenses that you would incur regardless, collecting the bonus points, and deploying those points for travel expenses. Someone who obtains a card offering sixty thousand points after spending three thousand dollars in three months, which they would have spent anyway on groceries, gas, and bills, has earned enough points for domestic round-trip flights or several nights of hotel accommodations. Multiple cards acquired systematically over time—spacing applications by three to six months to avoid concentrated hard inquiries on credit reports—generate hundreds of thousands of points annually that can fund significant portions of travel expenses.

The planning timeline determines whether you pay premium prices for mediocre availability or whether you capture optimal prices for better options. The one percent begin planning major trips six to twelve months in advance for international travel and three to six months for domestic travel. This advance planning allows booking flights during fare sales that offer thirty to fifty percent discounts compared to prices two weeks before departure. It allows booking preferred accommodations before they fill, often at early-booking discounts that hotels offer to encourage advance reservations. It allows researching activities and restaurants rather than wandering aimlessly and ending up in overpriced tourist traps because you did not know better options existed.

The flight booking strategy exploits the pricing algorithms airlines use to maximize revenue. Prices fluctuate based on demand, time until departure, competitive routes, and complex revenue management systems. The general patterns are that booking two to three months in advance for domestic flights and three to six months in advance for international flights typically produces lowest prices. Tuesday and Wednesday departures cost less than weekend departures because business travelers avoid these days. Flights with connections cost less than nonstop flights, and the time cost of connections must be weighed against the money saved. Shoulder season travel during spring and fall offers dramatically lower prices than summer and winter holiday periods while often providing superior weather and smaller crowds.

The use of flight comparison tools like Google Flights, Skyscanner, or Kayak allows searching across multiple airlines simultaneously and identifying lowest prices for your routes. The flexible date search features show price calendars revealing which departure dates offer substantially lower fares than others, allowing you to shift travel dates by a day or two to capture savings of hundreds of dollars. The price tracking features alert you when fares drop for routes you are monitoring, allowing you to book when sales occur rather than paying whatever price exists when you happen to search.

The accommodation strategy determines whether you spend one hundred fifty dollars nightly for generic hotel rooms or whether you spend fifty dollars nightly for superior apartments in residential neighborhoods where locals live. Hotels cater to tourists who book through familiar platforms and who pay premium prices for convenient locations near tourist attractions. Vacation rentals through platforms like Airbnb or VRBO provide apartments and homes in residential neighborhoods at fractions of hotel costs, often with kitchens that allow grocery shopping and cooking to avoid expensive restaurant meals. The one percent filter for highly-rated properties with numerous reviews, communicate with hosts before booking to verify that listings match descriptions, and book accommodations in neighborhoods where locals live rather than in tourist districts where every business caters to visitors paying inflated prices.

The extended stay strategy provides even greater savings for those with flexible work arrangements or who can combine vacation with remote work. Booking accommodations for one month rather than one week typically reduces nightly rates by thirty to fifty percent because hosts prefer longer stays that reduce turnover work and vacancy periods. Someone spending three weeks in a location might book for one month and pay less than they would for three weeks at weekly rates. This approach requires longer travel periods but dramatically reduces per-day costs while allowing deeper engagement with locations rather than rushing through multiple destinations trying to see everything.

The geographic arbitrage approach involves traveling to locations where cost of living is substantially lower than your home location, allowing you to maintain or improve lifestyle quality while spending far less than you would at home. Many locations in Southeast Asia, Central America, Eastern Europe, and parts of South America offer excellent infrastructure, safety, culture, and climate at costs of one thousand to two thousand dollars monthly for comfortable living including housing, food, transportation, and activities. Someone who can work remotely might spend three months in these locations, reducing their living expenses by two thousand dollars monthly compared to expensive U.S. cities while experiencing different cultures and climates.

The seasonal timing determines whether you pay peak prices for overcrowded experiences or whether you pay thirty to fifty percent less for superior experiences during shoulder seasons. Peak seasons for most tourist destinations align with summer months when families travel, winter holidays, and spring break periods. Traveling during shoulder seasons immediately before or after these peaks provides weather that remains excellent while crowds thin and prices drop dramatically. Someone visiting Europe in late April or early October rather than July pays substantially less for flights and accommodations while experiencing pleasant weather and avoiding crowds that make summer travel in popular cities miserable.

The destination selection based on cost efficiency rather than solely on interest allows more frequent travel on limited budgets. A week in expensive cities like London, Paris, or New York might cost three thousand to five thousand dollars for modest hotel, meals, and activities. The same budget funds three to four weeks in Southeast Asia or Central America with superior accommodations, food, and activities. The one percent consider cost-adjusted experiences rather than simply where they want to visit, recognizing that some destinations provide ten times the value of others when measured by experience quality per dollar spent.

The local living approach versus tourist infrastructure utilization determines both cost and experience quality. Tourists eat at restaurants near major attractions that charge premium prices for mediocre food because customers are one-time visitors who will never return. They stay in hotels in tourist districts surrounded by other hotels and tourist businesses rather than in neighborhoods where locals live. They participate in organized tours that cost fifty to one hundred dollars per person for experiences you could replicate independently for ten dollars with minimal research. They shop in stores catering to tourists rather than in markets where locals buy goods at fraction of tourist prices.

The one percent eat where locals eat, using Google Maps reviews filtered for highest-rated restaurants with local language reviews rather than English reviews from tourists. They use public transportation that locals use rather than taxis and tour buses that extract maximum money from time-constrained visitors. They shop in neighborhood markets rather than in tourist shopping districts. They walk through residential neighborhoods observing daily life rather than only visiting major attractions. These approaches provide more authentic cultural experiences while costing fractions of what tourists pay for sanitized experiences designed for mass consumption.

The activity prioritization based on value and interest rather than on tourist must-see lists allows focusing budgets on experiences that matter to you rather than checking boxes on generic itineraries. Every destination has activities and attractions that tourist literature suggests everyone must experience. Many provide minimal value while costing substantial money and time. The one percent research activities carefully through sources beyond tourist marketing—reading blogs from long-term travelers, asking locals for recommendations, identifying activities that align with their genuine interests rather than what they are told they should experience.

The free and low-cost activities that exist in every destination provide substantial value without consuming vacation budgets. Walking tours led by local guides working for tips provide excellent city orientation and history for ten to twenty dollars. Museums often have free or reduced admission days. Parks, beaches, markets, and neighborhoods cost nothing to explore. Cultural events and festivals provide authentic experiences at no cost. The one percent prioritize these experiences rather than paying hundreds of dollars for organized tours that commoditize culture.

The food strategy determines whether vacation food costs exceed home food costs by three times or whether you maintain reasonable food budgets while eating well. Eating three meals daily at restaurants catering to tourists costs fifty to one hundred dollars per person. Shopping at markets and cooking breakfast and lunch while eating dinner at local restaurants costs fifteen to twenty-five dollars per person for superior food. Someone traveling with family of four might spend four hundred dollars daily on tourist restaurant meals or one hundred dollars daily using hybrid approach of cooking some meals and eating others at local establishments. Over a two-week vacation, this difference is over four thousand dollars—enough to fund an additional vacation.

The travel hacking communities provide resources for learning optimization strategies that most travelers never discover. Websites like Nomadic Matt, The Points Guy, and various travel hacking blogs document specific strategies for maximizing credit card rewards, finding mistake fares, booking award travel optimally, and traveling extensively for minimal cost. The forums associated with these sites provide current information about which strategies work, which cards offer best rewards, and how to troubleshoot problems that arise during bookings. The one percent invest time learning from these communities rather than booking travel naively through methods that cost two to three times more for equivalent or inferior experiences.

The house-sitting and home exchange platforms provide free accommodations in exchange for caring for homes and pets while owners travel. Websites like TrustedHousesitters or HomeExchange connect travelers willing to stay in homes and care for properties with homeowners seeking responsible house-sitters. This arrangement provides free accommodations in residential neighborhoods while allowing you to live like a local rather than like a tourist. The requirements are establishing trustworthiness through profile building and references, flexibility about dates and locations, and willingness to care for homes and pets responsibly. For those who can meet these requirements, house-sitting eliminates accommodation costs entirely.

The group travel decisions determine whether social pressure forces expensive trips that do not align with your priorities or whether you maintain boundaries that protect your financial discipline. Friends suggest destination weddings requiring two thousand dollar flights plus expensive resort accommodations. Extended family proposes elaborate group vacations that cost five thousand dollars per person for experiences you could replicate independently for one thousand dollars. Colleagues organize trips to expensive destinations during peak seasons. The one percent evaluate these invitations based on actual relationship value and cost-adjusted experience quality rather than feeling obligated to participate because everyone else is going.

The communication about vacation choices with family and friends determines whether your strategic approach to travel creates friction or whether others respect your decisions. The ninety-nine percent either hide their strategies out of embarrassment about appearing cheap or they explain apologetically as if their choices reflect poverty rather than intelligent optimization. The one percent are direct about their approach without apology. When friends suggest expensive trips, they propose less expensive alternatives or they decline explicitly because the costs do not align with their priorities. They explain that they prefer traveling more frequently to less expensive destinations rather than traveling rarely to expensive ones. They maintain relationships without requiring identical vacation choices.

The vacation timing relative to work obligations and career considerations matters for those climbing corporate ladders or building businesses. The person who takes three-week vacations during critical project periods damages their career prospects regardless of their technical competence. The person who times vacations around work cycles and who ensures projects are in good hands before departing maintains professional reputation while still taking necessary rest. The one percent coordinate vacation timing with managers, communicate clearly about availability during time off, and establish coverage that prevents work crises from interrupting rest.

The balance between experiencing life now and building wealth for future requires conscious decision-making rather than defaulting to either extreme. The person who eliminates all discretionary spending including travel to maximize savings rate might accumulate wealth faster but at cost of relationships, experiences, and personal development that money cannot buy later. The person who refuses to constrain vacation spending because "you only live once" never builds wealth and faces decades of constrained choices because they prioritized immediate experiences over future freedom. The optimal path involves systematic vacation spending at levels that preserve high savings rates while allowing meaningful travel experiences. Someone maintaining forty percent savings rate who allocates six to eight percent of gross income to vacation spending can travel substantially while building wealth that creates permanent freedom.

The teaching of vacation values to children establishes patterns that persist through their lives. Children who experience only expensive resort vacations learn that travel requires luxury accommodations and organized entertainment. They develop expensive tastes that limit their future travel capacity when they must fund trips themselves. Children who experience budget travel involving hostels, street food, public transportation, and unstructured exploration learn that adventure and cultural immersion matter more than accommodation quality. They develop skills and confidence for independent travel that expands their future opportunities while requiring minimal resources. The one percent deliberately expose children to varied travel experiences that build capabilities rather than expectations for luxury.

The solo travel considerations apply for those without partners or families or for those who benefit from periodic independent experiences. Solo travel allows complete control over itinerary, budget, and pace. It forces social engagement with locals and other travelers rather than remaining insulated within your group. It builds confidence and problem-solving capabilities through navigating unfamiliar environments independently. The costs are lower than group travel because you make all decisions based on your preferences and budget without compromising. The one percent who travel solo do so strategically, staying in social hostels or attending events where meeting others occurs naturally, taking occasional tours or classes that provide structure, and maintaining reasonable safety awareness without paranoia.

The digital nomad lifestyle represents extreme version of geographic arbitrage where people work remotely while traveling continuously or while living in low-cost locations indefinitely. This lifestyle became accessible to increasing numbers of people during the 2020s as remote work normalized across industries previously requiring office presence. The one percent who can work remotely evaluate whether geographic arbitrage makes sense for their situations, potentially spending months or years in locations where five-thousand-dollar monthly budgets provide lifestyles that would require fifteen-thousand-dollar budgets in expensive U.S. cities. The savings can accelerate wealth building dramatically while providing international experience and cultural exposure.

The return on investment from vacation spending is difficult to quantify but real. The memories created during meaningful travel persist long after physical possessions are forgotten. The relationships strengthened through shared experiences provide value that exceeds the costs when those costs are reasonable and when the experiences are well-designed. The cultural exposure and perspective shifts that travel provides enhance decision-making and understanding in ways that create personal and professional value. The rest and recovery that proper vacations provide sustain decades of high performance that generate far more wealth than the vacation costs consumed. These returns justify reasonable vacation spending. They do not justify unlimited spending or vacation debt that undermines wealth building.

The lifetime vacation budget provides perspective on whether your annual spending aligns with your values and goals. Someone who spends five thousand annually on vacations for forty years spends two hundred thousand on travel over their lifetime. At ten percent returns, this two hundred thousand invested instead would become nine million dollars. This does not mean you should eliminate vacations and invest everything. It means understanding the true long-term cost of vacation spending and consciously choosing the balance between present experiences and future freedom. The one percent make this choice deliberately rather than spending reactively based on momentary desires or social pressures.

Matt Kepnes demonstrated through his decade of travel that extensive experiences do not require extensive spending. His success came from systematic application of optimization strategies that most travelers never learn despite their availability. He proved that the relationship between money and travel quality is not linear and that often the least expensive approaches provide the most authentic and memorable experiences. His business success came from teaching these strategies to others, creating value by closing the knowledge gap that causes most people to spend three times more than necessary for inferior experiences.

The principles apply regardless of whether you want to travel full-time like Kepnes or whether you want occasional vacations to rest and recharge while primarily remaining home building your career and business ventures. Vacations are not obstacles to wealth building when funded properly and optimized strategically. They are necessary components of sustainable high performance that allows decades of discipline required to build substantial wealth. The question is whether you will approach vacation spending with the same strategic thinking you apply to housing, transportation, food, and investments, or whether you will treat travel as the one expense category where discipline does not matter and where costs are whatever they happen to be.

The one percent systematize vacation spending through dedicated funds, through learning optimization strategies from travel hacking communities, through planning far in advance, through choosing cost-efficient destinations and seasons, through living locally rather than consuming tourist infrastructure, and through maintaining clear boundaries about what they will and will not spend on travel. These practices allow them to travel more frequently and more meaningfully than peers who spend two to three times more for inferior experiences. The frameworks have been provided. The implementation in your specific circumstances remains your responsibility. Whether you travel intelligently or whether you treat vacations as financial regression is your choice to make.

CHAPTER 27:
STUDENT LOAN STRATEGY—MANAGING EDUCATIONAL DEBT

In 2012, a physician named James Dahle finished his medical residency carrying two hundred thousand dollars in student loan debt at an average interest rate of 6.8 percent. He faced a decision that confronted millions of Americans with similar debt burdens: should he pay off the loans aggressively using every available dollar beyond basic living expenses, or should he make minimum payments while investing the difference in stock market index funds? His physician colleagues overwhelmingly advocated aggressive payoff based on the emotional appeal of becoming debt-free. Financial calculators suggested that paying extra principal would save him tens of thousands in interest over the life of the loans.

Dahle took a different approach. He analyzed the mathematics dispassionately rather than responding to the emotional weight of six-figure debt. His loans averaged 6.8 percent interest. Stock market index funds had returned approximately ten percent annually over the previous century. The marginal tax rate he faced as a physician exceeded thirty percent, making his student loan interest partially deductible and reducing his effective interest rate to approximately 4.8 percent after tax benefits. The mathematics indicated that paying minimum amounts on relatively low-interest debt while investing aggressively in higher-return assets would generate superior long-term outcomes despite feeling counterintuitive.

He established automated minimum payments on all student loans while directing every dollar beyond those minimums and beyond basic living expenses into stock market investments. His colleagues who chose aggressive payoff eliminated their loans in three to five years and then began investing heavily. Dahle maintained his loans for the full ten-year repayment period while investing consistently throughout. By the time his loans were finally paid off through minimum payments, his investment accounts had grown substantially beyond what his debt-free colleagues had accumulated because he had invested for the entire ten years while they had invested for only five to seven years after becoming debt-free.

The difference was not enormous in the short term but it was meaningful—approximately one hundred thousand dollars in additional investment wealth after ten years. More importantly, Dahle's approach established the principle that debt is not automatically bad and that financial decisions should be made mathematically rather than emotionally. He went on to found The White Coat Investor, a financial education platform teaching medical professionals how to manage their unique financial situations including substantial student debt. His message was that debt creates obligation but not emergency, that interest rates matter more than debt balances, and that the optimal strategy depends on specific numbers rather than on blanket rules about debt being evil.

This chapter addresses what has become one of the most contentious financial topics in American society: how to manage the student loan debt that affects over forty million Americans carrying a combined one point seven trillion dollars in obligations. The decision about how aggressively to pay down this debt affects wealth building for decades because every dollar directed toward debt payoff is a dollar not deployed into investments during the years when compound growth provides maximum benefit. Yet student loans carry psychological weight that exceeds their mathematical impact, making purely analytical approaches difficult to implement despite their financial superiority.

The framework for student loan strategy begins with understanding that not all debt is created equal and that the optimal approach to managing debt depends entirely on its interest rate, its tax treatment, and the opportunity cost of capital directed toward repayment. Student loans at three percent interest represent fundamentally different financial situations than credit card debt at twenty percent interest. The former is cheap financing that costs less than inflation-adjusted stock market returns. The latter is catastrophically expensive debt that must be eliminated immediately because no investment generates returns sufficient to justify paying twenty percent interest on borrowed money.

The interest rate threshold that determines strategy is approximately five to six percent. Student loans with interest rates below this threshold typically should be paid at minimum required amounts while excess capital is deployed into stock market investments that generate higher expected returns. Student loans with interest rates above this threshold typically should be paid aggressively because the guaranteed return from debt elimination exceeds expected investment returns after accounting for risk and taxes. This threshold is not rigid and it varies based on individual circumstances including tax situation, risk tolerance, and presence of employer matching in retirement accounts. But it provides the framework for making decisions mathematically rather than emotionally.

The federal student loan types include Direct Subsidized Loans that do not accrue interest while you are in school, Direct Unsubsidized Loans that accrue interest from disbursement, Direct PLUS Loans for graduate students and parents with higher interest rates, and consolidated loans that combine multiple loans into single payment streams. Each type has specific interest rates set by Congress that change annually for new borrowers but remain fixed for the life of loans once originated. Understanding which types of loans you hold and their specific interest rates is the first step in developing optimal repayment strategy because different loans within your portfolio might warrant different approaches.

The private student loans from banks and other lenders operate differently than federal loans and typically offer less flexible repayment options, no income-driven repayment plans, and no forgiveness programs. They often carry variable interest rates that fluctuate based on market conditions or fixed rates that are negotiated based on creditworthiness at origination. Private loans typically should be prioritized for refinancing or aggressive repayment because they lack the protections and flexibility that federal loans provide. The person carrying both federal and private loans should generally direct extra payments toward private loans first while maintaining minimum payments on federal loans that offer superior terms and protections.

The income-driven repayment plans for federal loans calculate monthly payments based on discretionary income rather than loan balance, potentially reducing required payments substantially for those with high debt relative to income. The plans include Income-Based Repayment, Pay As You Earn, Revised Pay As You Earn, and Income-Contingent Repayment, each with slightly different qualification requirements and payment calculations. These plans extend repayment periods to twenty or twenty-five years and forgive any remaining balance after that period, though the forgiven amount is currently treated as taxable income in the year of forgiveness.

The strategic use of income-driven repayment creates opportunities for those pursuing careers with relatively low income despite high educational debt. Someone with one hundred fifty thousand in student debt earning fifty thousand annually might face monthly payments of fifteen hundred dollars under standard ten-year repayment that consume thirty-six percent of gross income. Under income-driven plans, those payments might reduce to three hundred to five hundred dollars monthly based on family size and income, making the debt manageable while allowing the borrower to invest in retirement accounts and build emergency funds. The trade-off is that extending repayment to twenty-five years with minimal payments means the loan balance grows due to interest accrual exceeding monthly payments, and the eventual forgiven amount creates tax liability that must be planned for decades in advance.

The Public Service Loan Forgiveness program forgives remaining federal student loan balances after ten years of qualifying payments while working for government or nonprofit organizations. This program creates enormous value for those who genuinely intend to pursue public service careers long-term and who qualify for income-driven repayment plans that keep payments low relative to debt. Someone with two hundred thousand in debt working in public service earning sixty thousand annually might make total payments of sixty thousand over ten years before receiving forgiveness of the remaining one hundred eighty thousand including accumulated interest. This represents one hundred eighty thousand of tax-free debt elimination that makes public service financially competitive with private sector employment despite lower salaries.

The PSLF program has been notoriously difficult to navigate with high rejection rates due to administrative errors, loan type mismatches, and employment verification problems. The one percent who pursue PSLF document everything meticulously, submit employment certification forms annually rather than waiting until applying for forgiveness, ensure all loans are the correct federal loan types that qualify, and maintain income-driven repayment plan enrollment throughout. They treat PSLF as option that might work rather than as guarantee, maintaining backup plans if forgiveness is ultimately denied.

The refinancing of student loans through private lenders can reduce interest rates substantially for borrowers with strong credit scores and stable incomes. Private lenders offer refinancing that consolidates multiple loans into single loans with interest rates potentially two to four percentage points lower than original federal rates. Someone with one hundred thousand in federal loans at 6.8 percent interest might refinance to 3.5 percent, saving over three thousand dollars annually in interest. The total savings over ten years could exceed thirty thousand dollars, making refinancing highly valuable for those who qualify for favorable rates.

The trade-off with refinancing federal loans into private loans is that you forfeit all federal protections including income-driven repayment options, deferment and forbearance during hardship, and potential forgiveness programs. This trade is appropriate for high earners with stable employment who will never need income-driven repayment and who are not pursuing PSLF. It is inappropriate for those with uncertain income, those pursuing public service careers, or those who might need the flexibility federal loans provide. The one percent evaluate their specific situations honestly rather than refinancing automatically because lower rates seem attractive without considering what protections they are surrendering.

The employer student loan repayment assistance has emerged as employee benefit at some companies that make monthly contributions toward employee student loans as part of compensation packages. This benefit is treated as taxable income to employees but still provides substantial value by accelerating debt payoff without requiring employees to reduce take-home pay. Someone receiving two hundred fifty dollars monthly in employer loan repayment assistance receives three thousand dollars annually toward principal reduction that would otherwise have required four thousand dollars or more in pre-tax earnings to fund personally. The one percent considers this benefit when evaluating job offers and they maximize it when available.

The decision between aggressive payoff and minimum payments with investing depends on the specific mathematics of your situation and requires calculation rather than assumption. Someone with fifty thousand in student loans at four percent interest faces minimum monthly payments of approximately five hundred seven dollars over ten years. If they can afford to pay one thousand dollars monthly, they can pay off the loans in approximately four and a half years and save approximately two thousand five hundred dollars in interest. Alternatively, they can maintain minimum payments while investing the extra four hundred ninety-three dollars monthly in index funds. Over the same four and a half years, that four hundred ninety-three monthly becomes approximately thirty thousand dollars at ten percent returns. After the aggressive payer becomes debt-free and begins investing one thousand dollars monthly, both scenarios converge with the minimum payer having slightly more wealth due to earlier investment start despite carrying debt longer.

The calculations become more favorable for investing over aggressive payoff when loans carry lower interest rates or when the borrower's marginal tax rate is high enough that student loan interest deductions reduce effective interest rates substantially. They become more favorable for aggressive payoff when loans carry higher interest rates, when investment returns are expected to be lower than historical averages, or when the borrower values debt freedom for psychological reasons that justify accepting suboptimal financial outcomes. The one percent run these calculations with their specific numbers rather than following generic advice that ignores individual circumstances.

The emergency fund consideration affects student loan strategy because debt obligations create ongoing expenses that must be covered even during income interruption. The person aggressively paying down student loans while maintaining minimal emergency reserves faces catastrophe if they lose employment and cannot make loan payments, potentially triggering default with severe consequences. The person maintaining minimum loan payments while building robust emergency funds can weather income interruption through drawing on reserves while maintaining all debt obligations. The one percent typically prioritize emergency fund establishment to three to six months of expenses before pursuing aggressive debt payoff, though they might pursue aggressive payoff while simultaneously building emergency funds if cash flow permits.

The psychological component of student debt management cannot be ignored despite mathematical approaches suggesting optimal strategies. Many people experience significant stress and mental burden from carrying debt regardless of interest rates or opportunity costs. The anxiety from six-figure debt might impair work performance, decision-making, and overall wellbeing in ways that cost more than the mathematical suboptimality of aggressive payoff would cost. For these individuals, pursuing aggressive payoff despite mathematical disadvantage might be rational choice because the psychological benefits exceed the financial costs. The one percent acknowledge psychological realities while also questioning whether debt anxiety is legitimate constraint or whether it can be reframed through education about how strategic debt management actually works.

The marriage and family considerations affect student loan decisions because spouses' loans and incomes interact in income-driven repayment calculations. Filing taxes jointly versus separately affects discretionary income calculations that determine payments under income-driven plans. Having children affects family size variables that influence payment amounts. The presence of Parent PLUS loans that parents took to fund children's education creates complicated family dynamics about who should repay those loans. The one percent address these situations through explicit family discussions about responsibilities, through coordinating filing statuses to optimize payment calculations if pursuing income-driven plans, and through ensuring that student loan obligations and strategies are understood before marriage rather than creating surprises after.

The graduate school decision should be evaluated based on debt required relative to expected income increase from the degree. Law school costing three hundred thousand in tuition plus three years of forgone income requires analysis of realistic starting salaries for lawyers from schools at various tiers. Medical school costing similar amounts requires understanding physician compensation and the decade of training before earning full attending salaries. Master's degrees should be evaluated based on whether they create specific career advancement opportunities or whether they simply represent expensive credentialing that employers do not actually value. The one percent calculate expected lifetime earnings with and without degrees, compare against all-in costs including opportunity costs of years spent in school rather than earning, and make decisions based on realistic return on investment rather than on aspirational career fantasies.

The undergraduate institution decision affects student debt dramatically but affects career outcomes minimally for most fields outside of elite finance and consulting recruiting. The student who attends flagship state university for thirty thousand dollars total graduates with manageable debt and employment prospects nearly identical to the student who attends private university for two hundred fifty thousand. The difference in outcomes rarely justifies the six-fold cost difference. The one percent evaluate colleges based on realistic career impact rather than on prestige or on emotional attachment to particular schools. They consider community college for first two years before transferring to four-year institutions, which cuts costs by forty percent while producing identical degrees. They evaluate full scholarships at less prestigious schools versus partial aid at more prestigious schools based on total cost rather than on institutional rankings.

The prevention of student debt through work-study programs, scholarship applications, major selection based on earning potential, and realistic school selection matters more than optimizing repayment of debt already accumulated. The person who avoids seventy thousand in student debt has invested zero hours managing that debt over subsequent decades. The person who accumulates one hundred thousand in debt must manage it strategically for ten to twenty-five years. Prevention is superior to management, yet most high school students receive no financial education about evaluating college costs relative to expected earnings or about whether college is even necessary for their intended careers. The one percent who have children educate them explicitly about these trade-offs before college decisions are made rather than discovering debt problems after graduation.

The career selection based partly on student debt obligations determines whether debt remains manageable or whether it consumes decades of earnings. The student who accumulates one hundred fifty thousand in debt preparing for social work career earning forty thousand annually has created impossible mathematics that will require income-driven repayment and eventual forgiveness. The student who accumulates similar debt preparing for engineering career earning eighty thousand annually has created manageable situation where standard repayment consumes fifteen to twenty percent of gross income for ten years before elimination. The one percent evaluate career choices partly based on financial realities including debt service capacity rather than purely based on interest or passion disconnected from economic outcomes.

The side income strategies can accelerate debt elimination or investment accumulation when career income alone leaves minimal margin after basic expenses and minimum debt payments. Someone earning fifty thousand annually with fifteen hundred monthly going to minimum student loan payments and thirty-five hundred monthly required for basic living expenses has no margin for wealth building or aggressive debt payoff. The same person generating one thousand monthly through side business can deploy that income entirely toward debt elimination or investment, transforming their financial trajectory. The one percent pursue side income not because their career income is inadequate but because additional income streams accelerate wealth building beyond what career income alone can achieve, and this applies equally to those managing student debt.

The staying current on payments regardless of strategy choice is non-negotiable because student loan default creates catastrophic consequences that outweigh any financial benefit from redirecting payment money elsewhere. Default triggers wage garnishment, tax refund seizure, Social Security payment reduction, credit score destruction, and in extreme cases lawsuits and asset seizure. The one percent never miss student loan payments even if this requires reducing other expenses or temporarily pausing aggressive investing. They establish automatic payments that execute before they can spend money elsewhere, ensuring that loans remain current regardless of other financial pressures.

The company loan repayment programs and employer matching in retirement accounts interact with student loan repayment decisions. Someone whose employer offers four percent 401k match on six percent contribution should always contribute six percent to capture the full match before directing any extra money toward student loan payoff because the match provides one hundred percent immediate return that no debt payoff can match. Someone whose employer offers student loan repayment assistance should maximize this benefit before using personal income for extra loan payments. The one percent sequence these decisions to capture free money from employers before deploying personal resources toward debt or investments.

The federal loan versus private loan prioritization in portfolios containing both types generally favors keeping federal loans at minimum payments due to their flexibility while directing aggressive payments toward private loans that lack protections. Someone carrying fifty thousand in federal loans at 4.5 percent and thirty thousand in private loans at 6.5 percent should maintain minimums on federal loans while attacking private loans aggressively. This approach eliminates the higher-rate debt that lacks protections while preserving access to income-driven repayment and potential forgiveness on federal loans if circumstances change unexpectedly. The one percent evaluate their specific loan portfolios and prioritize payments based on interest rates and loan characteristics rather than paying all loans equally.

The windfall deployment toward student loans requires analysis of whether lump sum debt reduction generates better outcomes than investing windfalls. Someone receiving twenty thousand inheritance faces decision about whether to pay down student debt or to invest. The analysis is identical to the ongoing payment analysis: what is the interest rate on the debt and what are expected investment returns? If debt carries 6.5 percent interest, paying it down provides guaranteed 6.5 percent return. If investment returns are expected to average ten percent, investing provides better expected outcome despite uncertainty. The one percent run these calculations with each windfall rather than automatically directing all windfalls toward debt or automatically investing all windfalls regardless of specific circumstances.

The timeline to financial independence gets affected by student loan decisions because aggressive debt payoff delays investment accumulation during years when compound growth provides maximum benefit. Someone who spends five years aggressively paying debt before beginning investment has lost five years of compound growth that cannot be recovered. Someone who invests throughout while making minimum debt payments benefits from those five years of growth. The difference might be ten to fifteen years in time until financial independence for someone targeting forty percent savings rate. The one percent consider this timeline impact explicitly rather than assuming debt freedom must precede wealth building.

The loan forgiveness tax bomb planning applies to those pursuing income-driven repayment expecting eventual forgiveness. Current law treats forgiven amounts as taxable income in the year of forgiveness, creating potentially massive tax bills for those who have grown their balances through decades of interest accrual. Someone with three hundred thousand forgiven after twenty-five years of income-driven payments might face one hundred thousand in federal and state taxes due immediately. The one percent pursuing this strategy set aside money throughout the repayment period in dedicated accounts that will fund this eventual tax bill, treating it as deferred payment rather than as complete forgiveness. They track projected forgiveness amounts and adjust savings accordingly as balances grow.

The broader principle connecting student loan strategy to wealth building is that debt is tool that can be used intelligently or can be weapon that destroys financial futures. Student loans at reasonable interest rates represent acceptable financing of human capital development when the education funded actually increases earning capacity by amounts that justify the debt incurred. Student loans at any interest rate represent catastrophic mistakes when they finance degrees that provide no income increase or when they are accumulated at levels that cannot be serviced from realistic career earnings. The one percent make these decisions based on mathematics before accumulating debt rather than rationalizing decisions after debt exists.

James Dahle demonstrated through his systematic approach that emotional reactions to debt lead to suboptimal financial decisions when those reactions override mathematical analysis. His willingness to carry six-figure debt for ten years while investing aggressively generated superior outcomes compared to peers who prioritized debt freedom over investment. His success came not from superior intelligence or exceptional circumstances but from understanding the actual mathematics of debt versus investment and from maintaining discipline to implement the mathematically optimal strategy despite social pressure to eliminate debt aggressively.

The one percent make student loan decisions mathematically while acknowledging psychological realities that might justify suboptimal choices. They understand interest rates and opportunity costs. They calculate whether aggressive payoff or minimum payments with investing produces better outcomes in their specific situations. They refinance when appropriate while understanding what they forfeit. They pursue income-driven repayment and forgiveness programs when mathematics support those approaches. They pay loans on schedule regardless of strategy chosen. They evaluate education costs versus earning potential before accumulating debt rather than after. They integrate student loan management with overall wealth-building strategy rather than treating debt as isolated emergency requiring all resources.

The frameworks have been provided. The calculations are straightforward. Whether you approach student debt strategically or whether you make decisions based on anxiety and social pressure is your choice. The one percent choose strategy while the ninety-nine percent choose emotion. The outcome differential measured across decades reaches hundreds of thousands in accumulated wealth. You now understand how to manage student debt intelligently within your broader wealth-building framework.

CHAPTER 28:
PERSONAL LOANS AND DEBT MANAGEMENT—
ESCAPING THE TRAP

In 1992, a financial counselor named Dave Ramsey emerged from personal bankruptcy with a message that would eventually reach millions: debt is slavery, and freedom comes only through complete elimination of all consumer obligations regardless of interest rates or mathematical optimization. Ramsey had built a real estate portfolio worth over four million dollars during the 1980s using borrowed money and aggressive leverage. When his lenders were acquired by a larger bank that called all his notes simultaneously, he could not refinance quickly enough and lost everything. The experience transformed his relationship with debt from seeing it as useful tool for wealth building to seeing it as existential threat that must be eliminated completely before any other financial progress can occur.

His prescription was radical simplicity: list all debts from smallest balance to largest regardless of interest rates, make minimum payments on all debts except the smallest, attack the smallest debt with every available dollar until it is eliminated, then roll that payment plus the minimum to the next-smallest debt, repeating until all debt is gone. This "debt snowball" method violated mathematical optimization because it often meant paying low-interest small debts before high-interest large debts. Yet Ramsey insisted that personal finance is twenty percent math and eighty percent behavior, and that the psychological wins from eliminating debts completely provided motivation that pure mathematical approaches lacked.

Millions of people used Ramsey's system to eliminate consumer debt that had trapped them for years or decades. They celebrated each eliminated debt by cutting up the associated credit card or loan documents, creating emotional milestones that reinforced progress. They maintained intensity through the process because they could see progress measured in debts eliminated rather than in abstract balance reduction on large obligations. They developed hatred of debt through Ramsey's aggressive rhetoric that reframed borrowing from normal American behavior to moral failing requiring immediate correction.

The results were undeniable despite mathematical suboptimality. People who had carried debt for decades became debt-free within two to five years. They developed financial discipline that persisted after debt elimination, allowing them to build wealth they had never imagined possible. They often reported that becoming debt-free transformed their lives more significantly than subsequent wealth accumulation because freedom from debt obligations created psychological peace that money in investment accounts could not replicate.

Yet Ramsey's absolutism also created problems for some followers who interpreted his message too literally. People paid off three percent car loans aggressively while forgoing employer 401k matches providing one hundred percent returns. They eliminated all debt including mortgages at four percent interest rather than investing in stock market returning ten percent. They avoided strategic use of debt that could have accelerated wealth building because they had been taught that all debt is evil regardless of its cost or purpose. The one percent recognized that Ramsey's approach was designed for people trapped in consumer debt spirals who needed psychological intervention more than mathematical optimization, but that his principles did not apply equally to those already practicing financial discipline.

This chapter addresses how to manage and eliminate the personal loans, credit card debt, payday loans, and other consumer obligations that destroy wealth for those who carry them while acknowledging that not all debt is created equal and that the optimal strategy depends on specific circumstances including debt amounts, interest rates, and psychological relationship with debt. The framework begins with brutal honesty about whether you have consumer debt problem requiring emergency intervention or whether you have strategic debt that can be managed deliberately within broader wealth-building plan.

The definition of consumer debt problem includes carrying credit card balances month to month, taking payday loans or other high-interest short-term financing, making only minimum payments on multiple obligations while adding new debt, using debt to fund lifestyle that income cannot support, experiencing constant stress about debt obligations, or avoiding looking at account balances because the reality is too painful to face. Someone exhibiting any of these patterns has debt problem requiring immediate intervention before any other wealth-building activity can proceed effectively. The mathematics of consumer debt make wealth building impossible because interest charges at fifteen to twenty-five percent annually exceed any reasonable investment returns, meaning that every dollar invested while carrying high-interest debt is economically irrational.

The emergency debt elimination approach applies to those with consumer debt problems and requires complete halt to all wealth building beyond capturing employer retirement matches until consumer debt is eliminated entirely. This seems to contradict the systematic investment approach we have advocated throughout this book, but the reality is that investing while carrying debt at twenty percent interest is mathematical insanity that benefits only the lenders collecting that interest. Someone with ten thousand dollars in credit card debt at twenty percent interest pays two thousand dollars annually just in interest while their balance remains unchanged. The same two thousand dollars invested annually at ten percent returns becomes sixty-three thousand dollars over twenty years. The person who eliminates the debt immediately through stopping all investment and attacking debt aggressively frees two thousand dollars annually within five years that can then be invested for remaining fifteen years, generating forty-five thousand dollars in accumulated wealth. The person who maintains debt while investing generates eighteen thousand dollars in accumulated wealth while paying forty thousand in interest. The difference is catastrophic.

The debt inventory creation represents the first step in systematic elimination and requires listing every consumer debt with current balance, interest rate, minimum monthly payment, and payoff date if only minimum payments are made. This inventory creates visibility into total obligation and reveals the actual cost of debt service. Most people carrying multiple debts have never calculated total monthly obligations or total interest being paid annually. The creation of this inventory often shocks people into action by making abstract debt burden concrete. The one percent trapped in debt situations create this inventory immediately and update it monthly as they make progress, using the visibility to maintain motivation.

The spending audit identifies where money is going currently and where cuts can be made to generate cash flow for debt elimination. Someone claiming they have no money to pay down debt usually has substantial spending on consumption that could be eliminated temporarily while attacking debt. The audit involves exporting three months of transactions from all checking and credit card accounts, categorizing every expense, and identifying what is truly necessary versus what is discretionary. Necessary expenses include housing, basic food, essential transportation, minimum debt payments, and utilities. Everything else is discretionary and can be cut during debt elimination emergency.

The one percent in debt crises often identify one thousand to two thousand dollars monthly in discretionary spending that can be redirected toward debt payoff. This comes from eliminating restaurant meals, canceling subscriptions, stopping entertainment spending, deferring clothing purchases, and generally living with extreme frugality until debt is eliminated. This requires accepting that you are in financial emergency and that emergencies require emergency responses, not comfortable maintenance of lifestyle that created the debt problem. The person who insists on maintaining their lifestyle while paying down debt extends the process by years or never completes it at all because they never generate sufficient cash flow to make meaningful progress.

The debt snowball method that Ramsey popularized provides psychological advantages for those who need motivation more than mathematical optimization. You list debts from smallest balance to largest regardless of interest rates. You make minimum payments on all debts except the smallest. You attack the smallest debt with every available dollar beyond minimums until it is completely eliminated. You roll the payment from the eliminated debt plus its previous minimum payment to the next-smallest debt, creating a growing payment snowball. You repeat until all debts are eliminated. The method generates quick wins through completely eliminating debts within weeks or months, providing motivation through visible progress rather than through slow balance reduction on large debts.

The debt avalanche method provides mathematical optimization for those who maintain discipline without requiring psychological wins. You list debts from highest interest rate to lowest regardless of balance. You make minimum payments on all debts except the highest-interest debt. You attack the highest-interest debt with every available dollar until it is eliminated. You roll payments to the next-highest-interest debt. You repeat until all debts are eliminated. This method minimizes total interest paid and completes debt elimination faster in calendar time compared to snowball method, but it might require years before eliminating first debt if the highest-interest debt also has the largest balance.

The choice between snowball and avalanche depends on honest self-assessment about whether you need psychological wins to maintain intensity or whether you can persist based on knowing you are following mathematically optimal approach. Someone with six small debts and one large debt at highest interest might benefit from snowball approach that eliminates multiple debts within first year, providing motivation to persist through attacking the large debt subsequently. Someone with three debts where the highest-interest debt is also smallest might use avalanche approach because it provides both mathematical optimization and quick win. The one percent choose the method that they will actually complete rather than the theoretically superior method they will abandon.

The debt consolidation through personal loans converts multiple high-interest obligations into single lower-interest loan with fixed payment schedule. Someone carrying fifteen thousand across three credit cards at nineteen, twenty-two, and twenty-five percent interest might consolidate into single personal loan at twelve percent interest, reducing their interest burden by over one thousand dollars annually while simplifying payments to single monthly obligation. The consolidation makes sense only if the consolidation loan interest rate is meaningfully lower than weighted average of existing debts, if the borrower stops adding new debt to the credit cards after consolidating, and if fees for consolidation do not consume the interest savings.

The balance transfer offers from credit card companies provide zero percent or low promotional interest rates for twelve to twenty-one months, allowing aggressive debt payoff without interest accumulation during promotional period. Someone with ten thousand in credit card debt at twenty percent interest might transfer that balance to card offering zero percent for eighteen months with three percent transfer fee. The three hundred dollar transfer fee is easily justified by the three thousand dollars in interest saved over eighteen months if the borrower aggressively pays down the balance during the promotional period. The trap is that borrowers often make minimum payments during promotional period, fail to eliminate the balance before promotional rate expires, and face deferred interest or high ongoing rates on remaining balance after promotion ends. The one percent use balance transfers strategically by calculating exactly how much they must pay monthly to eliminate the entire balance before promotional period expires, then making those payments automatically without fail.

The credit counseling agencies provide debt management plans that consolidate payments and potentially reduce interest rates through agreements with creditors. These agencies are nonprofit organizations that negotiate with your creditors to reduce interest rates and create structured repayment plans, typically lasting three to five years. You make single monthly payment to the agency which then distributes payments to your creditors according to the negotiated plan. The advantages include reduced interest rates, simplified payments, and stopping collection calls. The disadvantages include fees charged by agencies, requirement to close credit card accounts which damages credit scores temporarily, and limited effectiveness if you have debt beyond what monthly payment plan can address within five years.

The debt settlement companies claim they can negotiate with creditors to accept less than full balance owed in exchange for lump sum payments. These companies are largely predatory operations that charge substantial fees while providing minimal value and often making situations worse. The process involves stopping payments to creditors while accumulating money in accounts, then offering creditors thirty to fifty percent of balance as settlement. This destroys credit scores, generates relentless collection calls, risks lawsuits, and may result in tax liability for forgiven debt amounts. Most people could negotiate directly with creditors for similar or better outcomes without paying settlement company fees. The one percent avoid debt settlement companies entirely and either negotiate directly with creditors if necessary or pursue bankruptcy if debt is truly unmanageable through normal repayment.

The negotiation with creditors directly provides opportunities for those facing genuine hardship to modify payment terms, reduce interest rates temporarily, or settle debts for less than full balance. Creditors prefer receiving reduced payments to receiving nothing through borrower bankruptcy. Someone facing job loss or medical emergency can contact creditors, explain the situation honestly, and request hardship programs that temporarily reduce payments or interest rates. Someone with debt they cannot repay in reasonable timeframe can offer lump sum settlement for less than full balance, particularly if they have access to funds through family assistance or windfall. The key is being honest about your situation, knowing what you can actually afford to pay, and making realistic offers rather than promises you cannot keep.

The payday loans and title loans represent predatory lending charging effective interest rates often exceeding three hundred percent annually when fees are annualized. These loans are marketed to desperate people with poor credit who cannot access traditional financing. They create debt traps where borrowers continuously roll over loans, paying fees repeatedly while never reducing principal. Someone borrowing five hundred dollars might pay seventy-five dollars in fees every two weeks, paying nine hundred seventy-five dollars annually in fees alone while the five hundred dollar principal remains unchanged. This is catastrophically expensive financing that no legitimate financial need justifies. The one percent never use these products under any circumstances because the cost is so extreme that virtually any alternative including borrowing from family, selling possessions, or negotiating payment plans with creditors is superior.

The rent-to-own furniture and electronics stores similarly charge extreme effective interest rates through weekly or monthly payments for items that could be purchased outright for fractions of the total payments. Someone paying thirty dollars weekly for a television accumulates fifteen hundred sixty dollars annually for an item that could be purchased for four hundred dollars cash. This is not financing but rather is extremely expensive rental that creates illusion of ownership while extracting maximum value from people who lack access to credit or who fail to calculate total costs. The one percent never use these services and instead save money for purchases, buy used items for cash, or simply go without until they can afford to buy outright.

The auto title loans where you pledge your vehicle as collateral for short-term loans combine high costs with risk of losing transportation if you default. These loans typically charge twenty-five percent interest per month or three hundred percent annually, making them only marginally better than payday loans while putting your vehicle at risk. Someone borrowing two thousand dollars against their car might pay five hundred dollars monthly in interest while their principal remains unchanged, and if they miss a payment the lender can seize the vehicle regardless of how much equity you have or how much you have already paid. The one percent view these loans as financial suicide to be avoided regardless of circumstances.

The medical debt represents unique category because it typically carries zero interest if you negotiate payment plans directly with providers, making it the least harmful debt to carry while you address higher-interest obligations first. Someone with five thousand in medical debt and ten thousand in credit card debt should make token payments to medical providers while aggressively attacking credit card debt because the credit card debt accumulates interest at twenty percent while medical debt typically does not if payment plans are established. The key is contacting medical providers proactively to establish payment plans before accounts go to collections, because once in collections the debt becomes far more difficult to manage and begins damaging credit scores.

The stopping of new debt accumulation during elimination phase is non-negotiable because paying down existing debt while adding new debt is running on treadmill that guarantees you never reach zero. Someone paying one thousand monthly toward debt elimination while adding five hundred monthly in new debt makes net progress of only five hundred monthly, extending their debt elimination timeline substantially. The one percent in debt elimination mode cut up credit cards, remove stored payment information from online shopping sites, implement waiting periods before any purchase over some threshold amount, and generally create friction in spending processes that prevents impulsive debt accumulation. This is temporary emergency measure during debt elimination, not permanent lifestyle, but it is essential for generating the intensity required to eliminate debt quickly rather than slowly.

The lifestyle downgrades during debt elimination provide additional cash flow for accelerated payoff and create psychological separation from the consumption patterns that created debt. Someone paying off debt might move to smaller apartment, get roommate, sell vehicle and use public transportation, stop eating at restaurants entirely, cancel all entertainment subscriptions, and eliminate discretionary spending completely. These downgrades seem extreme to those not in debt crisis, but they are appropriate emergency responses that generate five hundred to one thousand dollars monthly in additional debt payment capacity. The person who refuses lifestyle downgrades while claiming they want to eliminate debt has not accepted that they face genuine financial emergency requiring emergency response.

The side income generation during debt elimination accelerates progress beyond what cutting expenses alone can achieve. Someone generating five hundred dollars monthly through freelancing, part-time employment, or selling possessions can deploy that income entirely toward debt elimination, cutting months or years from the timeline. The objection that working additional hours is too difficult or that selling possessions is too painful reveals lack of seriousness about debt elimination. The one percent in debt crises work sixty to seventy hours weekly temporarily, sell everything not essential to basic functioning, and generally sacrifice comfort for speed in reaching zero debt. This is temporary intensity that creates permanent freedom rather than comfortable approach that extends debt servitude indefinitely.

The accountability structures through working with accountability partners, financial counselors, or supportive communities maintain motivation when the process becomes difficult. Debt elimination typically requires one to five years of sustained intensity depending on debt amount and income. Most people lose motivation during this period and return to old patterns that recreate debt. Having someone who knows your situation and checks your progress regularly creates external pressure that supplements internal motivation. The one percent seek accountability rather than trying to eliminate debt in isolation where lapses go unnoticed until substantial damage is done.

The celebration of milestones maintains motivation through long elimination process by marking progress. Each debt completely eliminated deserves recognition through inexpensive celebration that acknowledges progress without undermining elimination efforts. The person who eliminates their first debt might have a special meal at home celebrating the progress, not an expensive restaurant meal that adds new debt. The point is marking psychological progress that pure balance reduction on large debts does not provide. The one percent engineer motivation through these celebrations rather than relying solely on distant goal of complete debt freedom that might be years away.

The credit score impact during aggressive debt elimination is typically negative in the short term but positive in the long term. Closing accounts reduces available credit and affects credit utilization ratios. Consolidating debt creates hard inquiries. Settling debt for less than full balance damages scores for years. Yet becoming debt-free ultimately provides excellent credit scores because payment history improves, utilization drops to zero, and the absence of debt makes you attractive borrower. The one percent accept short-term credit score damage as price of debt elimination, recognizing that excellent credit serves no purpose if you never intend to borrow again anyway.

The transition from debt elimination to wealth building occurs when final consumer debt is eliminated and you suddenly have substantial cash flow available that was previously directed toward debt payments. Someone paying fifteen hundred dollars monthly toward debt elimination has fifteen hundred monthly available for investment once debt is gone. The key is redirecting this money immediately into automatic investment contributions rather than allowing lifestyle to inflate and consume the freed cash flow. The one percent establish automated investment transfers before making their final debt payment so that the money moves directly from debt elimination to wealth building without passing through spending accounts where lifestyle inflation can capture it.

The maintaining of debt-free status requires different behaviors than what led to debt accumulation originally, meaning that eliminating debt without changing underlying behaviors guarantees eventual return to debt. The person who eliminated debt through extreme frugality must maintain reasonable spending discipline after debt elimination even though they now have more cash flow available. The person who eliminated debt through side income should maintain that income and deploy it toward investments rather than lifestyle inflation. The one percent develop new identity as people who do not carry consumer debt rather than merely completing debt elimination project while maintaining identity as people who borrow for consumption.

The strategic debt usage after consumer debt elimination distinguishes between consumer debt that finances depreciating purchases versus strategic debt that finances appreciating assets or cash-flowing investments. The one percent who become debt-free eventually use debt again but only for mortgages on properties that generate rental income, for business expansion that generates returns exceeding interest costs, or for arbitrage opportunities where borrowed money can be deployed at returns exceeding borrowing costs. They never return to consumer debt for vehicles, vacations, clothing, entertainment, or other consumption that provides no financial return. This distinction is what separates wealth builders from those who cycle between debt elimination and reaccumulation throughout their lives.

The time value of money during debt elimination means that early debt elimination has far greater impact on lifetime wealth than later debt elimination because freeing cash flow early allows more years of investment compound growth. Someone who eliminates twenty thousand in debt at age thirty frees cash flow that can be invested for thirty-five years until retirement, generating three million dollars at ten percent returns. Someone who eliminates the same debt at age fifty has only fifteen years for investments to compound, generating five hundred thousand dollars. The one percent prioritize debt elimination early in their working years precisely because early elimination multiplies wealth-building capacity through providing more years of investment growth.

The teaching of debt avoidance to children through involving them in family debt elimination process creates powerful lessons that prevent them from repeating parents' mistakes. Children who observe parents sacrificing to eliminate debt, who participate in lifestyle downgrades, and who see the celebration when debt is finally eliminated learn viscerally that debt creates suffering and that avoiding it is essential. Children who are sheltered from family debt situations or who grow up in families where debt is treated as normal develop no resistance to borrowing for consumption and often accumulate debt as soon as they gain access to credit. The one percent use their debt elimination journeys as teaching opportunities rather than hiding financial struggles from children.

The bankruptcy consideration represents last resort for those with debt so overwhelming that normal repayment is impossible within reasonable timeframe. Someone with one hundred thousand in consumer debt earning forty thousand annually cannot repay that debt through income because the entire amount exceeds two years of gross income and the interest accumulation makes the balance grow rather than shrink even if they directed fifty percent of gross income to payments. Bankruptcy provides legal process for discharging debt and starting fresh, though it destroys credit for seven to ten years and carries psychological and sometimes professional consequences. The one percent consider bankruptcy when debt truly cannot be repaid, when creditors are pursuing legal judgments, or when debt service prevents meeting basic living needs. They consult bankruptcy attorneys to understand the process before filing rather than assuming bankruptcy is either automatic solution or forbidden option.

The broader principle connecting debt management to wealth building is that debt destroys wealth when used for consumption and when interest costs exceed returns you can generate through investing freed cash flow. Consumer debt at fifteen to twenty-five percent interest makes wealth building mathematically impossible because no investment generates returns sufficient to justify carrying that debt. The emergency elimination of consumer debt becomes prerequisite to wealth building rather than competing with it. Once consumer debt is eliminated, strategic debt for appreciating assets or cash-flowing investments becomes tool rather than burden, but this transition requires changed behavior and psychology that prevents return to consumption-based borrowing.

Dave Ramsey's lifetime work demonstrates that millions of people need psychological intervention more than mathematical optimization when dealing with consumer debt. His debt snowball method helps people make progress through generating quick wins even though it is mathematically suboptimal. His absolutist position on debt elimination before investing helps people develop hatred of debt that prevents future accumulation. His success with masses of people trapped in debt proves that behavior change matters more than technical optimization for those facing debt crises. Yet his principles apply less to those who never accumulated consumer debt or who use strategic debt for wealth building, revealing that context determines whether his approach is essential or overly restrictive.

The one percent avoid consumer debt entirely when possible through living below their means and paying cash for consumption. When circumstances or mistakes lead to consumer debt accumulation, they eliminate it systematically using either snowball or avalanche methods based on what they will actually complete. They use balance transfers and consolidation strategically when these reduce costs without creating new problems. They negotiate with creditors when necessary. They avoid predatory lending regardless of desperation. They stop adding new debt while eliminating existing debt. They downgrade lifestyle temporarily to generate cash flow for elimination. They generate side income for acceleration. They maintain intensity through accountability and celebration. They transition immediately to wealth building once debt is eliminated. They never return to consumer debt after elimination. They teach their children to avoid debt through involving them in elimination process.

The frameworks have been provided. The methods are proven by millions who have escaped debt using these approaches. Whether you currently carry consumer debt requiring emergency elimination or whether you have avoided debt through discipline, you now understand how to manage and eliminate debt systematically. The implementation and sustained behavioral change required to remain debt-free remain your responsibility. The one percent choose freedom through systematic elimination while the ninety-nine percent remain trapped through inaction or through continued accumulation. Your choice determines whether debt controls your life or whether you control your financial destiny.

CHAPTER 29:
READING PEOPLE—APPLIED PSYCHOLOGY

In 1993, an FBI negotiator named Chris Voss arrived at a Brooklyn apartment building where a man named Charlie had barricaded himself with a gun, threatening suicide while his wife and children sheltered in a neighbor's apartment. The NYPD had been negotiating for three hours without progress. Charlie was agitated, oscillating between rage at his circumstances and despair about his future. Every time officers tried to solve his problems or talk him down from the ledge, he became more entrenched in his position. Standard negotiation tactics—building rapport through finding common ground, offering solutions, emphasizing consequences of violence— were failing.

Voss took a different approach rooted in his emerging understanding of human psychology. Rather than trying to solve Charlie's problems or convince him to surrender, Voss simply labeled the emotions he heard in Charlie's voice. "It sounds like you're really angry." "It seems like you feel trapped." "It looks like nobody understands what you're going through." He did not offer solutions. He did not argue. He did not try to convince. He simply reflected back what Charlie was feeling, demonstrating that someone was actually listening rather than merely waiting for their turn to speak.

The effect was immediate. Charlie's voice changed from agitated to thoughtful. He began explaining his situation more calmly. He stopped repeating the same complaints and started exploring his options. Within forty minutes of Voss taking over negotiations, Charlie put down his weapon and exited the apartment peacefully. The transformation came not from brilliant argumentation or from offering deals but from tactical empathy—demonstrating that you understand someone's emotions before attempting to influence their decisions.

Voss spent the next two decades as the FBI's lead international kidnapping negotiator, handling hundreds of cases where lives depended on his ability to understand what people really wanted beneath what they said they wanted, to identify deception, to build trust with criminals and terrorists, and to guide conversations toward outcomes that served his objectives. His success rate was extraordinary not because he was better at arguing or because he had authority to make bigger offers, but because he understood human psychology more deeply than his adversaries expected and because he used that understanding systematically.

After retiring from the FBI, Voss founded a consulting company teaching his negotiation methods to business executives. He discovered that the same psychological principles that worked with hostage-takers and kidnappers worked equally well in salary negotiations, business deals, and everyday interactions. The human brain operates predictably when you understand its patterns. The person who studies these patterns gains advantages in every domain where human interaction determines outcomes—which is essentially every domain that matters for building wealth.

This chapter examines the psychological principles that govern how people actually make decisions, how to read people accurately rather than projecting your assumptions onto them, and how to influence outcomes ethically through understanding rather than through manipulation. These skills separate those who advance rapidly through corporate hierarchies, who negotiate superior compensation, who build successful businesses, and who avoid being exploited from those who remain trapped by their own psychological naiveté about how humans actually operate.

The foundation of reading people begins with understanding that humans are not rational actors making decisions based on logical analysis of available information. We are emotional beings who make decisions based on feelings and then rationalize those decisions with logic after the fact. The person who appeals to logic when someone has made an emotional decision will fail because they are arguing in the wrong domain. The person who addresses the emotions driving decisions while providing logical justification that allows the person to rationalize their emotional choice succeeds because they are working with human psychology rather than against it.

Robert Cialdini spent his career studying influence and compliance, eventually identifying six fundamental principles that trigger automatic compliance responses in human beings. These principles operate beneath conscious awareness, making people far easier to influence than they realize. The principles are reciprocity, commitment and consistency, social proof, liking, authority, and scarcity. Understanding how these principles work allows you to deploy them ethically to advance legitimate goals while also recognizing when others deploy them against you.

The reciprocity principle states that humans feel obligated to return favors and concessions. When someone does something for you, you experience psychological pressure to reciprocate even if you never requested the initial favor. This is why salespeople offer free samples—not because samples directly lead to sales but because samples create sense of obligation that increases purchase likelihood. In negotiation, making small concessions early creates pressure on the other party to reciprocate with their own concessions. In networking, providing value to others before asking for anything creates goodwill that makes people far more willing to help you when you eventually make requests.

The strategic application of reciprocity involves initiating value provision rather than waiting for others to offer first. The person who helps a colleague with a project without being asked, who makes introductions that benefit others without immediate return, or who shares useful information freely creates reservoir of goodwill that can be drawn upon when they need assistance. This is not manipulation but rather is how human social systems have operated for millennia. The person who only extracts value without providing it becomes known as taker and receives no help when needed. The person who provides value consistently becomes known as giver and receives disproportionate support because people want to reciprocate.

The commitment and consistency principle reveals that once people commit to something publicly, they experience strong pressure to act consistently with that commitment even when circumstances change. This is why salespeople ask series of small yes questions before requesting the purchase decision—each yes creates commitment that makes the final yes more likely. In negotiation, getting agreement on principles before discussing specifics makes it harder for the other party to reject specific proposals that align with already-agreed principles. In management, getting employees to commit publicly to goals increases follow-through compared to privately assigned goals because the public commitment creates social pressure for consistency.

The tactical use of commitment involves structuring conversations to establish agreements on small points before requesting agreement on larger points. Rather than opening a compensation negotiation by stating your desired salary, you might first establish agreement that your performance has exceeded expectations, that the company values retaining high performers, and that compensation should reflect value delivered. Once these points are agreed, your request for specific compensation that aligns with these agreed principles becomes far harder to reject because rejection would require the other party to act inconsistently with their own stated positions.

The social proof principle demonstrates that people determine correct behavior by observing what others do, particularly when they are uncertain about appropriate action. This is why testimonials and case studies work in marketing—not because people lack the ability to evaluate products independently but because observing that others made similar choices reduces perceived risk. In business, referencing how other companies in your industry handle similar situations makes your proposals seem safer. In negotiation, mentioning that others in similar positions receive certain compensation levels establishes those levels as normal rather than as exceptional requests.

The weaponization of social proof requires understanding which reference groups matter for specific decisions. The person trying to convince executives to adopt new technology should reference what other companies in their industry are doing rather than what companies in different industries are doing because executives care about competitive positioning within their industry. The person negotiating salary should reference compensation at comparable companies rather than at companies at different scales because the other party will dismiss irrelevant comparisons. The power of social proof lies in selecting the right comparison groups that the decision-maker considers relevant peers.

The liking principle reveals that people are more likely to comply with requests from people they like, and that liking is generated through similarity, compliments, and cooperation toward shared goals. This is why salespeople spend time finding commonalities with prospects before discussing products—the discovered similarities create liking that makes subsequent sales pitches more effective. In networking, expressing genuine interest in others and finding authentic connection points creates relationships that provide long-term value. In negotiation, building rapport before discussing terms makes the other party more willing to make concessions because they want to help someone they like rather than someone who treats the interaction as pure transaction.

The development of genuine liking rather than fake rapport requires actual curiosity about other people and willingness to find authentic connection points rather than manufacturing false commonalities. People detect insincerity quickly, and false rapport-building attempts backfire by signaling that you view them as marks to be manipulated. The one percent develop genuine interest in understanding what motivates different people, what challenges they face, and what they care about beyond immediate transaction. This authentic curiosity creates real connections that provide value across years rather than fabricated relationships that serve only immediate purposes.

The authority principle shows that people defer to perceived experts and authority figures even when they should not. This is why credentials, titles, and professional attire influence compliance—not because these things indicate actual competence but because they trigger automatic deference responses. In business, establishing expertise through speaking engagements, published articles, or recognized credentials makes your advice more likely to be followed. In salary negotiation, referencing external validation of your expertise through awards, publications, or competitive offers makes your requests more credible. In management, clear title and role definition makes your directives more likely to be followed because people defer to legitimate authority.

The ethical development of authority through actual competence rather than through false credentials separates influence from fraud. The one percent build genuine expertise in their domains, then ensure that expertise is visible through appropriate credentials, publications, speaking opportunities, and third-party validation. They do not claim expertise they lack or credentials they have not earned because false authority eventually gets exposed and destroys credibility permanently. They understand that real authority comes from demonstrated competence over time but that even real authority must be communicated effectively or it provides no influence advantage.

The scarcity principle demonstrates that people value things more when they are scarce or when they might lose access to them. This is why limited-time offers work in marketing and why competition for your services increases your perceived value in employment negotiation. In business, projects with limited availability attract more interest than identical projects available indefinitely. In negotiation, mentioning other opportunities you are considering creates urgency that prevents the other party from delaying decisions indefinitely. In management, the recognition and opportunities you control become more valued when employees understand they are selectively distributed rather than universally available.

The truthful application of scarcity requires that the limitations are real rather than fabricated. The person who invents competing job offers to create negotiating leverage commits fraud that destroys relationships when discovered. The person who genuinely has competing offers and communicates this reality creates legitimate urgency. The one percent create real scarcity through genuine options rather than manufacturing false scarcity through lies that eventually backfire.

Joe Navarro spent twenty-five years as FBI special agent and counterintelligence officer, specializing in nonverbal communication and behavior analysis. His work involved identifying foreign spies through observing behavioral anomalies, conducting interrogations where detecting deception determined whether intelligence was actionable, and reading people in high-stakes situations where mistakes had national security consequences. After retiring, Navarro wrote multiple books teaching civilians how to read nonverbal behavior in business and personal contexts.

His core insight was that the body reveals truth that words conceal. Humans evolved to read nonverbal signals because survival often depended on accurately assessing whether someone posed threats or offered opportunities. The person who reads only words while ignoring body language misses the majority of communication. The person who reads nonverbal behavior while integrating it with verbal content gains accurate understanding of what people actually think and feel regardless of what they claim.

The baseline establishment represents the first requirement for reading body language accurately because people display different behaviors normally and you cannot identify deviations without knowing their baseline. Someone who naturally fidgets appears anxious when they are actually comfortable. Someone who normally maintains rigid posture appears defensive when they are actually relaxed. The one percent spend time observing people in neutral situations before important conversations, noting their typical facial expressions, gestures, posture, and vocal patterns. This baseline allows them to identify changes during high-stakes discussions that indicate emotional shifts or deception.

The cluster observation prevents misinterpreting single behaviors that might have multiple explanations. Crossed arms might indicate defensiveness or might simply mean someone is cold. Avoiding eye contact might indicate deception or might indicate cultural norms about respectful listening. The one percent look for clusters of behaviors that together indicate specific emotions rather than jumping to conclusions based on isolated gestures. When someone crosses arms while leaning back, breaking eye contact, and reducing vocal responsiveness simultaneously, the cluster suggests withdrawal or disagreement. Any single behavior means nothing, but multiple behaviors reinforcing the same interpretation provide reliable signals.

The feet and legs provide the most honest nonverbal communication because people control them less consciously than facial expressions. Someone whose feet point toward the door rather than toward you while their face smiles politely is signaling that they want to leave regardless of what they say verbally. Someone whose feet are planted firmly and oriented toward you is engaged even if their arms are crossed. The one percent watch feet during conversations to understand whether people actually want to be present or whether they are merely being polite while wanting to escape.

The pacifying behaviors people display when experiencing stress include touching their necks, rubbing their faces, exhaling forcefully, or adjusting clothing repeatedly. These self-soothing gestures indicate psychological discomfort with the topic being discussed or with the situation they face. In negotiation, noticing pacifying behaviors when discussing specific terms reveals which terms create the most discomfort for the other party, suggesting where you have leverage. In interviews, displaying too many pacifying behaviors yourself signals anxiety that might reduce the interviewer's confidence in your competence.

The genuine versus fake smile distinction separates automatic emotional responses from manufactured displays. Genuine smiles involve both mouth and eyes, with crow's feet forming at eye corners and eyebrows raising slightly. Fake smiles involve only the mouth while eyes remain unchanged or even sad. The person displaying fake smiles is masking their true emotions behind socially appropriate expressions. This matters in situations where you need to know whether someone genuinely agrees with what you proposed or whether they are merely being polite before rejecting you later. The one percent watch eyes during conversations to understand whether enthusiasm is genuine or manufactured.

Paul Ekman spent decades studying facial expressions and emotions, eventually identifying seven universal emotions that appear identically across all cultures: anger, contempt, disgust, fear, happiness, sadness, and surprise. His research demonstrated that these emotions appear in micro-expressions lasting fraction of a second before people mask them with socially appropriate expressions. The person who learns to recognize micro-expressions gains access to true emotions that others work to conceal.

The practical training in micro-expression recognition requires deliberate practice using recorded videos where you can slow down footage and study facial changes frame by frame. Various online courses teach these skills systematically. The investment is hours rather than years, and the payoff is ability to read emotions that others think they are concealing successfully. In negotiation, catching a micro-expression of distress when you mention a specific term tells you that term creates problems for the other party even if they maintain poker face verbally. In hiring, catching micro-expressions of contempt when candidates discuss previous employers reveals attitudes that will likely transfer to your organization if you hire them.

The vocal tone, pace, and pitch changes communicate emotions more reliably than words themselves. Someone whose voice raises in pitch is experiencing stress regardless of what they claim verbally. Someone whose speaking pace accelerates is excited or anxious. Someone whose vocal volume decreases is withdrawing from conversation or losing confidence. The one percent listen to how things are said as carefully as to what is said, understanding that voice reveals emotional truth that careful word choice attempts to conceal.

The strategic use of silence creates space for others to reveal more than they intended because most people experience discomfort with conversational pauses and fill them by continuing to talk. In negotiation, staying silent after making your proposal rather than immediately justifying it or retreating forces the other party to respond first. Often they make counteroffers more favorable than you expected because the silence made them anxious. In interviews, staying silent after answering questions rather than continuing to elaborate nervously signals confidence that brief complete answers are sufficient. In sales, staying silent after stating price rather than immediately offering discounts or justifications forces the prospect to either accept or make the next move rather than waiting for you to negotiate against yourself.

Chris Voss's tactical empathy approach that saved Charlie's life in Brooklyn is applicable in business contexts where understanding and labeling emotions disarms resistance more effectively than logical argument. When someone resists your proposal, responding with "It seems like you're concerned about the implementation complexity" rather than with "But it's not that complex" acknowledges their feelings without arguing. This acknowledgment often causes them to explain their concerns more fully, giving you information about what would actually address their resistance rather than forcing you to guess.

The calibrated questions technique that Voss teaches involves asking open-ended questions beginning with "what" or "how" that force the other party to solve problems from your perspective. Rather than saying "You need to approve my budget increase," you ask "What would need to happen for you to feel comfortable approving this budget increase?" The question forces them to identify specific conditions that would lead to approval, giving you roadmap for getting what you want while making them feel ownership of the solution rather than feeling pressured by your demands.

The "that's right" moment that Voss identifies as critical in negotiation occurs when you summarize the other party's position so accurately that they respond with "that's right" rather than "you're right." The difference is that "that's right" indicates they feel truly understood while "you're right" indicates they are agreeing just to end the conversation. Getting to "that's right" requires patient listening to understand their actual position rather than listening selectively for points you can counter. Once someone feels truly understood, they become far more willing to consider your perspective because the human need to be understood has been satisfied.

The mirroring technique involves repeating the last few words someone said with upward inflection, encouraging them to elaborate without asking questions that might make them defensive. When someone says "I'm not sure this approach will work," responding with "Won't work?" with questioning tone prompts them to explain why rather than requiring you to guess their concerns and address them blindly. This technique keeps them talking and revealing information while requiring minimal input from you.

The accusation audit involves preemptively raising negative aspects of your position before the other party raises them, disarming their planned objections while demonstrating that you are honest rather than trying to hide problems. When asking for raise, you might open with "I know the company faces budget constraints this year and that timing might not be ideal..." before making your case. By acknowledging their likely objections first, you remove the force of those objections when they raise them later because you have already demonstrated awareness rather than seeming naïve.

Daniel Kahneman's research on cognitive biases revealed systematic errors in human judgment that can be exploited in negotiation and persuasion. The anchoring bias shows that people's estimates are influenced by initial numbers presented even when those numbers are arbitrary. In salary negotiation, the first number mentioned—whether by you or by the employer—serves as anchor that shapes the entire subsequent negotiation range. Research shows that whoever makes the first offer establishes advantageous anchor. The common advice to let employers state salary range first often backfires because it allows them to anchor low. The one percent research market rates thoroughly, then make the first offer at the top of reasonable range, establishing high anchor that shifts the entire negotiation upward.

The confirmation bias reveals that people seek information confirming their existing beliefs while discounting information contradicting those beliefs. In sales, establishing what problems a prospect thinks they face before presenting solutions ensures your solutions will be evaluated favorably because they confirm the prospect's own problem assessment. In negotiation, getting the other party to articulate why they should make concessions before you formally request concessions makes them generate arguments supporting your position, which their confirmation bias then reinforces. The one percent guide people to conclusions rather than forcing conclusions on them because people trust their own reasoning far more than they trust others' arguments.

The loss aversion bias demonstrates that people fear losses roughly twice as strongly as they value equivalent gains. Framing proposals in terms of what the other party stands to lose rather than what they stand to gain creates stronger motivation for action. Rather than telling your boss "Approving this project will generate five hundred thousand in profit," you might frame it as "Not approving this project means our competitor will capture five hundred thousand in market share we currently hold." The second framing triggers loss aversion while the first triggers gain attraction, and loss aversion is stronger motivator.

The sunk cost fallacy causes people to continue investing in failing projects because they have already invested substantially and do not want to "waste" previous investment. In negotiation, getting small agreements early makes the other party more likely to agree to larger requests later because abandoning the negotiation would waste the time and energy already invested. In employment, the years you have invested in a company make you reluctant to leave even when better opportunities exist because leaving feels like wasting your investment.

The one percent recognize sunk cost thinking in themselves and avoid it by evaluating decisions based on future expected returns rather than on past investment that cannot be recovered.

Frank Abagnale spent years in the 1960s successfully impersonating an airline pilot, doctor, and lawyer while cashing millions in fraudulent checks before being caught and imprisoned. His success came not from sophisticated forgery but from understanding human psychology. He wore pilot uniforms because people defer to authority figures without verification. He acted confident and entitled because confidence signals legitimacy while nervousness signals deception. He provided specific details that made his stories credible even when those details were fabricated. After serving prison time, Abagnale spent decades consulting with FBI and corporations on fraud prevention, teaching them that humans are easily manipulated through triggering automatic trust responses.

His most important insight was that people are far more trusting than they should be when presented with social proof, authority signals, and confident demeanor. Someone wearing a business suit and carrying briefcase can access most office buildings by following employees through security doors and claiming they are visiting someone on upper floors. Someone calling an employee and claiming to be from IT support can often get that employee to reveal passwords by sounding authoritative and providing reason why passwords are needed urgently. These attacks succeed not because victims are stupid but because humans evolved to trust apparent authority and to cooperate with people displaying confidence.

The defensive application of this knowledge involves recognizing when someone is using psychological principles against you. The salesperson creating false urgency through claiming limited availability is deploying scarcity principle. The negotiator making extreme initial demand before moderating to their actual desired outcome is using reciprocity through creating appearance that they made major concession. The colleague flattering you excessively before asking for favor is deploying liking principle. The one percent recognize these tactics when deployed against them, allowing them to evaluate decisions rationally rather than responding to psychological triggers automatically.

The ethical consideration in deploying these psychological principles is whether you are using them to guide people toward outcomes that serve their legitimate interests or whether you are manipulating them toward outcomes that benefit you at their expense. Using tactical empathy to understand a job candidate's actual career goals so you can determine whether your role serves those goals is ethical persuasion. Using the same techniques to manipulate someone into accepting role that does not serve their goals is unethical manipulation. The distinction lies in whether your goal is alignment of interests or exploitation of information asymmetry.

The one percent study psychology not to become manipulators but to become effective communicators who understand how humans actually make decisions rather than how we wish they made decisions. They use tactical empathy to understand others' perspectives and concerns. They recognize influence principles when deployed by others and evaluate decisions rationally rather than responding automatically. They structure their communications to work with human psychology rather than against it. They read nonverbal behavior to understand when words do not match emotions. They ask calibrated questions that help others solve problems from their perspective. They create genuine authority through competence and ensure that authority is visible. They provide value to others before requesting value, triggering reciprocity through authentic giving rather than through manipulation.

Chris Voss, Robert Cialdini, Joe Navarro, Daniel Kahneman, Paul Ekman, and Frank Abagnale each contributed to understanding how humans actually operate beneath the rational surface we present to ourselves and others. Their collective work reveals that reading people accurately and influencing outcomes ethically is not mysterious art but rather is learnable skill based on understanding systematic patterns in human behavior. The person who invests time studying these patterns gains advantages in negotiation, leadership, sales, networking, and every other domain where human interaction determines outcomes.

The principles are proven through decades of research and application. The one percent develop sophisticated understanding of psychology because advantages compound across hundreds of important interactions throughout careers and lives. The ninety-nine percent remain psychologically naïve and wonder why others seem to advance more easily despite comparable technical skills.

CHAPTER 30:
THE STAGE—MASTERING THE ART OF PERSUASIVE SPEECH

In January 2007, Steve Jobs walked onto a stage in San Francisco to introduce a product that would transform Apple from a computer company into the most valuable corporation in the world. The product was the iPhone, though the audience did not know that yet. Jobs wore his signature black turtleneck and jeans. He carried no notes. The presentation would run ninety minutes and include multiple live demonstrations of unfinished technology that could fail catastrophically in front of thousands of attendees and millions watching online. Most executives facing such stakes would be visibly nervous, would rely heavily on teleprompters, would hedge their claims with qualifications and caveats, and would generally communicate uncertainty through their body language and vocal tone even while claiming confidence with their words.

Jobs appeared completely relaxed. He smiled genuinely. He made eye contact with the audience rather than reading from screens. He paused deliberately after important statements, allowing the audience to absorb information rather than rushing nervously through his material. He modulated his vocal energy, speaking softly during explanatory sections and raising intensity during dramatic reveals. He physically demonstrated the product, touching and swiping the screen, showing rather than merely telling how the revolutionary interface worked. He structured the presentation as story with clear beginning, middle, and climax rather than as specification list. He used the rule of three repeatedly: "An iPod, a phone, and an internet communicator. . .these are not three separate devices, this is one device."

The audience response was electric. They interrupted repeatedly with applause and cheers. They laughed at his jokes. They gasped at demonstrations of features they had never seen. By the end of the presentation, everyone present understood that they had witnessed something historic. The iPhone went on to generate over one trillion dollars in revenue for Apple over the following seventeen years. But the product's success began with Jobs' ability to communicate its significance through a masterful presentation that persuaded skeptical technology journalists, excited early adopters, and convinced carriers and developers to bet on Apple's vision.

Jobs was not naturally gifted at public speaking. Early videos of his presentations in the 1980s show an awkward young man who rushed through material, failed to make eye contact, and generally communicated discomfort with being onstage. He became a master presenter through decades of deliberate practice, through studying presentation techniques, through rehearsing intensively before every major event, and through receiving candid feedback about what worked and what failed. His eventual mastery was not talent but rather was learned skill developed through years of focused effort because he understood that his ability to persuade audiences directly determined Apple's success.

This chapter examines how to communicate effectively when speaking to groups, whether you are making formal presentations to executives, teaching classes or workshops, motivating teams you manage, pitching to investors or customers, or speaking at conferences in your industry. These skills directly affect your career advancement because leaders must communicate vision and strategy to teams. They affect your business success because entrepreneurs must raise capital, recruit talent, and sell products through persuasive communication. They affect your earning potential because consultants and advisors are paid partly for expertise but mostly for ability to communicate that expertise effectively to clients who need it translated into actionable guidance.

The foundational principle of effective speaking is that your goal is never to demonstrate your knowledge or to impress the audience with your sophistication. Your goal is to change the audience in specific ways—to teach them information they did not know, to persuade them to take actions they were not planning to take, to inspire them to higher effort than they were giving, or to lead them toward outcomes that serve their interests even if they do not initially see why those outcomes matter. Every speech should have a clear specific change you want to create in the audience. The speaker who forgets this and focuses on displaying their expertise or defending their ego creates boring presentations that audiences tolerate without being changed.

The change-focused framework requires identifying exactly what you want audience members to think, feel, or do differently after your speech compared to before it. The executive presenting quarterly results wants the board to feel confident in management's strategy and to approve continued investment. The entrepreneur pitching to venture capitalists wants them to believe the market opportunity is large, the solution is defensible, the team can execute, and therefore they should commit capital. The consultant presenting to clients wants them to understand their problem clearly, to trust that the proposed solution will work, and to commit to implementing recommendations. The manager addressing their team wants them to understand why current approach is failing, to believe the new direction will succeed, and to commit emotionally to making difficult changes.

The one percent prepare every presentation by articulating the specific change they seek before considering what content to include. They write a single sentence describing the desired change: "After this presentation, the audience will understand why our current infrastructure cannot scale and will support the three million dollar investment in rebuilding it." This change statement determines everything else—what information to include, what to exclude, how to structure the argument, what stories to tell, and what call to action to make. The ninety-nine percent begin preparing by dumping everything they know about the topic into slides, creating presentations that inform without persuading and that demonstrate knowledge without creating change.

In 1940, Winston Churchill became Prime Minister of Britain as Nazi Germany conquered France and prepared to invade England. The British military had been humiliated at Dunkirk. The nation faced existential threat. Many in Parliament advocated negotiating peace with Hitler to avoid invasion and occupation. Churchill's first speech to Parliament as Prime Minister needed to unite the government behind continued resistance despite overwhelming odds against success. He could not reasonably promise victory. He could not minimize the danger Britain faced. He could only inspire commitment to fight regardless of consequences.

His speech was short—just seven hundred words delivered in thirteen minutes. But every element was crafted for maximum impact. He acknowledged reality brutally: "We have before us an ordeal of the most grievous kind. We have before us many, many long months of struggle and of suffering." He established that he was not naive about the challenges they faced. Then he pivoted to commitment: "You ask, what is our policy? I will say: It is to wage war, by sea, land and air, with all our might and with all the strength that God can give us." He used parallel structure and rhythmic repetition that made the speech memorable: "You ask, what is our aim? I can answer in one word: victory, victory at all costs, victory in spite of all terror, victory, however long and hard the road may be." He ended with the phrase that would define Britain's resistance: "I have nothing to offer but blood, toil, tears and sweat."

The speech accomplished exactly what Churchill needed. Parliament united behind continued resistance. The British people, hearing the speech through radio broadcasts, understood their government would fight rather than surrender. The speech set the tone for Churchill's leadership throughout the war—unflinching honesty about difficulties combined with absolute commitment to ultimate victory regardless of cost. Churchill delivered hundreds of speeches during the war, but this first speech established his credibility to lead through crisis by demonstrating that he understood the reality they faced while refusing to accept defeat as inevitable.

Churchill's mastery of language was not accidental. He spent hours crafting speeches, testing different word choices, reading drafts aloud to hear their rhythm, and rehearsing delivery. He understood that in moments of crisis, leaders must communicate with clarity and force that cut through fear and confusion. His speeches during World War II are studied eight decades later not as historical artifacts but as models of how language can inspire action when circumstances seem hopeless. His effectiveness came from preparation combined with understanding that speeches in moments of crisis require different approaches than speeches during normal times.

The structural framework for persuasive speeches follows a pattern refined over millennia of rhetoric: establish credibility, state the problem clearly, explain why the problem matters, present your solution, preempt objections, provide evidence supporting your solution, and close with clear call to action. This structure appears in Churchill's speech, in Jobs' product launches, and in every effective persuasive presentation regardless of context. The structure works because it mirrors how audiences process information—they must first trust the speaker before they will consider the argument, they must understand the problem before they will care about solutions, they must believe the solution addresses the problem before they will act.

The credibility establishment happens in the opening thirty to sixty seconds and determines whether the audience will listen openly or skeptically to everything that follows. Credibility comes from demonstrating that you understand the audience's situation, that you share their values or goals, and that you have relevant expertise or experience. The consultant opening a presentation to manufacturing executives might say: "I spent fifteen years managing production facilities before moving into consulting, so I understand firsthand the constraints you face with legacy equipment and the pressure you get from finance to minimize capital expenditures while somehow still improving output." This opening establishes shared experience that makes executives receptive to recommendations because the speaker is not an outsider imposing theoretical solutions.

The problem statement must be clear and specific enough that the audience recognizes it immediately without requiring explanation. Vague problem statements like "We need to improve efficiency" fail because efficiency means different things to different people. Specific problem statements like "Our order processing currently requires seventeen manual handoffs between five departments, creating an average of four point three errors per hundred orders and extending delivery times by nine days compared to competitors" create clarity that allows everyone to assess whether this is actually a problem worth solving. The one percent make problems concrete through specific data, through stories illustrating the problem's impact, or through comparison to standards the audience accepts. The ninety-nine percent describe problems abstractly in language that sounds impressive but that prevents the audience from visualizing the actual issue.

The explanation of why the problem matters prevents the common response of "so what?" to problem statements. Many real problems do not seem urgent until their consequences are made explicit. The executive hearing that order processing has seventeen handoffs might think this is how things have always been done and might not perceive urgency for change. The speaker who follows the problem statement with "This extended delivery time causes us to lose twenty-three percent of price-sensitive customers to competitors who deliver faster, costing us four point seven million annually in lost revenue" creates urgency by connecting the operational problem to financial consequences the executive cares about. The rule is that problems must be translated into consequences that matter to your specific audience—financial losses for executives focused on profit, customer dissatisfaction for teams focused on service quality, competitive disadvantage for organizations focused on market position.

The solution presentation should be clear and simple enough that the audience can understand and remember it without extensive explanation. Complex multi-step solutions requiring twenty slides to explain will not be remembered or implemented even if approved. Simple solutions that can be summarized in one sentence are far more likely to be adopted. "We will implement a unified order management system that eliminates fourteen of the seventeen handoffs by giving sales, fulfillment, and customer service access to the same real-time information" is clear and memorable. The details of how the system works can follow, but the core solution must be graspable immediately.

The preemptive objection handling addresses concerns the audience will have before they voice them, demonstrating that you have thought through the challenges rather than proposing naive solutions. Every solution has drawbacks or risks. The presenter who ignores these appears either ignorant or dishonest. The presenter who addresses them directly appears thoughtful and credible. "This will require three million dollars in software licensing and implementation costs, which I know seems expensive. But the four point seven million in annual revenue we are losing plus the one point two million in operational costs from error correction and delays means we recover the investment in seven months."

The evidence supporting your solution should combine data, expert opinion, and stories that make abstract arguments concrete. Data provides objective support—"Seventy-three percent of companies in our industry have implemented unified order management systems in the past five years." Expert opinion provides authority—"According to Gartner research, unified order management reduces order errors by an average of sixty-eight percent." Stories make the argument memorable—"Our competitor implemented this system two years ago. Their VP of Operations told me they reduced delivery times from fourteen days to five days and cut order errors by seventy-one percent. They recovered their implementation costs in eight months."

Bryan Stevenson, a lawyer who has argued multiple cases before the Supreme Court and who founded the Equal Justice Initiative, has delivered hundreds of speeches about criminal justice reform, racial inequality, and mass incarceration. His TED talk on injustice has been viewed over seven million times and is consistently rated among the most powerful TED talks ever delivered. Stevenson's effectiveness comes not from rhetorical flourishes or dramatic delivery but from his use of specific stories that make abstract injustices concrete and personal.

In one case he argued before the Supreme Court, Stevenson represented a defendant who had been sentenced to death by a jury from which all Black members had been systematically excluded. Rather than opening with legal arguments about constitutional violations, Stevenson told the story of his client's grandmother, who had attended every day of the trial despite being in her eighties and despite the defendant being her grandson facing execution. He described how she sat in the back of the courtroom praying and how the defendant would look back at her for strength. He described how when the verdict was read, she collapsed and had to be carried from the courtroom. Only after establishing the human reality did Stevenson present his legal arguments about jury selection violations.

The story served multiple purposes. It made the defendant human to justices who might otherwise see him as abstract legal case. It demonstrated that the defendant had family who loved him and who would suffer from his execution. It created emotional connection that pure legal argumentation cannot create. It established that Stevenson understood his client as a person rather than merely as vehicle for legal principle. The justices ruled in Stevenson's favor, and he later stated that establishing the human context through story was essential to victory.

The strategic use of stories transforms presentations from information delivery to persuasive communication. Stories are remembered when statistics are forgotten. Stories create emotional engagement when abstract arguments do not. Stories demonstrate that you understand the human reality of the issue rather than viewing it as merely technical problem. The one percent include stories in every important presentation—stories of customers who experienced problems, stories of employees who implemented solutions successfully, stories of competitors who succeeded or failed, stories from their own experience that establish credibility.

The effective story must be brief enough that it does not consume the entire presentation, specific enough that the audience can visualize the situation, and relevant enough that it directly supports the argument you are making. Rambling stories that meander without clear point destroy presentations by consuming time without advancing your argument. Stories disconnected from your core message confuse audiences by making them wonder why you told the story if it does not support your conclusion. The one percent craft stories deliberately, practicing delivery until they can tell them smoothly in two to three minutes, ensuring every detail supports their point and eliminating extraneous information that dilutes impact.

Hans Rosling was a Swedish physician and statistician who spent his career studying global health and economic development. He recognized that most people, including educated professionals and policymakers, held completely inaccurate beliefs about global poverty, health, and development. Their mental models were decades out of date, still reflecting the world of the 1960s when most of the world was desperately poor and when health outcomes in developing countries were catastrophic. They did not realize that dramatic improvements had occurred and that the majority of the world now lived at middle-income levels with life expectancies approaching wealthy nations.

Rosling could have addressed this ignorance through publishing research papers that few would read and fewer would understand. Instead, he became a presenter, delivering hundreds of speeches using animated data visualizations that made complex statistics intuitively comprehensible. His tools showed how countries had moved from poverty to prosperity over decades, with each country represented by a bubble whose size reflected population and whose position reflected life expectancy and income. As years advanced in the animation, audiences watched countries like China and India and dozens of others move from the bottom left of the graph toward the top right, representing improvements in both health and wealth.

These visualizations transformed abstract statistics into compelling stories about human progress. Audiences gasped when they realized how much improvement had occurred. They laughed when Rosling revealed how badly they had performed on quiz questions about global development compared to what random guessing would have produced. They left his presentations with completely transformed understanding of global conditions. Rosling's TED talks have been viewed over fifty million times, and his book "Factfulness" became an international bestseller. His impact came from recognizing that education requires more than presenting data—it requires translating data into forms that human brains can process and remember.

The lesson for anyone presenting data or technical information is that your responsibility is not to show how much you know but to ensure the audience understands what they need to know. This requires translating complexity into simplicity, using visualizations that make patterns obvious, and providing context that makes numbers meaningful. The engineer who presents server performance metrics as tables of numbers loses audiences who cannot interpret raw data. The engineer who shows graphs where green means good performance and red means problems that require attention communicates the same information in forms audiences can act on immediately.

The rule of three structures information in ways that human memory handles effectively. People remember three things far more reliably than they remember four or seven or ten things. Jobs used this in his iPhone introduction: "An iPod, a phone, and an internet communicator." Churchill used it throughout his speeches: "blood, toil, tears and sweat." The consultant presenting recommendations should organize around three key changes rather than seven initiatives. The executive explaining strategy should identify three priorities rather than five focus areas. This constraint forces you to identify what truly matters rather than listing everything you could possibly mention.

The vocal delivery determines whether audiences stay engaged or whether they drift into distraction despite excellent content. The common mistakes include speaking in monotone without vocal variety, speaking too quickly due to nervousness, filling pauses with "um" and "uh," and ending sentences with upward inflection that makes statements sound like questions. The one percent practice vocal delivery deliberately, recording themselves and listening critically, identifying verbal tics they need to eliminate, and working to vary their pace, volume, and pitch appropriately throughout presentations.

The power of pauses cannot be overstated. The amateur speaker fears silence and fills every gap with words or with filler sounds. The professional speaker uses pauses deliberately after important statements, giving audiences time to absorb information before moving forward. Jobs paused for several seconds after revealing each new iPhone feature, allowing the audience to react and discuss with neighbors before continuing. Churchill paused before his most important phrases, creating anticipation. Silence during presentations creates emphasis that constant talking cannot achieve. The one percent become comfortable with silence, using pauses strategically rather than rushing through material nervously.

The physical presence and body language communicate as much as words. The speaker who stands rigidly behind a podium gripping the edges appears nervous and defensive. The speaker who moves purposefully across the stage, uses hand gestures naturally, makes eye contact with different sections of the audience, and generally appears comfortable in their body communicates confidence that makes their arguments more persuasive. The research on body language shows that adopting confident postures—standing straight, occupying space, using open gestures—actually increases the speaker's own confidence through physiological feedback while simultaneously increasing the audience's perception of the speaker's credibility.

The one percent practice physical presence deliberately, often working with coaches to eliminate distracting mannerisms, to develop more purposeful movement, and to use gestures that emphasize key points rather than random movements that distract. They watch videos of their presentations and honestly assess what their body language communicates. They practice in the actual rooms where they will present when possible, becoming comfortable with the space. They wear clothing appropriate for the audience and occasion, understanding that inappropriate dress—either too casual or too formal—distracts from their message.

The slide design determines whether visuals support your argument or whether they undermine it through cluttered confusing layouts. The common mistake is creating slides filled with bullet points listing everything you plan to say, creating wall of text that audiences read rather than listening to you. Effective slides contain minimal text—perhaps one sentence or even just one word—combined with powerful images or clear data visualizations. Jobs' slides often showed only a product photo or a single word against black background. His slides supported his spoken words rather than competing with them.

The design principle is that slides should reinforce your verbal message, not replace it. If the audience can understand your entire argument by reading your slides without you speaking, your slides are doing your job and you are unnecessary. Your job is to explain, to provide context, to tell stories, to connect information to audience's situation. The slides provide visual reinforcement of key points, show images that make abstract concepts concrete, and display data that supports your arguments. The one percent often use slide designers to create professional visuals, understanding that investment in presentation quality generates returns through increased persuasiveness.

Tony Robbins built a coaching and seminar business worth over six hundred million dollars through his ability to motivate audiences during multi-day seminars where participants pay thousands of dollars for the experience. Robbins does not present technical information or complex frameworks that audiences could not understand without his guidance. He presents concepts about mindset, commitment, and action that are relatively simple intellectually. His value comes from his ability to create emotional states in audiences that cause them to commit to changes they have been avoiding.

His techniques include high-energy delivery with constant movement and vocal variety, audience participation exercises that create physical engagement, stories of transformation from people who applied his principles, and strategic use of music and lighting to manipulate emotional states. His seminars culminate with firewalking experiences where participants walk across hot coals, creating peak emotional experiences and sense of accomplishment that Robbins links to their ability to make other difficult changes they have been avoiding.

Whether you believe Robbins' methods are profound or simplistic, his commercial success demonstrates that motivational speaking requires different skills than informational or persuasive speaking. The goal is not primarily to teach or to convince through logic but rather to create emotional states that generate commitment to action. The manager trying to motivate discouraged team can learn from Robbins' techniques even if they never walk on coals—maintaining high energy, telling stories of past successes, getting people physically engaged through standing and movement, and linking abstract goals to concrete actions people can take immediately.

The opening thirty seconds determine whether audiences engage or tune out. The amateur speaker opens with apologies ("I'm not a great presenter but I'll do my best"), with agenda slides ("Today I want to cover three topics..."), or with background they think is necessary but that bores audiences ("Let me tell you about our company history..."). The professional speaker opens with content that immediately engages: a surprising statistic, a powerful story, a provocative question, or a clear statement of value ("In the next twenty minutes I'm going to show you how to reduce your customer acquisition costs by forty percent").

The one percent write and rewrite their openings repeatedly, testing different approaches, getting feedback from trusted colleagues, and ultimately selecting openings that create immediate engagement. They memorize opening two to three minutes so they can deliver them smoothly without notes, establishing confident presence. They practice openings more than any other section because they understand that if they lose the audience in the first minute, recovering attention becomes exponentially harder.

The closing call to action makes explicit what you want the audience to do as a result of your presentation. The amateur speaker ends with "Thank you for your time" or "Are there any questions?" without clearly stating what should happen next. The professional speaker ends with specific next steps: "I'm asking you to approve the three million dollar investment in the new order management system so we can begin implementation in Q3 and start capturing the four point seven million in annual revenue we are currently losing." The call to action removes ambiguity about what decision you want or what action you need.

The one percent craft calls to action that are specific enough to enable immediate response but reasonable enough that audiences can actually take the requested action. Asking a board to "approve a direction for the company" is too vague—approve what specifically? Asking them to "approve fifty-three initiatives requiring two hundred million in funding" is too large to generate immediate commitment. Asking them to "approve the top three strategic priorities and authorize management to develop detailed implementation plans for board approval next quarter" is specific yet achievable.

The handling of questions determines whether Q&A sections strengthen your presentation or undermine it. The common mistakes include becoming defensive when challenged, allowing hostile questioners to derail the presentation, admitting you do not know answers when you should know, and rambling in responses rather than answering concisely. The one percent prepare for likely questions before presenting, developing clear concise answers they can deliver confidently. When asked questions they cannot answer, they admit it directly—"I don't have that data with me but I'll get it to you by tomorrow"—rather than inventing answers or avoiding the question.

The techniques for handling hostile questions include acknowledging the concern before responding—"That's an important issue and I understand your concern about implementation costs"—then redirecting to your key messages—"What I'd emphasize is that the four point seven million we are losing annually makes the three million investment essential regardless of implementation challenges." The technique for handling questions you cannot answer is to be direct while offering to follow up: "I don't have that specific breakdown, but I'll send you the detailed financial model tomorrow that shows exactly where the savings come from."

The rehearsal time the one percent invest in important presentations would shock most people. Jobs rehearsed product launches for weeks, running through entire presentations repeatedly, adjusting timing, refining demonstrations, and ensuring every element was perfect. Churchill rewrote speeches multiple times and practiced delivery. Stevenson rehearses arguments extensively before Supreme Court appearances. The one percent understand that the first time you deliver a presentation should not be the actual presentation to your audience—it should be the tenth or twentieth run-through after you have refined content and delivery through repeated practice.

The feedback seeking from trusted colleagues before presenting to important audiences allows identifying problems while you can still fix them. The one percent present to small groups of colleagues or coaches who provide candid feedback about content, structure, delivery, and visual aids. They ask specific questions: "Did the opening engage you immediately?" "Was the problem statement clear?" "Were you convinced by the evidence?" "What objections did I fail to address?" This feedback reveals gaps in logic, unclear explanations, and delivery issues that the presenter cannot identify themselves because they are too close to the material.

The confidence without arrogance that characterizes effective speakers comes from preparation combined with genuine belief in your message rather than from ego. The speaker who is confident because they have rehearsed extensively and because they know their evidence supports their conclusions communicates differently than the speaker who is confident because they believe they are smarter than their audience. The first confidence is earned and appropriate. The second is arrogance that audiences detect and resent.

The one percent maintain confidence even when challenged because they know they have prepared thoroughly. They can defend their recommendations because they have thought through objections. They can answer questions because they have anticipated them. This genuine confidence based on preparation differs completely from false confidence based on bravado. The person who has not prepared can only bluster when challenged, which reveals their lack of substance and destroys credibility. The person who has prepared can respond substantively, which reinforces credibility.

The self-awareness about your speaking weaknesses allows improving them rather than hoping audiences won't notice. Everyone has verbal tics—some people say "um" constantly, some say "like" after every few words, some repeat "you know" habitually, some end sentences with "right?" seeking affirmation. These tics undermine credibility by making speakers appear nervous or uncertain. The one percent identify their specific tics through recording themselves, then work deliberately to eliminate them through conscious practice. This requires months of effort—you must catch yourself using the tic in real-time and consciously stop, eventually breaking the habit through repetition.

The context adaptation means preparing different presentations for different audiences even when covering the same material. The presentation to executives should emphasize business impact and financial outcomes. The presentation to technical staff should include implementation details that executives don't need. The presentation to frontline employees should emphasize how changes will affect their daily work. The one percent prepare core content once but customize framing, emphasis, and level of detail for each audience rather than delivering identical presentations regardless of who is listening.

The career leverage from speaking ability compounds across years because effective speakers get selected for high-visibility opportunities that ineffective speakers never receive. The executive who presents confidently to the board gets promoted to roles requiring regular board interaction. The consultant who presents effectively to clients gets selected for the most important client engagements. The entrepreneur who pitches effectively to investors raises capital that entrepreneurs with better products but worse presentation skills cannot raise. The manager who motivates teams effectively gets promoted to larger teams.

The one percent invest in developing speaking skills early in their careers because they understand these skills multiply the impact of their technical expertise. They join Toastmasters or similar organizations to practice in low-stakes environments. They volunteer for presentations at work even when nervous about speaking. They hire coaches when they can afford them. They study great speakers, analyzing what makes them effective. They record themselves and honestly assess their weaknesses. They practice deliberately rather than merely hoping they will improve through repeated exposure.

The underlying principle connecting all of these techniques is that speaking effectively is about serving your audience by helping them understand, by persuading them toward decisions that serve their interests, by motivating them to higher effort, or by leading them toward better outcomes. The speaker focused on displaying their knowledge or impressing the audience with their sophistication fails because they serve themselves rather than serving the audience. The speaker focused on creating specific changes in the audience succeeds because everything they do is oriented toward that change rather than toward ego gratification.

Steve Jobs, Winston Churchill, Bryan Stevenson, Hans Rosling, and Tony Robbins represent different types of speaking excellence—product launches, wartime leadership, legal argumentation, data-driven education, and motivational seminars. Yet they share common characteristics: they prepared intensively, they structured presentations around creating specific changes in audiences, they told stories that made arguments concrete and memorable, they used vocal variety and physical presence effectively, they opened with immediate engagement and closed with clear calls to action, and they demonstrated confidence based on preparation rather than on arrogance. These characteristics can be learned and developed through deliberate practice regardless of whether you possess natural charisma or comfort with public speaking.

The frameworks have been provided. The techniques are proven through decades of research and through the examples of effective speakers across contexts. Making the choice to master the stage is a necessary thing since it affects your career trajectory, your earning potential, your ability to build businesses, and your capacity to influence outcomes that matter to you. The one percent develops speaking effectiveness because they understand that leadership, sales, fundraising, and virtually every high-value activity requires ability to communicate persuasively to groups. The ninety-nine percent avoid speaking opportunities or present ineffectively when forced to speak, limiting their career potential regardless of their technical competence. You now understand what makes speaking effective and what techniques separate persuasive speakers from those who merely consume time without creating change. The practice and implementation remain your responsibility.

CHAPTER 31:
RAISING CHILDREN—PREPARING THE NEXT GENERATION

In 1918, a man named Sam Walton was born during the final months of World War I to a farm family in Oklahoma that would lose everything during the Great Depression. His childhood was marked by scarcity, frequent moves as his father chased work, and the understanding that survival required effort and ingenuity. Sam began contributing to family finances at age eight by selling magazine subscriptions and delivering newspapers. By high school he was earning more than many adults through his paper route and other ventures. The lessons he learned during these years—that money comes from work, that frugality enables opportunity, and that wealth is built through systematic effort rather than luck—would shape not only his eventual creation of Walmart but also how he raised his own children.

When Sam Walton became one of the wealthiest men in America through building Walmart into the largest retailer in the world, he faced the question that confronts everyone who builds substantial wealth: how do you raise children who will respect money, develop their own capabilities, and use inherited wealth responsibly rather than allowing it to destroy their character and initiative? His answer was radically different from how most wealthy people approach this question. His children grew up in a modest three-bedroom house in Bentonville, Arkansas long after the family could have afforded mansions. They wore ordinary clothes rather than designer brands. They worked in Walmart stores during summers alongside regular employees, stocking shelves and operating cash registers for minimum wage. They learned the business from the ground up through actual work rather than through merely inheriting positions.

Sam's philosophy was simple: his children would benefit from the wealth he built, but they would not be given everything without earning it, and they would not be insulated from understanding how businesses actually operate. He established trusts that provided financial security while requiring his children to work and contribute rather than living on dividends alone. He involved them in business decisions from young ages, teaching them to think like owners rather than like spoiled heirs. He modeled the values he wanted them to adopt through his own continued frugality and work ethic despite his wealth. When Sam Walton died in 1992, his children inherited one of the largest fortunes in American history. Yet they continued working in the business, continued living relatively modest lifestyles compared to their wealth, and continued the values their father had instilled through both teaching and modeling.

The Walton family today, three decades after Sam's death, ranks among the wealthiest families in the world with combined net worth exceeding two hundred billion dollars. Yet the third and fourth generations continue working productively, continue living with reasonable restraint despite their wealth, and continue managing the business and philanthropic foundations their grandfather established. This outcome is not accidental or lucky. It is the direct result of Sam Walton's deliberate approach to raising children who would respect wealth while not being destroyed by it. His approach demonstrates principles that apply whether you are building billions or building modest wealth to pass to the next generation.

This chapter addresses what may be the most important long-term question in wealth building: how do you prepare children to handle wealth responsibly so that what you build across your lifetime serves to strengthen rather than weaken them and their descendants? This is the chapter about legacy—not the legacy of dollars accumulated but the legacy of values transmitted, capabilities developed, and character formed. The wealthiest person who raises children ruined by entitlement and dependence has failed at the most important measure of success. The person of modest means who raises children who build their own wealth through applied principles has succeeded at what actually matters.

The partner selection precedes child-rearing in importance because your children will inherit genetic predispositions, personality traits, intelligence, and tendencies toward various behaviors from both parents. The choice of who you have children with is the single most important decision affecting your children's outcomes beyond your control after conception occurs. Sam Walton married Helen Robson, whose family owned a successful retail business and who shared his values about work ethic, frugality, and faith. This alignment created household where both parents modeled and reinforced the same principles, making it far more likely that children would adopt those principles rather than rebelling against them.

The one percent think about partner selection partly in terms of what kind of parent their partner will be and what characteristics their children will inherit. This is not about eugenics or about judging people's worth based on genetics. This is about recognizing reality that children inherit from both parents and that choosing a partner with characteristics you want your children to develop increases likelihood that your children will develop those characteristics. Intelligence has substantial genetic component. Conscientiousness has substantial genetic component. Tendency toward addiction has substantial genetic component. These facts are uncomfortable but they are facts nonetheless, and they matter enormously for your children's outcomes.

The prenatal health environment affects child development before birth in ways that shape lifetime outcomes. The person who smokes, drinks alcohol, uses drugs, experiences high stress, or maintains poor nutrition during pregnancy creates developmental environment that can impair child cognitive function, emotional regulation, and physical health permanently. The research on fetal alcohol syndrome, prenatal stress effects, and maternal nutrition impacts is unambiguous. The one percent treat pregnancy as the most important nine months of their child's development because it establishes biological foundations that no amount of excellent parenting after birth can fully compensate for if those foundations are damaged.

The maternal health optimization before pregnancy matters as much as health during pregnancy because egg quality, nutritional reserves, and metabolic health at conception affect fetal development throughout gestation. The woman who enters pregnancy overweight with poor metabolic health, nutritional deficiencies, or uncontrolled stress creates starting conditions that affect her child's lifelong health independent of choices made during pregnancy itself. The one percent who plan to have children optimize health before conception rather than waiting until pregnancy is confirmed to begin taking health seriously. This includes achieving healthy body composition, establishing excellent nutrition patterns, building fitness through regular exercise, managing stress effectively, and addressing any metabolic conditions like insulin resistance or thyroid dysfunction.

John D. Rockefeller raised his children in the late 1800s and early 1900s when he was building Standard Oil into the monopoly that would make him history's wealthiest individual. He faced the same question Sam Walton would face decades later: how do you raise children who will respect money when they have access to unlimited wealth? His approach established principles that wealthy families have studied and emulated for over a century. He gave his children allowances but required them to maintain account books documenting every penny spent and saved. He inspected these books weekly, discussing their spending decisions and requiring them to justify expenditures. He required them to give ten percent to church and save ten percent before spending the remaining eighty percent on anything else.

This system taught double-entry bookkeeping before children could understand why it mattered. It created habits of tracking expenses and income that persisted through their lives. It established giving as non-negotiable first priority rather than as optional activity when convenient. It required children to make spending decisions within budgets rather than merely requesting whatever they wanted whenever they wanted it. The system seems harsh by modern standards where parents give children money without accountability, but it produced children who managed the Rockefeller fortune responsibly across multiple generations rather than squandering it within one generation as the Vanderbilt heirs did.

The allowance structure that develops financial literacy should begin as soon as children can count, typically around ages four to six. The amounts are modest—perhaps one dollar per year of age weekly, so a six-year-old receives six dollars weekly. The money is divided into designated purposes before any spending occurs: ten percent to giving, ten percent to long-term savings, perhaps twenty percent to medium-term savings for larger purchases, and the remaining sixty percent available for immediate spending. The child maintains simple written records of income and spending, updated weekly with parent supervision.

This system teaches that money comes from somewhere—in this case from parents, though eventually from work as children age. It teaches that money has multiple purposes beyond spending. It teaches that saving precedes spending rather than saving whatever remains after spending. It teaches tracking income and expenses so you know where money goes rather than wondering vaguely why you never have money despite thinking you should. It teaches delayed gratification through accumulating medium-term savings for purchases requiring weeks or months of saving. It teaches generosity through giving before spending. Most importantly, it makes these lessons automatic through repetition during years when habits form easily rather than trying to teach them in adulthood when poor habits are already entrenched.

Warren Buffett famously declared that he would leave his children "enough money so that they would feel they could do anything, but not so much that they could do nothing." He has followed through on this philosophy, leaving the vast majority of his fortune to charitable foundations rather than to his children while providing his children with enough resources to pursue meaningful work without financial desperation. His daughter Susie, his son

Howard, and his son Peter all pursued careers in nonprofits, farming, and music respectively—fields they were passionate about but that did not generate substantial income. The financial support their father provided allowed them to pursue these passions while living comfortably, but it was not so much that they could live lavishly without working.

This balance is extraordinarily difficult to achieve because the appropriate amount varies by individual child based on their character, capabilities, and life circumstances. The child with strong work ethic and clear sense of purpose might handle substantial inherited wealth responsibly. The child lacking discipline or direction might be destroyed by access to resources that eliminate the necessity of developing those qualities through struggle. The one percent evaluate their children individually rather than applying blanket rules, adjusting support levels based on observed character and development rather than on equal distribution that treats different children identically despite different needs and capabilities.

The work requirement for children of wealthy families instills understanding that productivity matters regardless of financial necessity. Sam Walton's children worked in Walmart stores. Bill Gates requires his children to do chores and earn privileges. Many wealthy families require children to work regular jobs during summers rather than assuming their wealth exempts them from employment. This work serves multiple purposes beyond the income earned. It teaches that adults are expected to contribute productively to society. It exposes children to people who must work for living rather than insulating them only among the wealthy. It develops skills and work ethic that trustfunds cannot provide. It creates pride in earned money that inherited money never provides.

The one percent require their children to work from early ages through age-appropriate contributions. Young children complete household chores—not for allowance because family members contribute to household functioning without payment, but as expectations for being part of the family. Teenagers work part-time jobs during school years and full-time during summers. Young adults work in family businesses at market wages rather than at inflated salaries that would not be paid to non-family employees. This consistent expectation of productive contribution creates identity as workers rather than as idle wealthy, and this identity persists even when inherited wealth eventually provides financial independence.

The teaching of investment principles begins once children accumulate savings in their medium-term and long-term savings buckets. Rather than leaving money in savings accounts earning minimal interest, parents can help children open custodial investment accounts and begin learning how markets work. The child who saves fifty dollars might invest it in an S&P 500 index fund, then watch over months and years as it grows to sixty, seventy, eighty dollars. They learn viscerally that money can multiply itself through patient investment rather than only through earning and saving. They learn that markets fluctuate and that this is normal rather than catastrophic. They develop emotional tolerance for volatility during years when the amounts involved are small and losses are not devastating.

The one percent use their children's investment accounts as teaching laboratories for principles they will need to manage far larger amounts eventually. They review account statements together, discussing why balances increased or decreased. They explain the difference between temporary price fluctuations and permanent losses. They model discipline by not selling during downturns when children panic about declining balances. They explain how compound growth works by showing how the fifty dollar investment might become hundreds or thousands over decades if never withdrawn. These lessons using small amounts prepare children to eventually manage six or seven figure portfolios without the emotional mistakes that destroy wealth for those who never learned these principles.

The graduated responsibility for financial decisions teaches children to make choices and experience consequences while stakes are low enough that mistakes are educational rather than catastrophic. The young child chooses how to spend their sixty percent spending allocation from allowance, experiencing the regret of impulsive purchases that provide no lasting value. The teenager manages clothing budget for school year, learning to shop strategically or experiencing insufficient clothes if they blow the budget early. The young adult manages their spending completely beyond housing costs that parents cover during college or early career years, learning to budget or experiencing financial pressure from overspending.

This graduated system means children make mistakes while safety nets exist to prevent catastrophic failures, but consequences remain real enough to teach. The teenager who spends their clothing budget on expensive item in August and then lacks winter clothes in November learns about planning and delayed gratification through direct experience rather than through abstract lecture. The one percent allow these mistakes rather than rescuing children immediately, understanding that lessons learned through painful experience persist far longer than lessons learned through being told what to do.

The exposure to family wealth discussions from young ages prepares children to eventually participate in wealth management decisions rather than being surprised by inheritance or being unprepared to manage it. Many wealthy families maintain complete secrecy about their finances until parents die and children learn through inheritance that their family was wealthy. This approach creates multiple problems. Children who live modestly thinking their family has average means develop no understanding of wealth management. When they inherit substantial assets, they lack the knowledge and experience to manage them competently. They often either squander inherited wealth through poor decisions or they feel enormous guilt about having wealth when they did nothing to earn it, creating psychological problems that impair their wellbeing.

The one percent discuss family finances at age-appropriate levels beginning in early teenage years. The fourteen-year-old learns that the family has investments and that those investments fund the lifestyle the family maintains. The sixteen-year-old learns approximate family net worth and begins understanding what that means for their future. The eighteen-year-old learns about trust structures and estate plans so they understand what they will eventually inherit and under what conditions. The twenty-five-year-old participates in family financial meetings, learning how investment decisions are made and contributing to philanthropic allocation discussions. This progressive transparency prepares children across years rather than shocking them with information they are unprepared to process.

The teaching of philanthropy through involving children in giving decisions from young ages instills that wealth exists for purposes beyond consumption. The Rockefellers required children to give ten percent of allowances to church before spending on themselves. Many wealthy families establish donor-advised funds that children help allocate, teaching them to evaluate charitable organizations and to think about social impact. Some families volunteer together at nonprofits, exposing children to people in need and to work being done to address those needs.

The one percent understand that children who never learn that others suffer, who never see poverty or need directly, and who never give of their time or money to help others develop narcissistic worldviews where they are the center of the universe and everyone exists to serve them. This emotional and moral bankruptcy is far more destructive than financial bankruptcy, yet it is common among children raised with wealth who were insulated from hardship and never taught to think beyond themselves. The systematic involvement in giving and service prevents this outcome by making children aware that others exist, that those others face genuine hardship, and that our resources can help address that hardship.

The Vanderbilt family represents the cautionary tale of wealth destroyed through poor preparation of heirs. Cornelius Vanderbilt built shipping and railroad fortune that made him the wealthiest American of his era. He left almost his entire fortune to one son while giving minimal amounts to his other children, creating family conflict and ensuring that the concentrated wealth would face no diversification. His son and grandchildren built enormous mansions, threw lavish parties, and generally consumed wealth faster than investments could generate returns. Within three generations, the family fortune was largely gone. When 120 Vanderbilt descendants gathered for a family reunion in 1973, not one of them was wealthy. The family that had been America's wealthiest became a case study in how not to transfer wealth across generations.

The Vanderbilts failed because they never taught their children that wealth requires stewardship rather than consumption. They modeled lavish spending on assets that generated no returns—mansions that cost fortunes to maintain, yachts that depreciated, parties that provided temporary entertainment and permanent costs. Their children learned that being wealthy means spending ostentatiously rather than living below your means and investing the difference. When they inherited wealth, they continued these consumption patterns until the wealth was gone. No amount of money survives multiple generations of heirs who consume faster than assets grow.

The trust structures that protect inherited wealth from immature decisions provide legal frameworks that balance access with protection. The simplest trusts distribute income to heirs while protecting principal, ensuring that heirs cannot squander accumulated wealth while still benefiting from returns it generates. More sophisticated trusts might distribute increasing percentages of principal as heirs reach certain ages—perhaps twenty-five percent at age twenty-five, another twenty-five percent at thirty, additional amounts at thirty-five and forty, with full control at forty-five once children have demonstrated maturity and hopefully have established their own careers and financial discipline.

Some trusts include incentive provisions that match earned income dollar-for-dollar up to certain thresholds, rewarding productive work while discouraging idleness. A child earning fifty thousand annually through employment might receive fifty thousand from the trust, doubling their effective income and allowing comfortable lifestyle while ensuring they remain employed productively. These incentives prevent the trust from enabling dependence while still providing support that allows children to pursue meaningful work that might not generate high income. The one percent structure trusts through consultation with estate planning attorneys who specialize in multigenerational wealth transfer, ensuring that legal structures align with family values and goals rather than using generic templates that may not serve specific situations appropriately.

The family governance structures in wealthy families with substantial assets create processes for making decisions about shared wealth and for maintaining family cohesion across generations. Some families establish family councils that meet quarterly or annually, bringing all adult family members together to discuss investment strategies, philanthropic allocations, business operations if family businesses exist, and to maintain relationships across branches of extended families. Some families create family constitutions documenting shared values, decision-making processes, and expectations for family members. Some families require family members to complete financial education programs before gaining access to trust distributions or before voting on family council decisions.

These formal structures seem excessive for families with modest wealth, but the principles apply at any scale. The family with one million dollars can benefit from documenting their values, discussing their estate plans with adult children, and establishing expectations about how inherited wealth should be used. The family with ten million dollars probably needs more formal structures including trusts, family meetings, and documented governance processes. The family with one hundred million or more requires sophisticated structures rivaling corporate governance because the assets under management justify the complexity and because informal approaches that work with small amounts fail catastrophically when amounts become large enough that poor decisions destroy substantial value.

The teaching of delayed gratification through requiring children to wait for desired items rather than providing everything immediately forms the foundation for all future financial discipline. The marshmallow experiment conducted by Walter Mischel at Stanford in the 1960s demonstrated that children who could delay gratification—waiting fifteen minutes to receive two marshmallows rather than eating one immediately—went on to achieve better academic outcomes, healthier BMI, and better life outcomes measured across decades. The ability to delay gratification predicts success more reliably than intelligence, family wealth, or most other factors studied.

The one percent deliberately structure childhood to develop this capability rather than hoping it develops accidentally. The child who wants a toy is required to save allowance for weeks or months to purchase it rather than having parents buy it immediately. The teenager who wants expensive item must earn money through work to buy it rather than receiving it as gift. The young adult who wants car must save for down payment and maintain employment to afford payments rather than having parents buy vehicles outright. These requirements create repeated experiences of wanting something, working and waiting to obtain it, and then valuing it more because effort was required. The child who receives everything immediately never develops the neural pathways and emotional regulation that delayed gratification requires, remaining impulsive and present-focused through adulthood.

The exposure to different socioeconomic circumstances prevents wealthy children from developing distorted worldviews where they assume everyone lives as they do. Sam Walton's children worked alongside regular Walmart employees earning minimum wage, exposing them directly to people who depended on those jobs for survival rather than working for character development. Bill Gates limits his children's screen time and requires them to complete chores despite ability to hire help for any task, teaching them that basic life competencies matter regardless of wealth. Many wealthy families require children to attend public schools rather than exclusive private schools, exposing them to diversity of circumstances and preventing the bubble that forms when children only interact with other wealthy children.

The one percent understand that children who only know wealth, who never interact with people who struggle financially, and who never see how most people actually live develop both moral problems through narcissism and practical problems through incompetence. These children often become adults who cannot function independently because they have always had staff handling basic life tasks, who cannot relate to normal people because they have never interacted with them meaningfully, and who have no sense of how their wealth compares to typical circumstances because they have never been exposed to those circumstances. The systematic exposure to normal life prevents these outcomes while still allowing children to benefit from family wealth.

The mistake many wealthy parents make is assuming that private schools, exclusive activities, and isolation from normal circumstances will benefit their children through providing superior education and networking opportunities. This assumption is partly true—elite private schools do provide educational advantages and networking access that public schools rarely match. But the trade-off is that children develop in bubbles where distorted reality becomes their normal, where they never learn to relate to people unlike themselves, and where they develop values aligned with consumption and status rather than with stewardship and purpose. The one percent evaluate this trade-off consciously rather than automatically assuming expensive private education is optimal for their children's development.

The teaching of hard skills through requiring children to develop capabilities beyond what wealth might allow them to avoid creates competence that provides psychological benefits independent of financial utility. The child who learns to cook can feed themselves competently rather than depending on restaurants or staff. The teenager who learns basic home and auto maintenance can handle minor repairs rather than requiring professional help for routine tasks. The young adult who learns to manage household finances, to negotiate with service providers, and to make basic financial decisions develops confidence that wealth cannot provide.

These competencies seem unnecessary when family wealth could pay for services handling all these tasks. But the psychological benefits of competence—knowing you can handle basic life challenges independently—provide wellbeing that dependence undermines. The adult who must call parents or staff to handle every minor problem because they were never taught basic skills remains psychologically dependent regardless of their chronological age. The adult who can handle normal life challenges independently while choosing to pay for convenience when appropriate maintains healthy sense of agency. The one percent ensure their children develop competencies even though wealth might allow avoiding that development.

The discussion of how inherited wealth should be used occurs before inheritance rather than leaving children to figure this out themselves after assets transfer. Parents communicate their values about money, about work, about giving, and about stewardship. They explain why they structured trusts as they did. They discuss their hopes for how children will use wealth to accomplish meaningful goals rather than merely consuming it. They share their mistakes and lessons learned through building wealth. This communication provides guidance that shapes how children approach inherited wealth rather than leaving them to develop their own philosophies that might conflict with parents' intentions.

The one percent understand that financial wealth without values-based context often destroys children because they lack framework for making good decisions about resources they did not earn. The child who inherits two million dollars with no guidance about whether they should work, whether they should invest conservatively or aggressively, whether they should give charitably, and whether they should live on principal or only on income will likely make poor decisions because they lack experience and guidance. The child who inherits the same amount with clear communication about family values, about expectations for continuing to work productively, about investing systematically for long-term growth, about giving generously from abundance, and about living on investment returns while preserving principal has roadmap for making decisions that honor both the wealth received and the values of those who built it.

The modeling of values through parents' own behavior teaches more effectively than any verbal instruction can teach. Sam Walton lived modestly despite his wealth, drove old pickup trucks, and continued working productively until his death. His children learned that wealth does not require conspicuous consumption because their father demonstrated frugality despite obvious ability to spend lavishly. Warren Buffett lives in the same house he purchased in 1958 for thirty-one thousand five hundred dollars despite being among the wealthiest people in history. His children learned that housing is about function rather than status through observing his choices rather than through being lectured about appropriate housing.

The one percent who want their children to adopt particular values must model those values consistently rather than merely preaching them. The parent who lectures about frugality while driving luxury vehicles and buying expensive status symbols teaches children that stated values matter less than demonstrated behaviors. The parent who lives modestly despite wealth while explaining that they prioritize investing over consuming teaches children that delayed gratification and thoughtful resource allocation matter more than impressing others. Children observe and imitate what parents do far more than they internalize what parents say.

The preparation of children for leadership roles in family businesses or foundations requires different approach than preparing them merely to manage inherited wealth. The child who will eventually lead family business needs to understand that business from ground up through working in various roles, through understanding how different functions operate, and through demonstrating competence before being given authority based on family name. The child who will eventually serve on family foundation board needs to understand philanthropy, social impact measurement, and nonprofit operations through years of involvement before making allocation decisions affecting millions.

The one percent who have built businesses or established foundations begin this preparation during children's teenage years through summer employment in the businesses and through involving them in foundation activities. They require children to work in frontline roles serving customers or beneficiaries rather than starting in executive offices. They require demonstrated competence in lower roles before promoting to increased responsibility. They sometimes require children to work elsewhere for several years before joining family enterprises, ensuring that children develop skills and credibility through external validation rather than only through family connections. These requirements produce heirs capable of stewarding businesses and foundations competently rather than heirs who destroy them through incompetence disguised behind family names.

The communication about wealth amounts and estate plans should occur progressively as children mature rather than being sprung on them suddenly when parents die. The child who learns at age fourteen that their family has wealth can process this information and begin developing appropriate relationship with money across years before inheritance occurs. The child who learns at age thirty when parents die suddenly that they are inheriting millions experiences shock that impairs decision-making during the emotionally difficult period after losing parents. The one percent share information progressively, allowing children to adapt gradually to understanding their family's wealth and their eventual inheritance rather than overwhelming them with information they are unprepared to process.

The balance between providing advantage and creating dependence represents the central challenge in raising children with wealth. Every parent wants their children to benefit from resources the parents built. The question is whether those benefits strengthen children by providing opportunities to develop their capabilities or whether those benefits weaken children by eliminating the necessity of developing capabilities through struggle. The child who receives excellent education, summer enrichment programs, tutoring when needed, and support for pursuing genuine interests benefits from wealth that develops their capabilities. The child who receives unlimited spending money, luxury goods without earning them, rescue from every problem, and elimination of all struggle is harmed by wealth that prevents capability development.

The one percent err toward providing too little rather than too much during child-rearing years, understanding that slight hardship builds character while slight excess often destroys it. They provide education, enrichment, and support for developing capabilities. They limit spending money, require work for desired items, allow children to experience consequences of poor decisions, and generally maintain some pressure that forces children to develop resilience and competence. They understand that their goal is not to make childhood easy but rather to use childhood to build adults capable of handling wealth responsibly and living meaningful lives regardless of inherited resources.

The ultimate measure of success in raising children is not the size of the estate you leave them but whether they become people of character who use whatever resources they inherit to accomplish meaningful purposes rather than merely consuming those resources before passing nothing to subsequent generations. Sam Walton succeeded by this measure. The Rockefellers succeeded by this measure. Many wealthy families whose names are unknown succeed by this measure through raising children who steward wealth across generations. Many prominent families whose wealth disappeared within two generations failed by this measure through raising children who consumed rather than stewarded.

We have completed the comprehensive education about wealth building that this book was written to provide. We have examined every major domain from mindset through strategy through execution through the teaching of these principles to the next generation. This final chapter addresses what may be the most important question of all: what happens to what you build after you are gone? The answer depends entirely on whether you prepared your children to handle wealth wisely or whether you left them resources they were unprepared to steward.

The one percent think multigenerationally. They build wealth not just for themselves but for descendants they will never meet. They prepare their children to steward that wealth rather than to squander it. They establish values, instill discipline, teach capabilities, provide graduated responsibility, model appropriate behaviors, and communicate clearly about expectations and purposes. They understand that successful wealth transfer is measured not in how much money changes hands but in whether children use inherited resources to accomplish meaningful purposes while continuing to live productive lives.

The ninety-nine percent either have no wealth to transfer or they transfer it in ways that damage recipients through lack of preparation or through excess that eliminates necessity of developing capabilities. They either tell children nothing about family wealth or they provide everything without teaching how to manage it. They either model consumption or they model such extreme frugality that children rebel against it. They hope that children will somehow learn to handle wealth well despite never being taught or prepared. The proper perspective preserves significant wealth.

CHAPTER 32:

ADVANCED LEVERAGE AND ENTITY STRUCTURES—THE SOPHISTICATED ARSENAL

In 2008, a real estate investor named Eric was sitting in his financial advisor's office watching his net worth evaporate in real-time. The financial crisis had destroyed property values across his portfolio of rental properties. He had purchased fifteen properties over the previous five years using traditional mortgages with twenty percent down payments. His properties had collectively appreciated from three million to four point five million at the peak in 2007. By late 2008, they were worth two point eight million and falling. He had over two million in mortgage debt against assets now worth less than three million, and several properties were generating negative cash flow as tenants lost jobs and vacancies increased.

Eric faced a crisis that destroyed thousands of real estate investors during this period. If he sold properties to reduce debt, he would crystallize massive losses because sale prices were below his purchase prices. If he held properties hoping for recovery, he risked foreclosure on properties where negative cash flow exceeded his capacity to subsidize them. If he defaulted strategically, he would destroy his credit and potentially face deficiency judgments for the difference between property values and mortgage balances. Every option looked catastrophic.

What Eric did not face was forced liquidation of his stock portfolio. During the same period when his real estate holdings were collapsing, his investment accounts had also declined from one point two million to seven hundred thousand—a painful but less severe drawdown than the real estate experienced. Yet Eric never considered selling these investments because they were not collateralized. No lender could force him to sell stocks at depressed prices to satisfy margin calls or mortgage obligations. The investments simply sat in his accounts, declining in value but secure from forced liquidation, positioned to benefit from the eventual recovery.

This experience taught Eric a lesson that would transform his approach to leverage for the remainder of his career. Traditional debt against specific assets—mortgages against properties, margin loans against stock portfolios—creates forced liquidation risk during downturns because lenders can demand repayment or seize collateral when values decline below loan-to-value thresholds. But certain types of leverage separate the borrowed money from specific assets, allowing you to use debt strategically while avoiding forced liquidation risk. After recovering from the 2008 crisis, Eric restructured his entire approach to leverage using securities-based lines of credit that would allow him to borrow against his investment portfolio for real estate purchases without creating the direct collateralization that had nearly destroyed him.

By 2020, Eric had rebuilt his portfolio to include twenty rental properties worth over eight million dollars and investment accounts worth three million dollars. But the structure was completely different. Rather than using traditional mortgages requiring twenty percent down payments that tied each loan to specific properties, Eric used a securities-based line of credit against his investment portfolio to fund property down payments. The SBLOC allowed him to borrow up to fifty percent of his portfolio value at interest rates of three to four percent with no required monthly payments—interest could be added to the loan balance or paid monthly at his discretion. This structure meant that when the COVID-19 pandemic caused brief market disruption in March 2020, he faced no margin calls despite his portfolio declining by thirty percent because SBLOCs do not have the same forced liquidation triggers that margin loans have.

This chapter examines the advanced financial tools and entity structures that the one percent use to optimize their wealth-building operations while minimizing taxes, protecting assets, and maintaining flexibility. These are not beginner tools. They are sophisticated instruments that provide enormous advantages when used correctly but that can destroy wealth when misunderstood or misapplied. The decision about whether you need these tools depends on your specific circumstances, the complexity of your financial situation, and your ability to understand both their benefits and their risks.

The securities-based line of credit represents one of the most powerful and underutilized tools available to people with substantial investment portfolios. An SBLOC is a revolving line of credit collateralized by your investment account holdings, similar to a home equity line of credit but secured by stocks and bonds rather than by real estate. Major brokerages including Fidelity, Schwab, Morgan Stanley, and Merrill Lynch offer these products to clients with portfolios typically exceeding one hundred thousand dollars, though some institutions require higher minimums.

The mechanics are straightforward. You pledge your investment portfolio as collateral. The lender extends a line of credit typically ranging from fifty to seventy percent of your portfolio value depending on what you own—higher for stable assets like large-cap stocks and investment-grade bonds, lower for volatile assets like smallcap stocks or sector-specific holdings. You can draw on this line at any time by writing checks or making electronic transfers. Interest accrues only on amounts actually borrowed, not on the total available line. Interest rates are typically one to two percentage points above short-term rates, currently ranging from seven to nine percent in 2024 though these rates fluctuate with Federal Reserve policy.

The critical difference between SBLOCs and margin loans is that SBLOCs typically do not have maintenance requirements that trigger forced liquidation when portfolio values decline. Margin loans require maintaining specific loan-to-value ratios, and when your portfolio value drops below required thresholds, you receive margin calls requiring you to either deposit additional cash or sell securities to bring the loan-to-value ratio back to acceptable levels. These forced sales during market declines crystallize losses at the worst possible times. SBLOCs generally allow you to exceed standard loan-to-value ratios temporarily during market declines without forced liquidation, though the lender reserves the right to demand repayment if ratios become extreme.

The strategic uses of SBLOCs include funding real estate down payments without liquidating investments, covering large purchases without selling appreciated securities that would trigger capital gains taxes, providing emergency liquidity during income interruptions without disrupting investment strategy, and creating short-term bridge financing for business opportunities. Someone with one million dollar portfolio can access five hundred thousand through SBLOC, use that money to purchase rental property with traditional mortgage, and generate rental income that pays both the mortgage and the SBLOC interest while the original million dollar portfolio continues growing. This leverage allows deploying capital into multiple asset classes simultaneously rather than choosing between them.

The risks of SBLOCs center on interest cost and potential forced liquidation during extreme market declines. Borrowing five hundred thousand at eight percent costs forty thousand annually in interest. If the investments and rental properties funded with this borrowed money do not generate returns exceeding eight percent, you are destroying wealth by paying more for money than you earn on it. During severe market declines like 2008, even SBLOCs without formal maintenance requirements might result in lenders demanding repayment if your loan-to-value ratio exceeds seventy-five to eighty percent. The borrower who uses SBLOC to maximize leverage by borrowing the full available amount faces potential forced liquidation if markets decline thirty to forty percent.

The conservative use of SBLOCs involves borrowing well below maximum available amounts—perhaps using only twenty-five percent of portfolio value even though fifty percent is available—and ensuring that the assets purchased with borrowed money generate income exceeding interest costs. Someone with two million dollar portfolio might borrow two hundred fifty thousand against a five hundred thousand available line, using that money to purchase rental property generating seven percent cash-on-cash return. The fourteen thousand annual rental income covers the twenty thousand SBLOC interest with six thousand deficit that comes from other income sources. Meanwhile the two million portfolio continues generating ten percent returns adding two hundred thousand annually. The leverage allows deploying capital into real estate without liquidating stocks, and the modest borrowing ratio provides safety margin against market declines.

The tax optimization through SBLOCs occurs because borrowed money is not taxable income and because interest on money borrowed for investment purposes is often tax-deductible. Someone who wants to access two hundred thousand for real estate purchase faces choice between selling two hundred thousand in stocks or borrowing two hundred thousand against stocks. Selling triggers capital gains taxes of thirty thousand assuming fifteen percent long-term capital gains rate on one hundred thousand of gains. Borrowing triggers no taxes and generates sixteen thousand in annual interest at eight percent that may be tax-deductible if the borrowed money is used for investment purposes. The borrower pays sixteen thousand annually in interest but avoids thirty thousand in immediate taxes and maintains exposure to the two hundred thousand in stocks that continue growing.

The home equity line of credit operates similarly to SBLOCs but uses your primary residence or rental properties as collateral rather than investment portfolios. HELOCs allow borrowing typically up to eighty-five percent of home value minus any existing mortgage balance. Someone with home worth five hundred thousand and mortgage of two hundred thousand has three hundred thousand in equity. An HELOC might allow borrowing eighty-five percent of home value minus the mortgage, or two hundred twenty-five thousand. Interest rates on HELOCs are typically lower than SBLOC rates, currently ranging from eight to ten percent as of 2024, because real estate is considered more stable collateral than stock portfolios.

The strategic advantages of HELOCs include lower interest rates than unsecured debt, large borrowing capacity for major expenses, flexibility to draw funds only when needed and repay without penalties, and potential tax deductibility if funds are used for home improvements. Someone planning major renovation might establish HELOC before beginning work, draw funds as needed for contractor payments, and then repay over time rather than taking out fixed home equity loan with immediate full disbursement. The HELOC allows paying interest only on amounts actually used and allows repaying early if income allows without prepayment penalties.

The risks of HELOCs involve using your home as collateral for purchases that may not justify the risk. Someone who uses HELOC to fund vacations or consumption is borrowing against their home to finance lifestyle, creating situation where they might lose their home if they cannot repay consumption-based debt. Someone who uses HELOC to fund rental property purchase is using leverage strategically, borrowing against one asset to acquire another incomeproducing asset. The interest rate on the HELOC becomes merely the cost of capital for the rental property investment, and if the investment fails, the HELOC still must be repaid but at least the borrowed money was deployed attempting to generate returns.

The variable interest rate on most HELOCs creates risk during rising rate environments. Someone who borrows one hundred thousand on HELOC at six percent pays six thousand annually in interest. If rates rise to ten percent, the interest cost increases to ten thousand annually—a meaningful increase that might strain cash flow. The one percent who use HELOCs either maintain very conservative borrowing ratios that allow absorbing rate increases or they have sufficient income that rate fluctuations do not materially affect their budgets. They never borrow the maximum available on HELOCs and then hope that rates remain low, because this gamble often ends poorly.

The strategic comparison between SBLOCs and HELOCs depends on what assets you own and what you intend to use borrowed money for. Someone with large investment portfolio and modest home equity can access more capital through SBLOC. Someone with substantial home equity and modest investment portfolio can access more through HELOC. Someone with both might use HELOC for long-term borrowing at lower rates and SBLOC for short-term liquidity that will be repaid quickly. The one percent maintain access to both types of credit lines even when not using them because having established credit available provides optionality during opportunities that require quick capital deployment.

The business entity structures determine how you are taxed, what liability protection you have, what administrative requirements you face, and what flexibility you have in managing ownership and succession. The choice of entity structure should be made based on consultation with accountants and attorneys who understand your specific situation rather than based on generic advice that might not apply to your circumstances. However, understanding the basic characteristics of each entity type allows you to have informed conversations with professionals and to understand what they recommend and why.

The sole proprietorship is the simplest business structure, created automatically when you begin business activities without forming any legal entity. You report business income and expenses on Schedule C attached to your personal tax return. You pay self-employment taxes on net profit covering both the employer and employee portions of Social Security and Medicare taxes, currently totaling 15.3 percent of net earnings. You have no liability protection—creditors can pursue your personal assets for business debts and vice versa. You need no separate tax identification number and can use your Social Security number for business purposes. You maintain no corporate formalities, no separate bank accounts are legally required though they are advisable, and the business legally dies when you die.

The sole proprietorship works adequately for very small service businesses with minimal liability risk and modest profits. Someone providing freelance writing services earning twenty thousand annually faces little liability risk from their work and gains minimal benefit from more complex entity structures. The administrative simplicity and tax simplicity of sole proprietorship outweigh the modest benefits that formal entities would provide. However, someone earning one hundred thousand annually through their business should almost certainly form an entity for liability protection and potential tax benefits, making sole proprietorship suboptimal despite its simplicity.

The single-member limited liability company provides liability protection while maintaining tax simplicity similar to sole proprietorship. You file articles of organization with your state, typically costing one hundred to five hundred dollars depending on jurisdiction. The LLC is disregarded for federal tax purposes, meaning you still report income and expenses on Schedule C just as sole proprietors do. You still pay self-employment taxes on net profit. But you now have liability protection separating business debts from personal assets, assuming you maintain proper separation between business and personal finances and you do not commit fraud or gross negligence that pierces the corporate veil.

The administrative requirements for single-member LLCs are modest. You should obtain an Employer Identification Number from the IRS even though you have no employees, because using an EIN rather than your Social Security number for business purposes provides identity theft protection. You should maintain separate bank account for business finances even though commingling funds does not create tax problems for single-member LLCs. Some states require annual reports and fees ranging from fifty to eight hundred dollars annually. You should maintain basic records documenting that the LLC is separate entity even though you are the sole owner.

The multi-member LLC provides liability protection and partnership tax treatment when businesses have multiple owners. The LLC files Form 1065 partnership return reporting income and expenses, then issues K-1 forms to each member reporting their share of income, deductions, and credits. Members pay self-employment taxes on their distributive share of profits if they actively participate in the business. Members pay income taxes on their shares of profits regardless of whether cash distributions are actually made. The LLC provides flexibility in allocating profits and losses among members differently than ownership percentages if desired and documented properly in operating agreement.

The multi-member LLC requires more sophistication than single-member LLC because multiple owners create potential conflicts about distributions, management, admission of new members, and exit strategies. The operating agreement should address all these issues explicitly before conflicts arise rather than trying to resolve them during disagreements. The one percent forming multi-member LLCs work with attorneys to draft comprehensive operating agreements covering every foreseeable issue rather than using generic online templates that leave critical issues unaddressed.

The S corporation election allows certain corporations and LLCs to avoid double taxation while potentially reducing self-employment taxes. An S corporation files Form 1120-S reporting income and expenses, then issues K-1 forms to shareholders reporting their shares. Shareholders pay income taxes on their shares of profits regardless of whether distributions occur. The critical difference from LLCs is that S corporation shareholders who work in the business must pay themselves reasonable salaries subject to payroll taxes, but profits distributed beyond those salaries face only income taxes without additional self-employment taxes.

The self-employment tax savings drive most S corporation elections. Someone earning one hundred thousand through single-member LLC pays self-employment taxes of 15.3 percent on the full one hundred thousand, totaling fifteen thousand three hundred. The same person operating as S corporation pays themselves salary of sixty thousand subject to payroll taxes of nine thousand one hundred eighty and distributes remaining forty thousand as profits subject to no additional payroll taxes. The savings is approximately six thousand annually. As income increases, the savings increase proportionally until Social Security wage base is exceeded, after which only Medicare taxes continue.

The IRS scrutinizes S corporation salary levels because paying unreasonably low salaries to avoid payroll taxes is tax evasion. The determination of reasonable salary involves examining what comparable employees in similar roles at similar companies earn. Someone providing professional services earning three hundred thousand annually cannot pay themselves forty thousand salary and distribute two hundred sixty thousand as profits because forty thousand does not reflect reasonable compensation for generating three hundred thousand in revenue. They might pay themselves one hundred fifty thousand salary and distribute one hundred fifty thousand as profits, creating meaningful payroll tax savings while maintaining defensible salary level.

The administrative requirements for S corporations exceed simpler entity structures. You must run payroll for yourself, filing quarterly payroll tax returns and annual W-2 forms. You must file separate corporate tax return annually. You must maintain corporate formalities including documented meetings and written consents for major decisions. You must ensure you do not violate S corporation restrictions including having more than one hundred shareholders, having only individuals or certain trusts as shareholders, and having only one class of stock. These requirements justify the complexity only when payroll tax savings exceed the additional accounting costs of operating as S corporation.

The C corporation represents standard corporate structure taxed separately from owners. The corporation pays corporate income tax on profits at 21 percent federal rate. Shareholders pay personal income tax on dividends distributed from after-tax profits, creating double taxation that makes C corporations tax-inefficient for most small businesses. The advantages include unlimited number of shareholders, ability to have different classes of stock with different rights, and ability to retain earnings in the corporation at 21 percent tax rate rather than passing income through to owners who might face higher personal rates.

C corporations make sense primarily for businesses seeking venture capital investment or planning initial public offerings, because investors prefer C corporation structure and because C corporation stock qualifies for various tax incentives for early-stage company investors. Someone building software company hoping to raise millions from venture capital should form as C corporation from inception because converting from LLC to C corporation later triggers potential tax complications. Someone building service business they will operate personally should almost never use C corporation because the double taxation destroys value without providing offsetting benefits.

The employer identification number serves as tax identification number for business entities, similar to how Social Security numbers identify individuals. You obtain EINs free from IRS website in minutes by completing simple online application. You need EIN to open business bank accounts, to file business tax returns for entities other than sole proprietorships, to hire employees, and to establish business credit separate from personal credit. The one percent obtain EINs immediately upon forming any business entity and use EINs rather than Social Security numbers for all business purposes to compartmentalize business and personal identification.

The business bank account separates business finances from personal finances, providing clean records for tax reporting, providing liability protection through demonstrating that business is separate entity, and simplifying accounting by consolidating all business transactions in designated accounts. Someone operating as sole proprietorship might legally use personal checking account for business, but doing so creates accounting nightmares at tax time when trying to identify which transactions were business versus personal. The one percent open business checking accounts immediately upon starting businesses regardless of entity structure because the separation provides clarity worth far more than the modest account fees.

The business credit cards serve similar function to business checking accounts while providing rewards, short-term financing flexibility, and further documentation of business expense separation. Many business credit cards offer rewards programs generating two to five percent cash back on business spending. Someone spending fifty thousand annually on business expenses generates one thousand to twenty-five hundred in rewards. Business cards also begin establishing business credit history separate from personal credit, eventually allowing business to qualify for financing based on business financials rather than on personal guarantees.

The one percent apply for business credit cards after establishing business bank accounts and after generating initial business revenue, typically within first few months of operations. They use business cards exclusively for business expenses, paying balances in full monthly to avoid interest charges while maximizing rewards. They never use business cards for personal expenses because commingling funds undermines the entity separation that provides liability protection and because it complicates accounting and tax reporting.

The integration of these tools within comprehensive wealthbuilding strategy requires understanding how they complement each other rather than viewing them as isolated tactics. Someone building wealth might operate side business as single-member LLC taxed as S corporation once profits justify payroll tax optimization. They might maintain HELOC against primary residence and SBLOC against investment portfolio, providing access to substantial capital without having drawn any funds. They might use business credit cards for all business expenses, generating rewards while maintaining clean separation between business and personal finances. They might use SBLOC to fund rental property down payments, maintaining stock portfolio exposure while deploying leverage into real estate. They might establish C corporation for software startup seeking venture funding while maintaining separate LLC for consulting services.

This coordination of multiple entity structures and credit facilities creates financial architecture that optimizes taxes, protects assets through liability separation, provides liquidity through credit access, and maintains flexibility through choosing optimal structure for each purpose rather than forcing everything through single entity or single financing source. The person with consulting income, rental properties, investment portfolio, and startup equity faces completely different needs across these domains and should structure each optimally rather than using one-size-fits-all approach that suboptimizes everything.

The mistakes that destroy value through misuse of these tools are predictable. The first mistake is forming entities unnecessarily before business generates meaningful revenue, wasting money on formation costs and annual fees for entities providing no actual benefit. The second mistake is electing S corporation status prematurely before profits justify payroll tax savings that exceed additional administrative costs. The third mistake is borrowing maximum available amounts through SBLOCs or HELOCs without ensuring borrowed money generates returns exceeding interest costs. The fourth mistake is forming entities or borrowing money without understanding the obligations created, then facing problems when unable to meet those obligations. The fifth mistake is attempting to use entity structures for asset protection without actually maintaining separation between business and personal finances, resulting in pierced corporate veils that eliminate protection entirely.

The one percent avoid these mistakes through working with competent advisors who help them understand options and implications before making decisions. They form entities only when clear benefits justify costs. They elect S corporation status only when payroll tax savings are substantial and when they can handle administrative requirements. They borrow through SBLOCs and HELOCs conservatively, maintaining safety margins against market declines and ensuring borrowed money is deployed profitably. They maintain proper entity formalities and financial separation that makes liability protection effective rather than illusory. They understand that sophisticated tools provide advantages only when used correctly and that misuse creates worse outcomes than simple approaches would have produced.

The timeline for implementing these structures follows business growth and wealth accumulation rather than preceding them. Someone starting side business begins as sole proprietor or singlemember LLC, keeping structure simple while validating that business generates revenue. Once annual profits exceed fifty thousand to seventy-five thousand, they evaluate S corporation election based on payroll tax savings versus administrative costs. Once investment portfolio reaches two hundred fifty thousand to five hundred thousand, they explore SBLOC access as potential liquidity source. Once home equity reaches one hundred thousand or more, they consider establishing HELOC as emergency reserve. The structures grow in sophistication as wealth and business complexity justify them rather than implementing sophisticated structures prematurely when simple approaches suffice.

Eric's experience during the 2008 financial crisis taught him that leverage structure matters as much as leverage amount. Traditional mortgages that tied each loan directly to specific properties created forced liquidation risk that nearly destroyed him. Securities-based lines of credit that separated borrowed money from specific portfolio holdings eliminated forced liquidation risk while still allowing leverage use. His post-crisis portfolio structure demonstrates sophisticated use of these tools—maintaining substantial investment portfolio that provides SBLOC capacity, using SBLOC borrowing to fund rental property down payments that allow maintaining stock exposure, keeping SBLOC utilization well below maximum to provide safety margin, and generating rental income that covers both property mortgages and SBLOC interest while portfolios continue growing.

This sophisticated approach requires more knowledge and more active management than simply buying properties with traditional mortgages and buying stocks in cash accounts. The question is whether the benefits justify the complexity for your situation. Someone with one hundred thousand total wealth gains nothing from these tools because they lack the asset base to support meaningful credit lines and because their situation is simple enough that entity structures provide minimal benefit. Someone with two million in combined investment portfolio and rental property equity could potentially benefit substantially from SBLOCs that allow deploying capital simultaneously across multiple asset classes and from entity structures that optimize taxes and protect assets. The decision about whether to implement these tools should be based on your specific numbers rather than on whether they sound sophisticated or whether other people use them.

The consultation with tax advisors and attorneys before implementing any of these structures is essential because individual circumstances determine optimal approaches and because mistakes in formation or operation can be expensive to correct. The one percent budget thousands of dollars for proper professional guidance when forming entities, when making S corporation elections, when establishing credit facilities, and when coordinating multiple structures across their financial operations. They understand that professional fees of five to ten thousand dollars are bargains when they prevent mistakes costing fifty to one hundred thousand or when they optimize structures generating ten to twenty thousand in annual tax savings.

The frameworks have been provided. The tools have been explained. The benefits and risks are clear. Whether you need these sophisticated structures depends on your specific situation—the complexity of your income sources, the size of your investment portfolio and real estate holdings, your tolerance for administrative complexity, and your commitment to using tools correctly rather than merely using them because they seem advanced. The one percent implement these structures when clear benefits justify costs and complexity. The ninety-nine percent either never learn these tools exist or they implement them prematurely or incorrectly, wasting money on complexity that provides no benefit. You now understand the tools.

CHAPTER 33:
ESTATE PLANNING AND TRUSTS—ENSURING YOUR LEGACY SURVIVES YOU

In 2016, the musician Prince died suddenly at age fifty-seven from an accidental fentanyl overdose. He left behind an estate estimated at three hundred million dollars and no will, no trust, no documented estate plan of any kind. Within weeks of his death, dozens of people claiming to be heirs emerged seeking portions of his estate. Distant relatives he had never met filed claims. People claiming to be secret children produced questionable documentation. The legal battles consumed years and tens of millions in legal fees and costs. The probate proceedings were entirely public, exposing every detail of his finances and family disputes to media scrutiny. The estate paid approximately one hundred million dollars in federal and state taxes that could have been reduced or deferred through proper planning. Six years after his death, the estate was still not fully settled, with some disputes continuing through appeals.

Prince was a sophisticated businessman who had famously fought record labels over control of his music and who had meticulously managed his catalog and brand. Yet he apparently believed he would live longer or that estate planning was not urgent or that somehow his affairs would resolve themselves smoothly despite his complicated financial situation and lack of clear heirs. His failure to spend perhaps fifty to one hundred thousand dollars on proper estate planning during his life cost his estate over one hundred fifty million in taxes, legal fees, and reduced asset values, while creating years of public conflict that damaged his legacy.

Three years earlier, in 2013, James Gandolfini died suddenly at age fifty-one from a heart attack while on vacation in Italy. Gandolfini was best known for playing Tony Soprano in the acclaimed HBO series. He left an estate estimated at seventy million dollars and a will that distributed his assets according to his wishes. However, the structure he chose—leaving most assets through his will rather than through trusts—created tax consequences that estate planning attorneys later estimated cost his heirs twenty to thirty million in unnecessary taxes. His estate paid approximately thirty million in estate taxes when proper planning could have reduced that burden by half or more. The will was public record, exposing all details of his finances and bequests. The probate process took over a year to complete.

Gandolfini had done more than Prince by at least creating a will documenting his wishes. But he had not worked with estate planning specialists who could have structured his assets to minimize taxes and avoid probate. His executors later stated that he had worked primarily with his business manager and accountant who prepared a will without implementing the trust structures and other planning strategies that would have preserved substantially more wealth for his family.

In contrast, when Paul Walker died suddenly in 2013 at age forty from a car accident, his estate was settled quickly and privately. Walker had worked with estate planning attorneys to establish revocable living trust that held his assets and that distributed them according to detailed instructions upon his death. His fifteen-year-old daughter was the primary beneficiary, with distributions controlled through the trust until she reached various ages. Because the assets were held in trust rather than in his personal name, they avoided probate entirely. No public record exists of his asset values or distributions. The trust was administered privately by his designated trustee. His daughter received her inheritance according to the structured timeline he had established without court involvement, public exposure, or family disputes.

These three examples spanning three years demonstrate that estate planning is not about wealth level—Prince, Gandolfini, and Walker had comparable estates. It is about whether you take time during life to document your wishes, structure your assets appropriately, and ensure smooth transfer to intended beneficiaries after death. Prince's complete lack of planning created disaster. Gandolfini's partial planning through wills alone cost tens of millions unnecessarily. Walker's proper planning through trusts achieved the smooth private transfer that most people want but that few actually accomplish.

This chapter examines how to ensure that wealth you spend decades building actually reaches your intended beneficiaries rather than being consumed by taxes, legal fees, and family conflicts. Estate planning is not only for the wealthy—anyone with minor children, anyone who owns assets, anyone who wants to control who receives their possessions after death needs basic estate planning. The specific strategies vary based on estate size, but the fundamental need applies universally. The one percent implement comprehensive estate planning as soon as they have significant assets or young children. The ninety-nine percent avoid estate planning because thinking about death is uncomfortable, because they assume they have time to address it later, or because they mistakenly believe estate planning is only for multimillionaires.

The probate process represents what happens when people die without proper planning. Probate is the court-supervised process of validating wills, inventorying assets, paying debts and taxes, and distributing remaining assets to heirs. The process takes months to years depending on estate complexity and state procedures. It costs thousands to tens of thousands in court fees and legal expenses. It is entirely public record—anyone can review court filings to see what assets you owned, what debts you owed, who inherited what, and what family disputes arose. The court controls timing of distributions regardless of beneficiaries' needs. Executors cannot act without court approval for major decisions. The process consumes time and money that proper planning eliminates entirely.

The probate avoidance through proper titling and beneficiary designations costs nothing and requires minimal time but provides enormous benefits. Assets owned jointly with rights of survivorship pass directly to surviving owner without probate. Bank accounts with payable-on-death designations pass directly to named beneficiaries. Investment accounts with transfer-on-death designations similarly avoid probate. Life insurance policies and retirement accounts pass directly to named beneficiaries. Real estate owned by trusts or as joint tenants with rights of survivorship avoids probate. Someone who owns three hundred thousand in retirement accounts, two hundred thousand in life insurance, three hundred thousand in home equity, and one hundred thousand in other assets can structure everything to avoid probate through proper titling and beneficiary designations without creating a single trust.

The will represents the most basic estate planning document, stating who should receive your assets after death, who should serve as executor managing your estate, and who should serve as guardian for minor children if both parents die. Wills are critical for anyone with minor children because guardianship designations can only be made through wills, not through any other document. Someone with young children who dies without a will leaves the court to decide who raises those children based on state law rather than on parents' wishes. This alone justifies creating wills immediately upon having children regardless of asset levels.

The limitations of wills are that they only control assets titled in your personal name without beneficiary designations, and they require probate to implement. The will itself is not self-executing—executors must file the will with probate court, which validates it, supervises asset distribution, and ultimately closes the estate once everything is distributed. This process is public, expensive, and slow. The one percent use wills primarily for guardianship designations and as backup documents catching any assets not properly titled or designated elsewhere, while structuring most assets to avoid probate through trusts and beneficiary designations.

The revocable living trust serves as will substitute that avoids probate while maintaining complete control during your lifetime. You create the trust document naming yourself as trustee, you transfer assets into the trust by retitling them in the trust's name, and you continue managing those assets exactly as before because you control the trust as trustee. Upon your death, your designated successor trustee assumes control and distributes assets according to your instructions without court involvement. The trust document remains private—no public filing occurs and no one except the trustee and beneficiaries ever sees the terms. The successor trustee can act immediately rather than waiting for court approval. The process is faster, cheaper, and private compared to probate.

The revocable living trust creation requires working with estate planning attorney to draft trust document, then systematically retitling assets into the trust. The house becomes titled to "John Smith, Trustee of the John Smith Revocable Living Trust dated January 1, 2024" rather than simply to "John Smith." Bank accounts, investment accounts, and business interests are similarly retitled. Life insurance and retirement accounts typically should not be retitled to the trust during your lifetime but should name the trust as beneficiary to maintain tax advantages those accounts provide. The process takes several hours of work retitling assets and costs one thousand to three thousand in legal fees for basic trust depending on estate complexity and location.

The revocable nature means you maintain complete control—you can amend or revoke the trust at any time, add or remove assets, change beneficiaries or distributions, and generally modify any provision. The trust provides no asset protection during your lifetime because creditors can reach assets you control. The trust provides no tax benefits because the IRS treats revocable trusts as transparent—you report income and gains as if you owned the assets directly. The sole benefit is probate avoidance, but this benefit alone justifies the modest cost for anyone with significant assets.

The one percent establish revocable living trusts typically once their estates exceed five hundred thousand including home equity, life insurance, and retirement accounts, or earlier if they have complex situations like multiple properties, business interests, or children from multiple marriages. They retitle assets systematically into the trust, update beneficiary designations appropriately, and amend the trust as circumstances change. They review and update trusts every three to five years or after major life changes like marriages, divorces, births, or moves to different states where laws might differ.

The pour-over will serves as companion to revocable living trusts, catching any assets not properly titled to the trust at death and "pouring" them into the trust to be distributed according to trust terms. Someone who establishes trust but forgets to retitle one bank account will have that account pass through probate via the pour-over will, but it will ultimately be distributed according to trust provisions rather than according to separate will provisions. This failsafe prevents assets from being distributed contrary to intentions due to oversight in retitling. Every person with revocable living trust should also have pour-over will as backup.

The irrevocable trust surrenders control in exchange for asset protection and tax benefits that revocable trusts cannot provide. Once you transfer assets to irrevocable trust, you cannot serve as trustee, you cannot amend or revoke the trust, and you cannot reclaim the assets. An independent trustee controls the assets according to trust terms you established at creation. This loss of control is precisely what provides benefits—because you no longer own or control the assets, they are protected from your creditors, they are removed from your taxable estate for estate tax purposes, and they can achieve various tax benefits depending on trust structure.

The irrevocable life insurance trust represents the most common type of irrevocable trust, removing life insurance death benefits from your taxable estate. Life insurance owned by the insured is included in taxable estate—someone with two million in other assets who owns five million life insurance policy has seven million taxable estate. If they transfer the policy to ILIT owned by and payable to the trust, the five million is excluded from their estate. For estates exceeding estate tax exemption amounts, this creates estate tax savings of forty percent of the policy value—two million in tax savings on a five million policy. The trust receives the death benefit and distributes it to beneficiaries according to trust terms, often providing structured distributions over time rather than lump sums.

The ILIT creation requires working with estate planning attorney and insurance agent to coordinate policy ownership transfer or new policy acquisition by the trust. You cannot serve as trustee—typically spouse, adult children, or professional trustee serves. You can fund premiums through annual gifts to the trust up to gift tax annual exclusion amounts, currently eighteen thousand per beneficiary per year. The trust is irrevocable—once established you cannot reclaim the policy or change fundamental terms, though some flexibility for trust modifications might be built into modern trust drafting. The cost is two thousand to five thousand in legal fees plus ongoing trustee fees if professional trustee is used.

The one percent with estates approaching or exceeding estate tax exemption levels establish ILITs for large life insurance policies to avoid forty percent estate tax on death benefits. They understand that paying three thousand in legal fees to establish trust that saves two million in eventual estate taxes represents one of the highest return investments possible. They structure trusts carefully to maintain access to cash value in certain policies while removing death benefits from estates. They coordinate with insurance advisors and estate attorneys to ensure policies are structured optimally for estate planning purposes.

The charitable remainder trust provides income during lifetime while ultimately benefiting charities, creating current tax deductions while deferring capital gains taxes on appreciated assets. You transfer appreciated assets—typically stock with large gains or appreciated real estate—to CRT. The trust sells the assets tax-free because it is tax-exempt entity. The trust pays you income for life or for term of years based on percentage of trust value, typically five to eight percent annually. At your death or at end of term, remaining trust assets pass to designated charities. You receive immediate tax deduction for present value of charity's eventual remainder interest, typically twenty-five to forty percent of assets contributed.

The CRT is particularly valuable for someone with highly appreciated assets generating little current income who wants to diversify without paying capital gains taxes. Someone with stock purchased for one hundred thousand now worth one million faces two hundred thousand in federal and state capital gains taxes if sold. Transferring to CRT allows the trust to sell tax-free and reinvest in diversified portfolio. The donor receives immediate tax deduction of perhaps three hundred thousand depending on age and payout rate, saving one hundred thousand or more in taxes in contribution year. The donor receives annual income of five to eight percent on one million, or fifty to eighty thousand annually. At death, perhaps five hundred thousand to seven hundred thousand remains for charity depending on how long income was received. The donor has converted non-income-producing concentrated stock into diversified income-producing portfolio while generating large tax deduction.

The qualified personal residence trust removes home value from taxable estate while allowing continued residence for specified term. You transfer your home to QPRT while retaining right to live there rent-free for term of years, typically ten to twenty years. At end of term, the home passes to trust beneficiaries, usually children. If you die during the term, the home returns to your estate as if the trust never existed. If you survive the term, the home's value is removed from your estate at the value it had when transferred to trust, which is typically far below current value because the transfer is discounted for your retained interest.

The QPRT is valuable for someone with large estate and expensive home who expects to live beyond the trust term. Someone with three million dollar home who expects to live fifteen more years might transfer home to fifteen-year QPRT. The discounted gift value might be one million five hundred thousand, using gift tax exemption space but removing three million from eventual estate. If the home appreciates to four million by end of term, that four million passes to children outside the estate despite only one million five hundred thousand gift tax impact. The parent can continue living in the home after the term expires by paying fair market rent to children who now own it, which has the added benefit of transferring additional wealth through rent payments.

The grantor retained annuity trust provides similar benefits to QPRTs but for financial assets rather than residences. You transfer assets to GRAT while retaining right to receive fixed annuity payments for term of years. At end of term, remaining assets pass to beneficiaries. If the assets appreciate faster than the IRS assumed interest rate, the excess growth passes to beneficiaries tax-free. If you die during term, assets return to estate. GRATs are used by wealthy individuals to transfer appreciating assets to next generation with minimal gift tax impact.

The GRAT is particularly effective during low interest rate environments when IRS assumed rates are low, making it easier for assets to outperform those rates. Someone might transfer one million to two-year GRAT structured to return approximately one million plus IRS assumed interest rate of three percent through annuity payments. If the assets actually appreciate at ten percent, approximately one hundred forty thousand passes to beneficiaries tax-free at end of term. The strategy works best with volatile assets likely to appreciate substantially and can be structured with multiple sequential GRATs to maximize odds that some perform well.

The special needs trust provides for disabled beneficiaries without disqualifying them from government benefits like Medicaid and Supplemental Security Income that have strict asset limits. Someone with disabled child who will require lifelong care faces dilemma— leaving assets directly to the child disqualifies them from government benefits until assets are spent down, but leaving nothing denies them quality-of-life improvements government benefits do not cover. The special needs trust holds assets for child's benefit, paying for expenses beyond what government programs cover like therapy, equipment, travel, entertainment, while preserving eligibility for government benefits that cover basic needs.

The special needs trust drafting requires significant expertise because strict rules govern what trust can pay for without affecting benefit eligibility. Paying for housing or food from trust can reduce government benefits dollar-for-dollar. Paying for supplemental items does not affect benefits. The trust must include specific language required by benefit programs. The trustee must understand rules governing distributions. Someone with disabled child should work with attorney specializing in special needs planning rather than using general estate planning attorney who might not understand the complexities.

The dynasty trust extends beyond one generation to benefit multiple generations while avoiding estate taxes at each generational transfer. Assets are transferred to trust structured to continue for as long as state law allows, sometimes perpetually in states that have abolished the rule against perpetuities. The assets grow inside the trust, with income and principal distributed to current generation beneficiaries as needed while preserving principal for future generations. Because assets are held in trust rather than owned outright by beneficiaries, they are excluded from beneficiaries' taxable estates, avoiding estate tax at each generational death.

The dynasty trust makes sense for extremely wealthy families wanting to provide for multiple generations while minimizing estate taxes paid across those generations. Someone transferring twenty million to dynasty trust pays gift or estate tax once on that transfer. The assets might grow to one hundred million over fifty years and pass through three generations of beneficiaries, all without additional estate tax because the assets remain in trust rather than becoming owned by each generation. The trade-off is complexity—the trust requires sophisticated trustee and administrator, and family members receive benefits from trust rather than owning assets outright.

The spendthrift provisions included in most trusts protect trust assets from beneficiaries' creditors and from beneficiaries' own poor judgment. The provisions prohibit beneficiaries from assigning their trust interests to third parties, prevent creditors from reaching assets before they are distributed to beneficiaries, and allow trustees to withhold distributions if beneficiaries would use them irresponsibly. Someone leaving assets to child with substance abuse issues or with poor financial management might include spendthrift provisions allowing trustee to make distributions for specific needs like housing, education, and medical care while prohibiting lump sum distributions that might be squandered.

The health and education exclusions from gift taxes allow unlimited transfers for medical and educational expenses paid directly to providers without consuming gift tax exemption. Someone wanting to help grandchildren with college costs can pay tuition directly to universities without gift tax implications regardless of amount. Someone wanting to help aging parents with medical costs can pay medical bills directly to hospitals and doctors without gift tax concerns. The payments must be made directly to the institutions rather than given to the beneficiary who then pays, and they must be for qualifying medical or educational expenses rather than for living costs.

The one percent use these exclusions systematically to transfer wealth while preserving gift tax exemption for other transfers. They pay grandchildren's private school tuition directly to schools, pay college tuition directly to universities, and pay medical expenses directly to providers, potentially transferring hundreds of thousands over years without gift tax impact. They combine these unlimited exclusions with annual exclusion gifts of eighteen thousand per recipient per year, systematically transferring wealth during lifetime rather than waiting for death when estate taxes might apply.

The annual exclusion gifts allow transferring eighteen thousand per recipient per year (as of 2024, adjusted periodically for inflation) without gift tax reporting or exemption usage. Married couples can combine their exclusions to give thirty-six thousand per recipient. Someone with three children and six grandchildren can give one hundred sixty-two thousand annually with spouse, or almost one million six hundred twenty thousand over ten years, removing that amount from eventual taxable estate while retaining use of gift tax lifetime exemption for larger transfers.

The unified estate and gift tax exemption currently stands at thirteen point six one million per person (as of 2024, adjusted annually for inflation), scheduled to sunset to approximately seven million in 2026 unless Congress extends it. Amounts transferred during life through taxable gifts or at death through estate transfers exceeding this exemption face forty percent federal tax. The one percent with estates approaching exemption levels engage in systematic lifetime gifting to children and grandchildren, reducing their eventual taxable estates. They make annual exclusion gifts, pay medical and education expenses directly, establish trusts, and generally transfer wealth during life when they can see it benefit recipients rather than waiting for death when estate taxes might consume forty percent.

The estate tax planning for extremely large estates involves sophisticated strategies including intentionally defective grantor trusts, family limited partnerships with valuation discounts, installment sales to trusts, and other advanced techniques requiring significant legal expertise. Someone with fifty million estate faces potential twenty million estate tax bill without planning. Sophisticated planning might reduce that to five to ten million through combination of strategies. The planning requires working with specialized estate planning attorneys and might cost fifty to one hundred thousand in legal and accounting fees, but saves millions in eventual taxes.

The powers of attorney for finances and healthcare allow designated agents to make decisions if you become incapacitated. The financial power of attorney allows your agent to manage your bank accounts, pay bills, file taxes, and handle financial matters if you cannot. The healthcare power of attorney allows your agent to make medical decisions if you cannot communicate your wishes. The living will documents your wishes about life-sustaining treatment if you are terminally ill or permanently unconscious. These documents are essential for everyone regardless of wealth level because incapacity can strike anyone at any age.

The one percent execute powers of attorney and healthcare directives when they create their basic estate plans, typically in their thirties or forties when they first establish revocable living trusts. They update these documents every five to ten years as circumstances change and as relationships with designated agents evolve. They discuss their wishes with designated agents so that agents understand what decisions to make if incapacity occurs. They store original documents with estate planning attorneys while keeping copies at home where agents can access them if needed.

The beneficiary designation review represents critical maintenance task that many people neglect, creating unintended results after death. Retirement accounts, life insurance, and some bank accounts pass directly to named beneficiaries regardless of what wills or trusts specify. Someone who creates comprehensive estate plan leaving everything to trust but forgets to update life insurance beneficiary designation will have the life insurance pass directly to whoever was named originally—often ex-spouse or parents—rather than to trust as intended. The result undermines the entire estate plan for assets that often represent largest components of estates.

The one percent review beneficiary designations on all accounts annually, updating them after major life events like marriages, divorces, births, and deaths of beneficiaries. They typically name their revocable living trusts as beneficiaries of life insurance policies to ensure coordinated distribution according to trust terms. They name individual beneficiaries on retirement accounts when appropriate to provide stretch IRA benefits, or name trusts as beneficiaries when beneficiaries need protection or structured distributions. They document beneficiary designations in their estate planning files so executors and trustees can verify that accounts pass as intended.

The family meetings to discuss estate plans prevent surprises and conflicts after death by ensuring family members understand your wishes and reasoning. The person who establishes trust leaving different amounts to children or distributing assets unequally without explanation creates resentment and potential litigation when children learn about unequal treatment after death. The person who discusses their reasoning while alive—perhaps one child received more financial help during life, or one child has greater needs, or one child is more financially responsible—allows family members to understand decisions and hopefully accept them even if they disagree.

The one percent hold family meetings with adult children to discuss estate plans once children reach sufficient maturity to process the information, typically when children are in their thirties or forties. They explain what assets exist, how they will be distributed, who will serve in what roles, and why they structured plans as they did. They allow questions and discussion while making clear that their decisions are final unless they choose to modify them. They update family members when material changes occur rather than allowing outdated information to create false expectations. These conversations are uncomfortable but they prevent far worse discomfort after death when surprised heirs receive less than expected or learn about arrangements they disagree with.

The periodic review and updating of estate plans ensures they remain aligned with current wishes, current laws, and current asset values. Tax laws change—the estate tax exemption has varied from one million to over thirteen million over past twenty years. Family circumstances change—marriages, divorces, births, deaths, and changed relationships require plan modifications. Asset values change—someone who created plan when estate was two million might need different strategies when estate reaches ten million. State residency changes require updating plans to comply with new state laws. Trustees and executors die or become unable to serve, requiring designation of new fiduciaries.

The one percent review estate plans every three to five years with their attorneys even when no major life events occur, ensuring plans remain current. They update plans immediately after major life events rather than postponing updates that might never happen if sudden death or incapacity occurs. They maintain relationships with estate planning attorneys who contact them about significant law changes affecting their plans. They treat estate planning as ongoing process rather than one-time task completed and forgotten.

The common mistakes that undermine estate plans include failing to fund trusts by retitling assets, forgetting to update beneficiary designations after divorces or remarriages, designating minor children as direct beneficiaries rather than to trusts, failing to coordinate retirement account beneficiaries with overall estate plan, not updating plans after moving to different states, designating executors or trustees who are incapable or unwilling to serve, creating overly complex plans that trustees cannot administer efficiently, and failing to communicate plans to family members who will be surprised and potentially litigious after death.

The one percent avoid these mistakes through systematic implementation with their attorneys, through maintaining checklists of tasks required after executing estate planning documents, through annual reviews of beneficiary designations, and through periodic meetings with attorneys to review and update plans. They understand that estate planning is worthless if documents are created but not implemented properly through retitling assets and updating beneficiaries. They treat implementation as seriously as document creation because both are essential to achieving intended outcomes.

The costs of comprehensive estate planning vary based on estate complexity and location but generally range from two thousand to ten thousand for most people. Simple wills, powers of attorney, and healthcare directives might cost one thousand to two thousand. Revocable living trust with pour-over will and other basic documents typically costs three thousand to five thousand. Complex plans involving multiple trusts, business succession planning, and sophisticated tax strategies might cost ten thousand to twenty-five thousand. These costs are trivial compared to probate costs, estate taxes, and family conflicts that result from failing to plan properly.

The one percent view estate planning costs as insurance premiums—small certain costs that prevent uncertain but potentially catastrophic future costs. They work with attorneys specializing in estate planning rather than with general practice attorneys who draft basic documents without sophisticated planning. They budget for periodic updates every few years. They understand that the cheapest plan is often the most expensive long-term if it fails to achieve goals or if it creates problems requiring expensive correction after death.

Prince, James Gandolfini, and Paul Walker each faced the reality that life ends suddenly without warning and that the plans you make during life determine what happens after death. Prince's complete failure to plan created disaster costing his estate over one hundred fifty million and creating years of public conflict. Gandolfini's partial planning through wills cost tens of millions in unnecessary taxes and created public probate process. Walker's proper planning through trusts achieved smooth private transition exactly as most people want but few achieve. The difference between these outcomes was not wealth level or sophistication but simply whether each person took time to work with competent estate planning attorneys to document wishes and structure assets appropriately.

You now understand why estate planning matters, what documents you need, how trusts work, what strategies exist for minimizing taxes and avoiding probate, and what mistakes undermine even well-intentioned plans. The one percent implement comprehensive estate planning because they understand that failing to plan means planning to fail. The ninety-nine percent avoid estate planning because death seems distant or because the process seems complicated or expensive, then their estates pay exponentially more in probate costs, taxes, and legal fees while their families suffer through conflicts that proper planning would have prevented.

CHAPTER 34:

PRINCIPAL VERUS INTEREST—THE MATHEMATICS OF DEBT DESTRUCTION

In 2004, a couple named John and Sally from Michigan took out a thirty-year mortgage for two hundred fifty thousand dollars at six percent interest to purchase their first home. Their monthly payment was one thousand four hundred ninety-eight dollars for principal and interest. They made their first payment in January 2004 and planned to make their final payment in December 2033, ultimately paying a total of five hundred thirty-nine thousand four hundred eighty dollars—two hundred fifty thousand in principal to pay back what they borrowed, plus two hundred eighty-nine thousand four hundred eighty dollars in interest paid to the lender for the privilege of borrowing the money.

In January 2004, their first payment of one thousand four hundred ninety-eight dollars was divided as follows: two hundred forty-eight dollars went toward principal and one thousand two hundred fifty dollars went toward interest. They had just paid the lender five times more in interest than they paid down on their actual loan balance. This ratio would persist for years. By December 2004, after making twelve payments totaling seventeen thousand nine hundred seventy-six dollars, they had reduced their loan balance by only three thousand seventy dollars. They had paid fourteen thousand nine hundred six dollars in interest—they gave the bank fourteen thousand nine hundred six dollars for the year while reducing what they owed by only three thousand seventy dollars.

Sally found these numbers disturbing. She understood intellectually that mortgages work this way, but seeing the actual breakdown of where their payments went bothered her deeply. She began researching mortgage amortization and discovered that their payment allocation would slowly shift over the thirty years. By year fifteen, roughly halfway through the mortgage, their monthly payment would finally divide approximately equally between principal and interest. By year twenty-five, most of each payment would go toward principal. In the final year, in 2033, nearly all of their one thousand four hundred ninety-eight monthly payment would reduce principal with only minimal amounts going to interest.

This structure meant that if they simply made their scheduled payments for thirty years, they would pay the lender almost as much in interest as they borrowed originally. Sally calculated that every dollar they borrowed would actually cost them one dollar and sixteen cents by the time they finished paying. But she also discovered something that changed everything: any extra payment they made would go entirely toward principal, permanently reducing the loan balance and therefore reducing all future interest charges calculated on that balance. A single extra principal payment of one thousand dollars in year one would save them approximately three thousand dollars in interest over the life of the loan because that thousand dollars would no longer be accumulating interest for thirty years.

John and Sally decided to make extra principal payments whenever possible. They started by paying an extra two hundred dollars monthly beyond their required payment. This extra two hundred dollars, which totaled twenty-four hundred annually, reduced their thirty-year mortgage to approximately twenty-three years. They saved over seventy thousand dollars in interest and gained their house free and clear seven years earlier. When they received tax refunds or work bonuses, they made lump sum principal payments, accelerating the payoff even further. They refinanced once when rates dropped to four point five percent, but they continued making the same total monthly payment as before—the required payment decreased but they maintained their previous payment level, with the difference going entirely to principal.

By 2019, just fifteen years after taking out their thirty-year mortgage, John and Sally made their final payment. They owned their home outright forty-four years before they turned sixty-five, eliminating their largest expense and freeing up substantial cash flow for investment. The extra payments that made this possible required modest sacrifice during their thirties and forties—they drove older cars, took less expensive vacations, and generally maintained spending discipline. But the result was entering their fifties with zero housing payment, allowing them to save over fifty percent of their income and reach financial independence by age fifty-eight.

This chapter examines the mathematics of how debt actually works, why understanding the distinction between principal and interest matters enormously for your financial outcomes, and what specific strategies allow you to destroy debt years or decades faster than standard payment schedules require. These are not exotic strategies requiring sophisticated financial knowledge. They are straightforward applications of basic mathematics that anyone can implement. The one percent understand these mechanics and use them systematically. The ninety-nine percent make minimum payments for decades without understanding that modest extra principal payments would save them years of debt servitude and tens of thousands in interest charges.

The amortization schedule reveals exactly where every payment goes throughout the life of any loan. Banks are required to provide these schedules showing every payment date, the amount going to principal, the amount going to interest, and the remaining balance after each payment. Most borrowers never look at these schedules. The one percent study them immediately upon taking any loan because the schedule reveals opportunities for strategic extra payments and because it makes viscerally clear how much you are actually paying for borrowed money.

The amortization mathematics follow simple principles. The lender calculates interest on the outstanding balance. On a two hundred fifty thousand dollar loan at six percent annual interest, the monthly interest is calculated as two hundred fifty thousand multiplied by point zero six (six percent) divided by twelve months, equaling one thousand two hundred fifty dollars for the first month.

Your payment of one thousand four hundred ninety-eight dollars covers this one thousand two hundred fifty in interest, with the remaining two hundred forty-eight reducing principal. Next month, the balance has declined to two hundred forty-nine thousand seven hundred fifty-two dollars, so interest is calculated on that lower amount, equaling one thousand two hundred forty-nine dollars. Your same payment now allocates two hundred forty-nine dollars to principal—one dollar more than the previous month.

This process continues for three hundred sixty months if you make only the required payments. The interest portion declines slowly as principal is paid down, while the principal portion increases by the same amount. In month one hundred eighty, halfway through the mortgage, your payment might allocate seven hundred dollars to interest and seven hundred ninety-eight dollars to principal. In month three hundred, your payment might allocate two hundred dollars to interest and one thousand two hundred ninety-eight dollars to principal. The total payment remains constant, but the allocation shifts dramatically.

The critical insight is that any extra payment reduces principal, which then reduces all future interest calculations based on that lower principal balance. The person who pays an extra one hundred dollars toward principal in month one has reduced their balance to two hundred forty-nine thousand six hundred fifty-two rather than two hundred forty-nine thousand seven hundred fifty-two. This one hundred dollar difference seems trivial. But that one hundred dollars would have accumulated interest at six percent for the remaining twenty-nine years and eleven months if not paid early. The compound interest saved over that period exceeds the original one hundred dollars by two to three times. The earlier you make extra principal payments, the greater their impact because they eliminate more years of compound interest accumulation.

The power of one extra payment annually demonstrates how modest additional payments create disproportionate results. Someone with the two hundred fifty thousand mortgage at six percent making one extra payment per year—just one thousand four hundred ninety-eight extra annually beyond the required twelve payments—reduces the thirty-year mortgage to approximately twenty-four years. This single extra payment saves approximately fifty thousand dollars in interest and eliminates six years of payments. The borrower who makes this extra payment has effectively earned a return of over thirty times their investment when measured by total interest saved divided by extra payments made.

The bi-weekly payment strategy achieves similar results through converting monthly payments to every-two-weeks payments. Instead of paying one thousand four hundred ninety-eight monthly (twelve payments annually), you pay seven hundred forty-nine every two weeks. Because there are fifty-two weeks in a year, you make twenty-six bi-weekly payments totaling thirteen monthly payment equivalents. You have made one extra full payment annually without feeling like you made extra payments because you simply divided your monthly payment in half and paid that amount every time you received a paycheck if paid bi-weekly.

The administrative implementation of bi-weekly payments requires either setting this up through your lender, which many lenders now offer, or making your own extra payments manually. The lenders who offer bi-weekly payment programs sometimes charge enrollment fees and processing fees that reduce the benefit. The person who simply makes one extra payment annually achieves essentially the same result without fees. The one percent typically make extra payments manually rather than enrolling in lender programs that extract fees, but the specific method matters less than the consistency of making extra payments systematically rather than hoping to make them whenever convenient.

The targeting of specific loans within portfolios containing multiple debts determines whether your extra payments generate maximum impact or whether they are deployed suboptimally. Someone carrying mortgage at four percent, car loan at seven percent, and credit card balance at eighteen percent should direct all extra payments toward the credit card because the eighteen percent interest means that debt is costing far more than the value generated by paying down lower-interest obligations. The guaranteed return from paying off eighteen percent debt exceeds any investment return you can generate reliably. Only after the credit card is eliminated should extra payments flow toward the seven percent car loan. The four percent mortgage should be paid off last because the interest cost is low enough that investing extra money often generates superior returns.

This mathematical optimization conflicts with the psychological approach popularized by Dave Ramsey's debt snowball method that we discussed in Chapter Thirty. Ramsey advocates paying smallest balances first regardless of interest rates, generating quick wins that maintain motivation. The mathematical optimization approach pays highest interest rates first regardless of balance size, minimizing total interest paid. Someone with twenty thousand in credit cards at eighteen percent, fifteen thousand car loan at seven percent, and two hundred thousand mortgage at four percent should mathematically attack the credit cards first. But if the credit cards are split across four cards with balances of two thousand, three thousand, seven thousand, and eight thousand, the snowball approach of eliminating the two thousand dollar card first might provide psychological benefit that helps maintain intensity.

The one percent generally follow mathematical optimization because they maintain discipline without needing psychological wins from eliminating small balances. But they acknowledge that for people who have struggled with debt and who need motivation more than optimization, the psychological approach might produce better results by maintaining engagement. The worst outcome is abandoning debt elimination entirely due to lack of motivation, making the psychologically optimal approach better than the mathematically optimal approach that you cannot maintain. The second-worst outcome is continuing to make minimum payments for years when either approach would dramatically accelerate payoff. Choose the approach you will actually implement rather than the theoretically superior approach you will abandon.

The mortgage recasting represents a lesser-known strategy for reducing required monthly payments after making lump sum principal payments while maintaining the same interest rate and remaining loan term. Someone who pays fifty thousand extra principal on their mortgage can request that the lender recast the loan, recalculating the monthly payment based on the new lower principal balance while keeping the original interest rate and remaining term. This reduces required monthly payments, though you can continue making the original payment amount with all extra going to principal.

The benefit of recasting is flexibility. Someone who pays large amount of principal might want lower required payments for cash flow management while retaining the option to pay more when possible. Recasting typically costs two hundred to five hundred dollars in lender fees and is only available on conventional mortgages, not on FHA or VA loans. Not all lenders offer recasting. The one percent who make large principal payments sometimes recast to reduce required payments while continuing to make the same total payment, gaining flexibility to reduce payments temporarily if income interruptions occur.

The refinancing decision requires analyzing whether new interest rate savings exceed the costs of refinancing and whether you will remain in the home long enough to recover those costs. Refinancing typically costs two to five percent of loan amount in fees including origination, appraisal, title insurance, and various charges. Someone with two hundred thousand remaining mortgage balance might pay four thousand to ten thousand in refinancing costs. If the new interest rate is one percentage point lower, they save approximately two thousand annually in interest. They break even in two to five years, after which all savings are net benefit.

The calculation must also account for whether you restart the thirty-year clock on a loan you have already paid down. Someone fifteen years into a thirty-year mortgage has fifteen years remaining. If they refinance to a new thirty-year mortgage, they extend their debt by fifteen years even if the interest rate is lower. The mathematically correct approach is refinancing to a new fifteen-year mortgage to maintain the original payoff timeline while capturing the lower rate. The fifteen-year mortgage will have higher monthly payments than a thirty-year refinance, but it prevents extending debt servitude by fifteen years.

The one percent refinance when rates drop by at least half a percentage point and when they plan to remain in the property for at least three to five years to recover closing costs. They refinance to the shortest term they can afford rather than defaulting to thirty years merely because that produces the lowest payment. They sometimes pay points upfront to reduce interest rates further if they plan very long holds. They calculate break-even periods before refinancing rather than reflexively refinancing whenever rates drop slightly. They avoid cash-out refinancing that extracts home equity for consumption, recognizing that this converts home equity to debt for no productive purpose.

The prepayment penalty clauses in some mortgages prohibit or penalize paying loans off early. These clauses protect lenders from losing expected interest income if borrowers pay loans off within the first three to five years. Someone who pays off two hundred fifty thousand mortgage in year three after paying only minimal principal might trigger a prepayment penalty of two to five percent of the original balance, or five thousand to twelve thousand five hundred dollars. This penalty can exceed the interest savings from early payoff, making extra payments counterproductive during the penalty period.

The one percent review loan documents before taking loans to identify prepayment penalties and to negotiate their removal. Most residential mortgages no longer include prepayment penalties, but some refinanced loans and many commercial loans still have them. The person who understands they might pay their loan off early should refuse to accept loans with prepayment penalties, or should at least limit penalties to very short periods like one to two years. The person who discovers after the fact that their loan has prepayment penalties should calculate whether paying during the penalty period still makes sense or whether delaying extra payments until penalties expire generates better outcomes.

The interest-only period option on some mortgages allows paying only interest for initial years, with no principal reduction. Someone with two hundred fifty thousand mortgage might pay only interest for the first five to ten years, with payments of one thousand two hundred fifty monthly at six percent interest, then convert to fully-amortizing payments for the remaining term. These loans appeal to people who cannot afford full payments initially or who plan to sell before interest-only period ends. But they are financial traps for most borrowers because you build no equity during the interest-only period and because the required payments spike dramatically when the loan converts to fully-amortizing.

The one percent avoid interest-only mortgages for primary residences because building equity through principal paydown is a key benefit of homeownership. They might use interest-only financing strategically for investment properties where the goal is maximizing cash flow rather than building equity, or where they plan definite exit within the interest-only period. They never use interest-only financing for consumption or for affording homes they could not otherwise buy, because this represents living beyond their means through financial engineering that delays but intensifies the day of reckoning.

The adjustable-rate mortgage offers initial interest rates below fixed-rate mortgages in exchange for rate uncertainty after the initial period. A five-year ARM might offer four percent for five years when fixed-rate mortgages are six percent, saving substantial interest initially but facing potential rate increases after year five. Someone with two hundred fifty thousand mortgage saves four thousand annually during the five-year fixed period compared to fixed-rate mortgage. If they definitely plan to sell before year five or if they can afford substantially higher payments if rates increase, the ARM provides clear benefit.

The risk is that rates spike after the initial period and that the borrower cannot afford the new payment or cannot refinance due to changed financial circumstances or property value decline. Someone who took a five-year ARM in 2003 faced their first rate adjustment in 2008 when the financial crisis made refinancing impossible and when job losses made higher payments unaffordable. Many of these borrowers lost homes to foreclosure. The one percent use ARMs only when they have specific plans to exit before rate adjustments or when they have sufficient financial cushion to absorb rate increases without strain. They never use ARMs to afford homes they could not afford with fixed-rate mortgages.

The loan modification programs during financial hardship allow renegotiating loan terms to avoid foreclosure. Someone who loses job or faces medical expenses might negotiate temporary payment reduction, interest rate reduction, or term extension to make payments manageable during crisis. Lenders prefer modification to foreclosure because foreclosure costs them more than temporary payment concessions cost. The government periodically creates formal modification programs during crises like the 2008 financial crisis or the COVID-19 pandemic that establish frameworks for modifications.

The one percent use modification as last resort to avoid foreclosure, not as first response to temporary cash flow problems. They maintain emergency funds covering six months of expenses to weather job losses or income reductions without requiring modification. They communicate with lenders early if problems are developing rather than missing payments first and then seeking help. They understand that modification damages credit scores and should be avoided when alternative solutions exist like drawing from savings or reducing other expenses temporarily.

The secured versus unsecured debt distinction determines whether the lender can seize collateral if you default. Mortgages and auto loans are secured by the property purchased—if you default, the lender forecloses or repossesses. Credit cards and personal loans are unsecured—if you default, the lender can sue you and garnish wages or seize assets through court judgment, but they cannot automatically take property. Secured debt typically carries lower interest rates because the collateral reduces lender risk. Unsecured debt carries higher rates reflecting greater risk.

The strategic default consideration involves intentionally stopping payments on underwater mortgages where you owe more than the property is worth. Someone with four hundred thousand mortgage on a property now worth two hundred fifty thousand is one hundred fifty thousand underwater. Continuing to pay the mortgage means paying four hundred thousand for an asset worth two hundred fifty thousand. Strategic default allows walking away from the property and the debt, though it destroys credit for years and might result in deficiency judgment for the difference between property value and loan balance depending on state law.

The one percent rarely face strategic default decisions because they purchase properties conservatively with substantial down payments, maintain emergency funds that prevent defaults during temporary income interruptions, and prioritize debt service above discretionary spending. When they do face underwater properties, they evaluate whether the property will recover value over time frames they can sustain payments, whether the debt is recourse or non-recourse, what credit score impacts will cost them, and whether they have other assets that creditors might seize through deficiency judgments. Strategic default is legitimate option in extreme circumstances but should be evaluated carefully with legal counsel rather than chosen impulsively.

The impact of credit scores on interest rates makes debt more expensive for those with poor credit and cheaper for those with excellent credit. Someone with 760 credit score might qualify for four percent mortgage while someone with 640 score faces six percent on the same loan. On two hundred thousand mortgage, this two percentage point difference costs approximately three hundred dollars monthly and over one hundred thousand over thirty years. The person with poor credit pays one hundred thousand dollars more for the same house purely because of their credit score.

The one percent maintain excellent credit scores above 760 through paying all bills on time, maintaining low credit utilization ratios below thirty percent of available credit, having long credit histories with diverse account types, and avoiding derogatory marks. They understand that excellent credit saves tens of thousands in interest costs over lifetimes and they protect their credit accordingly. They check credit reports annually for errors and dispute inaccuracies immediately. They never miss payments on any account because the long-term cost exceeds any short-term benefit from keeping money for other purposes.

The calculation of total interest paid over loan life reveals the true cost of borrowing and often shocks people into making extra payments. Someone with three hundred thousand mortgage at five percent for thirty years makes monthly payments of one thousand six hundred ten dollars. Total payments over thirty years equal five hundred seventy-nine thousand seven hundred sixty—three hundred thousand in principal plus two hundred seventy-nine thousand seven hundred sixty in interest. They pay nearly as much in interest as they borrowed. The person who pays just two hundred dollars extra monthly reduces total interest to one hundred ninety-four thousand and pays off the loan in twenty-one years instead of thirty. The extra payments of two hundred dollars monthly for twenty-one years total fifty thousand four hundred, but they save eighty-five thousand seven hundred sixty in interest—they invest fifty thousand and receive eighty-six thousand return.

This return calculation should be made for every loan you carry. Calculate how much total interest you will pay if you make only minimum payments. Calculate how much you save through extra payments. Compare the return on extra payments to returns you could generate by investing the money instead. For loans with interest rates above seven percent, extra payments almost always generate superior risk-adjusted returns compared to investing. For loans below four percent, investing often generates better returns. For loans between four and seven percent, the decision depends on your risk tolerance and your confidence in achieving investment returns that exceed your loan interest rate.

The psychological benefit of debt elimination deserves consideration even when mathematical analysis suggests investing generates superior returns. The person who pays off their mortgage early experiences reduced financial stress even if they could theoretically have accumulated more wealth by investing instead. The person who becomes debt-free eliminates risk that loss of employment might lead to foreclosure. The person who owns their home outright enters retirement without housing payments that many retirees struggle to cover from limited retirement income. These psychological and risk-reduction benefits have real value that pure mathematical optimization ignores.

The one percent make these decisions based on individual circumstances and preferences rather than following rigid rules. Someone thirty years from retirement earning twelve percent returns through their business might rationally carry a four percent mortgage indefinitely because their capital generates far more when deployed in their business than when used to pay down cheap debt. Someone five years from retirement might rationally pay off their mortgage aggressively to enter retirement debt-free even if this is mathematically suboptimal. The optimal strategy depends on your timeline, your alternative uses for capital, your risk tolerance, and your psychological relationship with debt.

John and Sally's decision to aggressively pay down their mortgage transformed their financial lives by eliminating their largest expense years before retirement. They made this choice despite financial advisors suggesting they would accumulate more wealth by maintaining the mortgage and investing the extra payment money. Their reasoning was that home equity provides psychological security that investment accounts do not provide, that mortgage payoff was guaranteed return while investment returns were uncertain, and that they valued becoming debt-free more than they valued maximizing theoretical wealth accumulation. By age fifty-eight, their lack of mortgage payment allowed them to retire early because their living expenses were fifty percent lower than they would have been with mortgage payments continuing until age sixty-eight.

Their experience demonstrates that understanding principal versus interest mathematics allows you to make informed decisions about debt management rather than passively making minimum payments for decades. Whether you choose to pay debt aggressively like John and Sally or to maintain debt while investing depends on your specific situation, but that choice should be made consciously after analyzing the numbers rather than by default because you never examined the alternatives. The frameworks have been provided. The mathematics are straightforward. The implementation through consistent extra principal payments, through targeting highest-interest debts first, through refinancing strategically when beneficial, and through maintaining excellent credit that minimizes interest costs remains your responsibility.

The one percent understand that debt is tool that can be used strategically or weapon that destroys wealth depending on how you manage it. They understand principal versus interest mechanics. They study amortization schedules. They make extra principal payments systematically. They refinance when mathematics justify it. They maintain excellent credit to minimize costs. They target highest-interest debts for elimination first. They never pay more in debt service than necessary, and they never carry debt longer than required when they have capacity to eliminate it faster.

The ninety-nine percent make minimum payments for decades without understanding where their money goes. They never examine amortization schedules. They never make extra principal payments despite having capacity to do so. They refinance without calculating break-even periods. They allow credit scores to decline through carelessness. They carry high-interest debt for years while making minimum payments. They accept thirty-year mortgages automatically without considering fifteen-year alternatives. They pay hundreds of thousands in unnecessary interest over their lifetimes because they never learned the mathematics that would have saved them years of debt servitude.

You now understand how debt actually works, why principal versus interest distinction matters, and what specific strategies allow destroying debt faster. Your decision regarding how you pay off debt should be made consciously based on mathematics rather than unconsciously through inertia. The years you spend in debt versus the years you live debt-free fundamentally determine your financial trajectory and your quality of life during the decades when housing payments either consume substantial income or cease entirely because you own your home outright. Choose wisely and calculate precisely.

CHAPTER 35:

THE POWER OF SILENCE—WHY THE WEALTHY SAY NOTHING

In 2013, a lottery winner named Abraham Shakespeare was found buried beneath a concrete slab in Florida. He had won thirty million dollars in the state lottery in 2006, taken a lump sum of seventeen million, and within months had become locally famous in his small town of Lakeland. He bought a large house in an upscale neighborhood. He purchased a Nissan Altima, then upgraded to multiple luxury vehicles. He loaned money to friends and family who asked. He invested in business ventures proposed by acquaintances he barely knew. He told everyone who would listen about his good fortune.

By 2009, Abraham was exhausted. Hundreds of people he had never met asked him for money. Friends he thought he had turned out to be opportunists who disappeared once he stopped giving. Family members sued him over money they claimed he promised them. Business partners stole from him because they knew he had difficulty reading contracts and managing complex finances. The woman who would eventually murder him, Dorice Moore, had befriended him by claiming she would help him manage the constant requests for money. Instead she swindled him out of millions before killing him and burying his body to cover her crimes.

Abraham Shakespeare's death was extreme, but the pattern that led to it is depressingly common. He broadcast his wealth. He told everyone about his windfall. He could not distinguish genuine relationships from opportunistic ones because his sudden wealth attracted swarms of people pretending friendship while seeking money. He trusted the wrong people with information about his assets. He was targeted because he made himself a visible target. His murder could have been prevented by a single behavioral change: saying nothing about his wealth to anyone beyond immediate family and professional advisors bound by fiduciary duty.

In 2012, a Maryland couple in their fifties won a Mega Millions jackpot of 218 million dollars—at the time, one-third of the largest lottery jackpot in history. They made a different choice than Abraham Shakespeare. They hired attorneys before claiming the prize. They established trusts to hold the winnings. They created a management structure with professional advisors. They gave no interviews. They released no photos. They kept their names out of media as much as state law allowed. They told almost no one about the win, including most of their extended family. They continued living in their same modest home. They continued working their regular jobs for two years before quietly retiring.

The Maryland couple understood what Abraham Shakespeare never learned: wealth broadcasts danger. The moment people know you have substantial money, you become target for theft, for lawsuits, for manipulation, for violence. You attract people whose interest in you is purely financial. You create envy in people who were previously your peers. You receive constant requests for help that you can never fulfill completely because there are always more people with problems than you have resources to solve. The wealthy who remain safe and who maintain genuine relationships do so by keeping their wealth invisible to everyone except the small circle of professionals who must know.

This chapter examines why silence about your wealth, your income, your investments, and your financial strategies provides advantages that disclosure destroys. It explains why you cannot save people who do not want to be saved and why attempting to do so wastes your energy while damaging relationships. It provides frameworks for determining what to share with whom and for recognizing when someone is genuinely ready to hear financial guidance versus when they are merely complaining without intending to change. Most importantly, it explains why the one percent move in silence while the ninety-nine percent broadcast everything, and how this behavioral difference compounds advantages over decades.

The fundamental principle is that money attracts problems in direct proportion to how many people know you have it. The person whose wealth is invisible to neighbors, coworkers, and extended family faces none of the requests, envy, targeting, or relationship complications that the person with visible wealth faces. This is why truly wealthy people often live far below their means in ways that make them indistinguishable from upper-middle-class professionals. They drive nice but not ostentatious cars. They live in comfortable but not palatial homes. They wear quality clothing without logos broadcasting luxury brands. They travel but without posting every five-star resort visit on social media. They have become invisible millionaires or billionaires who draw no attention.

Warren Buffett has lived in the same house in Omaha, Nebraska since 1958, when he purchased it for thirty-one thousand five hundred dollars. The house is comfortable but modest—fifty-six hundred square feet in a middle-class neighborhood, nothing that would signal that its occupant is one of the wealthiest people in human history. He drives himself in a Cadillac XTS, a nice car but not a vehicle that announces wealth. He eats at local restaurants rather than at exclusive establishments. He shops at regular grocery stores. If you encountered Warren Buffett in public in Omaha, nothing about his appearance or behavior would indicate that he controls hundreds of billions in assets.

This invisibility is strategic, not accidental. Buffett understands that visible wealth creates problems while invisible wealth creates freedom. No one asks Warren Buffett for money because almost no one encounters him randomly, and those who do encounter him have no idea who he is unless they recognize his face from media appearances. He receives no constant solicitations from strangers because he is not visibly wealthy in his daily environment. He maintains genuine friendships from decades ago because those relationships were formed before he became wealthy and because his lifestyle does not constantly remind people of wealth differences between him and his friends.

The contrast with people who broadcast wealth could not be starker. The entrepreneur who leases a Lamborghini the moment their startup raises venture capital announces to everyone they encounter that they have accessed money. The employee who buys a Mercedes immediately after receiving a promotion tells their colleagues exactly how much that promotion must have paid. The investor who posts about their real estate purchases on social media invites everyone who follows them to calculate their net worth. These broadcasts create multiple problems simultaneously: they attract opportunists seeking money, they create envy among peers who earned less, they establish you as target for theft or lawsuits, and they communicate insecurity about your status that undermines the respect you sought through displays.

The psychology of broadcasting wealth stems from status insecurity and from the need for external validation. The person confident in their financial position does not need others to know about it because their security is internal rather than dependent on others' perception. The person insecure about their status broadcasts wealth to convince themselves and others that they have achieved success. This broadcasting reveals the very insecurity it attempts to conceal. The one percent recognize this pattern—when they encounter someone broadcasting wealth through luxury purchases and social media posts, they understand immediately that this person is insecure rather than secure, that the displays signal weakness rather than strength.

In 1987, a drug dealer in Detroit named Demetrius Holloway became one of the most successful cocaine distributors in the Midwest, generating millions in monthly revenue. He drove a fleet of luxury vehicles. He wore diamond jewelry. He threw lavish parties. He carried thick stacks of cash visibly when he went to clubs. He dated high-profile women. He made himself highly visible in Detroit's social scene. His lifestyle and displays made him famous in the city, which he apparently enjoyed because it provided the status and recognition that his illegal business could never provide legitimately.

His visibility also made him a priority target for law enforcement. The FBI and DEA had no difficulty identifying his associates, tracking his movements, or building cases against him because he operated in plain sight. In 1989, Holloway was murdered by rivals who knew exactly where to find him because his routine was predictable and his locations were public. He was twenty-four years old. His money, his cars, and his jewelry did not protect him. His visibility killed him because it gave both law enforcement and rivals clear targets. If he had moved silently, lived modestly, and avoided broadcasting his wealth, he might have survived and eventually transitioned his capital into legitimate businesses. Instead, his need for recognition and status destroyed him.

The legitimate businessman or professional can learn from this extreme example despite operating in legal industries. The principle is identical: broadcasting wealth creates problems while silence creates safety. The executive who brags to colleagues about their bonus invites resentment that undermines their relationships and their effectiveness leading teams who know exactly how much more they earn than the people they manage. The investor who tells friends about their portfolio gains invites requests for loans, investment advice they are not qualified to give, and skepticism when markets decline and gains evaporate. The entrepreneur who posts on social media about their business success invites competitors to study their strategies, attracts regulatory scrutiny, and establishes expectations they may not meet consistently.

The one percent establish clear boundaries about financial disclosure. They share specific information only with specific people who have legitimate need to know. They tell their accountants and financial advisors everything because these professionals need complete information to provide competent guidance. They tell their spouses everything because financial partnership requires transparency between partners. They might tell their parents or adult children general information about their planning but not specific account balances or net worth figures that serve no purpose. They tell their friends nothing about their specific financial situation beyond what is necessarily revealed through their lifestyle choices. They tell their coworkers nothing about their compensation beyond what is required to negotiate effectively for themselves.

The determination of who deserves financial information follows a simple framework: does this person need this information to help me or to make decisions that affect both of us? Your accountant needs to know your income to file your taxes correctly. Your spouse needs to know your financial situation to make joint decisions about housing, children, and retirement. Your mortgage broker needs to know your income and assets to process your loan application. Your boss does not need to know your investment portfolio. Your coworkers do not need to know your salary unless you are sharing information strategically to help them negotiate better for themselves. Your friends do not need to know your net worth. Your extended family does not need to know your income unless you are supporting them financially.

The one percent also recognize that unsolicited financial advice is universally unwelcome and usually ignored regardless of how sound it is. The person who tries to convince their friends to save more, invest systematically, minimize expenses, and build wealth discovers quickly that their advice is met with resistance, excuses, and often resentment. This is not because the advice is wrong—it is exactly what their friends need to hear. It is because people do not change behaviors based on advice from peers. They change when they experience enough pain from their current behaviors that they become ready to try something different, or when they encounter information at exactly the moment they are searching for solutions.

David Bach, the personal finance author who popularized the "Latte Factor" concept, tells the story of how his advice was completely ignored by his own father for years. Bach would explain his investment strategies, share his success, and explicitly tell his father what to do. His father would nod, agree that the advice made sense, and then do nothing. Years later, after a health scare and forced early retirement, his father finally implemented the exact strategies Bach had been recommending for years. The difference was not the quality of the advice—it was identical advice he had ignored previously. The difference was that his father had become ready to hear it because his circumstances created urgency that abstract advice never created.

The lesson is that you cannot save people who are not ready to save themselves. The friend who complains about being broke while spending four hundred dollars monthly on restaurant meals is not seeking advice—they are seeking sympathy. The family member who asks for money repeatedly while refusing to change spending patterns is not seeking help—they are seeking enablement. The coworker who envies your financial progress while refusing to implement any of the strategies you have shared is not interested in replicating your success—they are interested in feeling victimized by circumstances rather than taking responsibility for changing those circumstances.

The one percent recognize these patterns and stop trying to convince people who demonstrate through their actions that they do not want to change. This recognition is not callous or uncaring. It is realistic assessment that allows you to deploy your energy toward people who are ready to hear guidance rather than wasting it on people who will not implement anything you suggest. The person who asks specific questions about how you achieved results is potentially ready to learn. The person who vaguely wishes they could achieve similar results but who deflects every suggestion with excuses is not ready and will not be ready until their circumstances create enough pain that change becomes less painful than continuation.

In 2004, Chris Gardner published his memoir "The Pursuit of Happyness" describing his journey from homelessness to becoming a successful stockbroker and eventually a multimillionaire entrepreneur. The book became a bestseller and was adapted into a film starring Will Smith. Gardner's story is inspiring and his financial advice is sound. Yet if you read interviews Gardner gave before his book's success, he describes spending years trying to help people in his old neighborhood understand how to build wealth, how to invest systematically, how to think long-term rather than focusing only on immediate needs. Almost none of them implemented his advice. Many resented him for "thinking he was better than them" because he had escaped the poverty they remained trapped in.

Gardner eventually realized that he could not save his old neighborhood through advice or through his example. The people there were not ready to hear what he had to say, or they resented him for his success, or they simply had too many immediate crises to think about long-term wealth building. He stopped trying to convince people who did not want to be convinced. He focused instead on writing his book, which found the audience of people who were actively seeking solutions and who were ready to implement guidance when they found it. The book sold millions of copies and helped many people who were ready to be helped. His years trying to convince his old neighbors had helped almost no one because they were not ready.

The application to your situation is direct: if you implement the principles in this book and begin building wealth, you will encounter people who notice your progress and who ask how you are achieving it. Some of these people are genuinely asking because they are ready to learn. Most are asking out of curiosity or envy without any intention of changing their behaviors. The one percent learn to distinguish between these groups through simple observation. The person ready to learn asks specific questions: "What index funds do you invest in?" "How much should I save before buying property?" "Should I pay off debt or invest first?" The person not ready to learn makes vague statements: "I wish I could save like you do." "I could never live that frugally." "I just don't have your discipline."

When you encounter someone making vague statements without asking specific questions, the correct response is to offer basic encouragement without providing detailed guidance they will not use. "You could definitely build wealth if you decided to make it a priority" is sufficient. Do not explain your entire investment strategy. Do not share specific numbers about your net worth or savings rate. Do not try to convince them that they could do what you are doing if only they made different choices. They are not ready to hear it, your advice will not be implemented, and your sharing of specific strategies merely broadcasts information that could create problems for you through envy or through others sharing your information without your permission.

When you encounter someone asking specific questions, you can share more detailed information while still maintaining boundaries about specific numbers. "I invest primarily in index funds through my 401k and Roth IRA" is helpful without disclosing account balances. "I keep my housing costs below twenty-five percent of gross income by living in a smaller place than I could afford" is actionable without revealing your income. "I paid off my student loans in four years by making extra principal payments whenever I received bonuses" is instructive without specifying loan amounts or bonus sizes. The specific tactical information allows them to implement similar strategies without requiring you to disclose personal financial details that serve no purpose and that create unnecessary vulnerability.

The social media amplification of broadcasting behaviors has made financial privacy far more difficult than it was in previous generations. The person who posts photos of their new car, their vacation to expensive resort, their recent home purchase, or their restaurant meals creates permanent public record of their spending that anyone can access indefinitely. These posts allow acquaintances to calculate approximate income levels, to track lifestyle inflation over time, and to assess net worth within reasonable ranges. The posts also broadcast security vulnerabilities—the vacation posts tell potential burglars when homes are empty, the purchase posts reveal what valuable items are in homes, the restaurant check-ins reveal routine patterns that make people predictable targets.

The one percent maintain minimal social media presence or they carefully curate what they share to avoid broadcasting wealth. They post about experiences rather than about purchases. They share ideas rather than possessions. They avoid location tagging that reveals where they are or where they live. They never post about financial achievements, investment gains, or business successes publicly because these posts create only problems without providing any benefit. The temporary validation from likes and comments does not compensate for the permanent problems created by broadcasting financial information to hundreds or thousands of people, most of whom are acquaintances rather than genuine friends.

The testing of relationships through selective disclosure reveals who you can trust with sensitive information. The person who tells their friend about a financial success and who then hears that information repeated by someone else who should not know it has identified someone who cannot be trusted. The person who mentions they are considering purchasing an investment property and who then receives unsolicited negative opinions from multiple people discovers that their "friend" has been discussing their finances with others. These tests are unpleasant but necessary because you need to identify the small number of people who can keep information confidential versus the majority who will share anything interesting they hear.

The one percent perform these tests deliberately by sharing information of varying sensitivity with different people and observing what remains confidential versus what gets broadcast. They might tell one friend they are considering a new job without specifying compensation, tell another friend they made a good investment without specifying amounts, and tell a third friend nothing about their finances. If they later discover that people who should not know about the job or investment somehow heard about them, they have identified which friend cannot be trusted with information. This sounds manipulative, but it is practical risk management. Your financial privacy is valuable and you need to know who will protect it versus who will violate it.

The family complications created by wealth differences are among the most difficult to navigate because you cannot simply distance yourself from family as you can from untrustworthy friends. The person who builds substantial wealth while their siblings remain financially struggling faces constant pressure to help, explicit or implicit guilt about their success, and often resentment regardless of whether they provide assistance. The correct approach is to establish clear boundaries about what you will and will not do financially for family members, to communicate those boundaries explicitly, and to maintain them consistently even when pressure intensifies.

The one percent typically establish rules like "I will help with genuine emergencies but not with ongoing subsidizing of lifestyle choices" or "I will match any money you save toward specific goals but I will not simply give money without corresponding effort on your part" or "I will pay for education expenses but not for consumer purchases." These rules create structure that prevents resentment on both sides—you are helping in ways that feel appropriate to you without enabling dependency, and family members understand what they can and cannot expect. The rules also prevent the pattern where family members who refuse to manage their finances effectively continuously drain resources from family members who do manage finances effectively.

The guilt that successful people feel about their achievement relative to struggling family members is often weaponized by those family members to extract money and assistance. The sibling who says "It must be nice to be able to afford vacations while I can barely pay rent" is attempting to create guilt that obligates you to help them. The appropriate response is not to defend your success or to feel guilty about it, but rather to recognize the manipulation and to maintain your boundaries: "I structured my life to allow me to take vacations by living below my means and saving systematically. You could do the same if you chose to." This response is direct without being cruel, and it places responsibility where it belongs—on the person making choices that create their circumstances.

The extended family dynamics become even more complicated when elderly parents favor less successful children with financial help while expecting more successful children to understand that they need help less. The parent who gives ten thousand dollars to the child who is "struggling" while giving nothing to the child who is "doing fine" creates resentment when the struggling child is struggling because of poor choices rather than because of circumstances beyond their control. The one percent address this explicitly rather than allowing resentment to fester: "I notice you give substantial financial help to my sibling regularly while I receive no help. I understand they earn less than I do, but they earn less partly because they refuse to work consistently or to manage money responsibly. I am not asking for money, but I am asking you to recognize that your help enables their dysfunction rather than addressing it."

This conversation is difficult and risks damaging relationships, but it is necessary if you are going to maintain respect within family systems where success is penalized and failure is rewarded. The alternative is silently accepting that your discipline and success entitle you to no support while your sibling's lack of discipline and failure entitle them to continuous subsidy. This is not a dynamic that healthy relationships can sustain long-term, and the one percent refuse to participate in it even at the risk of being labeled as selfish or uncaring by family members benefiting from the dysfunctional system.

The workplace disclosure about compensation and financial success is particularly fraught because coworkers who learn that you earn substantially more than they do often cannot separate that knowledge from their professional interactions with you. The colleague who discovers you earn thirty thousand more than they do for comparable work begins every interaction with that knowledge coloring their perception. They are more likely to resent your success, to minimize your contributions, to resist your leadership if you manage them, and to generally see you as overpaid rather than as having negotiated effectively. This is why the one percent never discuss compensation with coworkers except in limited circumstances where sharing information helps others negotiate better for themselves.

The exception to this rule is when you are sharing information strategically to help others understand their market value. The person who discovers their coworker doing similar work earns thirty percent more gains valuable information that allows them to negotiate effectively or to recognize they should find a new employer. Sharing compensation information in this context serves the person you are sharing it with rather than serving your ego. The one percent make these decisions deliberately—they might tell a coworker what they earn if that coworker is being substantially underpaid and needs data to negotiate, but they do not broadcast their compensation to everyone in their department to establish status.

The neighborhood selection partly determines whether your wealth remains invisible or becomes conspicuous. The person earning two hundred thousand who lives in a neighborhood where average household income is eighty thousand appears wealthy to their neighbors regardless of how modestly they live. Their house is likely nicer than surrounding houses, their cars are likely newer, and their lifestyle is likely more comfortable than their neighbors can afford. This visibility creates the problems that visibility always creates—requests for help, envy, potential targeting for theft. The person earning two hundred thousand who lives in a neighborhood where average household income is two hundred fifty thousand appears normal or even modest to their neighbors. Their house is average for the area, their cars are typical, and their lifestyle does not stand out.

The one percent often choose to live in neighborhoods where they are average or below-average wealth rather than in neighborhoods where they are the wealthiest residents. This allows them to maintain privacy while still living in areas with good schools, low crime, and strong property values. It prevents the complications that come from being obviously wealthier than everyone around you. It allows genuine relationships with neighbors based on compatibility rather than relationships colored by wealth differences. The decision to live among peers rather than to live as the wealthiest person in a less expensive neighborhood is partly about privacy and partly about quality of life.

The charitable giving creates similar visibility issues because public donations establish you as person with resources to give. The one percent often give anonymously or through donor-advised funds that keep their names private from recipient organizations. They might give publicly to causes they want to champion where visibility helps the cause, but they default to anonymity rather than to publicity. This prevents the pattern where making one substantial gift leads to solicitations from hundreds of other organizations who learned about your giving and who add you to their fundraising lists. It also prevents social pressure from friends and acquaintances who learn about your giving and who expect you to support their preferred causes at similar levels.

The transition from invisibility to visibility that occurs when wealth reaches levels that cannot be completely hidden requires conscious strategy about what to reveal and how to reveal it. The person who builds a fifty-million-dollar business cannot remain completely invisible because their role in that business is public record. The person who accumulates twenty million through systematic investing can remain invisible indefinitely because their wealth is held in private accounts that no one can discover without their disclosure. The one percent who cannot remain invisible due to business success manage visibility carefully—they give interviews sparingly, they share general business metrics without detailing personal finances, they live modestly relative to their actual wealth to avoid becoming high-profile targets, and they maintain privacy for their families even when they accept some public visibility for themselves.

The teaching of silence to children represents one of the most important lessons wealthy parents can transmit because children who broadcast their family's wealth create problems for the entire family. The child who tells classmates about expensive vacations, valuable possessions, or parents' business success invites targeting of the family by criminals, creates social complications as other parents make assumptions about your wealth, and establishes the child as person from wealthy family rather than as individual. The one percent teach children explicitly that family finances are private information not to be discussed outside the family. They explain that discussing money makes them targets for people who want money. They model financial privacy through their own behavior. They praise children when they demonstrate discretion and they correct children when they broadcast information inappropriately.

The historical examples of families destroyed by broadcasting wealth are numerous enough that patterns emerge clearly. The person who displays wealth attracts opportunists who befriend them solely for access to resources. These opportunists are often skilled at manipulation because they have practiced on previous targets. They identify your emotional vulnerabilities and exploit them. They create dependence by making themselves indispensable. They isolate you from people who might warn you about them. They steal as much as they can before you discover the theft. Abraham Shakespeare's murderer spent years executing exactly this pattern before finally killing him when he began to question her control over his finances.

The one percent protect themselves from these patterns through maintaining privacy about their wealth, through using professional advisors with fiduciary obligations rather than trusting friends who offer to help manage money, through maintaining relationships with people they knew before they became wealthy rather than accepting new friendships uncritically, and through recognizing that sudden new friends after visible wealth acquisition are probably opportunists rather than genuine friends. This sounds cynical and it is depressing to realize that wealth attracts false friends. But the alternative—trusting everyone and being exploited repeatedly—is far worse than maintaining healthy skepticism about others' motives.

The one percent understand that true friends are people who knew you before you achieved success and who treat you the same afterward. They are not people who suddenly appear after you become successful. They are not people who constantly need favors or money. They are not people whose primary interest seems to be your wealth or your connections rather than you as a person. The maintenance of genuine friendships requires being selective about who you trust with information about your success and being willing to distance yourself from people who demonstrate through their behavior that they see you as resource rather than as friend.

The contrast between the Maryland lottery winners who moved silently and Abraham Shakespeare who broadcast everything demonstrates that silence is not about paranoia or antisocial behavior. It is about recognizing reality that visible wealth creates problems while invisible wealth creates freedom. The Maryland couple is still alive and presumably living comfortably. Abraham Shakespeare is dead and his money is gone. The difference was not luck. It was behavior. They chose silence and professional management. He chose visibility and trust in people who had not earned it. The outcomes were predictable from those behavioral choices.

You face similar choices about whether to broadcast your financial progress or to build wealth silently. You will encounter people who seem genuinely interested in how you are achieving success. Most of them are curious without being ready to implement what you would teach them. Some of them are opportunists seeking to exploit your information or your resources. A tiny minority are genuinely ready to learn and would benefit from your guidance. The one percent learn to distinguish among these groups through observation rather than through optimistically assuming everyone who asks questions has good intentions.

The frameworks have been provided. You understand why silence protects while disclosure creates problems. You understand why you cannot save people who are not ready to save themselves and why attempting to do so wastes your energy while creating resentment. You understand how to determine what information to share with whom and how to recognize when someone is genuinely ready to implement guidance versus when they are merely making conversation. You understand why the one percent move invisibly while the ninety-nine percent broadcast everything they achieve.

The implementation requires discipline to resist natural human desires for recognition, for status, and for helping everyone who seems to need help. You must accept that your wealth is private information to be shared only with people who need to know. You must accept that most people in your life will not build wealth regardless of how much you try to help them because they are not ready to change their behaviors. You must accept that genuine success requires no external validation and that seeking validation through sharing your achievements undermines the achievements themselves. You must accept that the people who knew you before you achieved success are your real friends while people who appear after you achieve success are probably opportunists.

Move in silence. Build wealth invisibly. Share information selectively. Help people who are ready to be helped. Accept that most people are not ready and that this is not your responsibility to fix. Maintain privacy that protects you and your family. Recognize that true security comes from resources that no one knows you have rather than from displays that broadcast vulnerability. The one percent understand these principles and they implement them consistently. The ninety-nine percent broadcast everything and wonder why they attract problems, why their advice is ignored, and why people seem more interested in what they have than in who they are. You now understand the distinction. The decision to move silently or to broadcast everything is yours. Choose wisely because this choice affects not only your privacy but also your safety and the authenticity of every relationship you maintain.

CHAPTER 36:
THE SCIENCE OF SELLING—HOW TO MARKET ANYTHING TO ANYONE

In 1923, a man named Claude Hopkins was earning the modern equivalent of over three million dollars annually as an advertising copywriter when most Americans earned less than two thousand dollars per year. Hopkins wrote advertisements for products ranging from beer to toothpaste to automobiles, and nearly everything he touched became phenomenally successful. Schlitz beer went from fifth place to tied for first in its market within months of Hopkins writing their campaign. Pepsodent toothpaste became the best-selling toothpaste in America despite being unknown before his involvement. Goodyear tires, Quaker Oats, and dozens of other brands achieved market dominance through Hopkins' advertising.

Hopkins' success was not accidental or artistic. While other advertisers of his era treated advertising as creative expression focused on clever wordplay and aesthetic beauty, Hopkins treated it as science with measurable results. He tested every element of his advertisements—headlines, body copy, offers, layouts—through running multiple versions simultaneously and tracking which versions produced the most sales. He insisted that advertising must be measured by sales generated rather than by aesthetic appeal or by how many people could recite clever slogans. He pioneered the use of coupons in advertisements specifically to track which publications and which ad variations produced results.

His most important insight was that people do not buy products—they buy outcomes those products create. Women did not buy Pepsodent toothpaste because they wanted toothpaste. They bought it because Hopkins' advertisements convinced them that the film on their teeth made them ugly and that Pepsodent removed that film, making them attractive. The product was toothpaste. The outcome was attractiveness. Hopkins sold outcomes while his competitors sold product features. This distinction made him the highest-paid advertising writer in the world and established principles that effective marketers still follow a century later.

Hopkins documented his methods in a short book called "Scientific Advertising" published in 1923 that David Ogilvy, the legendary advertising executive, later called "the most important book ever written about advertising." The book is ninety pages and contains more actionable wisdom about selling than most people learn in entire careers. Hopkins' core principle was simple: "The only purpose of advertising is to make sales. It is profitable or unprofitable according to its actual sales." Everything else—creativity, aesthetics, entertainment value, awards from advertising industry peers—was irrelevant if the advertising did not generate more revenue than it cost.

This chapter examines how to sell effectively whether you are selling products through advertisements, selling services through proposals, selling ideas through presentations, or selling yourself through resumes and interviews. These are not separate skills but applications of identical principles to different contexts. The person who understands how selling actually works gains advantages in every domain where persuasion determines outcomes—which is essentially every domain affecting wealth building. The one percent understand that they are always selling something, and they study the science of persuasion systematically rather than hoping charisma or luck will carry them through.

The foundational principle of all selling is that people make decisions emotionally and then justify those decisions rationally. This is not how people think they make decisions. If you ask people how they choose products, they will describe rational processes involving feature comparisons, price analysis, and logical evaluation of alternatives. But brain imaging studies and behavioral research reveal that emotional centers activate first during purchase decisions, with rational centers activating afterward to generate justifications for decisions already made emotionally.

Someone buying a luxury car tells themselves they selected it because of safety ratings, reliability statistics, and resale value. The reality is they bought it because driving it made them feel successful, attractive, and elevated in status relative to driving a less expensive alternative. The safety ratings and reliability statistics are post-purchase rationalizations that make them comfortable with the emotionally-driven decision they already made. The salesperson who appeals only to rational features misses the emotional drivers that actually determine purchase decisions. The salesperson who creates emotional desire while providing rational justification for that desire closes sales that purely rational approaches never close.

In 1984, Apple released a commercial during the Super Bowl introducing the Macintosh computer. The ad showed dystopian scene inspired by George Orwell's "1984" with mindless drones watching a screen showing Big Brother speaking to them. A woman runs into the room carrying a sledgehammer, throws it at the screen, destroying it and freeing the drones. A narrator says: "On January 24th, Apple Computer will introduce Macintosh. And you'll see why 1984 won't be like '1984.'"

The ad showed no computer. It mentioned no features. It provided no price information. It contained no rational argument for why someone should buy a Macintosh instead of an IBM PC. Yet it is widely considered one of the most effective advertisements ever created, driving enormous demand for Macintosh computers and establishing Apple as the rebellious alternative to the corporate computing establishment represented by IBM. The ad worked entirely through emotional positioning—buying a Macintosh meant you were a rebel, an individual, someone who refused to conform to corporate drones using IBM computers. The emotional desire to see yourself as rebellious individual drove the purchase decision. The technical features of the Macintosh provided post-purchase rationalization.

Jobs understood what Claude Hopkins understood sixty years earlier: people buy outcomes and identities, not features and specifications. The outcome is not owning a computer—it is being the kind of person who owns that computer and what that ownership signals about your identity. Apple has used this emotional positioning consistently for forty years. They do not primarily sell features. They sell identity. You are not buying a phone when you buy an iPhone—you are buying membership in a tribe of people who value design, simplicity, and innovation. You are signaling to others and to yourself that you are sophisticated enough to recognize quality and willing to pay for it.

The application to your situation is direct: whatever you are selling, you must understand what outcome the buyer actually wants and what identity the purchase allows them to adopt. The consultant selling their services is not selling hours of work or even expertise—they are selling the outcome of solving the client's problem while allowing the client to appear competent to their organization because they hired the right expert. The employee selling themselves in a job interview is not selling years of experience or technical skills—they are selling the outcome of making their future boss successful while allowing that boss to feel smart for recognizing their talent. The entrepreneur selling software is not selling features—they are selling the outcome of saving time or making money while allowing users to feel sophisticated for using advanced tools.

The one percent identify the emotional outcomes and identity associations their offering provides before attempting to sell anything. They ask themselves: What does buying this allow the customer to become? What problem does it solve that creates emotional relief? What status does it convey? What identity tribe does it provide membership in? What fear does it address? What aspiration does it fulfill? These emotional drivers matter far more than rational features, yet most people trying to sell focus exclusively on features because features are easier to articulate than emotions.

In 1976, a vacuum cleaner salesman named Joe Girard was listed in the Guinness Book of World Records as the world's greatest salesman. He had sold 13,001 cars at a single Chevrolet dealership over fifteen years—an average of 6 cars per day every working day for over a decade. This record has never been broken. Girard did not sell through discounting—he sold cars at full price. He did not sell through manipulation—his customers sent him referrals and returned to buy from him repeatedly. He sold through understanding that people buy emotionally and through systematic follow-up that kept him in their awareness.

Girard's system began with his "250 rule"—he believed every person knows approximately 250 people well enough that those people would attend their funeral. This meant that every customer he treated well would potentially tell 250 people about their positive experience, while every customer he treated poorly would tell 250 people about their negative experience. He treated every interaction as though 250 future sales depended on it because they did. He sent birthday cards, anniversary cards, and holiday cards to every customer every year. He called customers months after purchases to ensure they were happy. He sent referral cards to satisfied customers offering them gift certificates if they sent him buyers. He created systems that kept him in customers' minds so that when they or anyone they knew needed a vehicle, they thought of Joe Girard first.

His success came not from superior product knowledge—many salespeople knew cars better than he did. It came not from better location or better inventory—other salespeople at his dealership had identical access. It came from understanding that selling happens in the relationship rather than in the transaction, and that the sale is often the beginning of the relationship rather than the end. The one percent study Girard's methods because they demonstrate that systematic follow-up and relationship maintenance generate far more revenue than focusing exclusively on closing immediate transactions.

The customer research required for effective selling means understanding your target customer better than they understand themselves. This is not hyperbole—through systematic research into their problems, fears, aspirations, and objections, you can understand patterns in how they think and what they need better than any individual customer understands their own situation. Claude Hopkins would spend weeks living with typical customers of products he advertised, observing their daily routines, asking about their problems, and understanding their context before writing a single word of advertisement. This research allowed him to identify the emotional drivers that rational analysis would never reveal.

The modern equivalent involves interviewing existing customers to understand why they actually bought, what problems they were trying to solve, what alternatives they considered, what objections nearly prevented purchase, and what outcomes they achieved. These interviews reveal language customers use to describe their problems—language you should use in your marketing because it matches how they think. They reveal fears you need to address in your sales process. They reveal outcomes you should emphasize because those are the outcomes customers actually care about rather than outcomes you assume they care about.

The one percent invest substantial time in customer research before creating marketing or sales materials. They interview dozens of customers. They read online reviews of their competitors' products to understand what customers like and dislike. They join online communities where their target customers discuss their problems. They study demographics and psychographics to understand who their customers are and what values they hold. This research allows them to create marketing that resonates because it speaks directly to customers' actual situations rather than to situations the marketer imagines.

In 1957, a copywriter named Eugene Schwartz wrote an advertisement for a book called "The Complete Guide to Successful Card Playing" that generated over two million dollars in sales—equivalent to over twenty million in modern currency. The advertisement was ten pages of dense text with minimal images. It began: "Little known card secrets anyone can learn. Experts get rich at the card table—why not you?" The headline promised an outcome—getting rich through card playing—rather than describing the product. The body copy built desire through describing specific techniques readers would learn, through providing social proof of others who had succeeded, through addressing objections about whether card skills could actually be learned, and through creating urgency through limited-time pricing.

Schwartz understood market sophistication—the concept that markets become increasingly resistant to advertising claims as they mature. The first advertisement for a revolutionary product can make bold claims that readers accept because they have never seen similar claims. The hundredth advertisement for a similar product faces skeptical readers who have heard exaggerated claims repeatedly and who have been disappointed by products that failed to deliver. Schwartz identified five levels of market sophistication, each requiring different advertising approaches:

Level One: The market has never seen this type of product. You can make direct claims about the benefit the product provides. "This pill makes you lose weight" is sufficient because readers have never encountered weight loss pills before.

Level Two: The market has seen similar products and skepticism has developed. You must explain your mechanism differently than competitors explain theirs. "This pill makes you lose weight by blocking carbohydrate absorption rather than by increasing metabolism like other pills" differentiates your product while acknowledging that readers have seen weight loss pills before.

Level Three: The market has seen every possible mechanism claimed. You must focus on proof rather than on mechanism. "This pill makes you lose weight—here are the clinical trial results showing average weight loss of thirty-seven pounds in twelve weeks" provides evidence rather than merely making claims readers have heard before.

Level Four: The market is saturated and highly skeptical. You must change the conversation entirely by identifying new prospects or by reframing the problem. "This pill makes losing weight effortless so you can focus on enjoying life rather than obsessing about diet" shifts focus from the pill to the lifestyle enabled by not struggling with weight.

Level Five: The market is exhausted. You cannot say anything that moves them because they have heard everything. You must either find new markets or create entirely new products that restart the cycle at level one.

The one percent assess market sophistication before creating marketing because the level determines what approach will work. The market for productivity software is highly sophisticated—readers have seen thousands of tools claiming to improve productivity and they are skeptical of all claims. Marketing productivity software at level one by simply claiming it improves productivity will fail. You must operate at level three or four by providing proof of specific improvements or by reframing productivity entirely. The market for a genuinely novel technology might be at level one, allowing simpler direct claims that would fail in mature markets.

David Ogilvy founded an advertising agency in 1948 that became one of the largest agencies in the world, representing major brands including Rolls-Royce, Dove, and American Express. Ogilvy's work for Rolls-Royce included an advertisement with the famous headline: "At 60 miles an hour the loudest noise in this new Rolls-Royce comes from the electric clock." This headline accomplished multiple things simultaneously: it demonstrated the quietness of the vehicle through specific measurable claim, it established Rolls-Royce as meticulous about engineering details down to the clock, and it created image of luxury and refinement.

Ogilvy documented principles for effective advertising based on his decades of testing what worked versus what failed. His principles include: headlines are critical because five times as many people read headlines as read body copy, making headline the primary determinant of advertisement effectiveness. Photographs work better than drawings because people perceive photographs as more credible than illustrations. Captions under photographs are read by twice as many people as read body copy, making them valuable real estate for important messages. Long copy sells better than short copy for expensive or complex products because people considering major purchases want detailed information. Testimonials from satisfied customers provide credibility that corporate claims cannot match.

These principles seem obvious once stated, but they were revolutionary when Ogilvy published them because most advertisers operated on intuition and aesthetic preference rather than on tested results. The one percent apply Ogilvy's principles systematically: they invest disproportionate effort in crafting headlines because headlines determine whether anyone reads further. They use photographs of real results rather than stock images because photographs provide proof. They include detailed information for expensive offerings rather than assuming people want brief summaries. They collect and display testimonials prominently because social proof influences decisions more than corporate claims.

The sales funnel framework structures the journey from initial awareness to completed purchase, recognizing that most people do not buy immediately upon first exposure to your offering. The funnel stages include:

Awareness: The prospect becomes aware that you or your offering exists. This happens through advertising, content marketing, social media, word of mouth, or other channels that put your name in front of potential customers.

Interest: The prospect wants to learn more. They visit your website, read your content, watch your videos, or otherwise engage with information about your offering. They are evaluating whether this might solve their problem or fulfill their need.

Consideration: The prospect actively compares you to alternatives. They are reading reviews, checking competitors, calculating costs, and determining whether your offering is their best option. Most prospects never reach this stage—they lose interest before getting here.

Purchase: The prospect completes the transaction. This might be immediate for low-cost items or might require multiple interactions for expensive or complex offerings.

The critical insight is that different stages require different marketing approaches. Someone at the awareness stage needs to understand quickly what you offer and whether it might be relevant to them. Someone at the consideration stage needs detailed information addressing objections and demonstrating why you are superior to alternatives. The one percent create different content for each stage rather than using identical marketing for everyone regardless of where they are in the funnel.

In 1986, a copywriter named Gary Halbert was in federal prison for mail fraud when he wrote "The Boron Letters"—a series of letters to his son teaching him about copywriting and marketing. Despite being written in prison as instruction to a teenager, the letters became legendary in direct marketing circles because they condensed decades of Halbert's experience into clear actionable principles. One principle he emphasized was that the most valuable asset in any business is a list of customers who have bought from you previously— what he called the "customer list."

Halbert explained that acquiring new customers is expensive because you must spend money on advertising to people who mostly will not buy. The people who have already bought from you once are far more likely to buy from you again because they already trust you and they already know your offerings provide value. The profitability in most businesses comes not from initial sales but from repeat purchases by existing customers. Therefore, the primary goal of marketing should be to acquire customers even at break-even or loss on initial sale, knowing that profits will come from subsequent sales.

This framework revolutionizes how you think about customer acquisition costs. The person who calculates that they spend one hundred dollars in advertising to acquire a customer who buys a fifty-dollar product concludes they are losing money and that their marketing is failing. The person who understands lifetime customer value recognizes that losing fifty dollars to acquire a customer who will buy six more times over the next year, generating four hundred dollars in total revenue on one hundred dollars in product costs, is phenomenally profitable. The initial loss of fifty dollars generates ultimate profit of two hundred fifty dollars.

The one percent build businesses around maximizing lifetime customer value rather than around maximizing profit on initial transactions. They invest heavily in customer acquisition even when initial transactions are barely profitable or unprofitable, knowing that the real profits come from repeat purchases, upsells to more expensive offerings, and referrals to new customers. They track lifetime value meticulously rather than only measuring initial transaction value. They invest in retention and satisfaction because keeping existing customers is far cheaper than acquiring new ones.

The headline formula that Hopkins, Ogilvy, and other great copywriters developed through testing follows patterns that work reliably across contexts. Effective headlines typically include:

Specificity: "How to Earn $10,000 Monthly Working Part-Time from Home" works better than "How to Make Money from Home" because the specific number creates credibility while vague claims create skepticism.

Benefit: "Lose 30 Pounds in 60 Days Without Exercise" focuses on the outcome the reader wants rather than on the mechanism that delivers it.

Curiosity: "The One Productivity Habit That Billionaires Use Daily" creates gap between what reader knows and what headline promises to reveal, compelling them to read further to close the gap.

Urgency or Scarcity: "Limited Time: Save 50% Before Friday" creates pressure to act now rather than postponing indefinitely.

Social Proof: "Join 50,000 People Who Have Already Transformed Their Finances" reduces perceived risk through demonstrating that many others have already taken the action you are asking them to take.

The one percent test multiple headlines for important marketing by running small-scale tests to determine which headlines generate the most engagement before investing heavily in broader distribution. They understand that headlines determine whether anyone reads further and that spending hours crafting and testing headlines generates enormous returns through increased response rates.

The objection handling in marketing must address concerns before prospects articulate them because unaddressed objections prevent purchases even when prospects do not vocalize their concerns. Common objections include: "This is too expensive," "This will not work for me," "I don't have time," "I tried something similar before and it failed," "I don't trust this company," "I need to think about it." These objections are predictable across most offerings, allowing you to address them systematically in marketing materials.

The price objection is addressed not by discounting but by demonstrating value that exceeds price. The consultant charging ten thousand dollars for services addresses price objection by showing that their work generates one hundred thousand in value to the client, making the ten thousand fee a bargain rather than an expense. The software company charging two hundred dollars monthly addresses price objection by showing that their software saves five hours weekly, which for someone earning fifty dollars hourly is worth one thousand dollars monthly in time savings. The framework is to make price seem small relative to value rather than to make price objectively small.

The skepticism objection is addressed through social proof—testimonials from satisfied customers who achieved results, case studies documenting specific outcomes, endorsements from credible third parties, and money-back guarantees that reduce perceived risk. Someone skeptical that your offering works will trust other customers who report success far more than they will trust your claims about your own product. The one percent collect testimonials systematically by asking every satisfied customer to document their results and by making providing testimonials easy through templates and prompts.

The timing objection—"I need to think about it"—is addressed through creating urgency that makes delaying more painful than buying immediately. Urgency can be created through limited-time pricing, through limited availability, through bonuses that expire, or through emphasizing the cost of continued delay. "Save $500 if you enroll by Friday" creates urgency through disappearing discount. "Only 50 spots available" creates urgency through scarcity. "Every month you delay implementing this system costs you $2,000 in lost productivity" creates urgency by quantifying cost of inaction.

The one percent understand that ethical urgency involves real constraints rather than manufactured false scarcity. The discount that expires Friday must actually expire—if prospects learn that "limited time" offers are always extended, they will never respond to urgency appeals. The 50 spots must actually be limited—if unlimited people can enroll, the scarcity claim is fraud. The $2,000 monthly cost must be accurate calculation rather than invented number. Ethical urgency increases response rates while maintaining trust. False urgency might increase short-term response but destroys credibility when exposed.

In 1999, a marketer named Frank Kern was broke, living with his parents, and working odd jobs when he discovered he could sell information products online. He created simple ebooks teaching what he was learning about online marketing and sold them through basic websites. His first product generated a few thousand dollars. He invested that money in learning more about marketing and creating better products. Within five years he was generating millions annually. Within ten years he had built multiple businesses generating eight figures collectively and had become one of the most influential figures in online marketing.

Kern's success came partly from his marketing skills but primarily from his understanding that selling is about telling stories that allow prospects to see themselves achieving the outcomes you are selling. His sales letters did not focus on features of his courses—they told stories of people who had been broke or struggling and who had transformed their lives through implementing the strategies he taught. The stories were specific: "Sarah was working as a waitress earning $30,000 annually when she discovered this system. Six months later she quit her job because her online business was generating $8,000 monthly." These stories allowed prospects to imagine themselves as Sarah, achieving similar results through buying his course.

The story structure Kern used follows the hero's journey framework: the protagonist faces a problem, encounters obstacles, discovers a solution, implements the solution despite challenges, and ultimately achieves transformation. This structure is effective because it matches how humans process information and because it creates emotional engagement that pure information cannot create. The prospect reading about Sarah's transformation from waitress earning $30,000 to entrepreneur earning $96,000 annually experiences vicarious emotion that makes them want to achieve similar transformation.

The one percent use storytelling systematically in sales and marketing. They collect customer success stories documenting specific journeys from problem to solution. They structure case studies as narratives rather than as dry recitations of results. They tell their own stories of overcoming obstacles to achieve success, making themselves relatable rather than positioning themselves as naturally gifted people whose success cannot be replicated. They understand that "Sarah increased her income from $30,000 to $96,000 in six months" is less compelling than the story of Sarah's specific journey including her fears, her challenges, and her ultimate breakthrough.

The landing page structure for online marketing follows tested patterns that maximize conversion rates—the percentage of visitors who take desired action. Effective landing pages include:

Headline: Captures attention and communicates primary benefit in 10 words or fewer.

Subheadline: Expands on headline by providing additional detail about the outcome offered.

Hero Image or Video: Shows product being used or shows outcomes achieved, making abstract offering concrete.

Benefits: Lists 3-5 primary outcomes the buyer achieves, focusing on benefits to them rather than on product features.

Social Proof: Displays testimonials, case studies, logos of impressive clients, or statistics about satisfied customers.

Objection Handling: Addresses common concerns through FAQ section or through specific copy addressing price, skepticism, timing, or other objections.

Guarantee: Reduces perceived risk through money-back guarantee, free trial, or other mechanism that allows risk-free evaluation.

Call to Action: Makes completely clear what action you want them to take—"Buy Now," "Schedule Demo," "Download Free Guide"— using button that stands out visually and that is repeated multiple times throughout the page.

The one percent test every element of landing pages systematically through A/B testing where half of visitors see version A and half see version B, with results tracked to determine which version generates more conversions. They test headlines, images, copy length, button colors, guarantee wording, and every other variable. Small improvements in conversion rate compound enormously—increasing conversions from 2% to 3% increases revenue by 50% from the same traffic, making testing one of the highest-return activities in marketing.

The follow-up sequence for prospects who do not buy immediately determines whether you capture the majority who need multiple exposures before purchasing or whether you leave that money on the table. Research consistently shows that most purchases require 5-12 touchpoints before completion—someone must see your offering multiple times before they buy. The salesperson who gives up after one contact misses most potential sales. The salesperson who systematically follows up through email sequences, retargeting advertisements, phone calls, or direct mail generates far more revenue from identical initial prospect pool.

The one percent build automated follow-up sequences that continue engaging prospects for weeks or months after initial contact. Someone who visits their website but does not buy immediately is added to email sequence that sends valuable content every few days while occasionally making offers. Someone who abandons their shopping cart receives automated emails reminding them of items

551

they were considering and perhaps offering limited-time discount to complete purchase. Someone who attends a webinar but does not buy receives follow-up sequence addressing objections and providing additional information that moves them toward purchase. These automated sequences generate revenue that would never be captured through hoping prospects remember you and return on their own.

The pricing psychology affects perceived value and purchase likelihood more than actual price in many contexts. A product priced at $97 is perceived as significantly less expensive than the same product priced at $100 despite only $3 difference, because the first digit drops from 1 to 0. A product priced at $1,997 is perceived as "in the thousands" while a product priced at $2,003 is perceived as "over two thousand," making the $1,997 price seem psychologically cheaper despite only $6 difference. Services priced at $247 monthly rather than $3,000 annually convert better because the smaller monthly number seems more affordable even though the annual cost is higher ($2,964 paid monthly versus $3,000 paid annually).

The anchoring effect means that the first price mentioned establishes reference point against which all subsequent prices are judged. Someone told that a consultation costs $500 perceives that as expensive or cheap based on their expectations. Someone told that consultations typically cost $1,000 but that you are offering yours for $500 perceives $500 as a bargain because the $1,000 anchor established expectation that was then beaten. The one percent use anchoring strategically by mentioning the full retail price before offering their actual price, by mentioning competitor prices before showing their lower price, or by showing premium options before showing the option they actually want customers to buy, making that option seem reasonably priced by comparison.

The guarantee structure reduces perceived risk and often increases sales more than it increases refunds, making strong guarantees profitable despite some customers requesting refunds. A 30-day money-back guarantee increases conversions because prospects feel they can evaluate the product risk-free and request refunds if disappointed. A 60-day or 90-day guarantee increases conversions further because longer guarantee period signals even greater confidence in the product. An unconditional guarantee with no requirements for refund ("If you're not satisfied for any reason, we'll refund your money, no questions asked") converts better than conditional guarantees requiring specific conditions for refunds.

The one percent often offer stronger guarantees than competitors because they understand that guarantees primarily affect purchase decisions rather than refund rates. Someone confident their product delivers value expects low refund rates regardless of guarantee strength, so offering stronger guarantee captures more sales without proportionally increasing refunds. Someone unsure about product quality should fix quality rather than offering weak guarantees that fail to address quality concerns while also failing to maximize conversions.

The scarcity and urgency distinction matters because they create pressure through different mechanisms. Scarcity is about limited availability—"Only 50 spots available" or "Only 3 items remaining in stock." Urgency is about limited time—"Offer expires Friday" or "Price increases in 24 hours." Both increase conversion rates by making prospects fear missing out if they delay, but they work through different psychological mechanisms. Scarcity triggers competition for limited resources. Urgency triggers time-based pressure to act before opportunity disappears.

The one percent use both scarcity and urgency but only when real constraints exist. Real scarcity exists when consulting capacity is genuinely limited, when workshop attendance is capped by venue size, when products are limited edition by design. Real urgency exists when prices actually increase after deadline, when bonuses actually expire, when enrollment windows actually close. False scarcity and false urgency—claiming limits that do not exist—work short-term but destroy trust when discovered and turn customers into enemies who warn others about your dishonesty.

In 2014, a former Google employee named Neil Patel started a marketing agency that grew to 8-figure annual revenue within several years. Patel built his business almost entirely through content marketing—creating extensive blog posts, videos, and tools teaching digital marketing strategies. His content was consistently higher quality and more detailed than competitors provided. People searching for marketing information discovered his content, found it valuable, began trusting him as expert, and eventually hired his agency when they needed professional help implementing strategies he taught.

Patel's approach demonstrates the content marketing principle: provide so much free value that people trust your expertise and want to work with you despite having access to free information explaining how to do things themselves. This seems counterintuitive—why would someone pay for services when you have taught them how to do those services themselves? The answer is that knowing how to do something does not mean having time or capability to do it yourself, and that someone who has taught you valuable information for free has established trust that makes you confident they will deliver value when you pay them.

The one percent who build service businesses create extensive content teaching their methodologies because this content generates trust faster than sales pitches ever could. The consultant who publishes detailed case studies explaining exactly how they helped clients generate results positions themselves as expert while attracting similar clients who want the same results. The coach who creates videos explaining their frameworks teaches people their methodology while demonstrating expertise that makes prospects confident hiring them. The content creates inbound leads—people contacting you asking to work together—rather than requiring outbound selling where you contact prospects who do not know you.

The sales conversation structure for high-value offerings follows predictable patterns that effective salespeople use consistently. The structure includes:

- **Rapport Building:** Establishing personal connection before discussing business, making the prospect comfortable and creating foundation for relationship rather than treating interaction as pure transaction.

- **Situation Assessment:** Asking questions to understand the prospect's current situation, their challenges, their goals, and their constraints before proposing solutions.
- **Pain Point Identification:** Helping prospect articulate specific problems they face and the costs of those problems, creating emotional motivation to solve them rather than assuming problems are obvious or that their importance is understood.
- **Solution Presentation:** Explaining how your offering addresses the specific problems identified, focusing on outcomes rather than on features and connecting directly to the pain points discussed.
- **Objection Handling:** Addressing concerns the prospect raises without becoming defensive, acknowledging their validity while explaining why they should not prevent purchase.
- **Closing:** Asking directly for the sale rather than hoping the prospect will volunteer to buy—"Should we move forward with this?" or "When would you like to start?"

The one percent follow this structure rather than jumping directly to solution presentation before understanding the prospect's situation. They understand that people buy to solve their problems rather than to acquire your offering, and that you cannot position your offering as solution until you understand what problems they need solved. They ask more questions than they answer during initial conversations, uncovering information that allows them to position their offering optimally rather than delivering generic sales pitches that might not address what matters to specific prospects.

The refund handling for inevitable situations where customers request their money back affects future revenue more than current revenue because how you handle refunds determines whether disappointed customers become enemies who damage your reputation or whether they remain neutral or even positive because you handled their refund graciously. The one percent process refunds immediately without making customers jump through hoops, without interrogating them about why they are requesting refunds, and without creating negative experiences that turn disappointed customers into active opponents.

Someone who requests a refund and receives it quickly with no friction might still recommend you to others even though your offering was not right for them, because you demonstrated integrity through hassle-free refund process. Someone who requests a refund and faces resistance, delays, or accusations of trying to cheat the system becomes enemy who posts negative reviews and who warns others away from your business. The short-term cost of processing refunds graciously is far less than the long-term cost of creating enemies through difficult refund processes.

The principle connecting all of these frameworks is that effective selling serves the buyer by helping them get what they actually want while making profit for yourself through creating value rather than through extracting value. The salesperson focused on commission checks uses manipulation and pressure tactics that might generate short-term sales but that create resentful customers who never buy again and who warn others away. The salesperson focused on solving customer problems uses education and consultation to help customers make decisions that serve them, generating initial sales plus repeat purchases plus referrals that compound over time.

Claude Hopkins, Joe Girard, David Ogilvy, Gary Halbert, Eugene Schwartz, Frank Kern, and Neil Patel each built legendary success through understanding that selling is about understanding what people actually want, communicating how your offering delivers what they want better than alternatives, and building trust through delivering promised value consistently. Their methods work across any product, service, or idea because they are based on psychology rather than on specific tactics. The psychology is universal—people buy emotionally then justify rationally, people need multiple exposures before buying, people trust social proof more than corporate claims, people respond to stories more than to features, people fear loss more than they desire gain.

The frameworks have been provided. You understand that you are always selling something whether you realize it or not—selling yourself in job interviews, selling your ideas to colleagues, selling products to customers, selling services to clients. You understand the psychological principles that determine whether people buy or whether they decline. You understand the practical techniques that increase response rates—crafting effective headlines, telling compelling stories, addressing objections preemptively, creating urgency ethically, following up systematically, and pricing strategically. The implementation through creating actual marketing materials, running actual sales conversations, testing actual headlines and offers, and measuring actual results remains your responsibility.

The one percent study marketing and sales systematically because these skills multiply the value of everything else they do. The engineer who cannot sell their ideas remains unrecognized while the engineer who can sell their ideas advances rapidly. The consultant with superior expertise who cannot sell their services earns less than the consultant with adequate expertise who sells effectively. The entrepreneur with the best product who cannot market it fails while the entrepreneur with adequate product who markets brilliantly succeeds. You now understand how to sell effectively. The one percent choose to learn and implement these skills because they understand that value not communicated is value not captured. The ninety-nine percent avoid learning to sell because they view it as beneath them or because they hope quality alone will generate success. The outcomes generated by these different choices compound across careers and lives, creating enormous differences in wealth and impact.

CHAPTER 37:
IMPLEMENTATION—THE ONLY THING THAT MATTERS

In 1989, a psychology professor named Richard Wiseman began a decades-long research project investigating why some people consistently experience good fortune while others seem perpetually unlucky. He advertised in national newspapers asking people who considered themselves either exceptionally lucky or exceptionally unlucky to contact him for study participation. Over the following years, he interviewed hundreds of self-identified lucky and unlucky people, conducted experiments to test their behaviors and responses, and analyzed what separated these groups beyond their own perceptions of their fortune.

The results were striking. Lucky people were not actually experiencing more positive random events than unlucky people when objective measures were applied. They were experiencing the same frequency of opportunities, setbacks, and neutral events as everyone else. The difference was entirely in how they responded to circumstances and in patterns of behavior that increased their exposure to positive possibilities. Lucky people maintained networks that provided access to opportunities. They tried new experiences that created chances for unexpected discoveries. They noticed opportunities that others missed because they maintained optimistic attitudes that kept them scanning for possibilities rather than dwelling on problems. They turned bad luck into good fortune by finding positive aspects of negative situations and by refusing to abandon efforts after initial setbacks.

Unlucky people exhibited opposite patterns. They maintained small social circles that limited exposure to opportunities. They avoided new experiences, preferring comfort of familiar routines. They missed opportunities because they focused on searching for specific outcomes rather than remaining open to unexpected possibilities. They interpreted setbacks as evidence that nothing works rather than as learning experiences providing direction for adjustment. Most tellingly, the groups' behaviors were completely within their conscious control. When Wiseman taught unlucky people to adopt behaviors typical of lucky people—expanding networks, trying new activities, reframing setbacks positively—their self-reported luck improved dramatically within weeks.

This research demonstrates the fundamental principle that has been illustrated through every chapter of this book: outcomes are not primarily determined by circumstances, intelligence, education, or luck. Outcomes are determined by consistent patterns of behavior sustained over extended time periods. The one percent who build substantial wealth are not smarter, better educated, or luckier than the ninety-nine percent who accumulate little despite comparable or higher incomes. They implement different patterns of behavior across dozens of domains, and the compound effect of these behavioral differences creates wealth outcomes that diverge by millions of dollars over working lifetimes.

You have now received comprehensive education about those behavioral patterns across every major domain affecting wealth building. We began in Chapter One by establishing that wealth is built through stewardship of resources rather than through consumption, through long-term perspective rather than short-term gratification, and through systematic implementation of known principles rather than through searching for secret strategies or exceptional opportunities. We examined in Chapter Two how values and priorities determine which behaviors you will sustain when they conflict with immediate pleasure or social expectations. We established in Chapter Three the mindset differences between the one percent who believe wealth building is entirely within their control and the ninety-nine percent who believe wealth results from luck, circumstances, or exceptional talents they lack.

These foundational chapters were not inspirational fluff. They were establishing that before tactical strategies matter, you must develop the underlying perspective that allows sustained implementation of those strategies. The person who reads about optimal investment approaches but who lacks discipline to maintain them during market volatility will achieve worse results than the person with adequate strategy and iron discipline. The person who understands exactly which behaviors build wealth but who cannot sustain those behaviors when peers make different choices will achieve the same outcomes as someone who never learned those behaviors. Knowledge without implementation produces identical results to ignorance.

The investment strategy chapters taught you that wealth is built through systematic deployment of capital into diversified index funds held in tax-advantaged accounts for decades while avoiding speculation disguised as investing. These are not complicated strategies requiring exceptional intelligence or access to privileged information. They are simple strategies that anyone earning income can implement. The difficulty is not understanding what to do. The difficulty is doing it consistently for thirty to forty years while markets fluctuate, while peers chase hot investments, while countless distractions promise better returns through less boring approaches. The one percent implement these simple strategies without deviation. The ninety-nine percent understand the strategies but fail to implement them, or implement them briefly before abandoning them during volatility or being seduced by alternatives that promise excitement or superior returns.

The real estate chapters established that property ownership provides multiple simultaneous sources of wealth building through mortgage paydown, appreciation, cash flow, and tax benefits, but only if you select properties wisely, manage them competently, and maintain them for extended periods. The strategies for identifying good properties, for estimating cash flow accurately, for managing tenants, for optimizing taxes, and for deciding when buying makes sense versus renting are all knowable and implementable. None require genius or exceptional luck. They require research before purchase, discipline during operation, and patience to allow years of compound benefits to accumulate. The one percent implement these strategies when appropriate for their situations. The ninety-nine percent either never consider real estate investing because it seems complicated, or they purchase properties emotionally without proper analysis and then struggle with negative cash flow or management problems that could have been avoided through basic due diligence.

The spending optimization chapters addressed housing, vehicles, food, and other major expense categories that determine whether your income generates high savings rates or whether it is consumed entirely by expenses that feel normal because everyone around you maintains similar patterns. The strategies for minimizing these costs without sacrificing fundamental quality of life are straightforward. Live in less expensive housing than cultural norms suggest you should occupy at your income level. Drive older paid-off vehicles rather than financing new cars every few years. Cook meals at home rather than eating restaurant meals regularly. These are not complicated strategies. They are uncomfortable strategies because they make you visibly different from peers and because they require daily discipline rather than one-time decisions. The one percent implement them regardless of discomfort because they prioritize long-term wealth over short-term status signaling. The ninety-nine percent reject them as extreme or unnecessary despite understanding intellectually that the compound effects determine whether wealth accumulation is possible.

The career advancement chapters taught that income growth is the engine that funds wealth building and that career progression is not meritocracy but political system with knowable rules. You advance by demonstrating capabilities beyond your current role before receiving promotions, by making your bosses successful, by building cross-functional relationships, by taking on high-visibility projects, by documenting and communicating accomplishments, and by asking directly for advancement rather than waiting to be noticed. You interview successfully by researching employers thoroughly, by constructing narratives connecting your background to their specific needs, by asking strategic questions demonstrating understanding, and by negotiating compensation based on market rates rather than accepting initial offers. These are learnable skills that anyone can develop through study and practice. They are not practiced by the majority because most people hope that competent performance and likability will suffice and because actively managing career advancement seems manipulative or unseemly. The one percent implement these strategies systematically and advance accordingly. The ninety-nine percent avoid them and plateau at some middle level where their income remains modest despite competent performance.

The health and business chapters addressed two domains that operate differently from other components of wealth building but that profoundly affect outcomes. Health maintenance through basic exercise, nutrition, and sleep determines whether you sustain earning capacity for forty years or whether health problems force early retirement that prevents you from benefiting from the wealth you spent decades building. Side businesses provide mechanism to increase income beyond employment limits while building equity that employment never provides. Both domains require consistent implementation of simple principles over extended periods. The one percent invest modest time in health maintenance and in rational business building because they understand the returns dwarf the costs. The ninety-nine percent neglect health until problems force attention and either never attempt entrepreneurship or attempt it recklessly through quitting stable employment to chase uncertain dreams.

The tool and system chapters on credit cards, taxes, and cash management addressed how to optimize the financial instruments and systems that facilitate wealth building. These optimizations generate meaningful returns—thousands to tens of thousands over working years—but they matter far less than the major decisions about earning, investing, and spending. The one percent optimize these details after addressing major domains because marginal improvements to sound foundations produce real benefits. The ninety-nine percent either ignore these optimizations entirely or focus on them while neglecting major domains, producing situations where they are maximizing credit card rewards while carrying high-interest debt or optimizing cash management while maintaining spending patterns that prevent meaningful wealth accumulation.

The pattern across all domains is identical. The strategies are simple and knowable. The difficulty is sustained implementation despite discomfort, despite social pressure, despite countless temptations to abandon discipline for immediate gratification or for alternatives promising easier paths. The one percent implement strategies consistently across decades. The ninety-nine percent learn strategies but fail to implement them, implement them inconsistently, or abandon them when circumstances make continuation difficult.

This brings us to the only question that actually matters: will you implement what you have learned or will this book become one more source of knowledge that fails to produce changed behavior? The information you have received throughout these chapters is worthless if it produces no change in your actions. Reading about optimal investment strategies while continuing to consume your income without systematic savings generates identical wealth to never reading about investing at all. Understanding exactly how to minimize major expenses while maintaining spending patterns that prevent wealth accumulation produces the same outcome as remaining ignorant of those strategies. Knowing how to advance your career through systematic networking and skill demonstration while waiting passively for recognition leads to the same plateau as never learning that career advancement requires active management.

The transformation from knowledge to implementation requires several components that most people never develop. First is genuine acceptance that your current patterns are producing outcomes you claim not to want. The person who says they want to build wealth while spending ninety-five percent of their income has not accepted that their spending patterns are incompatible with wealth building. They are hoping to discover strategies that allow wealth building without changing spending, which is impossible. The person who says they want career advancement while performing their defined role competently and then going home has not accepted that advancement requires demonstrating next-level capabilities and actively managing their visibility and relationships. They are hoping that merit will be recognized automatically, which is false. The acceptance of reality rather than hoping reality will accommodate your preferences is the first requirement for behavioral change.

Second is willingness to endure discomfort that results from living differently than peers and from delaying gratification for years before benefits materialize. The person who will not tolerate living in less expensive housing than they could technically afford cannot implement spending discipline that generates high savings rates. The person who will not tolerate driving an older car when peers drive new vehicles cannot minimize transportation costs that represent the second-largest expense category. The person who will not tolerate the social awkwardness of declining expensive activities with friends cannot maintain spending discipline when peer pressure makes consumption tempting. The question is whether you can tolerate years of discomfort during building years in exchange for decades of financial freedom that your peers who chose comfort will never achieve. Most people cannot tolerate this, which is precisely why most people never build substantial wealth.

Third is establishment of systems and automation that make optimal behaviors automatic rather than depending on making correct decisions repeatedly when alternatives are tempting. The person who attempts to save whatever remains after spending will save nothing because nothing remains after spending. The person who establishes automatic transfers moving predetermined percentages to investment accounts immediately upon receiving paychecks saves consistently because the money never exists as available funds for spending temptation. The person who attempts to eat healthy through willpower while maintaining kitchens full of junk food will fail during moments of hunger or stress. The person who systematically shops for healthy food and who simply does not purchase junk food succeeds because the discipline occurred once during shopping rather than requiring ongoing willpower at home.

Fourth is tracking and measurement that provides feedback about whether your actions are producing intended results. The person who does not track net worth quarterly does not know whether their financial behaviors are actually building wealth or whether they are merely treading water while feeling like they are making progress. The person who does not track savings rates and investment returns does not know whether they are on track to reach financial independence or whether their timeline assumptions are wildly optimistic. The person who does not track career progression does not know whether their advancement strategies are working or whether they are spinning wheels while peers advance past them. The one percent measure outcomes systematically and adjust behaviors when measurements reveal problems. The ninety-nine percent avoid measurement because they fear confirming that their actions are not producing results they hope for.

Fifth is long-term perspective that allows sustained effort across years and decades when benefits are not immediately visible. The person who expects to see meaningful wealth accumulation after six months of saving will become discouraged and abandon the effort when their account balances remain modest. The person who understands that wealth builds slowly through compound growth over decades maintains discipline through the years when progress seems minimal. The person who expects immediate career advancement after implementing better strategies for six months becomes frustrated when promotions do not materialize quickly. The person who understands that career advancement requires years of consistent networking, skill demonstration, and visibility management maintains effort across the time periods required for results. The one percent maintain perspective that allows sustained implementation despite slow visible progress. The ninety-nine percent abandon efforts when immediate results do not materialize.

The mathematical reality of wealth building is that small differences in behavior compound into enormous differences in outcomes across working lifetimes. Someone earning seventy-five thousand annually who saves fifteen percent achieves dramatically different outcomes than someone earning the same amount who saves forty percent. The difference is eighteen thousand seven hundred fifty annually, which seems meaningful but not life-changing. Over thirty years at ten percent returns, this eighteen thousand seven hundred fifty annual difference compounds into approximately three million dollars in accumulated wealth difference. The person saving forty percent reaches financial independence in their fifties. The person saving fifteen percent works until forced retirement. The behavioral difference is small—living on forty-five thousand versus living on sixty-three thousand seven hundred fifty annually. The outcome difference is the distinction between financial freedom and lifetime employment.

Someone who advances their career systematically by building relationships, demonstrating next-level capabilities, and asking explicitly for promotions might increase their income from sixty thousand to one hundred fifty thousand over fifteen years. Someone with identical starting position who performs their job competently while waiting to be noticed might see their income increase to eighty thousand over the same period. The income differential by year fifteen is seventy thousand annually. Over remaining working years, this compounds into millions in differential lifetime earnings and tens of millions in differential investment wealth through investing that additional income. The behavioral differences are modest—spending time networking, volunteering for visible projects, preparing for interviews, negotiating compensation. The outcome differences determine entirely different life trajectories.

Someone who maintains basic health practices through thirty minutes of resistance training three times weekly, ten thousand daily steps, adequate protein and vegetable consumption, and seven to eight hours of sleep might work productively until age seventy-five. Someone who neglects these practices might face forced retirement at sixty due to health problems. The fifteen additional working years at one hundred thousand annual income represent one million five hundred thousand in direct earnings. The compound investment returns on that income over subsequent decades represent several million more. The behavioral differences are modest—three hours weekly of exercise and attention to basic nutrition and sleep. The outcome differences are the distinction between extended productive years and forced early retirement with inadequate resources.

These examples demonstrate that the distinction between the one percent who build substantial wealth and the ninety-nine percent who accumulate little is not found in dramatic differences in intelligence, education, opportunities, or luck. The distinction is found in modest behavioral differences sustained consistently across decades. The accumulation of these small differences through compound effects creates outcome differentials that reach millions of dollars. This is why the frameworks provided throughout this book matter despite their simplicity. They identify the specific behavioral patterns that produce wealth building versus the patterns that prevent it. The implementation of the wealth-building patterns consistently across years and decades is the only thing that actually matters.

The choice before you is whether to implement these patterns or to continue the patterns you have maintained that have produced your current financial situation. If you are satisfied with your current trajectory toward financial outcomes that your current patterns produce, you need change nothing. If you are dissatisfied with that trajectory and want different outcomes, you must change behaviors to align with the patterns the one percent demonstrate. There is no third option where you maintain current behaviors while hoping for different outcomes. That is delusion rather than strategy.

The implementation must begin immediately rather than at some future date when circumstances improve or when you feel more prepared. The person who waits until they earn more to begin saving finds that expenses rise with income and that no income level feels sufficient to begin. The person who waits until they have more time to begin exercising discovers that free time never materializes and that health continues deteriorating while they wait. The person who waits until they feel confident to begin networking or asking for promotions never develops that confidence through waiting and watches peers advance while they remain stuck. The one percent begin implementing optimal behaviors immediately with whatever resources and circumstances they currently have. The ninety-nine percent wait for perfect conditions that never arrive.

The specific actions you should take immediately upon finishing this book depend on your current situation and which domains need most attention. If you have consumer debt, your first priority is eliminating that debt before addressing any other financial strategy because interest rates on consumer debt exceed returns from any investment you might make. If you are not contributing to employer retirement accounts to capture full company match, establish automatic contributions to capture that match because this is free money providing immediate returns. If you maintain lifestyle consuming ninety-five percent or more of income, establish automatic savings transfers that force you to live on eighty-five to ninety percent so that you begin building investment capital rather than consuming everything you earn.

If your career has stagnated with no promotions or meaningful raises in several years, schedule meetings with your manager to discuss explicit advancement criteria and establish visible projects that demonstrate next-level capabilities. If your major expense categories of housing, transportation, and food consume seventy-five percent or more of gross income, develop plans to reduce those categories by twenty to thirty percent through the specific strategies provided in relevant chapters. If you have no side income beyond employment and you have time available beyond work obligations, identify service or product opportunities you could pursue to generate additional income that accelerates wealth building beyond employment income alone.

If you neglect health through sedentary lifestyle, poor nutrition, and inadequate sleep, establish basic exercise routine of resistance training three times weekly and ten thousand daily steps while improving nutrition through adequate protein and substantial vegetables at every meal. If you maintain checking account balances far exceeding transaction needs or if emergency funds sit in accounts earning essentially nothing, move those funds to high-yield savings accounts offering four to five percent returns. If you have never met with tax advisor to discuss planning strategies or if you make major financial decisions without considering tax implications, retain competent advisor and establish year-round communication about tax optimization.

These immediate actions are not comprehensive wealth-building strategies. They are first steps that begin changing behavioral patterns from consumption and passivity toward accumulation and active management. The comprehensive implementation requires sustained effort across all domains we have examined. The person who optimizes investments while neglecting career advancement leaves substantial wealth unrealized. The person who maximizes income while consuming it all through poor spending discipline builds no wealth despite high earnings. The person who achieves everything perfectly in financial domains while destroying health through neglect might never benefit from the wealth accumulated. The integration across domains is what produces outcomes that transform lives rather than merely marginally improving finances.

The obstacles you will face during implementation are predictable because they are the same obstacles that prevent most people from building wealth. Social pressure from peers making different choices will tempt you to abandon discipline for conformity. Delayed gratification required while benefits accumulate will tempt you to abandon long-term strategies for immediate consumption. Complexity of managing multiple domains simultaneously will tempt you to simplify through ignoring domains that seem less urgent. Slow visible progress during early years will tempt you to abandon efforts that seem to produce inadequate results. Unexpected setbacks will tempt you to interpret difficulties as evidence that strategies do not work rather than as normal obstacles requiring adjustment.

The one percent who successfully implement wealth-building behaviors overcome these obstacles through several practices. They reduce social pressure by cultivating relationships with people making similar choices rather than expecting peers pursuing different paths to support their priorities. They maintain long-term perspective by tracking progress toward multi-decade goals rather than evaluating success based on monthly results. They manage complexity through systems and automation that make optimal behaviors automatic rather than requiring constant decision-making. They interpret setbacks as learning opportunities providing information about necessary adjustments rather than as evidence of futility. They maintain conviction in the soundness of their approach even when progress seems minimal because they understand the mathematics of compound growth.

The timeline from beginning implementation to achieving financial independence varies based on income level, savings rate, and starting point but follows predictable mathematical patterns. Someone earning sixty thousand annually and saving forty percent can accumulate sufficient wealth to support retirement at fifty thousand annual spending within approximately twenty-five years. Someone earning one hundred thousand annually and saving fifty percent can reach the same wealth level supporting seventy thousand annual spending within approximately eighteen years. Someone earning one hundred fifty thousand annually and saving sixty percent can reach financial independence supporting eighty thousand annual spending within approximately thirteen years. These timelines assume ten percent average annual returns and assume you begin from zero wealth, so higher initial wealth shortens timelines while lower returns extend them.

The achievement of financial independence does not require extraordinary income or exceptional investment returns. It requires ordinary income managed through high savings rates sustained across years sufficient for compound growth to build portfolios that generate withdrawal rates supporting your lifestyle. The person earning sixty thousand who saves forty percent will reach financial independence. The person earning two hundred thousand who saves ten percent will not. The income level matters far less than the savings rate and the discipline to sustain that rate across decades.

The life that financial independence provides is not one of luxury consumption or complete leisure. It is life of optionality where you make choices based on what you want to do rather than based on what you must do to generate income. You might continue working because you find your work meaningful, but you work on your terms rather than on employers' terms because you do not need the income to survive. You might pursue creative projects or charitable work that provides no income because you can fund your lifestyle from investment returns. You might take extended time to travel or to spend with family without concern about employment gaps on resume. You might start businesses with no immediate profit potential because you can afford to build slowly without requiring revenue for survival.

This optionality is the actual goal of wealth building rather than accumulated dollars in accounts. The dollars are merely the mechanism that purchases freedom from having to trade time for money according to others' requirements. The one percent understand this and optimize for years until freedom rather than for maximum accumulated wealth. They might reach their freedom number and stop aggressive wealth accumulation even when they could continue building larger portfolios because additional wealth provides no additional optionality beyond what they have already secured. The ninety-nine percent who never reach financial independence never experience this optionality regardless of whether they earn comfortable incomes because they remain dependent on employment income until forced retirement.

Richard Wiseman's research on luck demonstrated that people who experience consistent good fortune do so through patterns of behavior entirely within their conscious control. They maintain networks, try new experiences, notice opportunities, reframe setbacks positively, and persist despite difficulties. These are choices available to anyone regardless of circumstances or resources. The wealth-building journey you have been educated about throughout this book operates identically. The outcomes are determined by behavioral patterns entirely within your control. You choose whether to save or spend. You choose whether to invest systematically or consume income as it arrives. You choose whether to live below your means or according to cultural expectations. You choose whether to advance your career actively or wait passively for recognition. You choose whether to maintain health or neglect it. You choose whether to implement what you have learned or to hope that knowledge alone produces different outcomes.

The one percent make different choices than the ninety-nine percent across dozens of domains, and the compound effect of those choices creates wealth outcomes that diverge by millions of dollars. You have been provided complete education about what those different choices are, why they matter, and how to implement them. The education is worthless without implementation. The implementation is entirely your responsibility. No one will force you to establish automatic savings. No one will prevent you from purchasing vehicles you cannot afford. No one will stop you from eating restaurant meals daily. No one will make you ask for promotions or build side businesses or maintain health practices or optimize taxes.

The choice is yours to make and yours alone. You can implement the frameworks provided and build wealth that creates freedom and optionality. You can acknowledge the frameworks while continuing patterns that prevent wealth building and accepting the lifetime employment those patterns produce. Or you can deceive yourself that knowledge without implementation somehow produces results different from ignorance. The first path leads to financial independence and the life optionality that independence provides. The second and third paths lead to the same destination—dependence on employment income until forced retirement, modest accumulated wealth insufficient to provide meaningful freedom, and the realization that the life you wanted was achievable if you had implemented what you knew rather than merely learning it.

The one percent implement. The ninety-nine percent learn, admire, appreciate, and fail to act. You now know everything required to join the one percent. The only remaining question is whether you will act on that knowledge or whether you will become one more person who knows exactly what to do while doing something else entirely. That choice and its consequences over your remaining working years and into retirement are entirely yours. Choose wisely. Implement consistently. Build wealth systematically.

CHAPTER 38:
LEGACY—WHAT WEALTH IS FOR

In 1990, a man named Chuck Feeney stood in his modest apartment in San Francisco looking at financial statements that confirmed what he already knew. Over the previous decades, he had built a retail empire called Duty Free Shoppers that had made him a billionaire several times over. His personal wealth exceeded eight billion dollars, placing him among the wealthiest people in America. Most people in his position were purchasing estates, yachts, private jets, and other displays of accumulated wealth. Feeney owned none of these things. He lived in a rented apartment. He flew commercial in economy class. He wore an inexpensive watch. His entire lifestyle could be funded by a modest middle-class income, despite having accumulated billions.

Feeney had made a decision years earlier that profoundly shaped how he viewed his wealth. He did not consider the billions to be his in any meaningful sense beyond legal title. He viewed himself as temporary steward of resources that should be deployed for maximum positive impact rather than consumed for personal pleasure or hoarded for dynastic wealth transfer. He had established The Atlantic Philanthropies in 1982 and had quietly transferred his entire stake in Duty Free Shoppers to this foundation, retaining for himself only enough to maintain his modest lifestyle. The foundation would eventually give away over eight billion dollars to causes including education, healthcare, human rights, and scientific research, making it one of the largest philanthropic efforts in history.

What made Feeney's approach radical was not the scale of giving but the philosophy behind it. He practiced what he called "Giving While Living," insisting that charitable foundations should deploy their resources during the lifetimes of their founders rather than existing in perpetuity. He gave anonymously for decades, refusing recognition or naming rights that most major donors demand. He required the foundation to spend down all assets and close its doors by 2020, which it did after giving away its final grants. His reasoning was straightforward: money does good when it is deployed to solve problems, not when it sits in foundation accounts generating returns for distant future use. The problems of today require resources today, and the person who built the wealth should see it deployed during their lifetime rather than creating perpetual institutions that might or might not use resources effectively after they are gone.

This chapter addresses the question that follows naturally from everything we have discussed throughout this book: what is wealth for once you have built it? We have examined every strategy for accumulating wealth through high savings rates, systematic investing, career advancement, real estate, side businesses, and optimization of every major expense category. We have established that disciplined implementation of these strategies over decades produces wealth that provides financial independence and life optionality. But to what end? What should you do with wealth once you have accumulated it? How should you think about legacy and impact beyond your own consumption and security?

These questions matter because wealth building without purpose beyond accumulation produces empty achievement that fails to create meaning or lasting impact. The person who reaches financial independence with two million in investment accounts and no sense of what that wealth enables beyond personal security has succeeded financially while failing to engage with the deeper questions about what resources are for. The person who builds businesses generating substantial income while consuming all of it on progressively more expensive lifestyle has built nothing of lasting significance despite the apparent success. The one percent who build wealth most effectively also think most carefully about what that wealth should accomplish beyond providing for their own material needs.

The framework for thinking about wealth purpose begins with the stewardship principle established in Chapter One. You do not create wealth from nothing. You create it by combining your labor and intelligence with resources, institutions, and infrastructure that society provides. The education that made your career possible was funded largely by others through taxes and philanthropy. The legal system that protects property rights and enforces contracts was built over centuries and is maintained by everyone who respects rule of law. The markets that allow you to invest and build wealth exist because of regulatory frameworks and social trust that you did not create. The businesses that employ you or purchase your products exist within economic systems that countless people built and maintain. Your wealth is not purely the product of your individual effort despite your hard work contributing significantly to its creation.

This understanding does not diminish your achievement or suggest you lack rights to wealth you built legally. It establishes appropriate perspective that you are steward of resources created through interaction between your efforts and the broader systems and resources that society provides. This stewardship carries responsibilities that extend beyond maximizing personal consumption or dynastic wealth transfer. How you deploy wealth you have accumulated affects not only your own wellbeing but potentially the wellbeing of countless others who benefit from or are harmed by how you use resources under your control.

The immediate family provision represents the first circle of responsibility for deployed wealth. You have obligations to ensure your children receive education that prepares them for adult life, that they have healthcare when they need it, and that they reach adulthood without being hobbled by financial circumstances of their childhood. You have obligations to your spouse or partner if you have made commitments to share life together. You have potential obligations to parents or siblings if they face hardships that you have capacity to address. These familial obligations are real and they represent legitimate uses of wealth beyond your own consumption.

The challenge with family provision is determining where appropriate support ends and where wealth transfer that damages recipients begins. The child who receives everything they want without effort or achievement learns helplessness and entitlement rather than capability and agency. The adult child who receives substantial ongoing financial support never develops self-sufficiency or discovers what they are capable of achieving independently. The family member who faces manufactured crisis repeatedly because they know you will bail them out never learns to manage their own affairs responsibly because your intervention prevents natural consequences that would force learning.

The one percent who successfully pass wealth to next generations do so through education and opportunity rather than through elimination of all struggle or provision of unlimited resources. They fund education that develops capabilities. They provide seed capital for business ventures after children have demonstrated commitment and competence. They allow children to experience failure and difficulty while standing ready to prevent catastrophic outcomes. They model the behaviors and values that built wealth rather than merely transferring money and expecting values to somehow transmit through inheritance. They establish trust structures that provide access to resources over time rather than in lump sums that can be squandered quickly. They communicate explicitly about family wealth, about where it came from, about responsibilities that accompany it, and about expectations for how it should be used.

The ninety-nine percent either have no wealth to transfer or they transfer it in ways that damage recipients. They either tell children nothing about family wealth, creating complete surprise when inheritance materializes, or they flaunt wealth in ways that create entitlement expectations. They either give children nothing, forcing them to struggle unnecessarily when help would enable legitimate opportunities, or they give everything, preventing development of capabilities that struggle creates. They provide no education about money management, investment principles, or values that should guide wealth deployment, and then wonder why inheritors squander resources quickly.

The Warren Buffett principle that you should leave children "enough money so they can do anything, but not so much that they can do nothing" captures appropriate balance. The amount that allows adult children to pursue meaningful work or entrepreneurship or creative pursuits without financial desperation while not being so large that they never need to work or create value themselves. This amount varies by individual and by what you know about each child's character and capabilities. Some children can handle substantial wealth responsibly. Others would be damaged by access to large resources before they have developed maturity and discipline to deploy those resources well.

The education of children about money should begin early through age-appropriate involvement in family financial discussions and decisions. Young children learn through earning small amounts for completing tasks, through saving for things they want, and through experiencing both the satisfaction of achieved goals and the disappointment of spending on things that provide no lasting value. Teenagers learn through managing clothing budgets, through earning money through employment, through maintaining checking accounts, and through understanding family discussions about major financial decisions like vehicle purchases or college planning. Young adults learn through managing larger sums, through facing real financial consequences of decisions, and through explicit instruction about investment principles, tax planning, and long-term wealth building.

The one percent involve children in philanthropy from young ages, allowing them to participate in decisions about which causes to support and requiring them to research organizations and explain why particular giving makes sense. This teaches that wealth exists for purposes beyond personal consumption and it develops judgment about how to evaluate organizations and causes. The ninety-nine percent either never expose children to giving or they give without explanation, failing to develop charitable inclination or judgment about effective deployment of resources for social benefit.

The extended family and friendship circles represent more complex questions about obligations and appropriate support. The person who builds wealth often faces requests from relatives and friends facing financial difficulties. These requests range from legitimate temporary assistance for people facing genuine hardship through preventable crises resulting from poor decisions that the requester has made repeatedly. The distinction matters because appropriate assistance helps people through difficult periods so they can resume self-sufficiency, while misguided assistance enables continuing dysfunction by preventing natural consequences of poor choices.

The framework for evaluating requests is asking whether this assistance addresses genuine temporary hardship, whether the recipient is willing to change behaviors that created the situation, whether you can provide assistance in ways that create accountability for improvement, and whether saying no might actually serve the person better by forcing them to solve their own problems rather than depending on your intervention. The one percent help people facing genuine hardship who demonstrate commitment to changing the patterns that created their situations. They refuse to enable people whose crises result from repeated poor choices and who show no willingness to change those patterns. They understand that saying no can be the most compassionate response when yes would merely delay necessary learning while consuming resources that could help others facing legitimate hardship.

The charitable giving during wealth building years should begin even when resources are modest because the habits and values established during building years persist after wealth accumulates. The person who gives nothing while building wealth will likely give nothing after achieving wealth because they have established consumption patterns that expand to absorb all available resources regardless of how much they accumulate. The person who maintains systematic giving from the beginning, even when giving five percent of modest income, establishes that wealth exists for purposes beyond personal consumption and develops judgment about effective giving through years of practice with smaller amounts before facing decisions about deploying larger resources.

The percentage of income devoted to giving varies based on values, obligations, and circumstances. Many religious traditions suggest ten percent as appropriate baseline, though the specific percentage matters less than establishing systematic practice of giving rather than consuming all income beyond what you save. Someone might give five percent during years of building wealth aggressively while maintaining high savings rates, then increase to ten or twenty percent during later years when wealth building needs are less acute. The person who reaches financial independence and who requires only three to four percent withdrawal rates to fund their lifestyle might give away the difference between what their investments generate and what they need, potentially giving away half or more of investment returns annually while maintaining or growing principal.

The selection of causes to support should reflect thoughtful analysis about where resources can generate maximum positive impact rather than responding to emotional appeals or social pressure. The most effective giving typically supports organizations with proven track records of accomplishment in their domains, with clear metrics for measuring impact, with low overhead costs that ensure donated resources fund programs rather than administration, and with approaches that build capacity and self-sufficiency rather than creating dependency on continuing donations.

The evaluation of charitable organizations requires examining their financial statements to understand what percentage of donations fund programs versus overhead, reading independent evaluations from organizations like Charity Navigator or GiveWell that analyze effectiveness and financial health, understanding their specific approaches and whether those approaches are supported by evidence of effectiveness, and ideally visiting organizations to observe their work directly and to meet leadership and staff who execute the mission. The person who gives based on emotional appeals or familiar names without evaluating effectiveness wastes resources that could produce far greater impact if deployed to organizations actually accomplishing meaningful results efficiently.

The donor-advised funds provide tax-efficient vehicles for systematic giving that separate the timing of tax deductions from the timing of gifts to specific charities. You contribute cash or appreciated securities to a donor-advised fund, receiving immediate tax deduction for the full contribution. The assets grow tax-free within the fund. You recommend grants from the fund to qualified charities at whatever schedule you choose, potentially years after making the contribution. This allows you to bunch multiple years of giving into single tax years when itemizing deductions provides benefit, while distributing actual grants to charities over multiple years according to their needs and your preferences.

The appreciated securities donations provide additional tax benefits because you avoid capital gains taxes on appreciation while receiving charitable deduction for full market value. If you hold stock purchased for twenty thousand dollars that has appreciated to fifty thousand dollars, donating the stock directly to charity or to donor-advised fund provides fifty thousand dollar charitable deduction while avoiding capital gains tax on the thirty thousand dollar appreciation. If you instead sold the stock and donated cash, you would pay capital gains taxes on the thirty thousand dollar gain, reducing the amount available for charitable donation. The tax savings from donating appreciated securities rather than cash can reach fifteen to twenty percent of contribution amount for high earners, effectively allowing you to give more to charity at no additional after-tax cost.

The family foundations provide alternative structures for charitable giving that offer more control than donor-advised funds but that require more administrative complexity and cost. Foundations can be established with minimums as low as one hundred thousand to two hundred fifty thousand dollars in many states, though amounts below one million often cannot justify administrative costs. Foundations allow family involvement in grantmaking decisions, can employ family members in foundation operations, and continue across generations if structured appropriately. The trade-offs are substantial administrative burdens including annual tax filings, required minimum distributions of five percent of assets annually, and potential scrutiny of investments and grantmaking to ensure compliance with tax exemption requirements.

The decision between donor-advised funds and family foundations depends on asset levels devoted to charitable giving, desire for family involvement and continuity across generations, and tolerance for administrative complexity. For most people giving less than several million over their lifetimes, donor-advised funds provide better combination of simplicity and tax benefits. For those devoting tens of millions or more to charitable purposes and who want maximum family involvement and perpetual structures, foundations might justify their additional complexity and cost.

The impact investing represents approach to deploying wealth that seeks both financial returns and positive social or environmental outcomes. Rather than separating wealth building through market-rate investments from charitable giving through donations that provide no financial return, impact investing attempts to achieve both objectives simultaneously by investing in businesses or funds that address social problems while generating profits. Examples include affordable housing developments that provide both community benefit and reasonable investment returns, renewable energy projects that advance environmental goals while generating income, or businesses in developing countries that create employment while producing profits.

The challenge with impact investing is that most opportunities generate returns below what you could achieve through conventional investing while requiring more sophisticated analysis to evaluate both financial and impact components. The person who accepts two percent returns from impact investments when they could achieve eight percent returns through index funds has foregone six percent annually, which compounds over decades into substantial wealth difference. This foregone return represents the true cost of the impact investment. Whether that cost is justified depends on whether the impact generated exceeds what you could accomplish by earning higher returns through conventional investments and donating the difference to effective charities. In many cases, the latter approach produces both more wealth and more social benefit than attempting to achieve both through single investment vehicle.

The legacy thinking should extend beyond one generation to consider what values, capabilities, and resources you are establishing for descendants you will never meet. The person who builds substantial wealth and transfers it to children without education about stewardship or without structures ensuring responsible use across generations often creates wealth that is squandered within one or two generations. The adage that wealth lasts three generations—the builder who creates it, the inheritor who preserves it, and the spender who destroys it—is not inevitable outcome but rather is result of failing to establish values and structures that promote stewardship across generations.

The one percent who build wealth intended to benefit multiple generations do so through several mechanisms. They establish trust structures that provide access to income while protecting principal across generations. They require education about investment principles, philanthropy, and family values before beneficiaries gain full control of assets. They involve each generation in family business or philanthropic activities so that stewardship and purpose transmit through participation rather than merely through inheritance. They communicate family history and the principles that built wealth so descendants understand where resources came from and what responsibilities accompany them. They establish family governance structures that bring generations together to make decisions about shared resources and about family direction.

The teaching of wealth-building principles to others beyond your immediate family represents form of legacy that costs nothing beyond time while potentially transforming countless lives. The person who builds wealth through systematic implementation of known principles possesses knowledge that most people lack despite that knowledge being potentially life-changing for anyone who implements it. The decision about whether to hoard that knowledge or to share it freely determines whether your achievement benefits only you and your immediate family or whether it creates ripple effects through all the people you teach who then teach others.

The objections to teaching others usually involve fear that sharing knowledge reduces your competitive advantages or that teaching requires expertise or platforms you lack. These objections are misguided. The wealth-building principles we have examined throughout this book are not zero-sum competitive advantages that lose value when others learn them. More people investing in index funds does not reduce your returns. More people living below their means and building wealth does not prevent you from doing the same. The world benefits when more people build financial stability rather than living in precarious financial situations. You sacrifice nothing by teaching principles that helped you while potentially providing enormous benefit to others who implement what you share.

The teaching platforms include informal conversations with friends and family who ask about your financial decisions, mentoring younger colleagues or community members who could benefit from your experience, writing about principles and strategies through blogs or social media, creating courses or resources that systematically teach wealth-building frameworks, or supporting organizations that provide financial education to underserved communities. The specific platform matters less than the willingness to share knowledge rather than hoarding it. The one percent who have built wealth through knowledge-based principles generally share that knowledge freely because they understand that it costs them nothing while potentially changing lives for people who implement what they learn.

The maintenance of perspective about wealth's role in meaningful life prevents the tragedy of building wealth at expense of everything else that matters. The person who sacrifices health, relationships, integrity, or spiritual development in pursuit of wealth often achieves financial success while destroying the very things that make life worth living. The person who reaches financial independence at age fifty after working eighty-hour weeks for three decades while neglecting family, losing health, and abandoning all interests beyond work has made catastrophically bad trade-offs even if they accumulated substantial wealth. The wealth provides no benefit if you have destroyed everything that makes wealth valuable through the process of building it.

The one percent who build wealth most successfully maintain balance by understanding that wealth building does not require complete sacrifice of present wellbeing for future security. The strategies we have examined allow wealth building through living below your means, through systematic investing, through career advancement, and through side businesses while maintaining relationships, health, and engagement with interests beyond finance. These are not eighty-hour-per-week strategies. They are strategies for disciplined living sustained over decades without requiring complete sacrifice of present experience for future benefit.

The danger is not that wealth building requires these sacrifices but rather that some people choose to make them despite not being necessary. The person who could build wealth working forty to fifty hours weekly at their career while maintaining side business in evenings and weekends might instead work seventy hours weekly convinced that more work produces proportionally more wealth. This is often false because beyond certain thresholds additional work produces declining marginal returns while the costs to health, relationships, and wellbeing accelerate. The person sacrificing everything for marginal wealth increases often discovers too late that the trade-offs were profoundly unwise.

The spiritual dimensions of wealth stewardship matter for those who hold religious or philosophical frameworks giving life meaning beyond material success. For the author and for many readers, these dimensions include understanding that resources are gifts to be stewarded rather than possessions to be hoarded, that generosity reflects values deeper than financial optimization, that purpose extends beyond personal security to include serving others and honoring the One who provides all resources ultimately. These perspectives shape how wealth is built, how it is used, and what is considered success beyond mere accumulation.

The specific religious framework matters less than maintaining some conception of purpose and responsibility that extends beyond personal consumption and that provides meaning to the entire wealth-building enterprise. The person who views wealth purely as mechanism for personal security and consumption loses the sense of purpose that makes discipline sustainable and that makes achievement meaningful beyond selfish benefit. The person who views wealth as means to accomplish purposes beyond themselves maintains motivation through difficulties and maintains perspective that prevents wealth from becoming end rather than means.

The ultimate question is what you want to accomplish during your finite lifetime with the finite resources you will accumulate through implementation of the strategies this book has provided. You could accumulate the maximum possible wealth through extreme frugality and aggressive optimization across every domain, dying with the most money but perhaps with damaged relationships, compromised health, and unfulfilled potential in dimensions beyond finance. You could consume everything you earn on immediate pleasure and status signaling, dying with minimal accumulated wealth but perhaps with rich relationships and experiences. The optimal path lies between these extremes, building substantial wealth through disciplined implementation of key strategies while maintaining health, relationships, and engagement with purposes beyond accumulation.

Chuck Feeney demonstrated through his giving while living philosophy that wealth exists to be deployed for positive impact rather than to be hoarded indefinitely or to create dynastic fortunes that corrupt descendants. His approach required conviction that giving away billions during his lifetime while living modestly himself produced more social benefit and more personal satisfaction than building perpetual fortune for descendants or consuming wealth on luxury lifestyle. Most people will never face decisions about deploying billions, but the principles apply equally whether your resources are millions, hundreds of thousands, or modest wealth accumulated through decades of disciplined implementation of the strategies we have examined.

The question is whether you will view wealth you build as belonging to you for your consumption or whether you will view it as resources you temporarily steward for purposes that extend beyond your own security and pleasure. The former perspective leads to progressive lifestyle inflation consuming all available resources regardless of how much you accumulate. The latter perspective leads to maintaining sufficient lifestyle to fund health and wellbeing while deploying resources beyond those needs to benefit family, community, and causes that matter to you. The first path produces empty achievement. The second path produces meaning and impact that extend beyond your lifetime.

We have completed the comprehensive education about wealth building that this book was written to provide. You understand the foundations of stewardship perspective and long-term thinking. You understand the specific strategies for earning income, investing systematically, minimizing major expenses, advancing your career, building businesses, and optimizing the systems and tools that facilitate accumulation. You understand that knowledge without implementation produces no different outcomes than ignorance. You understand that the one percent who build substantial wealth do so through systematic implementation of simple principles sustained over decades rather than through exceptional intelligence, luck, or access to secret strategies.

The final understanding is that wealth is not the end goal but rather is means to other ends that provide meaning and purpose. Those ends might include providing for family across generations, supporting causes you believe in, creating opportunities for people who lack them, teaching others to build their own wealth and security, or simply achieving freedom to spend your time according to your values rather than according to financial necessity. The strategies build wealth. The purposes determine whether building that wealth was worthwhile. You have been provided complete education about building the wealth. The determination of worthy purposes and the implementation of strategies to achieve those purposes remain entirely your responsibility. Deploy it meaningfully.

CONCLUSION:
THE CHOICE BEFORE YOU

In 1997, two men named David and Michael graduated from the same university with engineering degrees. They were roommates, friends, and nearly identical in background and capabilities. Both accepted jobs at technology companies in their city earning forty-two thousand annually. Both were intelligent, hardworking, and ambitious. Both spoke about building wealth and achieving financial independence. Both read personal finance books and discussed investment strategies over beers on weekends. To outside observers, their trajectories appeared identical and their outcomes would likely be similar.

Twenty-seven years later, in 2024, David retired at age fifty with net worth of four point three million dollars. His investment portfolio generated one hundred seventy thousand annually in income at conservative four percent withdrawal rates, exceeding what he needed to maintain his lifestyle. He owned his home outright. He had no debt. He could structure his days however he wanted because employment income was optional rather than mandatory. He continued working part-time on projects he found meaningful, but the work was chosen rather than required. He had achieved complete financial independence before age fifty-one through systematic implementation of principles that he had learned years earlier.

Michael, his college roommate and friend, was still working full-time at age fifty with net worth of three hundred eighty thousand dollars. His retirement accounts held two hundred twenty thousand. He had one hundred sixty thousand in home equity on a house with remaining mortgage of one hundred ninety thousand. He carried fifteen thousand in credit card debt and twenty-eight thousand in auto loans. His employment income of ninety-five thousand was entirely consumed by his lifestyle plus modest retirement contributions. He could not envision retiring for at least fifteen more years, and even then he was uncertain whether his savings would prove sufficient. He remained trapped in employment not because he loved his work but because he could not afford to stop working.

The divergence between these two outcomes—one man retiring at fifty financially independent while the other man facing fifteen more years of mandatory employment—did not result from different starting points, different intelligence, different opportunities, or different luck. Both men earned similar starting salaries. Both received comparable raises and promotions over their careers, with each eventually reaching low six-figure incomes. Both experienced the same market returns on their investments. Both faced the same economy, the same job markets, the same life challenges. The difference in their outcomes, which measured four million dollars in accumulated wealth by age fifty, resulted entirely from different behavioral patterns sustained across twenty-seven years.

David saved forty percent of his gross income starting from his first paycheck. Michael saved ten percent when he remembered to increase his 401k contributions and zero percent for several years when he paused contributions to "catch up" on expenses. David invested exclusively in low-cost index funds held in tax-advantaged accounts and never sold during market downturns. Michael chased hot stocks, sold during the 2008 panic, and kept substantial cash in checking accounts earning nothing. David lived in a modest house that he purchased for one hundred eighty thousand dollars, putting twenty percent down and paying it off in fourteen years through aggressive extra principal payments. Michael bought a house for three hundred fifty thousand with minimal down payment, traded up to a four hundred fifty thousand house after seven years, and still owed one hundred ninety thousand after twenty-seven years.

David drove used cars that he purchased with cash and maintained until they required replacement, spending perhaps six thousand every five to seven years on vehicles. Michael financed new cars every four years, always carrying four hundred to six hundred monthly payments and spending over two hundred thousand on vehicles across twenty-seven years. David cooked most meals at home, took modest vacations funded from separate savings accounts, and maintained lifestyle on roughly fifty percent of his gross income throughout his career. Michael ate lunch out daily, ordered dinner several times weekly, took expensive vacations funded by credit cards, and spent essentially everything he earned despite increasing income.

The divergent outcomes were completely predictable from the behavioral patterns each man maintained. David implemented the principles that create wealth: high savings rates, systematic index fund investing, minimal major expenses through buying modest housing and used vehicles, aggressive debt elimination, and sustained discipline across decades regardless of income increases or peer choices. Michael knew these principles—he had read the same books David read and they had discussed these concepts explicitly over the years. But Michael never implemented what he knew. He always intended to start saving more aggressively next year after he paid off current debts. He always planned to simplify his lifestyle eventually after enjoying his current phase. He always meant to stop trading stocks and switch to index funds after he recovered from his latest losses. His knowledge was comprehensive but his implementation was nonexistent.

By age fifty, David was free while Michael remained trapped. The four million dollar difference in their net worth was not the most important difference. The most important difference was that David controlled his time while Michael sold his time for income he could not afford to lose. David chose his activities based on meaning and interest while Michael chose his activities based on economic necessity. David faced the second half of his life with options while Michael faced it with obligations. This divergence, created by twenty-seven years of different daily choices about saving, investing, spending, and debt, had transformed two nearly identical starting points into completely different life outcomes.

This conclusion brings us back to the question posed in this book's introduction: what separates those who build substantial wealth from those who work until they die despite comparable incomes and opportunities? We have examined the answer across thirty-five chapters covering every domain affecting wealth building. The answer is not secrets or exceptional intelligence or luck or access to privileged information. The answer is systematic implementation of known principles sustained across decades despite discomfort, despite social pressure, despite temptations to abandon discipline for immediate gratification. David implemented these principles. Michael knew these principles but failed to implement them. You now know these principles through the comprehensive education this book has provided. The only remaining question is whether you will implement what you know or whether you will become another person who understands exactly what to do while doing something else entirely.

The knowledge you have received throughout these chapters is comprehensive. You understand that wealth building begins with proper mindset—stewardship rather than ownership, long-term perspective rather than short-term gratification, personal responsibility rather than victim mentality. You understand that investment returns come from systematic deployment of capital into diversified index funds held in tax-advantaged accounts for decades, not from stock picking or market timing or chasing performance. You understand that real estate builds wealth through multiple simultaneous mechanisms including mortgage paydown, appreciation, cash flow, and tax benefits when properties are selected wisely and held long-term. You understand that major expense categories of housing, transportation, and food determine whether high income generates high savings or whether income is consumed entirely regardless of its level.

You understand that career advancement requires active management including demonstrating next-level capabilities, making bosses successful, building networks, taking visible projects, and explicitly asking for advancement rather than waiting to be noticed. You understand that optimal taxation requires using every available tax-advantaged account, understanding how different income types are taxed, maintaining records supporting deductions, and working with competent advisors. You understand that health maintenance through basic exercise and nutrition sustains earning capacity for decades and prevents medical costs from destroying accumulated wealth. You understand that side businesses accelerate wealth building by increasing income beyond employment limits while building equity that employment never provides.

You understand how to optimize credit card usage for rewards without carrying balances, how to manage student debt strategically based on interest rates and opportunity costs, how to eliminate consumer debt systematically through focusing on highest-interest obligations first, how to read people and use psychological principles ethically in negotiation and advancement, how to raise children who will steward inherited wealth responsibly rather than squandering it, how to use sophisticated leverage through SBLOCs and HELOCs when appropriate, how to structure business entities to optimize taxes and protect assets, how to implement estate plans ensuring smooth wealth transfer to intended beneficiaries, and how to understand principal versus interest mechanics that allow destroying debt years faster than standard payment schedules require.

This knowledge is valuable only if implemented. The person who reads this entire book, understands every principle, agrees intellectually that these strategies work, but fails to change any behaviors has wasted their time reading it. They will generate the same outcomes they would have generated had they never read it because knowledge without implementation produces identical results to ignorance. This is why we have emphasized throughout every chapter that implementation is the only thing that matters. Understanding optimal investment strategy while continuing to consume your entire income produces zero accumulated wealth. Understanding how to minimize major expenses while maintaining spending patterns that prevent savings produces the same outcome as never understanding expense optimization at all. Understanding career advancement strategies while waiting passively for recognition produces the same career plateau that befalls those who never learned these strategies.

The barriers preventing implementation are not knowledge gaps—you now have the knowledge required. The barriers are psychological, social, and habitual. The psychological barriers include loss aversion that makes you fear reducing current consumption despite understanding that this enables future abundance. They include present bias that makes immediate pleasures seem more valuable than distant future benefits despite mathematical proof that delayed gratification produces superior outcomes. They include optimism bias that makes you assume you have unlimited time to begin implementing optimal behaviors despite knowing intellectually that time is finite and that delay costs compound.

The social barriers include peer pressure to maintain consumption patterns your friends maintain despite understanding that their patterns prevent wealth building. They include family expectations that you spend on housing, vehicles, weddings, and holidays at levels that feel normal within your social circle despite understanding that normal spending patterns produce normal outcomes. They include status competition where you signal success through consumption rather than through accumulated wealth that remains invisible. They include the discomfort of being visibly different from your peers through living below your means, driving older vehicles, declining expensive activities, and generally prioritizing future freedom over current status.

The habitual barriers include the momentum of existing spending patterns that feel normal because you have maintained them for years. They include the automatic nature of consumption decisions made without conscious thought because you have always made them this way. They include the difficulty of establishing new patterns like automated savings transfers, systematic investment contributions, meal preparation routines, and exercise schedules when your current patterns include none of these things. They include the sheer effort required to change dozens of behaviors simultaneously rather than continuing comfortable existing patterns.

These barriers are real and they are why most people fail to build wealth despite having access to all necessary knowledge. The barriers are why the ninety-nine percent remain the ninety-nine percent despite living in the most prosperous society in human history with access to unlimited information about how to build wealth. The barriers are why Michael earned six figures for years while building minimal wealth despite understanding exactly what David did differently. Knowledge is necessary but insufficient. Implementation requires overcoming these barriers through mechanisms that make optimal behaviors automatic rather than depending on daily willpower.

The implementation mechanisms that make success likely rather than merely possible include automated systems that remove decisions from your conscious control. You establish automated transfers from checking to investment accounts on paydays before you can spend the money. You establish automated investment purchases that execute regardless of market conditions or your emotional state. You establish automated bill payments that prevent late fees and credit score damage. You establish automated extra mortgage payments that destroy debt faster than standard schedules without requiring monthly decisions. These automated systems implement optimal behaviors mechanically rather than hoping you will implement them consciously when behavioral economics research proves that conscious implementation fails reliably when competing with immediate temptations.

The social environment management makes optimal behaviors easier by surrounding yourself with people making similar choices rather than swimming against current while your social circle pulls you toward consumption. You cultivate relationships with people who prioritize wealth building over status signaling. You distance yourself from people whose spending patterns would undermine your discipline if you remained closely connected. You seek mentors who have achieved what you want to achieve rather than accepting advice from people whose outcomes you do not want to replicate. You join communities focused on financial independence where your choices seem normal rather than extreme. This environmental engineering reduces the constant friction that destroys discipline when every social interaction reinforces consumption-based values you are trying to reject.

The measurement and tracking create visibility into whether your actions produce intended results or whether you are deluding yourself about making progress. You track net worth quarterly to verify that it increases according to your expectations rather than assuming you are building wealth without confirming it. You track savings rates monthly to verify that you actually save the percentages you claim to save rather than vaguely thinking you save enough without measuring precisely. You track investment returns to verify that you achieve market-rate returns rather than underperforming through poor fund selection or behavioral mistakes. You track expense categories to verify that you actually minimize spending where you believe you minimize it rather than suffering from optimistic assumptions about your frugality. This measurement prevents years of suboptimal behaviors that would have been corrected immediately if you had been tracking outcomes rather than operating on faith that you were doing the right things.

The staged implementation prevents overwhelming yourself through attempting simultaneous change across all domains while increasing the likelihood that some changes stick rather than attempting everything and abandoning everything when the effort proves unsustainable. You might begin by establishing automated savings transfers and by tracking spending for three months without attempting to change spending yet. Once savings automation is habitual and spending visibility is established, you might tackle housing costs through refinancing or through planning eventual downsizing. Once housing is addressed, you might focus on vehicle costs through driving current vehicles longer and through planning to purchase used rather than new next time replacement is required. This staged approach over one to two years implements comprehensive changes more reliably than attempting overnight transformation that proves unsustainable.

The commitment devices create costs for failing to maintain discipline, making continued discipline easier than breaking commitment. You might commit publicly to fitness goals where failure means admitting defeat to people whose respect you value. You might establish joint accountability with friend or spouse where you report progress or setbacks regularly. You might create financial penalties for failing to meet savings targets—perhaps committing to donate substantial amount to organization you oppose politically if you fail to save forty percent of income for the quarter. These commitment devices work by making the immediate cost of abandoning discipline exceed the immediate benefit of the temptation that would cause you to abandon discipline. They transform distant abstract costs of failure into immediate concrete costs that influence present behavior.

The one percent implement these mechanisms because they understand that behavioral change requires engineered environments and automatic systems rather than depending on willpower and intention. They understand that Michael failed not because he lacked knowledge or intention but because he never implemented systems making optimal behaviors automatic. They understand that David succeeded not because he had superior willpower but because he automated savings and investments before he could spend money, because he cultivated relationships with people making similar choices, because he measured outcomes quarterly to verify progress, and because he implemented changes systematically rather than attempting overnight transformation.

The stakes of choosing implementation versus choosing continued inaction extend far beyond net worth figures in accounts. The stakes are whether you spend forty years selling time for money according to employers' terms or whether you achieve financial independence allowing you to spend time according to your values. The stakes are whether you face retirement hoping modest savings prove sufficient or whether you enter retirement with resources providing security and options. The stakes are whether you live in constant financial stress wondering if emergency expenses will trigger crisis or whether you maintain reserves eliminating financial anxiety. The stakes are whether you pass to your children the lessons and resources that enable them to build wealth or whether you pass the financial dysfunction that keeps them trapped.

The mathematical reality is that small behavioral differences compound into enormous outcome differences across working lifetimes. The difference between saving fifteen percent and saving forty percent seems modest in any single year—perhaps fifteen thousand annually for someone earning sixty thousand. Over thirty years at ten percent returns, this fifteen thousand annual difference compounds into three million dollars in differential accumulated wealth. The person saving forty percent retires financially independent. The person saving fifteen percent works until forced retirement. The behavior that creates this three million dollar difference is living on thirty-six thousand versus living on fifty-one thousand annually—a fourteen percent difference in lifestyle that creates a sixteen hundred percent difference in retirement security.

The difference between investing systematically in index funds versus chasing performance and trading frequently might produce two percentage points of differential annual returns—eight percent versus ten percent. On investments of twenty thousand annually over thirty years, this two percentage point difference compounds to seven hundred thousand dollars. The person who earned ten percent accumulates three point six million. The person who earned eight percent accumulates two point nine million. The behavior that creates this seven hundred thousand dollar difference is buying index funds and never selling versus constantly trading and trying to beat the market through stock selection.

The difference between eliminating mortgage debt in fifteen years through aggressive extra payments versus maintaining debt for full thirty-year term creates seven years of payment-free living before retirement plus over one hundred thousand in saved interest. The person who became debt-free at age forty-five can deploy mortgage payments toward investments for remaining twenty years of their career, accumulating perhaps five hundred thousand more than the person who maintained debt until age sixty. The behavior that creates this five hundred thousand dollar difference is paying an extra three hundred to five hundred monthly toward principal—a ten percent increase in monthly housing costs that generates permanent elimination of housing costs seven years earlier.

These examples demonstrate that the one percent who build substantial wealth do not earn dramatically more than the ninety-nine percent who accumulate little. They behave differently across every domain in ways that seem modest in any moment but that compound over decades into life-transforming outcome differences. They save five to fifteen percentage points more of income. They earn one to three percentage points higher investment returns through better fund selection and through avoiding behavioral mistakes. They eliminate debt five to fifteen years faster through extra payments. They minimize major expenses ten to thirty percent through strategic choices. The cumulative effect of these differences across thirty to forty years creates ten times more wealth than people earning identical incomes who make conventional choices in each domain.

The question before you is not whether you understand what creates wealth—you understand completely through the education provided across these thirty-five chapters. The question is whether you will join the one percent who implement what they know or whether you will join the ninety-nine percent who know what to do while doing something else entirely. This choice determines whether you build multiple millions in assets allowing early retirement and financial freedom or whether you work until forced retirement while hoping modest savings prove adequate. This choice determines whether your children inherit resources and lessons enabling them to build their own wealth or whether they inherit the financial patterns that kept you trapped. This choice determines whether you live the second half of your life with options or with obligations.

The implementation begins today with single action that moves you from knowledge to behavior. You log into your 401k account and increase your contribution percentage from whatever you contribute currently to five percentage points higher. You establish automated transfer from checking to investment account moving money on your payday before you can spend it. You list your debts with balances and interest rates and you commit to paying an extra one hundred dollars monthly toward the highest-interest obligation. You download expense tracking app and you commit to recording every expenditure for three months to establish visibility into where money actually goes. You call insurance agent and request quotes for higher deductibles that reduce premiums. You research used vehicles and commit to driving your current vehicle two more years while saving to purchase next vehicle with cash.

These individual actions seem trivial. They are not impressive accomplishments. They generate no immediate visible results. They provide no dopamine hit of transformation. They are boring, mechanical, unremarkable first steps. But they are the same first steps that David took twenty-seven years ago that eventually produced four point three million in net worth and retirement at age fifty. They are the steps that Michael never took despite understanding their importance and despite discussing them explicitly with David. They are the steps that separate the one percent who build wealth from the ninety-nine percent who remain trapped despite having identical knowledge about what they should do.

The path forward is clear and it is simple though not easy. You implement the foundational disciplines of high savings rates, systematic index fund investing, and minimized major expenses. You automate these behaviors to remove daily decision-making that invites failure. You measure quarterly to verify progress. You adjust behaviors when measurements reveal suboptimal results. You maintain discipline through market volatility and peer pressure and all the temptations to abandon long-term strategies for short-term comfort. You do this not for one year or five years but for twenty to forty years depending on your starting point and your retirement timeline. You do this while everyone around you makes different choices and while social pressure constantly suggests you are being too extreme in your discipline. You do this despite seeing no impressive results for the first five to ten years while compound growth remains too small to create obvious wealth.

The one percent maintain this discipline because they understand that the alternative is lifetime employment without escape and retirement dependent on hoping modest savings prove adequate. They understand that forty years of discipline creates thirty years of freedom. They understand that decades of living below their means enables decades of living according to their values rather than according to economic necessity. They understand that short-term sacrifice creates permanent advantage while short-term comfort creates permanent constraint. They make these trades consciously because they calculate the mathematics and they prefer the outcome that discipline produces to the outcome that comfort produces.

We close where we began—with the fundamental question of what separates those who build wealth from those who do not despite comparable circumstances. You now have complete answer to this question through comprehensive examination of every domain affecting outcomes. The separation occurs not through different knowledge or different opportunities or different luck but through different behavioral patterns sustained across decades. The one percent implement optimal behaviors systematically. The ninety-nine percent understand optimal behaviors theoretically while implementing suboptimal behaviors practically. You now understand the optimal behaviors completely. You understand the systems that make implementation reliable. You understand the barriers preventing implementation and the mechanisms that overcome those barriers. You understand the mathematics proving that modest behavioral differences compound into enormous outcome differences. You understand the stakes.

The only remaining variable is your choice. Will you implement what you now know or will you become another person who understands wealth building theoretically while accumulating little practically? Will you join the one percent through disciplined implementation sustained across decades or will you remain in the ninety-nine percent through continued conventional behaviors? Will you create the automated systems, establish the measurement practices, make the environmental changes, and maintain the discipline required to transform knowledge into wealth? Or will you read this book, agree with its principles, intend to implement them eventually, but never actually change anything because change is uncomfortable and current patterns are familiar even though they produce outcomes you claim not to want?

David and Michael were functionally identical in 1997. They are completely different in 2024. The divergence occurred through thousands of small choices compounded over twenty-seven years. David chose implementation. Michael chose continued intention without implementation. You now face the same choice they faced. You cannot claim ignorance—you have been provided complete education about what creates wealth and what prevents it. You cannot claim that circumstances prevent implementation—people with lower incomes than you currently earn have implemented these principles successfully. You cannot claim that you need more information—you have received comprehensive frameworks covering every relevant domain. The only remaining question is whether you will act on what you know.

The frameworks have been provided. The mathematics are clear. The path is simple. The choice is yours. The time to begin is now because every day you delay is day you cannot recover. The compound growth you forfeit through spending rather than investing this year is growth that would have compounded for all remaining years until retirement. The debt interest you pay this year through failing to make extra principal payments is interest that compounds across all remaining years of the loan. The career advancement you forfeit this year through passive waiting rather than active management is advancement that would have increased your income for all remaining years of your career. Time is not renewable and delay has permanent cost.

You know what to do. You know why it matters. You know how to do it. You know what prevents most people from doing it and you know how to overcome those barriers. You know the outcomes that implementation produces and you know the outcomes that failure produces. Everything necessary for success has been provided. The implementation is entirely your responsibility and yours alone. No one will force you to save. No one will prevent you from spending. No one will make you invest systematically. No one will stop you from consuming your income. The life you build through your choices over the next twenty to forty years is the life you will live. Choose wisely. Choose deliberately. Choose now. And above all, choose implementation over continued intention because intention without implementation produces nothing while implementation sustained over decades produces everything.

The one percent implement. The ninety-nine percent intend. You now know exactly what separates these groups. The only remaining question is which group you will join through your choices starting today and sustained across decades. This is not a question I can answer for you. This is not a decision anyone can make on your behalf. This is the defining choice of your financial life and you make it through your behaviors in every moment of every day for the rest of your working years. Make it well. The life you want to live in your fifties, sixties, seventies, and beyond depends entirely on whether you implement what you know starting immediately or whether you continue patterns that feel comfortable while producing outcomes you claim not to want.

The book is complete. The education has been provided. Your journey begins now. The distance between where you are and where you want to be is measured not in complexity but in consistent implementation across time. The path is simple. The execution is entirely yours. Begin today. Continue tomorrow. Persist for decades. Build wealth systematically. Create freedom deliberately. Live according to your values rather than according to economic necessity. This is how the one percent think. This is how the one percent act. This is how the one percent build lives of freedom while the ninety-nine percent remain trapped despite having access to identical knowledge. You now have the knowledge. You now have the frameworks. You now have the clarity about what separates success from failure. The implementation and all its consequences—positive or negative—are now entirely your responsibility. Choose to implement. Choose to persist. Choose to succeed. The alternative is choosing to fail through inaction disguised as intention. The choice is yours. The time is now. Begin.

GLOSSARY OF FINANCIAL TERMS:

Accredited Investor: A person or entity that meets SEC requirements to invest in certain private securities offerings, typically requiring $1 million net worth (excluding primary residence) or $200,000+ annual income ($300,000 jointly). Most wealth-building strategies in this book do not require accredited investor status.

Amortization: The process of paying off debt through regular payments over time. Each payment includes both principal and interest, with the proportion shifting over the loan term. Early payments are mostly interest; later payments are mostly principal.

Appreciation: The increase in an asset's value over time. Real estate and stocks typically appreciate over decades, though short-term volatility is common. Appreciation combines with cash flow and leverage to build wealth.

Asset: Anything of value that you own. Assets include cash, investments, real estate, business equity, and personal property. Your net worth equals total assets minus total liabilities.

Asset Allocation: How you divide investments among different asset classes (stocks, bonds, real estate, cash). A typical allocation might be 80% stocks, 20% bonds. Asset allocation is the primary determinant of portfolio returns and volatility.

Asset Protection: Legal strategies to shield wealth from lawsuits, creditors, and other claims. Techniques include liability insurance, business entities (LLCs, corporations), trusts, and retirement accounts with creditor protection.

Backdoor Roth IRA: A legal method for high earners to contribute to Roth IRAs despite exceeding income limits. You contribute to a traditional IRA (non-deductible) and immediately convert to Roth, paying minimal taxes if done promptly.

Basis Point: One-hundredth of one percent (0.01%). Used to describe small differences in interest rates or investment returns. An expense ratio of 0.50% is 50 basis points; 0.05% is 5 basis points.

Bear Market: A prolonged period of declining stock prices, typically defined as a 20%+ drop from recent highs. Bear markets create opportunities for those with capital to buy at discounted prices.

Beneficiary: The person or entity designated to receive assets from retirement accounts, life insurance policies, trusts, or estates upon the owner's death. Keeping beneficiary designations current is essential for estate planning.

Beta: A measure of how much an investment moves relative to the overall market. Beta of 1.0 means the investment moves with the market. Beta above 1.0 means higher volatility; below 1.0 means lower volatility.

Brokerage Account (Taxable): An investment account without tax advantages but also without withdrawal restrictions. You can access funds anytime without penalties, though you pay taxes on dividends, interest, and capital gains.

Bull Market: A prolonged period of rising stock prices. Bull markets eventually end, but they typically last longer than bear markets. The one percent invest systematically through both bull and bear markets.

Capital: Money or assets available for investment. Your capital includes cash, liquid investments, and borrowing capacity. Preserving capital during market crashes allows you to exploit opportunities.

Capital Expenditure (CapEx): Major expenses for replacing building systems or components: roofs, HVAC, water heaters, appliances. Real estate investors budget 1-2% of property value annually for CapEx to avoid being caught unprepared.

Capital Gains: Profit from selling an asset for more than you paid. Short-term gains (held less than one year) are taxed as ordinary income. Long-term gains (held over one year) receive preferential tax rates of 0%, 15%, or 20%.

Capital Stack: The layers of financing used to purchase an asset, typically ordered by payment priority. In real estate: senior debt (mortgage), mezzanine debt, preferred equity, common equity. Each layer has different risk and return characteristics.

Capitalization Rate (Cap Rate): Net operating income divided by property value. A property generating $20,000 annual net income with a value of $250,000 has an 8% cap rate. Higher cap rates suggest higher returns but often higher risk.

Cash Flow: The money remaining after all expenses are paid. Positive cash flow means income exceeds expenses; negative cash flow means expenses exceed income. Real estate should generate positive cash flow to avoid subsidizing tenants.

Cash-on-Cash Return: Annual cash flow divided by total cash invested, expressed as a percentage. If you invest $50,000 down payment and generate $5,000 annual cash flow, your cash-on-cash return is 10%. This measures actual money in your pocket relative to money you invested.

Compound Interest: Earning returns on both your original investment and on previous returns. The most powerful wealth-building force available. $10,000 invested at 10% for 40 years becomes $452,592 through compounding.

Correlation: How closely two investments move together. High correlation means they move in the same direction. Low or negative correlation provides diversification benefits. Stocks and bonds typically have low correlation.

Cost Basis: What you originally paid for an asset, adjusted for improvements (real estate) or reinvested dividends (stocks). Cost basis determines your capital gain when you sell. Higher basis means lower taxable gain.

Debt Service Coverage Ratio (DSCR): Net operating income divided by mortgage payment. Lenders typically require DSCR of 1.25 or higher for rental property mortgages, meaning income must exceed mortgage payment by 25%.

Depreciation: A tax deduction for the theoretical wearing out of property over time. Residential rental property is depreciated over 27.5 years, creating paper losses that offset rental income for tax purposes.

Diversification: Spreading investments across multiple assets, sectors, or strategies to reduce risk. Index funds provide instant diversification across hundreds or thousands of companies. The one percent diversify across asset classes: stocks, real estate, bonds, business equity.

Dividend: A portion of company profits paid to shareholders. Dividends provide cash flow from stocks. Qualified dividends receive preferential tax treatment. Index funds generate modest dividends that compound over time.

Donor-Advised Fund (DAF): A charitable investment account. You contribute and receive an immediate tax deduction, the money grows tax-free, and you recommend grants to charities over time. Allows tax-efficient giving and anonymous donations.

Down Payment: The portion of a property's price you pay in cash. Traditional mortgages require 20% down; FHA loans require 3.5% down. Larger down payments reduce mortgage payments and avoid PMI but reduce leverage benefits.

Due Diligence: Thorough investigation and analysis before making an investment or business decision. Proper due diligence on rental properties includes inspection, rental market analysis, expense verification, and title search.

Earnings Per Share (EPS): A company's profit divided by shares outstanding. Growing EPS typically indicates company health. Index investors don't analyze individual company EPS—they own the entire market.

Economies of Scale: The cost advantages that come from larger operations. A landlord with ten properties achieves economies of scale in property management, maintenance, and purchasing that a landlord with one property cannot access.

Emergency Fund: Liquid savings covering 3-6 months of expenses. Prevents forced sale of investments during emergencies and provides psychological security. Keep in high-yield savings accounts, not invested in stocks.

Equity: The portion of an asset you own outright. In real estate, equity equals property value minus mortgage balance. In stocks, equity means ownership shares. Building equity through appreciation and debt paydown creates wealth.

Escrow: A third-party account holding funds until conditions are met. Mortgage escrow accounts hold property tax and insurance payments. Real estate purchase escrow holds deposit until closing.

Estate Tax: Federal tax on estates exceeding $13.61 million per person (2024). Proper estate planning uses trusts, gifting, and other strategies to minimize estate taxes for high-net-worth individuals.

Expense Ratio: Annual fees charged by mutual funds or ETFs, expressed as a percentage of assets. A fund with 0.50% expense ratio charges $50 annually per $10,000 invested. Index funds typically charge 0.03-0.20%; actively managed funds charge 0.50-2.00%.

FICO Score: The most common credit scoring model, ranging from 300-850. Scores above 740 qualify for best interest rates. Scores below 620 indicate high risk. Your FICO score determines borrowing costs across your lifetime.

Fiduciary: A person or entity legally required to act in your best interest. Fee-only financial advisors are fiduciaries. Stockbrokers and insurance agents typically are not and may recommend products that benefit them rather than you.

Fixed-Rate Mortgage: A loan where the interest rate never changes. Payment stability protects you from rate increases. The one percent use fixed-rate mortgages on rental properties for predictable cash flow.

Foreclosure: Legal process where lenders repossess property after the borrower defaults on mortgage payments. Foreclosures destroy credit and result in loss of all equity. Proper cash flow analysis and reserves prevent foreclosures.

Front-End Ratio: Housing expenses (mortgage, taxes, insurance) divided by gross income. Lenders typically require front-end ratios below 28%. Keeping housing costs below 25% of gross income provides comfortable margin.

Geographic Arbitrage: Moving to locations where your money goes further. Someone earning $80,000 lives far better in Tulsa than in San Francisco. Remote work has made geographic arbitrage more accessible.

Gross Income: Total income before taxes and deductions. Your gross income determines contribution limits for retirement accounts, loan qualification amounts, and tax brackets.

Gross Rent Multiplier (GRM): Property price divided by annual gross rent. Lower GRM suggests better value. GRM is a quick screening tool but cash flow analysis is more important.

Health Savings Account (HSA): The most powerful tax-advantaged account available. Contributions are tax-deductible, growth is tax-free, and withdrawals for medical expenses are tax-free. The only triple-tax-advantaged account. Requires high-deductible health insurance.

High-Deductible Health Plan (HDHP): Health insurance with deductibles of at least $1,600 (individual) or $3,200 (family). Required for HSA eligibility. Lower premiums plus HSA benefits make HDHPs optimal for healthy individuals.

House Hacking: Living in a property while renting out other units. Reduces or eliminates your housing costs while building equity. The most accessible entry point into real estate investing for those with limited capital.

Index Fund: A mutual fund or ETF that tracks a market index (S&P 500, Total Stock Market, etc.) rather than trying to beat it. Low fees and broad diversification make index funds optimal for most investors. Passively managed rather than actively managed.

Inflation: The general increase in prices over time. Historical average is 3% annually. Inflation erodes purchasing power but assets like stocks and real estate typically outpace inflation over decades.

Interest Rate: The cost of borrowing money, expressed as an annual percentage. Lower rates reduce borrowing costs substantially. A 1% difference in mortgage rate on $300,000 saves approximately $65,000 over 30 years.

Internal Rate of Return (IRR): A calculation of investment return accounting for timing of cash flows. More sophisticated than simple ROI. Used in real estate and business valuation.

Joint Tenancy: Property ownership where two or more people own equal shares with right of survivorship. When one owner dies, their share automatically passes to surviving owners without probate.

1031 Exchange: Named after IRS code section 1031. Allows deferring capital gains taxes when selling investment real estate by purchasing replacement property of equal or greater value. Must use qualified intermediary and complete exchange within strict timeframes.

529 Plan: Tax-advantaged education savings account. Contributions grow tax-free and withdrawals for qualified education expenses are tax-free. Many states provide state tax deductions for contributions. Unused funds can roll to Roth IRA (up to $35,000 lifetime).

Leverage: Using borrowed money to amplify returns. Real estate leverage allows controlling $200,000 property with $40,000 down payment. 5% appreciation on full property value equals 25% return on your investment. Leverage magnifies both gains and losses.

Liability: A debt or obligation you owe. Liabilities include mortgages, student loans, credit card debt, car loans. Your net worth equals assets minus liabilities.

Lifestyle Inflation: Increasing spending as income rises. The primary destroyer of wealth-building potential. The one percent avoid lifestyle inflation by maintaining spending levels even as income grows, investing the difference.

Liquidity: How quickly an asset can be converted to cash without significant loss. Cash is perfectly liquid. Stocks are highly liquid. Real estate is illiquid—selling takes months and involves substantial costs.

Loan-to-Value Ratio (LTV): Loan amount divided by property value. An $160,000 mortgage on a $200,000 property is 80% LTV. Lower LTV means more equity and less risk. Lenders offer better rates for lower LTV loans.

Long-Term Capital Gains: Profit from selling assets held over one year. Taxed at preferential rates of 0%, 15%, or 20% depending on income. Far more favorable than ordinary income tax rates.

Margin: Borrowing money from a brokerage to purchase securities, using your portfolio as collateral. Margin magnifies gains and losses. The one percent use margin cautiously if at all—leverage in real estate is safer because tenants pay the debt.

Market Capitalization: Total value of a company's outstanding shares. Calculated as share price × shares outstanding. Large-cap stocks ($10B+), mid-cap ($2-10B), small-cap (under $2B). Index funds own companies across all market caps.

Market Timing: Attempting to buy before market rises and sell before it falls. Consistently fails because timing requires being right twice (when to sell and when to buy back in). The one percent stay invested through market cycles rather than timing them.

Marginal Tax Rate: The tax rate on your last dollar of income. A person in the 22% bracket pays 22% on income above the bracket threshold, not on all income. Understanding marginal rates is essential for tax planning.

Mortgage: A loan secured by real property. If you default, the lender can foreclose and take the property. Fixed-rate mortgages have constant payments; adjustable-rate mortgages have payments that change with interest rates.

Mortgage Insurance (PMI): Required insurance when down payment is less than 20%. Protects the lender if you default. Typically costs 0.5-1.0% of loan amount annually. Avoided by putting 20% down or by using piggyback loans.

Multiple Listing Service (MLS): Database of properties for sale, accessible to licensed real estate agents. Most online property sites (Zillow, Realtor.com) pull data from MLS feeds.

Net Operating Income (NOI): Rental income minus operating expenses (taxes, insurance, maintenance, management), but before mortgage payment. Used to calculate cap rate and DSCR. Essential metric for evaluating rental properties.

Net Worth: Total assets minus total liabilities. Your true financial position. Net worth should increase steadily year over year if you implement wealth-building behaviors consistently.

Non-Qualified Dividend: Dividends taxed as ordinary income rather than at preferential capital gains rates. Most dividends from REITs are non-qualified. Qualified dividends receive preferential rates.

Occupancy Rate: Percentage of time rental units are occupied. 95% occupancy means properties are rented 95% of the time. Budget for 92-95% occupancy when analyzing rental properties.

Opportunity Cost: The value of the next-best alternative you give up when making a choice. Money spent on luxury car has opportunity cost of investment returns you forfeited. Understanding opportunity cost prevents wasteful spending.

Passive Income: Income requiring minimal ongoing effort: rental income, dividends, business income from systems you've built. Building multiple passive income streams is the path to financial independence.

Percentage Point: Different from percent. If interest rates rise from 5% to 7%, they increased by 2 percentage points (or 40 percent). Distinguish percentage points from percent to avoid confusion.

Portfolio: Your collection of investments. A diversified portfolio might include index funds, rental properties, business equity, and bonds. Asset allocation determines portfolio characteristics.

Pre-Tax: Before taxes are deducted. Pre-tax contributions to 401(k) or HSA reduce current taxable income. Pre-tax income is different from after-tax income—always calculate percentages from gross income to maintain consistency.

Principal: The original loan amount or the portion of a payment that reduces loan balance. Early mortgage payments are mostly interest; later payments are mostly principal. Extra principal payments dramatically reduce total interest paid.

Private Mortgage Insurance (PMI): See Mortgage Insurance.

Pro Forma: Projected financial statements for a property or business. Pro forma rent rolls estimate future rental income. Always verify pro forma assumptions—sellers exaggerate to make properties look better.

Prospectus: Legal document describing a mutual fund's strategy, fees, risks, and historical performance. Always read prospectuses before investing, focusing on expense ratio and investment strategy.

Purchase Price Allocation: Dividing property purchase price between land (not depreciable) and improvements (depreciable). Proper allocation maximizes depreciation deductions for tax purposes.

Qualified Dividend: Dividends meeting IRS requirements for preferential tax treatment. Taxed at long-term capital gains rates (0%, 15%, 20%) rather than ordinary income rates. Most U.S. company dividends are qualified.

Qualified Education Expenses: Expenses eligible for tax-free withdrawal from 529 plans: tuition, fees, books, room and board at accredited institutions, up to $10,000 annually for K-12 tuition.

Rate of Return: Investment gain or loss expressed as a percentage of amount invested. A $10,000 investment growing to $11,000 has a 10% rate of return. Compound annual growth rate (CAGR) accounts for multiple years.

Real Estate Investment Trust (REIT): A company owning income-producing real estate. REITs trade like stocks, providing real estate exposure without property management responsibilities. Most REIT dividends are taxed as ordinary income.

Rebalancing: Periodically adjusting your portfolio back to target asset allocation. If stocks outperform bonds, your allocation shifts from 80/20 to 85/15. Rebalancing sells winners and buys losers, maintaining discipline.

Refinancing: Replacing an existing loan with a new loan, typically to reduce interest rate or change loan terms. Refinancing costs 2-3% of loan amount, so rate reduction must be substantial enough to justify costs.

Rent Roll: Document listing all rental units, current tenants, lease terms, and monthly rents. Essential for evaluating rental property. Verify rent rolls by reviewing actual leases—don't trust seller-provided data.

Return on Investment (ROI): Gain from investment divided by amount invested. $5,000 gain on $50,000 investment equals 10% ROI. ROI measures efficiency of investments but doesn't account for time or risk.

Roth 401(k): Employer retirement plan accepting after-tax contributions with tax-free growth and withdrawals. Combines benefits of 401(k) (high contribution limits, employer match) with Roth benefits (tax-free withdrawals).

Roth IRA: Individual retirement account accepting after-tax contributions up to $7,000 annually ($8,000 if 50+). All growth and withdrawals are tax-free after age 59½. The most powerful wealth-building vehicle for those eligible.

S Corporation (S-Corp): Tax election allowing business owners to avoid some self-employment taxes. Profits flow through to personal returns. Requires reasonable salary. Beneficial for profitable small businesses.

Savings Rate: Amount saved divided by gross income. A person earning $80,000 who saves $32,000 has a 40% savings rate. Savings rate is the single most important factor determining wealth accumulation speed.

Securities-Based Lending: Borrowing against your brokerage account. Interest rates are typically lower than mortgages. Risky because market declines can trigger margin calls. The one percent might use for real estate down payments but only with substantial equity cushions.

Self-Directed IRA: IRA allowing alternative investments beyond stocks and bonds: real estate, private equity, precious metals. Provides flexibility but requires careful compliance with IRS rules prohibiting self-dealing.

Short-Term Capital Gains: Profit from selling assets held one year or less. Taxed as ordinary income, potentially 37% federal plus state taxes. Tax code incentivizes long-term holding.

Single-Family Rental (SFR): A standalone house rented to tenants. Easier to manage than multi-family but provides no economies of scale. Appreciation typically exceeds multi-family but cash flow is typically lower.

Standard Deduction: Amount you can deduct from taxable income without itemizing. $14,600 (single) or $29,200 (married filing jointly) for 2024. Most taxpayers take standard deduction rather than itemizing.

Stock Split:
Division of existing shares into multiple shares. A 2-for-1 split doubles your share count and halves the price. Splits don't change total value—purely cosmetic. Index investors ignore splits.

Superfunding: Contributing five years of 529 plan contributions in one year without triggering gift taxes. Allows moving large sums out of taxable estates while funding education. High-net-worth estate planning strategy.

Tax Bracket: Income range taxed at a specific rate. The U.S. uses progressive brackets: 10%, 12%, 22%, 24%, 32%, 35%, 37%. Income in each bracket is taxed at that bracket's rate. Only income above bracket thresholds is taxed at higher rates.

Tax-Deferred: Accounts where taxes are postponed until withdrawal: traditional 401(k), traditional IRA. Contributions may be tax-deductible. Growth is tax-free but withdrawals are taxed as ordinary income.

Tax Loss Harvesting: Selling investments at a loss to offset capital gains, reducing tax liability. Losses can offset gains plus $3,000 of ordinary income annually. Excess losses carry forward indefinitely.

Taxable Account: See Brokerage Account (Taxable).

Tenant Screening: Process of evaluating prospective tenants: credit check, criminal background check, employment verification, previous landlord references. Proper screening prevents most tenant problems before they occur.

Tenants in Common: Property ownership where multiple people own specified shares without automatic right of survivorship. Each owner can sell their share independently. Common for investment properties with multiple owners.

Time Value of Money: The principle that money available today is worth more than the same amount in the future because of its earning potential. $10,000 today growing at 10% for 10 years becomes $25,937. This principle underlies all investing mathematics.

Title Insurance: Insurance protecting against defects in property title: unpaid liens, boundary disputes, forged documents. One-time premium paid at closing. Essential for real estate purchases.

Total Return: Investment gain including both price appreciation and income (dividends, interest, rent). Dividend-paying stocks have total returns exceeding price appreciation alone.

Traditional 401(k): Employer retirement plan accepting pre-tax contributions up to $23,000 annually ($30,500 if 50+). Contributions reduce current taxable income. Growth is tax-deferred. Withdrawals are taxed as ordinary income.

Traditional IRA: Individual retirement account accepting pre-tax contributions up to $7,000 annually ($8,000 if 50+). Deductibility phases out at higher incomes. Withdrawals are taxed as ordinary income.

Triple Net Lease (NNN): Lease where tenant pays all property expenses: taxes, insurance, maintenance. Landlord receives net rent without operating costs. Common in commercial real estate. Preferred by passive investors.

Trust: Legal entity holding assets for beneficiaries. Revocable trusts avoid probate and provide privacy. Irrevocable trusts provide asset protection and estate tax benefits. Essential for estate planning.

Umbrella Insurance: Liability coverage beyond limits of auto and homeowners insurance. Policies typically provide $1-5 million coverage for $200-500 annually. Essential for anyone with assets worth protecting.

Underwriting: Process lenders use to assess risk: credit score, income verification, debt-to-income ratio, employment history, property appraisal. Strong underwriting profile gets better loan terms.

Vacancy Rate: Percentage of time rental units sit empty. 5% vacancy rate means units are vacant 5% of the time (about 18 days per year). Budget for 5-8% vacancy when analyzing rental properties.

Value Investing: Strategy of buying undervalued stocks expected to appreciate. Requires analysis, research, and market timing. Consistently underperforms index investing for most investors.

Vanguard: Investment company founded by John Bogle that pioneered index funds. Vanguard offers low-cost index funds across all asset classes. The one percent invest heavily with Vanguard or similar low-cost providers.

Variable Expenses: Costs that change month to month: groceries, utilities, entertainment. Harder to control than fixed expenses but offer the most optimization opportunity. Tracking variable expenses reveals wasteful spending.

Vesting: The process of gaining ownership rights over time. Employer 401(k) matches may vest over 2-6 years. Leaving before full vesting means forfeiting unvested contributions. Always stay long enough to fully vest.

Volatility: How much investment prices fluctuate. Stocks are more volatile than bonds. Volatility creates short-term risk but doesn't affect long-term returns for buy-and-hold investors. The one percent ignore volatility.

W-2: Tax form reporting employment wages and withholdings. Received annually from employers. Needed for tax filing. W-2 income faces full taxation—self-employment income offers more tax optimization opportunities.

W-4: Form used to adjust tax withholding from paychecks. Claim fewer allowances to increase withholding (bigger refund, less available monthly). Claim more allowances to decrease withholding (smaller refund, more monthly cash).

Wash Sale Rule: IRS rule preventing tax loss harvesting if you repurchase the same or substantially identical security within 30 days. Violation disallows the loss deduction. Avoid by purchasing similar but not identical securities.

Wealth: Net worth sufficient to sustain your desired lifestyle indefinitely without employment income. Wealth provides options, security, and the ability to serve Kingdom purposes. Wealth is not about ostentation but about freedom.

Withholding: Taxes removed from paychecks before you receive them. Adjust via W-4 form. Under-withholding causes tax bills; over-withholding provides interest-free loans to the government. Optimize to break even.

Yield: Income return on investment: dividends from stocks, interest from bonds, rent from real estate. Expressed as annual percentage. High yield doesn't always mean good investment—consider total return, not just yield.

Yield Curve: Graph showing relationship between bond yields and maturity dates. Normal curve slopes upward (longer bonds pay more). Inverted curve (short bonds pay more than long) often predicts recession.

Zero-Sum Game: A situation where one person's gain equals another's loss. Active stock trading is approximately zero-sum (minus fees)—winners' gains come from losers' losses. Index investing avoids zero-sum competition by owning the entire market.

Zoning: Local regulations governing property use: residential, commercial, industrial, mixed-use. Zoning affects what you can do with property. Check zoning before purchasing—restrictive zoning limits options; favorable zoning creates opportunities.

Note to Readers: This glossary defines terms as used in this book's context. Some terms have additional technical meanings in specific financial or legal contexts. Consult professionals when making significant financial decisions. Understanding these terms provides the vocabulary needed to implement the book's frameworks effectively—but implementation matters more than vocabulary mastery.

ABOUT THE AUTHOR

Maxwell is an aspiring entrepreneur who has dedicated years to studying the behavioral patterns that separate those who build substantial wealth from those who remain financially trapped despite comparable opportunities. He is currently working on attaining an associate's degree in business management and has pursued extensive self-directed education in finance, investing, real estate, marketing, and psychology.

His perspective on wealth building has been shaped by personal experience with both financial success and catastrophic failure. After making decisions that resulted in incarceration, he used that time to systematically study the principles that create wealth and to develop frameworks for implementing those principles regardless of starting circumstances.

Maxwell is a strong believer in Yeshua Messiah (Jesus Christ), devoutly serving Him through the Messianic Jewish faith, while maintaining deep respect for Torah and the Hebrew roots of faith. This perspective shapes his understanding of stewardship, wealth, and purpose—viewing money not as an end in itself but as a tool for advancing God's Kingdom on earth.

He is engaged to Sara, an educator who shares his commitment to biblical stewardship and Kingdom purpose. Together they plan to implement the principles outlined in this book, building rental property portfolios, investing systematically in index funds, developing side businesses, and raising children who understand wealth as responsibility rather than entitlement.

Beyond personal wealth building, Maxwell is committed to financial literacy education, particularly for underserved communities where lack of financial knowledge perpetuates cycles of poverty across generations. He teaches financial literacy to fellow inmates and possibly develop curriculum for use in in the future upon release.

Think Like a One Percenter represents the culmination of thousands of hours of research, study, and synthesis. It is both a guide for others seeking to build wealth and a commitment by the author to implement every principle it contains.

APPENDIX A:
RESOURCE GUIDE AND RECOMMENDED READING

Essential Books (Read These First)
Investing & Wealth Building:
- A Random Walk Down Wall Street by Burton Malkiel
- The Bogleheads' Guide to Investing by Taylor Larimore, Mel Lindauer, and Michael LeBoeuf
- The Millionaire Next Door by Thomas J. Stanley and William D. Danko
- Your Money or Your Life by Vicki Robin and Joe Dominguez
- The Simple Path to Wealth by JL Collins

Real Estate:
- The Book on Rental Property Investing by Brandon Turner
- The Millionaire Real Estate Investor by Gary Keller

Business & Career:
- The Lean Startup by Eric Ries
- Zero to One by Peter Thiel
- The $100 Startup by Chris Guillebeau

Psychology & Behavior:
- Thinking, Fast and Slow by Daniel Kahneman
- Influence: The Psychology of Persuasion by Robert Cialdini
- Atomic Habits by James Clear

Marketing & Sales:
- Scientific Advertising by Claude Hopkins
- Ogilvy on Advertising by David Ogilvy

- Breakthrough Advertising by Eugene Schwartz
- The Boron Letters by Gary Halbert
- Advanced Reading

Tax Strategy:
- Tax-Free Wealth by Tom Wheelwright
- The Power of Zero by David McKnight

Estate Planning:
- Beyond the Grave by Jeffrey L. Condon
- The Tools & Techniques of Estate Planning by Stephan R. Leimberg

Leverage & Entity Structures:
- Own Your Own Corporation by Garrett Sutton
- Asset Protection for Physicians and High-Risk Business Owners by Gideon Rothschild
- Websites & Tools

Investment Research:
- Morningstar.com (fund analysis)
- Bogleheads.org (investment forum and wiki)
- Portfolio Visualizer (backtesting tools)

Real Estate Analysis:
- BiggerPockets.com (forums, calculators, education)
- Rentometer.com (rental price comparisons)
- Zillow.com (property research)
- Tax & Financial Planning:
- IRS.gov (official tax information)
- Fairmark.com (tax guide for investors)

Calculators:
- Bankrate.com (comprehensive financial calculators)
- Investor.gov (SEC investor tools)
- SmartAsset.com (tax and investment calculators)

- Podcasts
- BiggerPockets Real Estate Podcast
- ChooseFI (financial independence)
- Afford Anything by Paula Pant
- The Mad Fientist (tax optimization)
- Radical Personal Finance by Joshua Sheats

Scripture References for Biblical Stewardship

- Proverbs 13:22 (leaving inheritance)
- Proverbs 21:5 (diligent planning)
- Proverbs 22:7 (the borrower is slave to the lender)
- Luke 14:28 (counting the cost)
- Matthew 25:14-30 (parable of the talents)
- 1 Timothy 5:8 (providing for family)
- Ecclesiastes 11:2 (diversification)
- Malachi 3:10 (tithing and provision)

APPENDIX B:
WORKSHEETS AND CALCULATORS

Net Worth Tracking Worksheet
Assets:
Cash and checking accounts: $_____
Savings accounts: $_____
Retirement accounts (401k, IRA, etc.): $_____
Taxable investment accounts: $_____
Real estate (current market value): $_____
Business equity: $_____
Vehicles (current value): $_____
Other assets: $_____
Total Assets: $_____
Liabilities:
Mortgage balance(s): $_____
Student loans: $_____
Auto loans: $_____
Credit card debt: $_____
Personal loans: $_____
Other debts: $_____
Total Liabilities: $_____
Net Worth (Assets - Liabilities): $_____
Track quarterly and compare to previous quarters to measure progress.

Monthly Budget Worksheet
Income:
Primary job (after taxes): $_____
Secondary job/side hustle: $_____
Investment income: $_____
Other income: $_____
Total Monthly Income: $_____
Fixed Expenses:

Rent/Mortgage: $_____
Property taxes (monthly): $_____
Insurance (home/renters): $_____
Car payment: $_____
Auto insurance: $_____
Health insurance: $_____
Other insurance: $_____
Minimum debt payments: $_____
Variable Expenses:
Groceries: $_____
Dining out: $_____
Gas/transportation: $_____
Utilities: $_____
Phone/internet: $_____
Entertainment: $_____
Clothing: $_____
Personal care: $_____
Miscellaneous: $_____
Savings & Investments:
401k contribution: $_____
IRA contribution: $_____
HSA contribution: $_____
529 contribution: $_____
Taxable investment account: $_____
Emergency fund: $_____
Total Monthly Expenses: $_____
Surplus/Deficit: $_____
Savings Rate: _____% (Total Savings ÷ Gross Income × 100)
Rental Property Analysis Worksheet
Purchase Information:
Purchase price: $_____
Down payment (% and $): % / $
Loan amount: $_____
Interest rate: _____%
Loan term: _____ years
Monthly Income:
Unit 1 rent: $_____
Unit 2 rent: $_____

Unit 3 rent: $_____

Other income: $_____

Total Monthly Income: $_____

Monthly Expenses:

Mortgage payment (P&I): $_____

Property taxes: $_____

Insurance: $_____

HOA fees: $_____

Property management (8-10%): $_____

Maintenance reserve (1% of value annually): $_____

Vacancy allowance (5-8% of rent): $_____

Capital expenditures (1-2% of value annually): $_____

Utilities (if owner-paid): $_____

Total Monthly Expenses: $_____

Monthly Cash Flow: $_____ (Income - Expenses)

Key Metrics:

Cash-on-cash return: _____% (Annual Cash Flow ÷ Down Payment × 100)

One percent rule: _____% (Monthly Rent ÷ Purchase Price × 100)

Cap rate: _____% (Annual Net Income ÷ Purchase Price × 100)

Retirement Savings Calculator

Current Information:

Current age: _____

Retirement age: _____

Years until retirement: _____

Current retirement savings: $_____

Monthly contribution: $_____

Expected annual return: _____%

Projected Retirement Savings:

Use online calculator at Bankrate.com or similar

Future value = $_____

Annual retirement income at 4% withdrawal rate: $_____

NOTES & SOURCES

Chapter 1: The Mindset

- Stanley, Thomas J., and William D. Danko. The Millionaire Next Door. Lanham, MD: Taylor Trade Publishing, 1996.

- Kahneman, Daniel. Thinking, Fast and Slow. New York: Farrar, Straus and Giroux, 2011.

- Dweck, Carol S. Mindset: The New Psychology of Success. New York: Random House, 2006.

Chapter 2: The Five Percent Rule

- Historical savings rate data: U.S. Bureau of Economic Analysis, Personal Savings Rate [PSAVERT], retrieved from FRED, Federal Reserve Bank of St. Louis.

- Morgan Housel. The Psychology of Money. Harriman House, 2020.

Chapter 3: Index Funds

- Malkiel, Burton G. A Random Walk Down Wall Street. New York: W.W. Norton & Company, 2019.

- Bogle, John C. The Little Book of Common Sense Investing. Hoboken: John Wiley & Sons, 2017.

- SPIVA U.S. Scorecard, S&P Dow Jones Indices, various years.

- Dimensional Fund Advisors research on factor investing.

Chapter 4: Tax-Advantaged Arsenal

- Peter Thiel Roth IRA reporting: ProPublica, "Lord of the Roths: How Tech Mogul Peter Thiel Turned a Retirement

Account for the Middle Class Into a $5 Billion Tax-Free Piggy Bank," June 2021.

- IRS Publication 969: Health Savings Accounts and Other Tax-Favored Health Plans.

- IRS Publication 590-A and 590-B: Contributions to and Distributions from IRAs.

- 529 plan data: Savingforcollege.com, College Savings Plans Network.

Chapter 5: Real Estate

- Turner, Brandon. The Book on Rental Property Investing. BiggerPockets Publishing, 2015.

- Keller, Gary, et al. The Millionaire Real Estate Investor. McGraw-Hill, 2005.

- Sam Zell biographical information: Zell, Sam. Am I Being Too Subtle? Portfolio, 2017.

- Historical real estate appreciation data: Case-Shiller Home Price Index, S&P Dow Jones Indices.

- Real estate tax law: IRS Publication 527, Residential Rental Property.

Chapter 6: Career Optimization

- Bureau of Labor Statistics, wage and employment data.

- LinkedIn Economic Graph research on career mobility.

- Salary negotiation research: Babcock, Linda, and Sara Laschever. Women Don't Ask. Princeton University Press, 2003.

Chapter 35: Principal Versus Interest

- Mortgage amortization mathematics: standard financial formulas for time value of money.

- Mortgage payment examples calculated using standard amortization formulas. Historical mortgage rate data: Freddie Mac Primary Mortgage Market Survey.

Chapter 36: The Stage

- Jobs, Steve. iPhone introduction keynote, Macworld 2007 (video available via Apple archives).

- Churchill war speeches: Churchill, Winston S. Never Give In!: The Best of Winston Churchill's Speeches. Hyperion, 2003.

- Bryan Stevenson information: Stevenson, Bryan. Just Mercy. Spiegel & Grau, 2014.

- Stevenson TED talk: "We Need to Talk About an Injustice," March 2012.

- Hans Rosling presentations and data: Rosling, Hans. Factfulness. Flatiron Books, 2018.

- Gapminder Foundation data visualization tools.

- Tony Robbins seminar methodology: Robbins, Anthony. Awaken the Giant Within. Free Press, 1991.

Chapter 37: The Power of Silence

- Abraham Shakespeare case: News reports from Tampa Bay Times and other Florida media, 2009-2010.

- Warren Buffett biographical information: Schroeder, Alice. The Snowball: Warren Buffett and the Business of Life. Bantam, 2008.

- Lottery winner statistics: National Endowment for Financial Education research on lottery winners.

Chapter 38: The Science of Selling

- Hopkins, Claude C. Scientific Advertising. 1923. (Public domain, multiple modern editions available)

- Ogilvy, David. Ogilvy on Advertising. Vintage Books, 1985.
- Schwartz, Eugene M. Breakthrough Advertising. Bottom Line Books, 1966.

- Halbert, Gary. The Boron Letters. TBOT LLC, 2013.

- Joe Girard sales record: Guinness Book of World Records, verified sales data.

- Frank Kern marketing information: Various interviews and published materials, 2000s-present.

- Neil Patel content marketing: NeilPatel.com blog archives and published case studies.

- Apple "1984" advertisement: Video available via YouTube and advertising archives.

- Cialdini, Robert B. Influence: The Psychology of Persuasion. Harper Business, 2006.

Biblical References

- All Scripture quotations from the Tree of Life Version (TLV), © 2015 by The Messianic Jewish Family Bible Society. Used by permission.

General Research

- Behavioral economics research: Kahneman and Tversky, various papers on prospect theory and cognitive biases.

- Tax code citations: Internal Revenue Code sections as noted in text.

- Historical financial data: Federal Reserve Economic Data (FRED), Bureau of Labor Statistics, Census Bureau.

- Investment performance data: Morningstar, S&P Dow Jones Indices, Dimensional Fund Advisors.

Author's Note on Sources

I have made every effort to cite sources accurately and to credit original research and ideas appropriately. Where concepts have become part of general financial literacy knowledge through widespread dissemination, I have not always been able to identify original sources. Any errors or omissions in attribution are unintentional and will be corrected in future